# Taste*of*Home.

# EASY
# EVERYDAY
# COOKING

## - 2023 -

© 2023 RDA Enthusiast Brands, LLC.
1610 N. 2nd St., Suite 102, Milwaukee WI
53212-3906
All rights reserved. *Taste of Home* is a
registered trademark of RDA Enthusiast
Brands, LLC.
Visit *tasteofhome.com* for other
*Taste of Home* books and products.

**International Standard Book Number:**
D 978-1-62145-912-5
U 978-1-62145-913-2
**Component Number:**
D 117800109H
U 117800111H

INSTANT POT is a trademark of Double
Insight Inc. This publication has not been
authorized, sponsored or otherwise
approved by Double Insight, Inc.

**Chief Content Officer, Home & Garden:**
Jeanne Sidner
**Content Director:** Mark Hagen
**Associate Creative Director:**
Raeann Thompson
**Senior Editor:** Christine Rukavena
**Editor:** Hazel Wheaton
**Senior Art Director:** Courtney Lovetere
**Art Director:** Maggie Conners
**Deputy Editor, Copy Desk:** Dulcie Shoener
**Copy Editor:** Elizabeth Pollock Bruch
**Contributing Designer:** Jennifer Ruetz
**Cover Photography:** Taste of Home
Photo Studio

**Pictured on front cover:**
Angel Berry Trifle (p. 250)
Heirloom Tomato Salad (p. 81)
Stuffed Pizza Rolls (p. 15)
Mexican-Inspired Chicken Soup (p. 58)
Hot Chocolate Cookies (p. 284)
Strawberry Shakes (p. 24)
Barbecued Chicken Salad
   Sandwiches (p. 58)
Asparagus & Shrimp with
   Angel Hair (p. 134)

**Pictured on back cover:**
Overnight Yeast Waffles (p. 193)
Canadian Cheese Soup (p. 63)
Chicken Provolone (p. 153)
Strawberry Watermelon Lemonade (p. 15)
Pressure-Cooker Lava Cake (p. 169)
Guacamole Chicken Salad
   Sandwiches (p. 69)
Sausage-Stuffed Shells (p. 115)

Printed in China
1 3 5 7 9 10 8 6 4 2

**Pictured on opposite page:**
Baba Ganoush (p. 10)
Blueberry Cantaloupe Salad (p. 36)
Basil Tomato Soup with Orzo (p. 75)
Thai Salad with Peanut Dressing (p. 90)
Shrimp Quesadillas (p. 104)
Grapefruit Gremolata Salmon (p. 133)
Sweet & Spicy Chipotle Chicken (p. 156)
Pressure-Cooker Salsa London Broil (p. 178)
Banana Crumb Pudding (p. 195)

MORE WAYS TO CONNECT WITH US

SHOP.TASTEOFHOME.COM

# EASY
# EVERYDAY
# COOKING

INTRODUCTION ........................................... 4

30-DAY MEAL PLANNER.......................... 6

APPETIZERS & BEVERAGES ................... 8

BREAKFAST & BRUNCH ........................ 32

FAVORITE SOUPS & SANDWICHES ......... 54

SIDES & SALADS................................ 76

COOKING FOR TWO ............................ 98

30-MINUTE DINNERS.........................118

GIVE ME 5 OR FEWER .......................138

INSTANT POT® & AIR FRYER................162

MAKE-AHEAD MARVELS.....................184

HOT OFF THE GRILL............................ 206

ONE-DISH RECIPES............................ 228

DELECTABLE DESSERTS ..................... 248

FEEDING A CROWD ........................... 272

INDEXES................................... 294

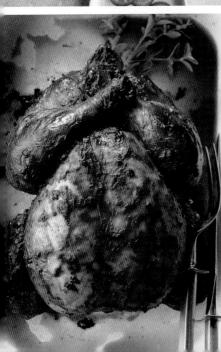

# HOME-COOKED MEALS ARE EASIER THAN EVER!

**Today's schedules are tighter than ever, so sitting down with the family is even more important. The all-new *Easy Everyday Cooking* lets you spend your time where it's most valuable—sharing a meal, not making it!**

## TAKE IT EASY — AND MAKE THEM HAPPY!

Why spend time in the kitchen when you can spend it with your family? With this new collection of recipes, you can treat your family to satisfying, delicious home cooking without devoting hours to preparation.

Slow-cooked meals with minimal prep time. Dinners that will be on the table in just 30 minutes. Comforting casseroles, satisfying side dishes and sweet desserts. Special chapters make the most of a streamlined approach perfectly suited to modern home cooks—five-ingredient recipes, one-dish wonders, and make-ahead options. Plus, a 30-day meal planner helps you get started budgeting your time and using your leftovers.

Every recipe in this book is accompanied by complete nutritional information, and easy-to-spot icons identify our healthiest recipes as well as freezer-friendly recipes, five-ingredient recipes and more. A special icon index makes it simpler than ever to find just the type of dish you're looking for—so you won't waste time shuffling through pages.

Shared by talented home cooks and approved by the experts in the *Taste of Home* Test Kitchen, the recipes in this volume prove that the best meals don't rely on time-consuming methods or complex steps. Instead, they're made with quality ingredients and prepared with care and confidence ... and the very best recipes of all are the ones you'll use again and again!

**Grilled Lobster Tails** (p. 223)

**One-Pot Dutch Oven Pasta Bake** (p. 247)

## ICONS IN THIS BOOK

- These **fast-fix recipes** are table-ready in just 30 minutes or less.

- Dishes that use **five or fewer ingredients** (they may also call for water, salt, pepper, canola or olive oil, and optional items).

- Our **healthiest recipes**, these dietitian-approved dishes are lower in calories, fat and sodium.

- **Freezer-friendly** items that include directions for freezing and reheating.

- Recipes that use a **slow cooker**—one of the most convenient kitchen tools.

- Recipes made in a handy **Instant Pot®** electric pressure cooker.

- For the flavor and crispness of fried but without added fat, try these **Air Fryer** recipes.

- With prep done the night before, these **overnight** dishes are easy to fit into your schedule.

Slow-Cooker Pina Colada Bananas Foster (p. 267)

Shrimp Patty Sandwiches (p. 71)

Easy Mediterranean Chicken (p. 129)

# CREATE FAMILY-FAVORITE DISHES WITH 450+ RECIPES & TIPS

IN THIS EDITION:

### MAKE-AHEAD MARVELS
Freezer-friendly recipes, slow-cooker meals, overnight breakfasts and more—these are dishes you can prepare in advance and have on the table in minutes. Come home to slow-cooked Beef Osso Bucco (p. 186) all ready to serve, while Banana Crumb Pudding (p. 195) waits in the fridge for dessert!

### ONE-DISH RECIPES
Stovetop skillet meals, sheet-pan dinners, savory delights that simmer away in a Dutch oven and more ... these recipes all save time in the kitchen and make cleanup a snap! Try a Bacon & Asparagus Frittata (p. 232) or North African Chicken & Rice (p. 234).

### GIVE ME 5 OR FEWER
Every recipe in this chapter calls for just a handful of items, saving you both time and money on your grocery trips. Dishes like BBQ Country-Style Ribs (p. 146) and Chicken with Shallot Sauce (p. 149) are budget friendly and easy to whip up on short notice.

### 30-MINUTE MAINS
These main courses hit the table in just half an hour or less, so they make dinner a breeze, even on busy nights. Check out Apple Cider Pork Chops (p. 133), Broiled Parmesan Tilapia (p. 120) or Classic Crab Cakes (p. 127).

### INSTANT POT® & AIR FRYER
These recipes use the newest, most popular kitchen gadgets to create soups, mains, desserts and more. Make Buffalo Chicken Wings (p. 176) or Pretzel-Crusted Catfish (p. 177) in the air fryer or try Balsamic Pork Tenderloin (p. 166) or Red Beans & Rice (p. 180) in the Instant Pot®.

### DELECTABLE DESSERTS
Whether it's Classic Creme Brulee (p. 262), a Heavenly Blueberry Tart (p. 254) or our Best Angel Food Cake (p. 259), you never have to skimp on sweets because of time!

# 30-DAY MEAL PLANNER

When making a meal plan, it helps to have a regular routine—like meatless Mondays, taco Tuesdays, or fish on Fridays. Leftovers from Sunday night's more elaborate meals can be used during the week—Mom's Roast Chicken (Day 1) provides the basis for both Super Quick Chicken Fried Rice (Day 4) and Chicken & Rice Casserole (Day 5); Baked Ham with Pineapple (Day 22) leaves enough for lunchtime sandwiches and Ham & Egg Pockets (Day 25) as a weeknight breakfast-for-dinner.

### DAY 1
**Mom's Roast Chicken, p. 152**
SERVE WITH
• Corn Pudding with Bacon & Cheddar, p. 200
• Garlic & Artichoke Roasted Potatoes, p. 95

### DAY 2
**Spinach Ravioli Bake, p. 161**
SERVE WITH
• Pesto Twists, p. 10
• Classic Wilted Lettuce Salad, p. 79

### DAY 3
**Taco Skillet Pizza with Cornbread Crust, p. 244**
SERVE WITH
Green Chile Corn Fritters, p. 83

### DAY 4
**Super Quick Chicken Fried Rice, p. 157**
SERVE WITH
• Easy Egg Rolls, p. 199
• Szechuan Sugar Snap Peas, p. 89

### DAY 5
**Chicken & Rice Casserole, p. 188**
SERVE WITH
Heirloom Tomato Salad, p. 81

### DAY 11
**Buffalo Chicken Chili, p. 64**
SERVE WITH
Spinach Salad with Hot Bacon Dressing, p. 92

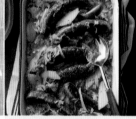

### DAY 12
**German Bratwurst with Sauerkraut & Apples, p. 278**
SERVE WITH
Swiss Potato Pancake, p. 87

### DAY 13
**Broiled Parmesan Tilapia, p. 120**
SERVE WITH
• Mashed cauliflower
• Italian Tomato Cucumber Salad, p. 94

### DAY 14
**BBQ Meat Loaf Minis, p. 145**
SERVE WITH
• Freezer Mashed Potatoes, p. 198
• Creamed Peas, p. 96

### DAY 15
**Beef Osso Bucco, p. 186**
SERVE WITH
Dreamy Polenta, p. 95

### DAY 21
**Spicy Chicken Nuggets, p. 154**
SERVE WITH
• Rosemary Sweet Potato Fries, p. 85
• Strawberry Shortcake Salad, p. 87

### DAY 22
**Baked Ham with Pineapple, p. 281**
SERVE WITH
• Old-Fashioned Macaroni & Cheese, p. 280
• Sweet Potato Pone, p. 82

### DAY 23
**Slow-Cooker Veggie Lasagna, p. 107**
SERVE WITH
Green Chile Prosciutto Rolls, p. 23

### DAY 24
**Spinach Pizza Quesadillas, p. 59**
SERVE WITH
Mexican-Inspired Chicken Soup, p. 58

### DAY 25
**Ham & Egg Pockets, p. 48**
SERVE WITH
Ramen Corn Chowder, p. 61

**DAY 6**
**Cilantro-Topped Salmon,**
**p. 140**

**SERVE WITH**
Roasted Fall
Vegetables, p. 293

**DAY 7**
**Pizza Monkey Bread,**
**p. 31**

**SERVE WITH**
Zucchini Fries, p. 93

**DAY 8**
**Rosemary-Apricot Pork**
**Tenderloin, p. 157**

**SERVE WITH**
Walnut Cranberry
Orzo, p. 89

**DAY 9**
**Eggplant Casserole,**
**p. 201**

**SERVE WITH**
Cashew Rice Pilaf,
p. 276

**DAY 10**
**Easy Shrimp Tacos,**
**p. 124**
**SERVE WITH**
• Elote (Mexican Street
Corn), p. 211
• Southwestern Rice,
p. 235

**DAY 16**
**White Bean, Sweet**
**Potato & Pepper Ragout,**
**p. 240**

**SERVE WITH**
Garlic bread

**DAY 17**
**Mexican-Style Chicken**
**Manicotti, p. 116**

**SERVE WITH**
Arroz con Gandules,
p. 287

**DAY 18**
**Best Ever Grilled Cheese**
**Sandwiches, p. 75**

**SERVE WITH**
Basil Tomato Soup
with Orzo, p. 75

**DAY 19**
**Chicken & Vegetable**
**Curry Couscous, p. 146**

**SERVE WITH**
• Toasted pita bread
• Radish Cucumber Salad,
p. 85

**DAY 20**
**Veg Jambalaya, p. 236**

**SERVE WITH**
Grapefruit Lettuce Salad,
p. 83

**DAY 26**
**Pork Schnitzel with**
**Sauce, p. 120**

**SERVE WITH**
Skillet Cabbage, p. 94

**DAY 27**
**Honey-Mustard Glazed**
**Salmon, p. 142**

**SERVE WITH**
Syrian Green Beans
with Fresh Herbs, p.91

**DAY 28**
**Chicken Thai Pizza, p. 137**

**SERVE WITH**
Thai Salad with
Peanut Dressing, p. 90

**DAY 29**
**Roast Leg of Lamb with**
**Rosemary, p. 159**

**SERVE WITH**
• Harvard Beets, p. 84
• Balsamic Brussels
Sprouts with Pears, p. 78

**DAY 30**
**Lemon-Basil Grilled**
**Shrimp & Couscous,**
**p. 225**

**SERVE WITH**
Zucchini Patties, p. 90

# - 1 -

# APPETIZERS & BEVERAGES

Snack time with the family, game-day gatherings or an evening in with a close circle of friends—you'll find the perfect dishes to serve in this collection of dips, spreads, beverages and small-plate appetizers.

**Easy Pimiento Cheese** (p. 19) **Cajun Crab Poppers** (p. 12) **Frozen Margaritas** (p. 17)
**Blueberry Iced Tea** (p. 21) **Blue Cheese Garlic Bread** (p. 26) **Green Chile Prosciutto Rolls** (p. 23)
**Bacon Cheeseburger Balls** (p. 16) **Pineapple Smoothies** (p. 30) **Creamy Red Pepper Dip** (p. 29)

⏱ 5️⃣
## PESTO TWISTS

Make pesto with basil straight from your kitchen garden or purchase prepared pesto from the grocery store to create these easy appetizers.
—*Jaye Beeler, Grand Rapids, MI*

------------------------------------------

**TAKES:** 25 min. • **MAKES:** 12 twists

- 1 pkg. (17.3 oz.) frozen puff pastry, thawed
- ½ cup prepared pesto
- ½ cup shredded Parmesan cheese
  Marinara sauce, warmed, optional

**1.** Preheat oven to 400°. Unfold puff pastry sheets on a lightly floured surface. Roll each sheet into a 12-in. square. Spread pesto onto 1 pastry sheet to within ¼ in. of edges. Sprinkle with cheese. Top with the remaining pastry sheet, pressing down lightly.
**2.** Cut into twelve 1-in.-wide strips. Twist each strip 4 times. Place 2 in. apart on parchment-lined baking sheets, pressing down ends. Bake until golden brown, 12-15 minutes. Serve warm with marinara sauce, if desired.
**1 TWIST:** 265 cal., 17g fat (4g sat. fat), 6mg chol., 270mg sod., 24g carb. (0 sugars, 3g fiber), 6g pro.
**CHEDDAR TWISTS:** Beat 1 egg and 1 Tbsp. water; brush over both sheets of pastry. Top 1 sheet with ¾ cup shredded cheddar cheese. Top with remaining pastry, egg wash side down. Cut and bake as directed.
**SWEET ALMOND TWISTS:** Beat 1 egg and 1 Tbsp. water; brush over both sheets of pastry. Top 1 sheet with ¼ cup almond cake and pastry filling; sprinkle with 1 cup sliced almonds. Top with remaining pastry, egg wash side down. Cut and bake as directed.

## 🍎 BABA GANOUSH

Baba ganoush (also spelled baba ghanoush or baba ghanouj) is a smoky-flavored Lebanese dip made with roasted eggplant. It's typically served as a starter with pita bread or fresh vegetables.
—*Nithya Narasimhan, Chennai, India*

------------------------------------------

**PREP:** 15 min. • **BAKE:** 20 min + cooling
**MAKES:** 8 cups

- 1 medium eggplant
- 3 Tbsp. olive oil, divided
- ¾ tsp. salt, divided
- ½ tsp. paprika
- 2 Tbsp. tahini
- 1 garlic clove, minced
- 1 tsp. lemon juice
  Chopped fresh parsley

**1.** Preheat oven to 450°. Cut eggplant in half lengthwise. Place halves cut side up on an ungreased baking sheet. Brush 1 Tbsp. olive oil over cut sides. Sprinkle with ½ tsp. each salt and paprika. Bake until dark golden brown, 20-25 minutes. Remove from pan to a wire rack to cool.

**2.** Peel skin from eggplant; discard. Place flesh in a food processor and pulse to mash; transfer to bowl. Stir in tahini, garlic, lemon juice and the remaining ½ tsp. salt. Spoon into serving dish. Drizzle with additional olive oil. Sprinkle with parsley and additional paprika.
**2 TBSP. DIP:** 89 cal., 8g fat (1g sat. fat), 0 chol., 224mg sod., 5g carb. (2g sugars, 2g fiber), 1g pro.

**TIPS**

- As an alternative to baking, you can grill the eggplant whole on medium-high heat, turning occasionally until the skin is charred, 25 to 35 minutes. When cool enough to handle, halve the eggplant and scoop out the meat.
- This vegan recipe is already healthy, but you can lighten it up further by using a little less oil or reducing the salt by ¼ tsp. Serve it with vegetables instead of pita bread, and you'll have yourself a good-for-you appetizer!

## CAJUN CRAB POPPERS

My brother moved to New Orleans, and I love visiting him and his family whenever I can. These easy jalapeno poppers are stuffed with crab, Cajun seasonings and bacon. They're a little hot and spicy, just like a visit to New Orleans!
—*Elizabeth Lubin, Huntington Beach, CA*

**PREP:** 20 min. • **BAKE:** 15 min. • **MAKES:** 16 poppers

- 4 oz. cream cheese, softened
- 1 large egg, lightly beaten
- 2 Tbsp. minced fresh parsley
- 1 garlic clove, minced
- ½ tsp. Cajun seasoning
- 1½ cups shredded sharp cheddar cheese
- 1 can (8 oz.) lump crabmeat, drained
- 2 bacon strips, cooked and crumbled
- 8 jalapeno peppers

**1.** Preheat oven to 375°. In a small bowl, beat the first 5 ingredients until blended. Stir in shredded cheese, crab and bacon.

**2.** Cut jalapenos in half lengthwise and remove seeds. Spoon filling into the pepper halves. Place on an ungreased baking sheet; bake until lightly browned, 15-20 minutes. Sprinkle with additional parsley.

**NOTE:** Wear disposable gloves when cutting hot peppers; the oil can burn skin. Avoid touching your face.

**1 POPPER:** 88 cal., 7g fat (4g sat. fat), 41mg chol., 187mg sod., 1g carb. (1g sugars, 0 fiber), 6g pro.

## MANGO LASSI

Learn how to make a mango lassi, the perfect summer drink any mango lover will love. This sweet and refreshing treat only needs 5 ingredients (not counting the ice cubes)!
—*Namrata Telugu, Terre Haute, IN*

**TAKES:** 10 min. • **MAKES:** 2 servings

- 1 cup fat-free plain yogurt
- 1 medium mango, peeled and cubed
- 2 cups ice cubes
- 3 Tbsp. sugar
- 5 fresh mint leaves
- 2 cardamom pods, crushed, optional

In a blender, combine the yogurt, mango, ice, sugar, mint leaves and, if desired, cardamom pods. Cover and process for 30-60 seconds or until blended. Pour into 2 chilled glasses; serve immediately.

**1½ CUPS:** 226 cal., 1g fat (0 sat. fat), 3mg chol., 73mg sod., 54g carb. (48g sugars, 3g fiber), 6g pro.

**TIP**

This drink is best enjoyed fresh, but it will keep until the next day in a covered jar in the refrigerator. To make a vegan mango lassi, switch the yogurt for a dairy-free option—we recommend using a coconut-based yogurt. You can adapt this recipe to other fruits as well, such as banana, strawberry, peach or cantaloupe.

## TOSTONES

I grew up eating many dishes from Puerto Rico, but tostones have always been a favorite dish for me. I still make the fried snacks when I miss my family.
—*Leah Martin, Gilbertsville, PA*

**PREP:** 15 min. + soaking • **COOK:** 5 min./batch • **MAKES:** 3 dozen

- 3 garlic cloves, minced
- 1 Tbsp. garlic salt
- ½ tsp. onion powder
- 6 green plantains, peeled and cut into 1-in. slices
  Oil for deep-fat frying

**SEASONING MIX**
- 1 Tbsp. garlic powder
- 1½ tsp. garlic salt
- ½ tsp. onion powder
- ½ tsp. kosher salt
  Optional: Guacamole and pico de gallo

**1.** In a large bowl, combine the garlic, garlic salt and onion powder. Add plantain slices; cover with cold water. Soak for 30 minutes.
**2.** Drain plantains; place on paper towels and pat dry. In a deep cast-iron or electric skillet, heat oil to 375°. Add plantains, a few at a time; cook until lightly browned, 30-60 seconds. Remove with a slotted spoon; drain on paper towels.
**3.** Place plantain slices between 2 sheets of aluminum foil. With the bottom of a glass, flatten to ½-in. thickness. A few at a time, fry until golden brown, 2-3 minutes longer.
**4.** Combine seasoning mix ingredients; sprinkle over tostones. If desired, serve with guacamole and pico de gallo.

**1 TOSTONE:** 63 cal., 3g fat (0 sat. fat), 0 chol., 103mg sod., 10g carb. (2g sugars, 1g fiber), 0 pro.

## FETA CHEESE & POMEGRANATE GUACAMOLE

Want to add a little flair to your bowl of guac? Top it off with chunks of feta and fresh pomegranate seeds. Since the cheese is so briny, we recommend cutting back on the amount of salt you use in the guacamole, or opting for reduced-sodium tortilla chips.
—*Taste of Home Test Kitchen*

**TAKES:** 15 min. • **MAKES:** 6 servings

- 3 medium ripe avocado, peeled and cubed
- 2 to 3 Tbsp. fresh lime juice
- ½ to 1 tsp. kosher salt
- ½ cup pomegranate seeds
- ½ cup crumbled feta cheese

In a bowl, mash avocados until almost smooth. Stir in lime juice and ½ tsp. salt. Let stand 10 minutes to allow flavors to blend. Adjust seasoning with additional lime juice and salt if desired. Top with pomegranate seeds and feta.
**¼ CUP:** 146 cal., 12g fat (2g sat. fat), 5mg chol., 256mg sod., 9g carb. (2g sugars, 5g fiber), 3g pro. **DIABETIC EXCHANGES:** 2 fat, ½ starch.

## VEGETARIAN STUFFED MUSHROOMS

Soy crumbles mixed with parsley, basil, oregano and bread crumbs make a delightful vegetarian filling for these savory stuffed mushrooms.
—*Arline Aaron, Brooklyn, NY*

-------------------------------------------------

**PREP:** 15 min. • **BAKE:** 25 min.
**MAKES:** 14 stuffed mushrooms

- 14 **large fresh mushrooms**
- 1 **small onion, finely chopped**
- 4 **tsp. canola oil**
- ¾ **cup soft bread crumbs**
- ½ **cup frozen vegetarian meat crumbles, thawed**
- 1 **tsp. minced fresh parsley**
- 1 **tsp. dried basil**
- ½ **tsp. dried oregano**
- ½ **tsp. salt**
- ½ **tsp. pepper**
  **Chopped fresh basil, optional**

**1.** Preheat oven to 350°. Remove stems from mushrooms and chop; set caps aside. In a large nonstick skillet, saute chopped stems and onion in oil until tender. Stir in bread crumbs, crumbles and the next +5 ingredients; cook until bread crumbs are lightly browned. Let cool slightly.
**2.** Stuff into mushroom caps. Place in a 15x10x1-in. baking pan coated with cooking spray. Bake for 25-30 minutes or until heated through and mushrooms are tender. If desired, top with chopped fresh basil. Serve warm.

**1 STUFFED MUSHROOM:** 34 cal., 2g fat (0 sat. fat), 0 chol., 111mg sod., 3g carb. (1g sugars, 1g fiber), 2g pro. **DIABETIC EXCHANGES:** ½ starch, ½ fat.

**TIP**

- The best mushrooms to use for this recipe are baby bella or white mushrooms—they have the best cap shape and can hold stuffing.
- To clean mushrooms, wipe with a damp paper towel or dish cloth. Don't run them under water; they already have moisture in them and you don't want them to absorb any more liquid.

## STUFFED PIZZA ROLLS

After trying a similar dish at a local restaurant, I came up with my own version. It is easy, delicious and fun for potlucks or parties.
—*Sarah Gilbert, Beaverton, OR*

- - - - - - - - - - - - - - - - - - - - - - - - - - - - - - - - - - - - - - - - - - - - -

**TAKES:** 30 min. • **MAKES:** 1 dozen

- 1    tube (13.8 oz.) refrigerated pizza crust
- ¼    cup prepared ranch salad dressing
- 6    oz. pepperoni, finely chopped
- 1    cup shredded pepper jack cheese
- ¼    cup shredded Romano cheese
- ¼    cup thinly sliced green onions
- ¼    cup chopped green pepper
- 4    cooked bacon strips, chopped
- 2    tsp. Italian seasoning
- 1    tsp. garlic powder
     Optional: Marinara sauce or Alfredo sauce, warmed

**1.** Preheat oven to 350°. Grease 12 muffin cups; set aside.
**2.** On a lightly floured surface, unroll pizza crust. Spread ranch dressing to within ½ in. of edges. Sprinkle with pepperoni, cheeses, green onions, green pepper, bacon and seasonings. Roll up jelly-roll style; pinch the edge closed. Cut crosswise into 12 slices. Place each slice into a prepared muffin cup.
**3.** Bake until lightly browned, 20-25 minutes. Serve warm with marinara or Alfredo sauce, if desired.

**1 PIZZA ROLL:** 234 cal., 14g fat (6g sat. fat), 28mg chol., 664mg sod., 17g carb. (2g sugars, 1g fiber), 10g pro.

## STRAWBERRY WATERMELON LEMONADE

The nutrition department at my local hospital inspired me to make this refreshing summer sipper. I tweaked their recipe slightly to create this drink full of sweet-tart flavor.
—*Dawn Lowenstein, Huntingdon Valley, PA*

- - - - - - - - - - - - - - - - - - - - - - - - - - - - - - - - - - - - - - - - - - - - -

**TAKES:** 20 min. • **MAKES:** 12 servings (3 qt.)

- ¼    cup sugar
- 2    cups boiling water
- ½    lb. fresh strawberries, hulled and quartered
     (about 2 cups)
- 12   cups cubed watermelon (about 1 medium)
- 1    can (12 oz.) frozen lemonade concentrate, thawed
- 3    Tbsp. lemon juice
     Ice cubes

Dissolve sugar in boiling water. Place strawberries and watermelon in batches in a blender; cover and process until blended. Pour blended fruit though a fine-mesh strainer; transfer to a large pitcher. Stir in lemonade concentrate, lemon juice and sugar water. Serve over ice.

**1 CUP:** 119 cal., 0 fat (0 sat. fat), 0 chol., 7mg sod., 34g carb. (30g sugars, 1g fiber), 1g pro.

## BACON CHEESEBURGER BALLS

The first time I served these, my husband and kids thought they were just plain meatballs. Then they cut into the flavorful filling inside!
—*Cathy Lendvoy, Boharm, SK*

**PREP:** 25 min. • **COOK:** 10 min. • **MAKES:** 3 dozen

- 1 large egg
- 1 envelope onion soup mix
- 1 lb. ground beef
- 2 Tbsp. all-purpose flour
- 2 Tbsp. 2% milk
- 1 cup shredded cheddar cheese
- 4 bacon strips, cooked and crumbled

COATING
- 2 large eggs
- 1 cup crushed saltines (about 30 crackers)
- 5 Tbsp. canola oil

**1.** In a large bowl, combine egg and soup mix. Crumble beef over mixture and mix well. Divide into 36 portions; set aside. In another large bowl, combine the flour and milk until smooth. Add cheese and bacon; mix lightly but thoroughly.

**2.** Shape cheese mixture into 36 balls. Shape 1 beef portion around each cheese ball. In a shallow bowl, beat eggs for coating. Place cracker crumbs in another bowl. Dip meatballs into beaten eggs, then coat with crumbs.

**3.** Heat oil in a large cast-iron or other heavy skillet over medium heat. Cook meatballs until meat is no longer pink and coating is golden brown, 10-12 minutes.

**1 MEATBALL:** 75 cal., 5g fat (2g sat. fat), 27mg chol., 137mg sod., 2g carb. (0 sugars, 0 fiber), 4g pro.

## LOBSTER TARTLETS

I love lobster, so I created these gems. They are the perfect appetizer for a cocktail party or family dinner. You can top them with chives or green onions for color.
—*Lorraine Caland, Shuniah, ON*

**TAKES:** 25 min. • **MAKES:** 25 tartlets

- ½ cup shredded white cheddar cheese
- ½ cup shredded provolone cheese
- ½ cup cooked lobster meat or 1 can (6½ oz.) flaked canned lobster meat, drained
- ⅓ cup finely chopped sweet red pepper
- 2 Tbsp. finely chopped green onion (white portion only)
- 2 Tbsp. mayonnaise
  Dash seafood seasoning
- 2 pkg. (1.9 oz. each) frozen miniature phyllo tart shells
  Paprika, optional

Preheat oven to 350°. In a small bowl, combine the first 7 ingredients. Spoon into tart shells. Place on an ungreased baking sheet. Bake until shells are lightly browned and filling is heated through, 12-15 minutes. If desired, sprinkle with paprika before serving.

**1 TARTLET:** 76 cal., 4g fat (1g sat. fat), 8mg chol., 78mg sod., 6g carb. (0 sugars, 0 fiber), 3g pro.

## BUFFALO BITES WITH BLUE CHEESE RANCH DIP

Low-carb cauliflower bites cook up fast in the air fryer, making them an easy snack or side dish. I serve them with a flavorful dip made with cottage cheese that's packed with protein compared to most dips. My teenagers happily eat their veggies with this recipe.
—Julie Peterson, Crofton, MD

-------------------------------------------------------------

**PREP:** 10 min. • **COOK:** 30 min. • **MAKES:** 6 servings

- 1   small head cauliflower, cut into florets
- 2   Tbsp. olive oil
- 3   Tbsp. Buffalo wing sauce
- 3   Tbsp. butter, melted

**DIP**
- 1½ cups 2% cottage cheese
- ¼   cup fat-free plain Greek yogurt
- ¼   cup crumbled blue cheese
- 1   envelope ranch salad dressing mix
     Celery sticks, optional

**1.** Preheat air fryer to 350°. In a large bowl, combine cauliflower and oil; toss to coat. In batches, arrange cauliflower in a single layer in air-fryer basket. Cook until florets are tender and edges are browned, 10-15 minutes, stirring halfway through.
**2.** In a large bowl, combine Buffalo sauce and melted butter. Add cauliflower; toss to coat. Transfer to a serving platter.
**3.** In a small bowl, combine dip ingredients. Serve with cauliflower and, if desired, celery sticks.
**1 SERVING:** 203 cal., 13g fat (6g sat. fat), 22mg chol., 1470mg sod., 13g carb. (4g sugars, 1g fiber), 8g pro.

## FROZEN MARGARITAS

One of my favorite summer drinks is a frozen margarita. What's not to love? This drink is great paired with tacos or chips and salsa.
—Caroline Stanko, Milwaukee, WI

-------------------------------------------------------------

**TAKES:** 15 min. • **MAKES:** 6 servings

- 6   lime wedges
     Kosher salt
- 1   cup tequila
- ½   cup Triple Sec
- ¼   cup lime juice (about 4 limes)
- ½   cup simple syrup or super fine sugar
- 6   to 9 cups ice cubes

**1.** Using lime wedges, moisten the rims of 6 margarita or cocktail glasses. Set aside lime wedges for garnish. Sprinkle salt on a plate; hold each glass upside down and dip rim into salt. Set aside. Discard remaining salt on plate.
**2.** In a blender, combine tequila, Triple Sec, lime juice, simple syrup and enough ice to reach desired consistency; cover and process until blended. Pour into prepared glasses. Garnish with lime wedges. Serve immediately.
**1 CUP:** 214 cal., 0 fat (0 sat. fat), 0 chol., 34mg sod., 24g carb. (22g sugars, 0 fiber), 0 pro.

**TIP**

If your blender isn't powerful enough to crush whole ice cubes, use pre-crushed ice instead. For a flavored margarita, replace a few of the ice cubes with frozen mango, strawberries or mixed berries.

## AIR-FRYER CALAMARI

You can make crispy calamari just like your favorite Italian restaurant's thanks to the air fryer! A quick coat in crunchy panko bread crumbs and a few minutes in the air fryer are all it takes to make this special appetizer.

—Peggy Woodward, Shullsburg, WI

PREP TIME: 20 min.
COOK TIME: 10 min./batch
MAKES: 5 dozen

- ½ cup all-purpose flour
- ½ tsp. salt
- 1 large egg, lightly beaten
- ½ cup 2% milk
- 1 cup panko bread crumbs
- ½ tsp. seasoned salt
- ¼ tsp. pepper
- 8 oz. cleaned fresh or frozen calamari (squid), thawed and cut into ½-in. rings
  Cooking spray

1. Preheat air fryer to 400°. In a shallow bowl, combine flour and salt. In another shallow bowl, whisk the egg and milk. In a third shallow bowl, combine bread crumbs, seasoned salt and pepper. Coat calamari with the flour mixture, then dip in the egg mixture and coat with the bread crumb mixture.
2. In batches, place calamari in a single layer on greased tray in air-fryer basket; spritz with cooking spray. Cook 4 minutes. Turn; spritz with cooking spray. Cook until golden brown, 3-5 minutes longer.
**1 PIECE:** 11 cal., 0 fat (0 sat. fat), 10mg chol., 28mg sod., 1g carb. (0 sugars, 0 fiber), 1g pro.

**TIPS**
- To clean calamari, first pull the skin off to reveal the white, slightly translucent flesh underneath. Rinse the tube of squid under cold water. For this recipe, slice the tube into ½-in. pieces.
- The best dipping sauces to pair with calamari are marinara, ranch, chipotle ranch or garlic lemon sauce.
- Like some other seafood recipes, calamari turns tough when it is overcooked. The key to keeping it soft is to cook it quickly with high heat.

BRIE WITH ALMONDS

## BRIE WITH ALMONDS

This nut-topped cheese is elegant and impressive for holiday occasions. No one will guess that the recipe is actually a snap to prepare.

—Mildred Aydt, Chanhassen, MN

TAKES: 15 min. • MAKES: 8 servings

- 1 round Brie cheese (8 oz.)
- 2 Tbsp. butter, melted
- ¼ cup sliced almonds
- 1 Tbsp. brandy, optional
  Assorted crackers or fresh vegetables

1. Preheat oven to 400°. Place Brie in an small ungreased cast-iron skillet or shallow 1-qt. baking dish. Combine the butter, almonds and, if desired, brandy; pour over Brie.
2. Bake, uncovered, until cheese is softened, 10-12 minutes. Serve with crackers or vegetables.
**1 SERVING:** 141 cal., 12g fat (7g sat. fat), 36mg chol., 199mg sod., 1g carb. (0 sugars, 0 fiber), 7g pro.

## EASY PIMIENTO CHEESE

Every good Southerner has their own version of pimiento cheese. It's wonderful on crackers, in a sandwich with a fresh summer tomato, inside a grilled cheese sandwich or plain with some crackers.

—Josh Carter, Birmingham, AL

PREP: 15 min. + chilling
MAKES: 16 servings

- 1⅓ cups mayonnaise
- 2 jars (4 oz. each) pimiento strips, chopped
- 1½ tsp. Worcestershire sauce
- ¼ tsp. cayenne pepper
- ¼ tsp. pepper
- 1 block (8 oz.) sharp cheddar cheese, shredded
- 1 block (8 oz.) extra-sharp cheddar cheese, shredded

In a large bowl, combine the first 5 ingredients. Add cheeses and stir to combine. Refrigerate, covered, at least 1 hour.
**¼ CUP:** 238 cal., 23g fat (7g sat. fat), 29mg chol., 286mg sod., 2g carb. (1g sugars, 0 fiber), 7g pro.

In a medium bowl, combine **6 plum tomatoes** (chopped), **1 small onion** (finely chopped), **½ cup chopped fresh cilantro**, **1 to 2 jalapeno peppers** (seeded and finely chopped), **3 Tbsp. lime juice**, **1 Tbsp. finely chopped cilantro stems**, **1 garlic clove** (minced) and **¼ tsp. salt.** Cover and refrigerate 1-2 hours before serving.

## - PICO DE GALLO -
Simple and quick to make, this classic salsa is a celebration of flavor!
Use the freshest, best-quality ingredients for the best results.

## AIR-FRYER THAI CHICKEN MEATBALLS

These meatballs make a great game-day snack. We also like to serve them as a main dish over stir-fried veggies.
—Merry Graham, Newhall, CA

- - - - - - - - - - - - - - - - - - - - - - - - - - - - - - - - - - - - - - - - - - - - - - - - - - - - -

**PREP:** 10 min. • **COOK:** 10 min./batch • **MAKES:** 12 servings

- ½ cup sweet chili sauce
- 2 Tbsp. lime juice
- 2 Tbsp. ketchup
- 1 tsp. soy sauce
- 1 large egg, lightly beaten
- ¾ cup panko bread crumbs
- 1 green onion, finely chopped
- 1 Tbsp. minced fresh cilantro
- ½ tsp. salt
- ½ tsp. garlic powder
- 1 lb. lean ground chicken

1. Preheat air fryer to 350°. In a small bowl, combine chili sauce, lime juice, ketchup and soy sauce. In a large bowl, combine egg, bread crumbs, green onion, cilantro, salt, garlic powder and 4 Tbsp. of the chili sauce mixture (reserve the remaining ½ cup for serving). Add chicken; mix lightly but thoroughly. Shape into 12 balls.
2. In batches, arrange meatballs in a single layer on greased tray in air-fryer basket. Cook until lightly browned, 4-5 minutes. Turn and cook until lightly browned and cooked through, 4-5 minutes longer. Serve with the reserved sauce; sprinkle with additional cilantro.
**1 MEATBALL:** 98 cal., 3g fat (1g sat. fat), 43mg chol., 369mg sod., 9g carb. (6g sugars, 0 fiber), 9g pro.

## BLUEBERRY ICED TEA

I enjoy coming up with new ways to use my slow cooker in the kitchen. If it's going to take up space, it needs to earn its keep! Serve this refreshing tea over plenty of ice and garnish with blueberries if desired. For fun, freeze blueberries in your ice cubes.
—Colleen Delawder, Herndon, VA

- - - - - - - - - - - - - - - - - - - - - - - - - - - - - - - - - - - - - - - - - - - - - - - - - - - - -

**PREP:** 10 min. • **COOK:** 3 hours + cooling • **MAKES:** 11 servings

- 12 cups water
- 2 cups fresh blueberries
- 1 cup sugar
- ¼ tsp. salt
- 4 family-sized tea bags
  Ice cubes
  Optional: Additional blueberries, lemon slices and fresh mint leaves

1. In a 5-qt. slow cooker, combine water, blueberries, sugar and salt. Cook, covered, on low heat for 3 hours.
2. Turn off slow cooker; add tea bags. Cover and let stand for 5 minutes. Discard tea bags; cool 2 hours. Strain and discard blueberries. Pour into pitcher; serve over ice cubes. If desired, top each serving with additional blueberries, lemon slices and fresh mint leaves.
**1 CUP:** 73 cal., 0 fat (0 sat. fat), 0 chol., 61mg sod., 19g carb. (18g sugars, 0 fiber), 0 pro.

## BASIL SHRIMP

My husband loves shrimp and agrees nothing beats this incredibly easy, enjoyable dish.
—Natalie Corona, Maple Grove, MN

TAKES: 30 min. • MAKES: 2 servings

- 1 Tbsp. minced fresh basil
- 1 Tbsp. olive oil
- 1 Tbsp. butter, melted
- 1 Tbsp. Dijon mustard
- 2 tsp. lemon juice
- 1 garlic clove, minced
  Dash salt and white pepper
- 8 uncooked shrimp (16-20 per lb.), peeled and deveined

**1.** In a small bowl, combine basil, oil, butter, mustard, lemon juice, garlic, salt and pepper. Pour 3 Tbsp. into a small shallow dish; set remaining marinade aside. Add shrimp to dish and turn to coat; let stand at room temperature 15-20 minutes.

**2.** Drain shrimp; discard marinade in dish. Thread shrimp onto 2 metal or soaked wooden skewers. Grill, covered, over medium heat until shrimp turn pink, 2-3 minutes on each side, basting occasionally with the reserved marinade. If desired, garnish with additional fresh basil.

**3 OZ. COOKED SHRIMP:** 159 cal., 9g fat (3g sat. fat), 133mg chol., 330mg sod., 1g carb. (0 sugars, 0 fiber), 17g pro. **DIABETIC EXCHANGES:** 3 lean meat, 2 fat.

> **TIP**
> To use frozen shrimp for this recipe, thaw them first. Place shrimp in a colander over a bowl, covered, in the refrigerator overnight. Alternatively, seal frozen shrimp in a resealable plastic bag, removing as much air as possible. Place bag in a bowl of cold water until completely thawed, 20-30 minutes, covering with a plate to keep the bag submerged. Pat shrimp dry with paper towels. Then peel and devein your shrimp. (You can leave the tails on or remove them—it's a matter of preference!)

## CHILI-LIME AIR-FRIED CHICKPEAS

Looking for a lighter snack that's still a crowd-pleaser? You've found it! These zesty, crunchy chickpeas will have everyone happily munching.
—Julie Ruble, Charlotte, NC

PREP: 10 min. • BAKE: 30 min. + cooling • MAKES: 1 cup

- 1 can (15 oz.) chickpeas or garbanzo beans, rinsed, drained and patted dry
- 1 Tbsp. olive oil
- 1½ tsp. chili powder
- 1 tsp. ground cumin
- ½ tsp. grated lime zest
- 1½ tsp. lime juice
- ¼ tsp. sea salt

**1.** Preheat air fryer to 400°. Spread chickpeas in a single layer on greased tray in air-fryer basket, removing any loose skins. Cook until very crunchy, 20-30 minutes, shaking basket every 5 minutes.

**2.** Meanwhile, whisk together remaining ingredients. Remove chickpeas from air fryer; let cool 5 minutes. Drizzle with oil mixture; toss to coat. Cool completely.

**¼ CUP:** 133 cal., 6g fat (0 sat. fat), 0 chol., 287mg sod., 17g carb. (3g sugars, 5g fiber), 4g pro.

# GREEN CHILE PROSCIUTTO ROLLS

I created these for my husband, who adores green chiles. He loves the rolls so much he could eat a whole pan.
—*Paula McHargue, Richmond, KY*

**TAKES:** 25 min. • **MAKES:** 14 rolls

- 1 tube (8 oz.) refrigerated crescent rolls
- 3 oz. cream cheese, softened
- 1 can (4 oz.) chopped green chiles, drained
- 1 Tbsp. sweet hot mustard
- ½ cup thinly sliced prosciutto, cooked and crumbled
- 1 large egg, beaten
- 3 Tbsp. grated Parmesan cheese

**1.** Preheat oven to 375°. Unroll crescent dough into 1 long rectangle; press perforations to seal. In a small bowl, beat cream cheese, green chiles and mustard. Spread over dough to within ½ in. of edges. Sprinkle with prosciutto. Roll up left and right long sides toward the center, jelly-roll style, until rolls meet in the middle. Cut into 1-in. slices.

**2.** Place on a parchment-lined baking sheet. Brush with egg; sprinkle with cheese. Bake until golden brown, 12-15 minutes. If desired, top with additional grated Parmesan cheese.

**1 ROLL:** 98 cal., 6g fat (2g sat. fat), 23mg chol., 258mg sod., 8g carb. (2g sugars, 0 fiber), 3g pro.

# LONG ISLAND ICED TEA

Smooth but potent describes this drink. Adjust the tequila to suit your taste. If you like a bolder flavor, use an ounce. If you would prefer a more mellow drink, use half an ounce.
—*Taste of Home Test Kitchen*

**TAKES:** 5 min. • **MAKES:** 1 serving

- 1 to 1¼ cups ice cubes
- 1 oz. vodka
- ½ to 1 oz. tequila
- 1 oz. light rum
- 1 oz. sour mix
- 1 oz. Triple Sec
- ½ oz. cola
  Lemon slice, optional

Place ice in a Collins or highball glass. Pour the remaining ingredients into the glass; stir. Garnish with a slice of lemon, if desired.

**⅔ CUP:** 330 cal., 0 fat (0 sat. fat), 0 chol., 3mg sod., 30g carb. (28g sugars, 0 fiber), 0 pro.

**TIP**

If you're serving a crowd, you can make a pitcher of Long Island iced tea by just increasing the quantities. To keep things fresh, mix up a batch of liquor starter—the vodka, tequila, rum, sour mix and Triple Sec—and let each guest add ice and cola to suit their own personal taste.

## STRAWBERRY SHAKES

Full of summer fruit, these thick berry blends are the perfect way to savor hot days. I serve them in tall glasses with sliced fresh strawberries as a garnish.
—*Ruby Williams, Bogalusa, LA*

------------------------------------------------

**TAKES:** 5 min. • **MAKES:** 4 servings

- ⅔ cup 2% milk
- 3 cups strawberry ice cream
- 1 cup fresh strawberries
- 2 Tbsp. strawberry syrup

In a blender, combine all ingredients; cover and process until smooth. Pour into chilled glasses. Serve immediately.
**1 CUP:** 253 cal., 10g fat (6g sat. fat), 34mg chol., 81mg sod., 38g carb. (9g sugars, 1g fiber), 5g pro.

## SAUSAGE CHEESE BALLS

These bite-sized meatballs are a favorite of mine. Feel free to swap in different cheese for the cheddar or to serve the balls with Dijon mustard instead of the barbecue and sweet-and-sour sauces.
—*Anna Damon, Bozeman, MT*

------------------------------------------------

**TAKES:** 30 min. • **MAKES:** 20 servings

- ½ cup shredded cheddar cheese
- 3 Tbsp. biscuit/baking mix
- 1 Tbsp. finely chopped onion
- 1 Tbsp. finely chopped celery
- ⅛ tsp. garlic powder
- ⅛ tsp. pepper
- ¼ lb. bulk pork sausage
  Optional: Sweet-and-sour and barbecue sauces

**1.** Preheat oven to 375°. Combine first 6 ingredients. Crumble sausage over mixture; mix lightly but thoroughly. Shape into 1-in. balls.
**2.** Place in a shallow baking pan coated with cooking spray. Bake, uncovered, until golden brown and no longer pink inside, 12-15 minutes. Drain on paper towels. Serve with sauces if desired.
**1 MEATBALL:** 30 cal., 2g fat (1g sat. fat), 6mg chol., 64mg sod., 1g carb. (0 sugars, 0 fiber), 1g pro.

**TIP**

To make these meatballs ahead of time, place the shaped, uncooked balls in a single layer on a sheet pan in the freezer. Once frozen, transfer to a freezer-safe container or bag in the freezer. When you're ready to bake them, take out as many as you need and bake from frozen until heated through, allowing for a little extra baking time.

# HOT ARTICHOKE-SPINACH DIP

One taste of this outrageously delicious dip and your guests will not stop eating it until it's gone. The savory blend of artichokes, spinach and Parmesan cheese is positively addictive! It tastes even better if you make it the night before and chill it in the fridge before baking.

—*Michelle Krzmarzick, Torrance, CA*

- - - - - - - - - - - - - - - - - - - - - - - - - - - - - - -

**TAKES:** 30 min. • **MAKES:** 3 cups

- 1 pkg. (8 oz.) cream cheese, softened
- ½ cup grated Parmesan cheese
- ¼ cup mayonnaise
- 1 garlic clove, minced
- 1 tsp. dried basil
- ¼ tsp. garlic salt
- ¼ tsp. pepper
- 1 can (14 oz.) water-packed artichoke hearts, rinsed, drained and chopped
- ½ cup frozen chopped spinach, thawed and squeezed dry
- ¼ cup shredded mozzarella cheese
  Assorted crackers

**1.** Preheat oven to 350°. In a large bowl, combine the cream cheese, Parmesan cheese, mayonnaise, garlic, basil, garlic salt and pepper; mix well. Stir in the artichokes and spinach. Transfer to a greased 9-in. pie plate. Sprinkle with mozzarella cheese.

**2.** Bake, uncovered, until bubbly and edges are lightly browned, 20-25 minutes. Serve with crackers.

**2 TBSP. DIP:** 68 cal., 6g fat (3g sat. fat), 13mg chol., 139mg sod., 2g carb. (0 sugars, 0 fiber), 2g pro.

**TIPS**

- Crackers are easy (and delicious), but you can also serve this dip fresh vegetables, garlic bread, tortilla chips or pita bread.
- If you prefer, trade the frozen spinach for 5 oz. of cooked fresh spinach—just make sure to blot it dry after cooking.
- To make this recipe lighter, use reduced-fat cream cheese and light mayo.

## SALMON DIP WITH CREAM CHEESE

Here's a delightful hors d'oeuvre that's excellent for any occasion. The combination of salmon, cream cheese and spices gives it terrific flavor.

—*Raymonde Hebert Bernier, Saint-Hyacinthe, QC*

---

**PREP:** 10 min. + chilling • **MAKES:** 1½ cups

- 6 oz. cream cheese, softened
- 3 Tbsp. mayonnaise
- 1 Tbsp. lemon juice
- ½ tsp. salt
- ½ tsp. curry powder
- ¼ tsp. dried basil
- ⅛ tsp. pepper
- 1 can (7½ oz.) salmon, drained, bones and skin removed
- 2 green onions, thinly sliced
  Crackers and chopped vegetables

In a bowl, combine the cream cheese, mayonnaise and lemon juice. Add the salt, curry powder, basil and pepper; mix well. Gently stir in salmon and onions. Cover and refrigerate for at least 1 hour. Serve with crackers and vegetables.

**2 TBSP. DIP:** 78 cal., 7g fat (2g sat. fat), 17mg chol., 234mg sod., 1g carb. (0 sugars, 0 fiber), 4g pro.

> **TIP**
> This dip will last for up to 5 days in the refrigerator. We don't recommend freezing it—cream cheese dips like this one typically don't hold up well in the freezer.

## BLUE CHEESE GARLIC BREAD

This is an irresistible way to dress up an ordinary loaf of bread. Serve slices as an appetizer or with a meal.

—*Kevalyn Henderson, Hayward, WI*

---

**TAKES:** 30 min. • **MAKES:** 10 servings

- ½ cup butter, softened
- 4 oz. crumbled blue cheese
- 2 Tbsp. grated Parmesan cheese
- 1 Tbsp. minced chives
- 1 tsp. garlic powder
- 1 loaf (1 lb.) unsliced French bread

1. Preheat oven to 350°. In a small bowl, combine the first 5 ingredients. Cut into bread to make 1-in.-thick slices, but don't cut all the way through—leave slices attached at the bottom. Spread the cheese mixture between the slices.
2. Wrap loaf in a large piece of heavy-duty foil (about 28x18 in.); fold foil around bread and seal tightly. Bake until heated through, about 20 minutes. Serve warm.

**1 PIECE:** 250 cal., 14g fat (8g sat. fat), 34mg chol., 546mg sod., 24g carb. (1g sugars, 1g fiber), 7g pro.

## APPLE MARTINI

You will feel like a movie star when you sip these fancy apple martinis. Guests will be impressed when you garnish each pretty drink with a green apple slice.
—Taste of Home *Test Kitchen*

------------------------------------------------------------

**TAKES:** 5 min. • **MAKES:** 1 serving

    Ice cubes
 2  oz. vodka
 1½ oz. sour apple liqueur
 1½ tsp. lemon juice
    Optional: Green apple slice

Fill a shaker three-fourths full with ice. Add the vodka, apple liqueur and lemon juice. Cover and shake for 10-15 seconds or until condensation forms on outside of shaker. Strain into a chilled cocktail glass. If desired, garnish with apple.

**⅔ CUP:** 285 cal., 0 fat (0 sat. fat), 0 chol., 1mg sod., 17g carb. (17g sugars, 0 fiber), 0 pro.

## SPARKLING GINGER LEMONADE

Chill out with this delightful cooler, perfect for springtime bridal showers or hot summer days on the deck. It's a quick fix you'll stir up time after time.
—Jodi Blubaugh, Eagle Mountain, UT

------------------------------------------------------------

**PREP:** 20 min. + cooling • **MAKES:** 5 servings

 2  cups water
 1  cup honey
 2  Tbsp. minced fresh gingerroot
 2  cups club soda, chilled
 1  cup lemon juice
    Optional: Lemon slices and fresh mint

**1.** In a saucepan, bring the water, honey and ginger to a boil. Remove from heat; cover and steep for 10 minutes. Strain, discarding ginger. Cool.
**2.** Transfer to a pitcher; stir in soda and lemon juice. Serve over ice. Garnish with lemon slices and fresh mint, if desired.

**1 CUP:** 217 cal., 0 fat (0 sat. fat), 0 chol., 23mg sod., 59g carb. (56g sugars, 0 fiber), 0 pro.

> **TIP** The flavor of fresh ginger is preferred, but if you don't have it on hand, you can use 1¼ tsp. of ground ginger instead of the 2 Tbsp. of fresh ginger.

## CREAMY CRAB WONTONS

How about a fast appetizer just for two? These hot, crispy little bites boast a rich, creamy filling with a hint of crab. They simply melt in your mouth. Serve wontons with plum sauce or sweet-and-sour sauce for dipping.
—Robin Boynton, Harbor Beach, MI

----------------------------------------

**TAKES:** 20 min. • **MAKES:** 2 servings

- 2 oz. cream cheese, softened
- 2 Tbsp. canned crabmeat, drained, flaked and cartilage removed
- 2 tsp. chopped green onion
- 6 wonton wrappers
  Oil for frying
  Sweet-and-sour sauce, optional

**1.** In a small bowl, combine the cream cheese, crab and onion. Place 1 rounded tsp. of filling in the center of each wonton wrapper. Moisten wrapper edges with water; fold in half lengthwise and press firmly to seal.
**2.** Keeping the filling in the center, again fold wonton wrapper lengthwise. Moisten the tops of the short edges with water. Bring the 2 top edges from opposite sides together, overlapping the edges; press and seal.
**3.** In a deep cast-iron or electric skillet, heat 1 in. oil to 375°. Fry wontons on each side until golden brown, 1-2 minutes. Drain on paper towels. Serve warm with sauce, if desired.

**3 WONTONS:** 226 cal., 16g fat (6g sat. fat), 39mg chol., 274mg sod., 16g carb. (1g sugars, 0 fiber), 6g pro.

**TIPS**
- The best dipping sauces for these appetizers are sweet-and-sour sauce, plum sauce, soy sauce, Japanese barbecue sauce, Sriracha, spicy mayo or spicy chili crisp.
- If you prefer, you can cook these wontons in an air fryer, fry them in a pan, or bake them in the oven. Just make sure you coat them with cooking spray if air-frying or baking.

## CRANBERRY ENDIVE APPETIZERS

You can pack a lot of flavor into an elegant appetizer by using the right combination of ingredients. I created this blue cheese filling for a holiday gathering, and everyone loved it.
—Margee Berry, White Salmon, WA

----------------------------------------

**TAKES:** 20 min. • **MAKES:** 2 dozen

- 4 oz. cream cheese, softened
- 2 Tbsp. apple jelly
- ⅓ cup crumbled blue cheese
- ¼ cup dried cranberries, chopped
- 24 leaves Belgian endive
- ¼ cup chopped pecans, toasted

In a large bowl, beat cream cheese and jelly until smooth. Stir in blue cheese and cranberries. Spoon a heaping teaspoonful of filling onto each endive leaf. Sprinkle with pecans.

**1 APPETIZER:** 40 cal., 3g fat (1g sat. fat), 7mg chol., 41mg sod., 3g carb. (2g sugars, 0 fiber), 1g pro.

## CREAMY RED PEPPER DIP
(SHOWN ON PAGE 9)

Roasted red peppers and cream cheese create the perfect combination in this zesty dip. Served in a sweet yellow pepper half, it makes a pretty presentation at parties.
—Linda Murray, Allenstown, NH

----------------------------------------

**TAKES:** 10 min. • **MAKES:** 1½ cups

- 1 garlic clove, peeled
- 1 pkg. (8 oz.) cream cheese, cubed
- ½ cup roasted sweet red peppers, drained
- 2 green onions, cut into 2-in. pieces
- 2 Tbsp. lemon juice
- ½ tsp. ground cumin
  Assorted fresh vegetables

In a food processor, process garlic until minced. Add the cream cheese, red peppers, onions, lemon juice and cumin; cover and process until smooth. Serve with vegetables.

**2 TBSP. DIP:** 72 cal., 7g fat (4g sat. fat), 19mg chol., 97mg sod., 2g carb. (1g sugars, 0 fiber), 1g pro.

CRANBERRY ENDIVE APPETIZERS

## FAVORITE MARINATED MUSHROOMS

Here's a great way to serve mushrooms as an appetizer. Sometimes I add them to salads for tangy flavor, or serve them as a side dish.

—*Brenda Snyder, Hesston, PA*

**PREP:** 15 min. + marinating • **MAKES:** 4 cups

- 2 lbs. fresh mushrooms
- 1 envelope (0.7 oz.) Italian salad dressing mix
- 1 cup water
- ½ cup olive oil
- ⅓ cup cider vinegar
- 2 Tbsp. lemon juice
- 1 Tbsp. sugar
- 1 Tbsp. minced fresh parsley
- 1 Tbsp. reduced-sodium soy sauce
- 2 tsp. crushed red pepper flakes
- 3 garlic cloves, minced
- ½ tsp. salt
- ⅛ tsp. pepper

**1.** Remove mushroom stems (discard or save for another use). Place caps in a large saucepan and cover with water. Bring to a boil. Reduce heat; cook for 3 minutes, stirring occasionally. Drain and cool.

**2.** In a small bowl, whisk the remaining ingredients. Place mushrooms in a large bowl; add dressing and stir to coat. Refrigerate, covered, 8 hours or overnight.

**½ CUP:** 166 cal., 14g fat (2g sat. fat), 0 chol., 602mg sod., 9g carb. (5g sugars, 2g fiber), 4g pro.

## PINEAPPLE SMOOTHIES

I got this recipe over 30 years ago and have been making it ever since. I've tried several diabetic recipes, and this is one of the best.

—*Margery Bryan, Moses Lake, WA*

**PREP:** 5 min. + freezing • **MAKES:** 5 servings

- 1 can (20 oz.) unsweetened pineapple chunks, undrained
- 1 cup buttermilk
- 2 tsp. vanilla extract
- 2 tsp. sugar or sugar substitute

Drain pineapple, reserving ½ cup juice. Freeze pineapple chunks. Place juice, buttermilk, vanilla, sugar and frozen pineapple in a blender; cover and process until smooth. Serve immediately.

**¾ CUP:** 96 cal., 0 fat (0 sat. fat), 2mg chol., 93mg sod., 19g carb. (18g sugars, 1g fiber), 3g pro. **DIABETIC EXCHANGES:** 1 starch.

**TIPS**

- If you're looking to sweeten this pineapple smoothie recipe without using added sugar, try using raw honey or agave nectar. Fruit is also naturally sweet, so first try making this smoothie without the sugar and see if you like it!

- You can also experiment with flavors. Try adding your favorite fruit—we suggest 1 cup of chopped strawberries or 1 small banana. If you want a more of a tropical flavor, you can use coconut milk instead of buttermilk.

## SAVORY CHEESE BALL

Blue cheese contributes a pleasant, tangy bite and olive a saltiness to this creamy cheese ball recipe. This cheese ball can be made a day in advance and kept, covered, in the refrigerator. For the optimum taste, let it stand at room temperature for 20 minutes before serving.
—*Jan Stawara, Howell, MI*

- - - - - - - - - - - - - - - - - - - - - - - - - - - - - - - - - - - - - - - - -

**PREP:** 15 min. + chilling • **MAKES:** 2 cups

- 1 **pkg. (8 oz.) cream cheese, softened**
- 1 **cup crumbled blue cheese**
- ¼ **cup butter, softened**
- 1 **can (4¼ oz.) chopped ripe olives**
- 1 **Tbsp. minced chives**
- ¾ **cup chopped walnuts**
  **Assorted crackers**

**1.** In a large bowl, beat the cream cheese, blue cheese and butter until smooth. Stir in olives and chives. Cover and refrigerate for at least 1 hour.

**2.** Shape cheese mixture into a ball; roll in walnuts. Cover and refrigerate for at least 1 hour. Serve with crackers.

**2 TBSP.:** 145 cal., 14g fat (6g sat. fat), 27mg chol., 204mg sod., 2g carb. (1g sugars, 1g fiber), 3g pro.

## PIZZA MONKEY BREAD

I cannot throw a party without making this recipe. It's fast and easy, and my kids love it.
—*Courtney Wilson, Fresno, CA*

- - - - - - - - - - - - - - - - - - - - - - - - - - - - - - - - - - - - - - - -

**PREP:** 15 min. • **BAKE:** 40 min. + cooling • **MAKES:** 16 servings

- ⅓ **cup olive oil**
- 1 **tsp. Italian seasoning**
- 1 **garlic clove, minced**
- ¼ **tsp. crushed red pepper flakes**
- 2 **cans (16.3 oz. each) large refrigerated flaky biscuits (8 count)**
- 2 **cups shredded part-skim mozzarella cheese**
- ¼ **cup grated Parmesan cheese**
- 20 **slices pepperoni, halved**
- ½ **cup marinara sauce**
  **Optional: Torn fresh basil leaves**

**1.** Preheat oven to 350°. In a large microwave-safe bowl, combine the first 4 ingredients; microwave, covered, on high for 30 seconds. Cool slightly.

**2.** Cut each biscuit into 4 pieces; add to oil mixture and toss to coat. Add cheeses and pepperoni; toss to combine. In a heavy 10-in. fluted tube pan coated with cooking spray, layer half of the biscuit mixture; drizzle with ¼ cup marinara sauce. Repeat layers.

**3.** Bake about 40 minutes or until golden brown. Cool in pan for 10 minutes. Run a knife around sides and center tube of pan. Invert onto a serving plate. Serve with additional marinara sauce, warmed. If desired, top with torn fresh basil, additional grated Parmesan cheese and additional red pepper flakes.

**1 SERVING:** 288 cal., 17g fat (5g sat. fat), 12mg chol., 723mg sod., 26g carb. (6g sugars, 1g fiber), 8g pro.

**TIPS**

Craving garlic breadsticks? Double or triple the amount of garlic. For another delicious twist, try replacing the marinara with pesto. Bonus—it's colorful!

# - 2 -

# BREAKFAST & BRUNCH

Rise and shine! Streamlining kitchen time doesn't mean skipping the most important meal of the day. Turn here when you need a hot and hearty breakfast or an impressive brunch-buffet addition. Not sure what to make for supper? Consider these dishes for a breakfast-for-dinner surprise.

**Cinnamon Swirl Quick Bread** (p. 50) **Oat Waffles** (p. 41) **Caramel Bubble Ring** (p. 45)
**Quick Stovetop Granola** (p. 39) **Fluffy Pancakes** (p. 49) **Buffet Scrambled Eggs** (p. 36)
**Gingerbread Coffee Cake** (p. 37) **Red Pepper Cornmeal Souffle** (p. 40) **Corned Beef Hash & Eggs** (p. 46)

## APPLE-CINNAMON BAKED FRENCH TOAST

When my wife and I hosted a breakfast for our church group, we wanted to avoid the last-minute rush of cooking. So we decided to try this make-ahead French toast. Everyone loved it and requested the recipe.
—*John Cashen, Moline, IL*

- - - - - - - - - - - - - - - - - - - - - - - - - - - - -

**PREP:** 20 min. + chilling • **BAKE:** 45 min.
**MAKES:** 6 servings

- 12 slices day-old French bread (¾ in. thick), divided
- 6 large eggs, lightly beaten
- 2¾ cups 2% milk
- ⅔ cup sugar, divided
- 1 Tbsp. vanilla extract
- 4 medium apples, peeled and thinly sliced
- 2 tsp. ground cinnamon
- ¾ tsp. ground nutmeg
- 1 Tbsp. butter
  Optional: Whipped cream and maple syrup

**1.** Arrange 6 slices bread in a greased 13x9-in. baking dish. Combine eggs, milk, ⅓ cup sugar and vanilla; pour half over the bread. Top with apples. Combine cinnamon, nutmeg and remaining ⅓ cup sugar; sprinkle over apples. Top with the remaining slices bread; pour remaining egg mixture over bread. Dot with the butter. Cover and refrigerate 8 hours or overnight.

**2.** Remove from refrigerator 30 minutes before baking. Preheat oven to 350°. Bake, uncovered, until a knife inserted in center comes out clean, 45-50 minutes. Let stand 5 minutes before serving. If desired, serve with whipped cream and syrup.

**1 PIECE:** 378 cal., 10g fat (5g sat. fat), 200mg chol., 352mg sod., 58g carb. (37g sugars, 3g fiber), 13g pro.

## BACON & EGG GRAVY

My husband, Ron, created this wonderful breakfast gravy. It's homestyle and old-fashioned. Sometimes we ladle the gravy over homemade biscuits. Served with fruit salad, it's a great breakfast.
—*Terry Bray, Winter Haven, FL*

- - - - - - - - - - - - - - - - - - - - - - - - - - - - -

**TAKES:** 20 min. • **MAKES:** 2 servings

- 6 bacon strips, diced
- 5 Tbsp. all-purpose flour
- 1½ cups water
- 1 can (12 oz.) evaporated milk
- 3 hard-boiled large eggs, sliced
  Salt and pepper to taste
- 4 slices bread, toasted

In a skillet, cook bacon over medium heat until crisp; remove to paper towels. Stir flour into the drippings until blended; cook over medium heat until browned, stirring constantly. Gradually add the water and milk. Bring to a boil; cook and stir for 2 minutes or until thickened. Add bacon, eggs, salt and pepper. Serve over toast.

**1 SERVING:** 905 cal., 55g fat (23g sat. fat), 396mg chol., 1066mg sod., 59g carb. (22g sugars, 2g fiber), 38g pro.

### TIPS

- A roux is the combination of fat and flour used to thicken sauces. In this case, bacon grease is used with the flour to thicken the gravy, but you may also find butter or oil as the fat in other roux recipes.
- Bacon grease lends a savory flavor to a roux. If you'd like save clean bacon grease to use for a future roux, you can keep it in the refrigerator. You can also use it to grease a casserole dish or season vegetables before baking. Try brushing some onto bread slices when making a grilled cheese sandwich.

## BUFFET SCRAMBLED EGGS

These are my favorite scrambled eggs. The white sauce, flavored with chicken bouillon, keeps the eggs creamy and moist. It's a tasty twist on a morning mainstay.
—*Elsie Beachy, Plain City, OH*

**TAKES:** 20 min. • **MAKES:** 8 servings

- 8 Tbsp. butter, divided
- ¼ cup all-purpose flour
- 2 cups whole milk
- 4 tsp. chicken bouillon granules
- 16 large eggs, lightly beaten
  Optional: Minced fresh parsley, tarragon and chives

1. In a small saucepan, melt 2 Tbsp. butter. Stir in flour until smooth. Gradually add milk and bouillon. Bring to a boil; cook and stir until thickened, about 2 minutes.
2. In a large skillet, melt remaining 6 Tbsp. butter. Add eggs; cook over medium heat until eggs begin to set, stirring occasionally. Stir in white sauce. Cook until eggs are completely set. If desired, sprinkle with parsley, tarragon and chives.

**¾ CUP:** 304 cal., 24g fat (11g sat. fat), 464mg chol., 692mg sod., 7g carb. (4g sugars, 0 fiber), 15g pro.

## BLUEBERRY CANTALOUPE SALAD

Add a fresh touch to any meal with these cute cups. The simple citrus dressing really jazzes up the fruit.
—*R. Jean Rand, Edina, MN*

**TAKES:** 10 min. • **MAKES:** 4 servings

- ¾ cup orange yogurt
- 1½ tsp. lemon juice
- ¾ tsp. poppy seeds
- ½ tsp. grated orange zest
- 2 cups diced cantaloupe
- 1 cup fresh blueberries

In a bowl, mix yogurt, lemon juice, poppy seeds and orange zest. To serve, divide cantaloupe and blueberries among 4 dishes; top with yogurt dressing.

**¾ CUP WITH 3 TBSP. DRESSING:** 76 cal., 1g fat (0 sat. fat), 1mg chol., 24mg sod., 17g carb. (15g sugars, 1g fiber), 2g pro. **DIABETIC EXCHANGES:** 1 fruit.

> **TIP**
> Blueberries contain more antioxidants than just about any other fruit. Eating them raw helps ensure you get all those benefits, so add them to salads and other recipes that don't require baking or cooking.

## GINGERBREAD COFFEE CAKE

At our house, we love gingerbread that's not too sweet. If you like things a bit sweeter, however, mix confectioners' sugar, milk and vanilla extract for an icing to drizzle on top.
—*Barbara Humiston, Tampa, FL*

**PREP:** 20 min. • **BAKE:** 20 min. + cooling • **MAKES:** 8 servings

- 1 cup all-purpose flour
- ½ cup plus 1 Tbsp. sugar, divided
- 1¾ tsp. ground cinnamon, divided
- 1 tsp. ground ginger
- ¼ tsp. salt
- ¼ tsp. ground allspice
- ¼ cup cold butter
- ¾ tsp. baking powder
- ½ tsp. baking soda
- 1 large egg, room temperature
- ½ cup buttermilk
- 2 Tbsp. molasses

1. Preheat oven to 350°. In a large bowl, mix flour, ½ cup sugar, ¾ tsp. cinnamon, ginger, salt and allspice; cut in butter until crumbly. Reserve ⅓ cup for topping.
2. Stir baking powder and baking soda into remaining flour mixture. In a small bowl, whisk egg, buttermilk and molasses. Add to flour mixture; stir just until moistened. Transfer batter to a greased 8-in. round baking pan.
3. Add remaining 1 Tbsp. sugar and 1 tsp. cinnamon to reserved topping; sprinkle over batter. Bake 20-25 minutes or until a toothpick inserted in center comes out clean. Cool completely in pan on a wire rack.

**1 PIECE:** 195 cal., 7g fat (4g sat. fat), 39mg chol., 283mg sod., 31g carb. (19g sugars, 1g fiber), 3g pro. **DIABETIC EXCHANGES:** 2 starch, 1½ fat.
OPTIONAL VANILLA ICING AND GINGER TOPPING: Mix ¾ cup confectioners' sugar, 1 Tbsp. 2% milk and ½ tsp. vanilla extract. Drizzle over cooled cake. Sprinkle with 2 Tbsp. finely chopped crystallized ginger.

## CINNAMON BREAKFAST BITES

These quick early-morning treats with a sweet, crispy coating are baked in the oven instead of deep-fried.
—*Ruth Hastings, Louisville, IL*

**TAKES:** 30 min. • **MAKES:** 1½ dozen

- 1⅓ cups all-purpose flour
- 1 cup crisp rice cereal, coarsely crushed
- 2 Tbsp. plus ½ cup sugar, divided
- 1 Tbsp. baking powder
- ½ tsp. salt
- ¼ cup butter-flavored shortening
- ½ cup 2% milk
- 1 tsp. ground cinnamon
- ¼ cup butter, melted

1. Preheat oven to 425°. In a large bowl, combine the flour, cereal, 2 Tbsp. sugar, baking powder and salt; cut in shortening until mixture resembles coarse crumbs. Stir in milk just until moistened. Shape into 1-in. balls.
2. In a shallow bowl, combine remaining ½ cup sugar and cinnamon. Dip balls in melted butter, then roll in cinnamon sugar.
3. Arrange in a single layer in an 8-in. cast-iron skillet or round baking pan. Bake until browned and a toothpick inserted in centers comes out clean, 15-18 minutes.

**1 PIECE:** 118 cal., 5g fat (2g sat. fat), 7mg chol., 178mg sod., 16g carb. (8g sugars, 0 fiber), 1g pro.

## HAM & SWISS BREAD PUDDING

This rich and hearty brunch dish is loaded with ham, mushrooms and cheese, plus layers of sliced French bread. It's a terrific choice when you have overnight guests.
—*Kelly Williams, Forked River, NJ*

**PREP:** 30 min. • **BAKE:** 50 min.
**MAKES:** 9 servings

- ¼ cup plus 3 Tbsp. butter, melted, divided
- 18 slices day-old French bread (¾ in. thick), divided
- ½ cup stone-ground mustard
- 1½ cups cubed fully cooked ham
- 1 cup sliced fresh mushrooms
- 2 garlic cloves, minced
- ¼ cup chopped green onions
- 2 cups shredded Swiss cheese
- 8 large eggs
- 4 cups heavy whipping cream
- ½ tsp. salt
- ½ tsp. pepper
- 2 Tbsp. minced fresh parsley
  Warm maple syrup, optional

**1.** Pour ¼ cup melted butter into a 13x9-in. baking dish; set aside. Spread both sides of the bread slices with mustard. Arrange 9 bread slices in the baking dish.
**2.** In a large skillet, saute the ham, mushrooms and garlic in remaining butter until mushrooms are tender. Add the onions; cook until crisp-tender, about 1 minute longer. Spoon ham mixture over the bread; sprinkle with cheese. Arrange remaining bread slices on top. In a large bowl, beat the eggs, cream, salt and pepper. Stir in parsley; pour over bread.
**3.** Place dish in a larger roasting pan; add 1 in. of hot water to larger pan. Bake at 325° until a knife inserted in the center comes out clean, 50-60 minutes. Let stand for 5 minutes before serving. Drizzle with maple syrup if desired.
**1 PIECE:** 858 cal., 69g fat (41g sat. fat), 415mg chol., 1152mg sod., 28g carb. (3g sugars, 3g fiber), 31g pro.

## QUICK STOVETOP GRANOLA

The fiber-rich oats in this granola will quell your cravings with just a small serving. Keep some handy in a small airtight container for moments when your stomach takes over. For even longer-lasting satisfaction, pair the treat with protein-packed yogurt.
—Taste of Home *Test Kitchen*

**TAKES:** 15 min. • **MAKES:** 3 cups

- 2 cups quick-cooking oats
- 2 Tbsp. brown sugar
- 2 Tbsp. honey
- 1 Tbsp. butter
- ¼ cup slivered almonds
- 2 Tbsp. golden raisins
- 2 Tbsp. sweetened shredded coconut

**1.** In a large nonstick skillet, toast oats over medium heat until golden brown. Remove and set aside. In the same skillet, cook and stir the brown sugar, honey and butter over medium-low heat until bubbly, 1-2 minutes.
**2.** Stir in the almonds, raisins, coconut and oats until coated. Cool. Store in an airtight container.
**¼ CUP:** 102 cal., 3g fat (1g sat. fat), 3mg chol., 14mg sod., 16g carb. (6g sugars, 2g fiber), 3g pro. **DIABETIC EXCHANGES:** 1 starch, ½ fat.

## PECAN PUMPKIN BISCUITS

Our two daughters love munching on these rich pecan-studded biscuits for breakfast. I make dozens and serve them piping-hot with butter and honey.
—Connie Bolton, San Antonio, TX

**TAKES:** 30 min. • **MAKES:** 1 dozen

- 2 cups all-purpose flour
- ¼ cup sugar
- 4 tsp. baking powder
- ½ tsp. salt
- ½ tsp. ground cinnamon
- ½ tsp. ground nutmeg
- ½ cup cold butter
- ⅓ cup chopped pecans, toasted
- ⅔ cup canned pumpkin
- ⅓ cup half-and-half cream
  Optional: melted butter and cinnamon sugar

In a large bowl, combine the first 6 ingredients. Cut in the butter until mixture resembles coarse crumbs. Stir in pecans. Combine pumpkin and cream; stir into dry ingredients. Turn onto a floured surface; knead 4 to 6 times. Roll to ½-in. thickness; cut with a 2½-in. biscuit cutter. Place on a greased baking sheet. Bake at 400° for 12-15 minutes or until golden brown. If desired, serve warm with melted butter and cinnamon sugar.
**1 BISCUIT:** 194 cal., 11g fat (5g sat. fat), 24mg chol., 313mg sod., 22g carb. (5g sugars, 1g fiber), 3g pro.

## RED PEPPER CORNMEAL SOUFFLE

I use the vegetables from our garden in all my cooking. Doing so adds from-scratch flavor that just can't be beat. Dotted with parsley and red pepper, this souffle is a favorite.
—Janet Eckhoff, Woodland, CA

PREP: 20 min. • BAKE: 35 min. • MAKES: 10 servings

  1  large onion, chopped
  1  cup chopped sweet red pepper
  ¼  cup butter
  3  cups whole milk
  ⅔  cup cornmeal
  1  cup shredded sharp cheddar cheese
  2  Tbsp. minced fresh parsley
  1  tsp. salt, divided
  ½  tsp. white pepper
  2  large egg yolks, beaten
  7  large egg whites, room temperature
  ½  tsp. cream of tartar

1. In a large saucepan, saute onion and red pepper in butter until tender. Add the milk. Bring to a boil. Gradually whisk in cornmeal; whisk constantly until thickened, about 5 minutes. Add cheese, parsley, ½ tsp. salt and pepper. Add 1 cup cornmeal mixture to the egg yolks; mix well. Return all to saucepan.
2. In a large bowl, beat egg whites, cream of tartar and remaining ½ tsp. salt until stiff peaks form. Fold into the cornmeal mixture. Transfer to a greased 2-qt. souffle dish.
3. Bake at 375° until golden brown, 35-40 minutes.
**1 SERVING:** 193 cal., 11g fat (7g sat. fat), 77mg chol., 427mg sod., 14g carb. (5g sugars, 1g fiber), 9g pro.

## SAUSAGE & EGG GRITS

I always eat my sausage, grits and eggs together, so I thought it would be great to mix them up in the same skillet. The resulting breakfast bombshell is loaded with down-home flavor—and it doesn't even use any butter!
—Jeannine Quiller, Raleigh, NC

PREP: 15 min. • COOK: 20 min. • MAKES: 6 servings

  4  breakfast turkey sausage links, casings removed
  1½  cups egg substitute
  1¼  cups whole milk, divided
  3  cups water
  ⅛  tsp. salt
  1  cup quick-cooking grits
  ¾  cup shredded reduced-fat cheddar cheese
  2  green onions, chopped
  ⅛  tsp. pepper

1. Crumble sausage into a large skillet; cook over medium heat until no longer pink. Remove to paper towels with a slotted spoon. Whisk egg substitute and ¼ cup milk; add to same skillet. Cook and stir until set; remove from the heat.
2. Meanwhile, in a Dutch oven, bring water, salt and remaining 1 cup milk to a boil. Slowly stir in grits. Reduce heat; cook and stir until thickened, 5-7 minutes.
3. Stir in half the cheese. Add the sausage, eggs, green onions and pepper; heat through. Serve in bowls; sprinkle with the remaining cheese.
**1 CUP:** 208 cal., 6g fat (3g sat. fat), 25mg chol., 369mg sod., 24g carb. (4g sugars, 1g fiber), 16g pro. **DIABETIC EXCHANGES:** 2 lean meat, 1½ starch.

## OAT WAFFLES

These family favorites have more fiber and less fat than standard waffles. My 2 year-old daughter loves them with fresh berries.
—*Karen Hayes, Danville, VA*

- - - - - - - - - - - - - - - - - - - - - - - - - - - - - - - - - - - - - - - -

**TAKES:** 10 min. • **MAKES:** 8 waffles (about 6½ in.)

- 1  cup all-purpose flour
- 1  cup oat flour
- 4  tsp. baking powder
- 1  Tbsp. sugar
- ½  tsp. salt
- 2  large eggs, room temperature
- 1¾ cups fat-free milk
- 2  Tbsp. canola oil
- 1  tsp. vanilla extract
-    Optional: Fresh fruit, maple syrup and powdered sugar

1. In a bowl, combine the first 5 ingredients. Combine the eggs, milk, oil and vanilla; stir into dry ingredients just until combined.
2. Pour batter by ½ cupfuls into a preheated waffle iron; bake according to manufacturer's directions until golden brown. Garnish with toppings as desired.

**1 WAFFLE:** 178 cal., 6g fat (1g sat. fat), 54mg chol., 307mg sod., 24g carb. (0 sugars, 2g fiber), 7g pro. **DIABETIC EXCHANGES:** 1½ starch, 1 lean meat.

> **TIP**
>
> As a substitute for 1 cup oat flour, you can process 1¼ cups quick-cooking or old-fashioned oats until finely ground.

## EARLY-RISER OVEN OMELET

Everyone will rush to the table when you serve this big fluffy omelet. Packed with tomato, broccoli, ham and cheese, it makes a hearty brunch dish that easily serves a crowd.
—*Wendy Fawcett, Gillam, MB*

- - - - - - - - - - - - - - - - - - - - - - - - - - - - - - - - - - - - - - - -

**PREP:** 15 min. • **BAKE:** 35 min. • **MAKES:** 6 servings

- 10 large egg whites
- 5  large eggs
- 1  cup fat-free milk
- ¼  tsp. seasoned salt
- ¼  tsp. pepper
- 1½ cups cubed fully cooked ham
- 1  cup chopped fresh broccoli
- 1  cup shredded reduced-fat cheddar cheese
- 1  medium tomato, seeded and chopped
- 3  Tbsp. finely chopped onion

In a bowl, beat egg whites, eggs, milk, seasoned salt and pepper. Pour into a greased 10-in. cast-iron or other ovenproof skillet. Sprinkle with ham, broccoli, cheese, tomato and onion. Bake, uncovered, at 350° until the eggs are almost set, 30-35 minutes. Broil 4-6 in. from the heat until the eggs are set and top is lightly browned, 1-2 minutes.

**1 PIECE:** 216 cal., 10g fat (4g sat. fat), 183mg chol., 805mg sod., 6g carb. (4g sugars, 1g fiber), 25g pro. **DIABETIC EXCHANGES:** 3 medium-fat meat, 1 vegetable.

## BREAKFAST ENCHILADAS

Draped in gooey cheese and a savory sauce, these enchiladas are a popular option at any brunch. Chorizo gives the hearty filling a Southwestern kick.
—*Tahnia Fox, Trenton, MI*

------------------------------------------------

**PREP:** 25 min. • **BAKE:** 25 min.
**MAKES:** 8 enchiladas

- ½ lb. uncooked chorizo or spicy pork sausage
- 1 small onion, finely chopped
- ½ medium green pepper, finely chopped
- 2 tsp. butter
- 6 eggs, beaten
- ¾ cup shredded cheddar cheese, divided
- ¾ cup shredded pepper Jack cheese, divided
- 1 can (10 oz.) enchilada sauce
- 8 flour tortillas (6 in.), room temperature
- 1 green onion, finely chopped

**1.** Preheat oven to 350°. Crumble chorizo into a large skillet; add the onion and green pepper. Cook over medium heat for 6-8 minutes or until sausage is fully cooked; drain.
**2.** In another skillet, heat butter over medium heat. Add the eggs; cook and stir until almost set. Remove from the heat; stir in the chorizo mixture and ⅓ cup of each cheese.
**3.** Spread ½ cup enchilada sauce into a greased 11x7-in. baking dish. Spoon 3 Tbsp. egg mixture down the center of each tortilla. Roll up and place seam side down in prepared dish.
**4.** Pour remaining enchilada sauce over the top; sprinkle with remaining cheeses.
**5.** Bake, uncovered, for 25-30 minutes or until heated through. Sprinkle with green onion.
**1 ENCHILADA:** 369 cal., 23g fat (10g sat. fat), 189mg chol., 1028mg sod., 20g carb. (2g sugars, 1g fiber), 20g pro.

## AUNT EDITH'S BAKED PANCAKE

My aunt made a mighty breakfast that revolved around a really big pancake. I always enjoyed watching as she poured the batter into her huge iron skillet, then baked the confection to perfection in the oven.
—*Marion Kirst, Troy, MI*

------------------------------------------------

**PREP:** 15 min. • **BAKE:** 20 min.
**MAKES:** 4 servings

- 3 large eggs, room temperature
- ½ tsp. salt
- ½ cup all-purpose flour
- ½ cup 2% milk
- 2 Tbsp. butter, softened
  Confectioners' sugar
  Lemon wedges

**1.** In a bowl, beat eggs until very light. Add salt, flour and milk; beat well. Thoroughly rub bottom and sides of a 10-in. cast-iron or other heavy skillet with butter. Pour batter into skillet.

**2.** Bake at 450° for 15 minutes. Reduce heat to 350° and bake until set, 5 minutes longer. If desired, remove pancake from skillet and place on a large hot platter. Dust with confectioners' sugar and serve immediately, with lemon wedges on side.
**1 PIECE:** 180 cal., 10g fat (5g sat. fat), 158mg chol., 407mg sod., 14g carb. (2g sugars, 0 fiber), 7g pro.

**DID YOU KNOW?**

A large pancake baked in an oven-safe skillet is frequently called a Dutch Baby, a moniker that is actually derived from its *Deutsch* (German) origins rather than the word *Dutch*. However, the Dutch are also known for making their own large skillet pancakes called *pannekoeken*. Unlike Dutch Babies, pannekoeken are not baked in the oven but rather on a stovetop, and they are thinner than traditional pancakes. Dutch Babies rise in the pan as they bake and, as a result, develop crisp, golden edges—unlike regular pancakes, which tend to be softer in texture throughout.

Place **2 cups unseasoned croutons** and **1 cup shredded cheddar cheese** in a greased 11-x7-in. baking dish. Combine **4 eggs**, **2 cups 2% milk**, ½ **tsp. salt**, ½ **tsp. ground mustard**, ⅛ **tsp. onion powder** and a **dash pepper**; pour into baking dish. Sprinkle with **4 strips cooked crumbled bacon**. Bake at 325° for 1 hour or until set.

# - BRUNCH EGG CASSEROLE -

This meal-in-one dish makes breakfast a snap. It's perfect for overnight guests, busy holiday mornings or any time you need an easy, hearty fix early in the day.

## CARAMEL BUBBLE RING

Lots of caramel topping make this quick pull-apart bread oh so gooey and delicious. It truly is a finger-lickin' good baked treat.
—*Laura Clifton, Wenatchee, WA*

- - - - - - - - - - - - - - - - - - - - - - - - - - - - - - - - - - - - - - - - - - - - - - - - - -

**PREP:** 15 min. • **BAKE:** 20 min. • **MAKES:** 16 servings

- ¾ cup sugar
- 4 tsp. ground cinnamon
- ½ cup caramel ice cream topping
- 2 Tbsp. maple syrup
- ⅓ cup chopped pecans, divided
- 2 tubes (11 oz. each) refrigerated breadsticks
- ⅓ cup butter, melted

**1.** Preheat oven to 350°. Combine sugar and cinnamon; set aside. Combine caramel topping and syrup; set aside. Sprinkle half the pecans into a greased 10-in. fluted tube pan. Drizzle with a third of the caramel mixture.

**2.** Open the tubes of breadstick dough (do not unroll). Cut each into 6 slices; dip in melted butter, then roll in cinnamon sugar. Place half in the pan; sprinkle with remaining pecans. Drizzle with half the remaining caramel mixture. Top with remaining dough. Drizzle with remaining caramel mixture.

**3.** Bake until golden brown, 20-25 minutes. Cool for 2 minutes. Invert onto a serving platter; serve warm.

**1 SERVING:** 176 cal., 7g fat (3g sat. fat), 10mg chol., 220mg sod., 28g carb. (18g sugars, 1g fiber), 2g pro.

## BROCCOLI & CHICKEN CHEESE STRATA

On our dairy farm, chores often delay dinner. That's when this strata comes in handy. I'll prepare it beforehand and later pop it in the oven for a quick and easy meal. Breakfast-for-dinner ease!
—*Margery Moore, Richfield Springs, NY*

- - - - - - - - - - - - - - - - - - - - - - - - - - - - - - - - - - - - - - - - - - - - - - - - - -

**PREP:** 15 min. + chilling • **BAKE:** 1 hour • **MAKES:** 8 servings

- 12 slices bread
- 2¼ cups shredded cheddar cheese, divided
- 3 cups frozen chopped broccoli, thawed and drained
- 2 cups diced cooked chicken
- 1 Tbsp. butter, melted
- 6 large eggs
- 3 cups 2% milk
- 2 Tbsp. finely chopped onion
- ¾ tsp. salt
- ½ tsp. ground mustard
- ¼ tsp. pepper

**1.** Using a doughnut cutter, cut 12 rings and holes in bread; set aside. Tear the remaining bread scraps and place in a greased 13x9-in. baking dish. Sprinkle with 2 cups cheese, broccoli and chicken. Arrange bread rings and holes on top; brush with melted butter.

**2.** Whisk together remaining 6 ingredients; pour over top. Refrigerate, covered, 8 hours or overnight.

**3.** Remove strata from refrigerator 30 minutes before baking. Preheat oven to 325°. Bake, uncovered, 55-60 minutes. Sprinkle with remaining cheese; bake until a knife inserted in center comes out clean, about 5 minutes longer. Let stand 5-10 minutes before cutting.

**1 PIECE:** 440 cal., 22g fat (10g sat. fat), 213mg chol., 794mg sod., 30g carb. (8g sugars, 3g fiber), 31g pro.

## CORNED BEEF HASH & EGGS

Sunday breakfasts have always been special in our house. It's fun to get in the kitchen and cook with the kids. No matter how many new recipes we try, the kids always rate this No. 1!
—*Rick Skildum, Maple Grove, MN*

**PREP:** 15 min. • **BAKE:** 20 min. • **MAKES:** 8 servings

|   |   |
|---|---|
| 1 | pkg. (32 oz.) frozen cubed hash browns |
| 1½ | cups chopped onion |
| ½ | cup canola oil |
| 4 | to 5 cups chopped cooked corned beef |
| ½ | tsp. salt |
| 8 | large eggs |
|   | Salt and pepper to taste |
| 2 | Tbsp. minced fresh parsley |

**1.** Preheat oven to 325°. In a large ovenproof skillet, cook hash browns and onion in oil until potatoes are browned and onion is tender. Remove from the heat; stir in corned beef and salt.
**2.** Make 8 wells in the hash browns. Carefully break 1 egg into each well. Sprinkle with salt and pepper. Bake, covered, for 20-25 minutes or until eggs reach desired doneness. Garnish with parsley.
**1 SERVING:** 442 cal., 30g fat (6g sat. fat), 242mg chol., 895mg sod., 24g carb. (3g sugars, 2g fiber), 20g pro.

**TIP**
You can make corned beef hash and eggs without an ovenproof skillet. Instead of transferring the pan to the oven after cracking the eggs into the hash, keep it on the stovetop. Simply put the lid on, and cook until the egg whites are set and the yolks reach desired doneness.

## BACON-CHEESE PUFF PIE

This recipe comes from my grandma, and it's one of my family's favorites—we love the combination of bacon, tomatoes and cheese. It's great for brunch at any time of year.
—*Sherry Lee, Sheridan, IN*

**PREP:** 20 min. + cooling • **BAKE:** 45 min. • **MAKES:** 6 servings

|   |   |
|---|---|
| 1 | pastry shell, unbaked |
| 1 | lb. sliced bacon, cooked and crumbled |
| 1 | large tomato, peeled and sliced |
| 1 | cup shredded cheddar cheese |
| 3 | large eggs, separated |
| ¾ | cup sour cream |
| ½ | cup all-purpose flour |
| ½ | tsp. salt |
|   | Paprika |

**1.** Line unpricked pastry shell with a double thickness of heavy-duty foil. Bake at 450° for 5 minutes. Remove foil. Bake 5 minutes longer. Cool completely.
**2.** Sprinkle bacon over the crust. Top with tomato and cheese. In a large bowl, beat the egg yolks, sour cream, flour and salt until smooth. In another large bowl, beat egg whites until stiff. Fold into sour cream mixture; spread over cheese. Sprinkle with the paprika.
**3.** Bake at 350° until a knife inserted in the center comes out clean, about 45 minutes. Let stand 5-10 minutes before cutting.
**1 PIECE:** 518 cal., 35g fat (17g sat. fat), 176mg chol., 901mg sod., 29g carb. (4g sugars, 1g fiber), 19g pro.

## BLUEBERRY CREAM MUFFINS

When most people think of Maine, they immediately think of lobster. But we who live here know of something equally as good: wild blueberries. Their flavor is unmatched, and they're especially great in these blueberry muffins with sour cream.
—*Lillian Van der Harst, Center Lovell, ME*

**PREP:** 15 min. • **BAKE:** 20 min. • **MAKES:** 2 dozen

- 4 **large eggs, room temperature**
- 2 **cups sugar**
- 1 **cup vegetable oil**
- 1 **tsp. vanilla extract**
- 4 **cups all-purpose flour**
- 1 **tsp. salt**
- 1 **tsp. baking soda**
- 2 **tsp. baking powder**
- 2 **cups sour cream**
- 2 **cups fresh blueberries**

Preheat oven to 400°. In a bowl, beat eggs. Gradually add sugar. While beating, slowly pour in oil; add vanilla. Combine dry ingredients; add alternately with the sour cream to the egg mixture. Gently fold in blueberries. Fill greased muffin cups three-fourths full. Bake until a toothpick inserted in center comes out clean, 18-20 minutes. Cool 5 minutes before removing from pans to wire racks.

**1 MUFFIN:** 282 cal., 14g fat (4g sat. fat), 45mg chol., 210mg sod., 35g carb. (19g sugars, 1g fiber), 4g pro.

## FESTIVE FRENCH PANCAKES

Not quite as thin as true crepes, these light-as-a-feather pancakes are topped with preserves and a dusting of confectioners' sugar. They're elegant and so easy to make, with a delicious French flair!
—*Diane Aune, Nine Mile Falls, WA*

**TAKES:** 15 min. • **MAKES:** 4 servings

- ⅔ **cup 2% milk**
- 2 **large eggs, room temperature**
- ⅓ **cup water**
- ½ **tsp. vanilla extract**
- ¾ **cup all-purpose flour**
- 2 **Tbsp. confectioners' sugar**
- 1 **tsp. baking powder**
- ½ **tsp. salt**
  **Preserves of your choice, optional**

**1.** In a blender, combine the milk, eggs, water and vanilla; cover and process until well blended. Combine the flour, confectioners' sugar, baking powder and salt; add to egg mixture. Cover and process until smooth.

**2.** Heat a lightly greased 8-in. nonstick skillet over medium heat; pour 2 Tbsp. batter into the center of skillet. Lift and tilt pan to coat bottom evenly. Cook until top appears dry; turn and cook 15-20 seconds longer. Remove to a wire rack.

**3.** Repeat with remaining batter, greasing skillet as needed. If desired, spread preserves over crepes; roll up. Sprinkle with additional confectioners' sugar if desired.

**2 CREPES:** 158 cal., 3g fat (1g sat. fat), 96mg chol., 470mg sod., 24g carb. (6g sugars, 1g fiber), 7g pro. **DIABETIC EXCHANGES:** 1½ starch, 1 medium-fat meat.

### HAM & EGG POCKETS

Refrigerated crescent roll dough make these savory breakfast pockets a snap to prepare.
—Taste of Home *Test Kitchen*

-------------------------------------------------------------

**TAKES:** 20 min. • **MAKES:** 2 pockets

| | |
|---|---|
| 1 | large egg |
| 2 | tsp. 2% milk |
| 2 | tsp. butter |
| 1 | oz. thinly sliced deli ham, chopped |
| 2 | Tbsp. shredded cheddar cheese |
| 1 | tube (4 oz.) refrigerated crescent rolls |

**1.** Preheat oven to 375°. In a small bowl, combine egg and milk. In a small skillet heat butter until hot. Add egg mixture; cook and stir over medium heat until egg is completely set. Remove from the heat. Fold in ham and cheese.

**2.** On a greased baking sheet, separate crescent dough into 2 rectangles. Seal perforations; spoon half the filling down the center of each rectangle. Fold in ends and sides; pinch to seal. Bake until golden brown, 10-14 minutes.

**1 POCKET:** 345 cal., 22g fat (8g sat. fat), 132mg chol., 756mg sod., 23g carb. (5g sugars, 0 fiber), 12g pro.

### PEANUT BUTTER BANANA OATMEAL

The classic flavors of peanut butter and banana come together in an oatmeal that's loved by kids and adults alike. My family has enjoyed this dish on many chilly mornings.
—Deborah Purdue, Westland, MI

-------------------------------------------------------------

**TAKES:** 15 min. • **MAKES:** 4 servings

| | |
|---|---|
| 3 | cups fat-free milk or water |
| ¼ | tsp. salt |
| 1½ | cups quick-cooking oats |
| 2 | large bananas, sliced |
| 2 | Tbsp. peanut butter |
| ½ | tsp. vanilla extract |

Place milk and salt in a large saucepan; bring just to a boil. Stir in oats; cook until thickened, 1-2 minutes, stirring occasionally. Remove from heat; stir in remaining ingredients.

**1 CUP:** 284 cal., 7g fat (1g sat. fat), 4mg chol., 260mg sod., 47g carb. (19g sugars, 5g fiber), 13g pro.

# FLUFFY PANCAKES

I found this fluffy pancake recipe among our old family favorites and adapted it to make a small amount. It's quick and easy to prepare, but we still consider it a special treat on Sunday mornings.
—*Eugene Presley, Council, VA*

- - - - - - - - - - - - - - - - - - - - - - - - - - - - - -

**TAKES:** 15 min. • **MAKES:** 8 pancakes

- 1 **cup all-purpose flour**
- 1 **Tbsp. sugar**
- 2 **tsp. baking powder**
- ½ **tsp. salt**
- 1 **large egg, room temperature**
- ¾ **cup 2% milk**
- ¼ **cup shortening or butter, melted**

**1.** In a small bowl, combine flour, sugar, baking powder and salt. Combine egg, milk and shortening; stir into the dry ingredients just until moistened.

**2.** Pour batter by ¼ cupfuls onto a greased hot griddle. Turn when bubbles form on top of pancakes; cook until the second side is golden brown.

**2 PANCAKES:** 274 cal., 15g fat (9g sat. fat), 82mg chol., 664mg sod., 29g carb. (5g sugars, 1g fiber), 6g pro.

**CHOCOLATE CHIP PANCAKES:** Stir ½ cup miniature chocolate chip into batter. Proceed as recipe directs.

**MAPLE PANCAKES:** Omit sugar. Add 1 Tbsp. maple syrup to milk mixture. Proceed as recipe directs.

> **TIP**
> If your pancakes aren't fluffy, the culprit is likely overmixing the pancake batter, which overworks the gluten in the flour. Use a gentle hand when folding the wet ingredients into the dry ingredients and mix just until incorporated. It's ideal to see some streaks and pockets of flour.

# CINNAMON SWIRL QUICK BREAD

While cinnamon bread is a natural for breakfast, we love it any time of the day. This one is a nice twist on traditional cinnamon swirl yeast breads.
—*Helen Richardson, Shelbyville, MI*

**PREP:** 15 min. • **BAKE:** 45 min. + cooling • **MAKES:** 16 pieces

- 2   cups all-purpose flour
- 1½  cups sugar, divided
- 1   tsp. baking soda
- ½   tsp. salt
- 1   cup buttermilk
- 1   large egg, room temperature
- ¼   cup canola oil
- 3   tsp. ground cinnamon

**GLAZE**
- ¼   cup confectioners' sugar
- 1½ to 2 tsp. 2% milk

**1.** Preheat oven to 350°. In a large bowl, combine flour, 1 cup sugar, baking soda and salt. Combine buttermilk, egg and oil; stir into dry ingredients just until moistened. In a small bowl, combine cinnamon and remaining ½ cup sugar.

**2.** Grease the bottom only of a 9x5-in. loaf pan. Pour half the batter into pan; sprinkle with half the cinnamon-sugar. Carefully spread with remaining batter and sprinkle with remaining cinnamon-sugar; cut through batter with a knife to swirl.

**3.** Bake 45-50 minutes or until a toothpick inserted in center comes out clean. Cool 10 minutes before removing from pan to a wire rack to cool completely. For the glaze: Combine confectioners' sugar and enough milk to reach desired consistency; drizzle over loaf.

**1 PIECE:** 179 cal., 4g fat (1g sat. fat), 14mg chol., 173mg sod., 34g carb. (21g sugars, 1g fiber), 3g pro.

❄

# MUSHROOM ASPARAGUS QUICHE

Loads of asparagus pieces add color and flavor to this hearty, creamy quiche. And the easy crescent roll crust means you'll have breakfast ready in a snap!
—*Sharon Fujita, Fontana, CA*

**PREP:** 20 min. • **BAKE:** 25 min. + standing • **MAKES:** 8 servings

- 1   tube (8 oz.) refrigerated crescent rolls
- 2   tsp. prepared mustard
- 1½  lbs. fresh asparagus, trimmed and cut into ½-in. pieces
- 1   medium onion, chopped
- ½   cup sliced fresh mushrooms
- ¼   cup butter, cubed
- 2   large eggs, lightly beaten
- 2   cups shredded part-skim mozzarella cheese
- ½   tsp. salt
- ½   tsp. pepper
- ¼   tsp. garlic powder
- ¼   tsp. each dried basil, oregano, parsley and rubbed sage

**1.** Separate crescent dough into 8 triangles. Place triangles in an ungreased 9-in. pie plate with points toward the center. Press dough onto the bottom and up the sides to form a crust; seal perforations. Spread with mustard; set aside.

**2.** In a large skillet, saute the asparagus, onion and mushrooms in butter until asparagus is crisp-tender. In a large bowl, combine the remaining ingredients; stir in the asparagus mixture. Pour into crust.

**3.** Bake at 375° for 25-30 minutes or until a knife inserted in the center comes out clean. Let stand for 10 minutes before cutting.

**FREEZE OPTION:** Cover and freeze unbaked quiche. To use, remove from freezer 30 minutes before baking (do not thaw). Preheat oven to 375°. Place quiche on a baking sheet; cover edge loosely with foil. Bake as directed, increasing time as necessary for a knife inserted in center to come out clean.

**1 PIECE:** 272 cal., 18g fat (8g sat. fat), 84mg chol., 580mg sod., 16g carb. (5g sugars, 1g fiber), 12g pro.

## PUMPKIN CHEESE COFFEE CAKE

This is one of my favorite recipes, especially in autumn. It is much easier to make than a traditional pumpkin roll—and it's always a crowd-pleaser!
—Carlene Jessop, Hildale, UT

- - - - - - - - - - - - - - - - - - - - - - - - - - - - - - - - - - - - -

**PREP:** 15 min. • **BAKE:** 35 min. • **MAKES:** 15 servings

- 2 cups sugar
- 2 large eggs, room temperature
- 1¼ cups canned pumpkin
- ¼ cup vegetable oil
- ½ tsp. vanilla extract
- 2¼ cups all-purpose flour
- 2 tsp. ground cinnamon
- 1 tsp. baking soda
- ½ tsp. salt

FILLING
- 1 pkg. (8 oz.) cream cheese, softened
- 1 large egg
- 1 Tbsp. sugar

TOPPING
- ¾ cup sweetened shredded coconut
- ½ cup chopped pecans
- ¼ cup packed brown sugar
- ¼ tsp. ground cinnamon

1. In a large bowl, beat sugar, eggs, pumpkin, oil and vanilla. Combine the flour, cinnamon, baking soda and salt; add to egg mixture and mix well. Pour into a greased 13x9-in. baking dish.
2. In a small bowl, beat cream cheese, egg and sugar until smooth. Drop tablespoonfuls over batter; cut through batter with a knife to swirl. Combine topping ingredients; sprinkle over top. Bake at 350° for 35-40 minutes or until a toothpick comes out clean. Cool on a wire rack.
**1 PIECE:** 344 cal., 15g fat (6g sat. fat), 59mg chol., 234mg sod., 50g carb. (33g sugars, 2g fiber), 5g pro.

## SHEEPHERDER'S BREAKFAST

My sister-in-law always made this delicious breakfast dish when we were camping. Served with toast, juice, and milk or coffee, it's a sure hit with the breakfast crowd. One-dish casseroles like this were a big help while I was raising my nine children, and now I've passed this recipe on to them.
—Pauletta Bushnell, Albany, OR

- - - - - - - - - - - - - - - - - - - - - - - - - - - - - - - - - - - - -

**TAKES:** 30 min. • **MAKES:** 8 servings

- ¾ lb. bacon strips, finely chopped
- 1 medium onion, chopped
- 1 pkg. (30 oz.) frozen shredded hash brown potatoes, thawed
- 8 large eggs
- ½ tsp. salt
- ¼ tsp. pepper
- 1 cup shredded cheddar cheese

1. In a large skillet, cook bacon and onion over medium heat until bacon is crisp. Drain, reserving ¼ cup drippings in pan.
2. Stir in hash browns. Cook, uncovered, over medium heat until the bottom is golden brown, about 10 minutes. Turn potatoes. With the back of a spoon, make 8 evenly spaced wells in potato mixture. Carefully break 1 egg into each well. Sprinkle with salt and pepper.
3. Cook, covered, on low until eggs are set and potatoes are tender, about 10 minutes. Sprinkle with cheese; let stand until cheese is melted.
**1 SERVING:** 354 cal., 22g fat (9g sat. fat), 222mg chol., 617mg sod., 22g carb. (2g sugars, 1g fiber), 17g pro.

> **TIP**
> This top-rated breakfast recipe can easily be adjusted to suit your tastes. Feel free to use country pork sausage instead of bacon or make it vegetarian by eliminating the meat and replacing the bacon drippings with oil or butter.

## CREAMY BANANA CREPES

My husband and I enjoy taking turns fixing weekend breakfasts. These crepes are frequently on our menus. The sweet-and-sour banana filling is delicious. You'll want to serve them for lunch, dinner and dessert!

—*Parrish Smith, Lincoln, NE*

------------------------------------------------

**PREP:** 10 min. + chilling • **COOK:** 10 min.
**MAKES:** 6 servings

- 2 large eggs, room temperature
- ¾ cup water
- ¾ cup 2% milk
- 2 Tbsp. butter, melted
- ½ tsp. vanilla extract
- 1 cup all-purpose flour
- 1 Tbsp. sugar
- ½ tsp. salt
- BANANA FILLING
- 3 Tbsp. butter
- 3 Tbsp. brown sugar
- 3 medium firm bananas, cut into ¼-in. slices
- SOUR CREAM FILLING
- 1 cup sour cream
- 2 Tbsp. confectioners' sugar
- ½ cup slivered almonds, toasted

**1.** In a small bowl, whisk eggs, water, milk, butter and vanilla. In another bowl, mix flour, sugar and salt; add to egg mixture and mix well. Refrigerate, covered, 1 hour.

**2.** Heat a lightly greased 8-in. nonstick skillet over medium heat. Stir batter. Fill a ¼-cup measure three-fourths full with batter; pour into center of pan. Quickly lift and tilt pan to coat bottom evenly. Cook until top appears dry; turn crepe over and cook 15-20 seconds longer or until bottom is cooked. Remove to a wire rack. Repeat with remaining batter, greasing pan as needed. When crepes are cool, stack them between pieces of waxed paper or paper towels.

**3.** In a small skillet, heat butter and brown sugar over medium heat until sugar is dissolved. Add bananas; toss to coat. Remove from heat; keep warm.

**4.** In a small bowl, combine sour cream and confectioners' sugar. Spread over half of each crepe. Top with banana filling and almonds; fold over filling. If desired, sprinkle with additional confectioners' sugar and almonds.

**2 CREPES:** 429 cal., 25g fat (12g sat. fat), 99mg chol., 327mg sod., 46g carb. (22g sugars, 3g fiber), 9g pro.

## COLORFUL BRUNCH FRITTATA

A friend called and asked me for a special recipe that he could serve at his daughter's wedding brunch. I created this recipe for the occasion, and he loved it. It's loaded with colorful veggies and looks beautiful on a buffet.

—*Kristin Arnett, Elkhorn, WI*

------------------------------------------------

**PREP:** 15 min. • **BAKE:** 50 min. + standing
**MAKES:** 12 servings

- 1 lb. fresh asparagus, trimmed and cut into 1-in. pieces
- ½ lb. sliced fresh mushrooms
- 1 medium sweet red pepper, diced
- 1 medium sweet yellow pepper, diced
- 1 small onion, chopped
- 3 green onions, chopped
- 3 Tbsp. olive oil
- 2 garlic cloves, minced
- 3 plum tomatoes, seeded and chopped
- 14 large eggs, lightly beaten
- 2 cups half-and-half cream
- 2 cups shredded Colby-Monterey Jack cheese
- 3 Tbsp. minced fresh parsley
- 3 Tbsp. minced fresh basil
- ½ tsp. salt
- ¼ tsp. pepper
- ½ cup shredded Parmesan cheese

**1.** Preheat oven to 350°. In a large skillet, saute asparagus, mushrooms, peppers and onions in oil until tender. Add garlic; cook 1 minute longer. Add the tomatoes; set aside.

**2.** In a large bowl, whisk eggs, cream, Colby-Monterey Jack cheese, parsley, basil, salt and pepper; stir into the vegetable mixture.

**3.** Pour into a greased 13x9-in. baking dish. Bake, uncovered, 45 minutes.

**4.** Sprinkle with Parmesan cheese. Bake 5 minutes longer or until a knife inserted in the center comes out clean. Let stand 10 minutes before cutting.

**1 PIECE:** 270 cal., 19g fat (10g sat. fat), 256mg chol., 377mg sod., 7g carb. (4g sugars, 1g fiber), 16g pro.

> **TIP**
> If your frittatas puff up while baking, the problem may be in the mixing. When you whisk the egg mixture, you're actually beating air into the eggs. If you overmix the egg mixture, you could incorporate too much air and cause the eggs to expand while baking.

# FAVORITE SOUPS & SANDWICHES

Whether you team them up for a lunch-counter classic meal or serve them solo, you'll love discovering these cozy soups and irresistible sandwiches.

**Spring Pea Soup** (p. 62) **Spinach Pizza Quesadillas** (p. 59) **Mexican-Inspired Chicken Soup** (p. 58)
**Smash Burgers** (p. 73) **Roasted Red Pepper Soup** (p. 70) **Guacamole Chicken Salad Sandwiches** (p. 69)
**Creamy Garlic & Mushroom Soup** (p. 67) **Chicken Florentine Panini** (p. 63) **Simple Shrimp Chowder** (p. 73)

## QUICK TANGY SLOPPY JOES

I adjusted and combined three different recipes to come up with this one. Kids like the tangy taste so much, they request the sandwiches for birthday parties.
—*Anna Adams, Chatsworth, CA*

- - - - - - - - - - - - - - - - - - - - - - - - - - - - - -

**TAKES:** 20 min. • **MAKES:** 6 servings

- 1 lb. ground beef
- 1 cup finely chopped onion
- ¾ cup finely chopped sweet red or green pepper
- ¼ cup finely chopped celery
- ½ cup ketchup
- 1 Tbsp. white vinegar
- 2 tsp. chili powder
- 1½ tsp. Worcestershire sauce
- 1 tsp. sugar
- 1 tsp. salt
- 6 hamburger buns, split

**1.** In a large cast-iron or other heavy skillet, cook and stir beef, onion, red pepper and celery over medium heat until meat is no longer pink and vegetables are crisp-tender; drain.
**2.** In a small bowl, combine the ketchup, vinegar, chili powder, Worcestershire sauce, sugar and salt; stir into the beef mixture. Simmer, uncovered, for 10 minutes, stirring occasionally. Serve on buns.

**1 SLOPPY JOE:** 314 cal., 12g fat (4g sat. fat), 50mg chol., 935mg sod., 32g carb. (8g sugars, 3g fiber), 20g pro.

## ITALIAN SAUSAGE BEAN SOUP

During the frigid months, I like to put on a big pot of this soothing soup. It cooks away while I do other things, such as baking bread, crafting or even cleaning.
—*Glenna Reimer, Gig Harbor, WA*

- - - - - - - - - - - - - - - - - - - - - - - - - - - - - -

**PREP:** 20 min. • **COOK:** 1½ hours
**MAKES:** 8 servings (3 qt.)

- 1 lb. bulk Italian sausage
- 1 medium onion, finely chopped
- 3 garlic cloves, sliced
- 4 cans (14½ oz. each) reduced-sodium chicken broth
- 2 cans (15 oz. each) pinto beans, rinsed and drained
- 1 can (14½ oz.) diced tomatoes, undrained
- 1 cup medium pearl barley
- 1 large carrot, sliced
- 1 celery rib, sliced
- 1 tsp. minced fresh sage
- ½ tsp. minced fresh rosemary or ⅛ tsp. dried rosemary, crushed
- 6 cups chopped fresh kale

**1.** In a Dutch oven, cook and stir sausage and onion over medium heat until meat is no longer pink. Add garlic; cook 1 minute longer. Drain.
**2.** Stir in the broth, beans, tomatoes, barley, carrot, celery, sage and rosemary. Bring to a boil. Reduce heat; simmer, covered, for 45 minutes.
**3.** Stir in kale; return to a boil. Reduce heat; cover and simmer until vegetables are tender, 25-30 minutes.

**1½ CUPS:** 339 cal., 9g fat (3g sat. fat), 23mg chol., 1100mg sod., 48g carb. (7g sugars, 11g fiber), 19g pro.

## MEXICAN-INSPIRED CHICKEN SOUP

This zesty soup is loaded with chicken, corn and black beans in a mildly spicy red broth. As a busy mom of three young children, I'm always looking for dinner recipes that can be prepared in the morning. The kids love the taco taste of this easy soup.
—Marlene Kane, Lainesburg, MI

**PREP:** 10 min. • **COOK:** 3 hours • **MAKES:** 6 servings

- 1½ lbs. boneless skinless chicken breasts, cubed
- 2 tsp. canola oil
- ½ cup water
- 1 envelope reduced-sodium taco seasoning
- 3 cans (11½ oz. each) V8 juice
- 1 jar (16 oz.) salsa
- 1 can (15 oz.) black beans, rinsed and drained
- 1 pkg. (10 oz.) frozen corn, thawed
  Optional: Shredded cheddar cheese, sour cream and chopped fresh cilantro

1. In a large nonstick skillet, saute chicken in oil until no longer pink. Add water and taco seasoning; simmer, uncovered, until chicken is well coated.
2. Transfer to a 5-qt. slow cooker. Stir in the V8 juice, salsa, beans and corn. Cover and cook on low for 3-4 hours or until heated through. If desired, serve with optional toppings.
**1½ CUPS:** 304 cal., 5g fat (1g sat. fat), 63mg chol., 1199mg sod., 35g carb. (11g sugars, 5g fiber), 29g pro.

## BARBECUED CHICKEN SALAD SANDWICHES

An impromptu picnic inspired this BBQ chicken salad sandwich. An instant summertime favorite, these dressed-up sandwiches have become a mainstay at our house.
—Linda Orme, Battleground, WA

**PREP:** 15 min. + marinating • **GRILL:** 15 min. + cooling
**MAKES:** 8 servings

- 1½ lbs. boneless skinless chicken breast
- ½ cup barbecue sauce
- 1 cup mayonnaise
- ½ cup finely chopped onion
- ½ cup chopped celery
- ¼ tsp. salt
- ¼ tsp. crushed red pepper flakes
- 8 kaiser rolls, split
- 8 tomato slices
- 8 lettuce leaves

1. Place the chicken in a shallow baking dish; add barbecue sauce. Turn to coat; cover. Refrigerate overnight.
2. Grill chicken, covered, over medium-high heat until a thermometer reads 165°, 6-8 minutes on each side. Cool; cover and refrigerate chicken until chilled.
3. Chop chicken; place in a large bowl. Stir in the mayonnaise, onion, celery, salt and pepper flakes. Serve on rolls with tomato and lettuce.
**1 SANDWICH:** 481 cal., 27g fat (4g sat. fat), 57mg chol., 712mg sod., 34g carb. (6g sugars, 2g fiber), 24g pro.

## RUSSIAN BORSCHT

Loaded with beets, carrots and cabbage, this recipe is great for gardeners like myself. Not only is it delicious, its brilliant color is eye-catching on the table.
—*Ginny Bettis, Montello, WI*

- - - - - - - - - - - - - - - - - - - - - - - - - - - - - - - - - - - - - - - -

**PREP:** 15 min. • **COOK:** 1 hour • **MAKES:** 8 servings (2 qt.)

- 2   cups chopped fresh beets
- 2   cups chopped carrots
- 2   cups chopped onion
- 4   cups beef or vegetable broth
- 1   can (16 oz.) diced tomatoes, undrained
- 2   cups chopped cabbage
- ½   tsp. salt
- ½   tsp. dill weed
- ¼   tsp. pepper
     Sour cream, optional

**1.** In a large saucepan, combine beets, carrots, onion and broth; bring to a boil. Reduce heat; cover and simmer for 30 minutes.
**2.** Add tomatoes and cabbage; cover and simmer until cabbage is tender, 30 minutes longer. Stir in salt, dill and pepper. Top each serving with sour cream if desired.
**1 CUP:** 71 cal., 1g fat (0 sat. fat), 0 chol., 673mg sod., 14g carb. (9g sugars, 4g fiber), 3g pro.

## SPINACH PIZZA QUESADILLAS

This simple five-ingredient dinner is special to me because my daughter and I created it together. You can make variations with other veggies you might have at home. It's a smart way to get kids to eat healthier.
—*Tanna Mancini, Gulfport, FL*

- - - - - - - - - - - - - - - - - - - - - - - - - - - - - - - - - - - - - - - -

**TAKES:** 20 min. • **MAKES:** 6 servings

- 6   whole wheat tortillas (8 in.)
- 3   cups shredded part-skim mozzarella cheese
- 3   cups chopped fresh spinach
- 1   can (8 oz.) pizza sauce

**1.** Preheat oven to 400°. On half of each tortilla, layer ½ cup cheese, ½ cup spinach and about 2 Tbsp. sauce. Fold other half over filling. Place on baking sheets coated with cooking spray.
**2.** Bake until cheese is melted, 10-12 minutes. If desired, serve with additional pizza sauce.
**1 QUESADILLA:** 301 cal., 13g fat (7g sat. fat), 36mg chol., 650mg sod., 29g carb. (3g sugars, 4g fiber), 19g pro. **DIABETIC EXCHANGES:** 2 starch, 2 medium-fat meat.

# VEGGIE BROWN RICE WRAPS

Salsa gives a bit of zip to the hearty brown rice and bean filling in these meatless tortilla wraps.
—Lisa Sullivan, St. Marys, OH

------------------------------------------

**TAKES:** 20 min. • **MAKES:** 6 servings

- 1 medium sweet red or green pepper, diced
- 1 cup sliced fresh mushrooms
- 1 Tbsp. olive oil
- 2 garlic cloves, minced
- 2 cups cooked brown rice
- 1 can (16 oz.) kidney beans, rinsed and drained
- 1 cup frozen corn, thawed
- ¼ cup chopped green onions
- ½ tsp. ground cumin
- ½ tsp. pepper
- ¼ tsp. salt
- 6 flour tortillas (8 in.), room temperature
- ½ cup shredded reduced-fat cheddar cheese
- ¾ cup salsa

**1.** In a large cast-iron or other heavy skillet, saute pepper and mushrooms in oil until tender. Add garlic; cook 1 minute. Add the rice, beans, corn, green onions, cumin, pepper and salt. Cook and stir until heated through, 4-6 minutes.

**2.** Spoon ¾ cup filling onto each tortilla. Sprinkle with cheese; drizzle with salsa. Fold sides of tortilla over filling; roll up. Serve immediately.

**1 WRAP:** 377 cal., 8g fat (2g sat. fat), 7mg chol., 675mg sod., 62g carb. (4g sugars, 7g fiber), 15g pro.

**TIP**

Green peppers are unripened versions of red, yellow or orange peppers. They are less expensive because they're quicker to get to market. Use a red or yellow pepper in this recipe if you prefer more sweetness.

## SUNDAY SUPPER SANDWICHES

Here's a great way to put a traditional dinner on the table with very little hands-on time. You can cook the meat in the slow cooker as well: Put all ingredients except bread cheese into a 4-quart slow cooker, cover and cook on low 8-10 hours or until meat is tender.
—*Elizabeth Godecke, Chicago, IL*

- - - - - - - - - - - - - - - - - - - - - - - - - - - - - - - - - - - - - - - - - -

**PREP:** 25 min. • **BAKE:** 2½ hours • **MAKES:** 8 servings

- 1    can (14 oz.) sauerkraut, rinsed and well drained
- 1    boneless pork shoulder butt roast (2½ to 3 lbs.)
- ½    tsp. salt
- ¼    tsp. pepper
- ¼    cup stone-ground mustard, divided
- 1    cup apple cider or unsweetened apple juice
- ¼    cup sweetened applesauce
- 8    slices rye bread, toasted
- 1    cup shredded Swiss cheese

**1.** Preheat oven to 325°. Place sauerkraut in an ovenproof Dutch oven. Sprinkle pork with salt and pepper; brush with 2 Tbsp. mustard. Place over sauerkraut. Add cider and applesauce.
**2.** Bake, covered, until pork is tender, 2½ to 3 hours. Remove roast; cool slightly. Drain sauerkraut mixture; set aside. Shred pork with 2 forks.
**3.** Place toast on an ungreased baking sheet. Spread with remaining 2 Tbsp. mustard. Top with pork, then sauerkraut mixture; sprinkle with cheese. Broil 4-6 in. from the heat until cheese is melted, 2-3 minutes.
**1 OPEN-FACED SANDWICH:** 403 cal., 20g fat (8g sat. fat), 96mg chol., 966mg sod., 25g carb. (8g sugars, 4g fiber), 31g pro.

## RAMEN CORN CHOWDER

This tastes so good, as if it simmered for hours, but it's ready in 15 minutes. I thought the original recipe was lacking in flavor, so I jazzed it up with extra corn and bacon bits.
—*Darlene Brenden, Salem, OR*

- - - - - - - - - - - - - - - - - - - - - - - - - - - - - - - - - - - - - - - - - -

**TAKES:** 15 min. • **MAKES:** 4 servings

- 2    cups water
- 1    pkg. (3 oz.) chicken ramen noodles
- 1    can (15¼ oz.) whole kernel corn, drained
- 1    can (14¾ oz.) cream-style corn
- 1    cup 2% milk
- 1    tsp. dried minced onion
- ¼    tsp. curry powder
- ¾    cup shredded cheddar cheese
- ⅓    cup cubed cooked bacon
- 1    Tbsp. minced fresh parsley
- 1    Tbsp. minced chives

**1.** In a small saucepan, bring water to a boil. Break noodles into large pieces. Add noodles and contents of seasoning packet to water. Reduce heat to medium. Cook, uncovered, until noodles are tender, 2-3 minutes.
**2.** Stir in the corn, cream-style corn, milk, onion and curry powder; heat through. Stir in the cheese, bacon, parsley and chives until blended. If desired, top with additional cheddar cheese and additional minced fresh chives.
**1 CUP:** 333 cal., 9g fat (5g sat. fat), 17mg chol., 1209mg sod., 49g carb. (13g sugars, 4g fiber), 13g pro.

## REUBEN SANDWICHES

My daughter shared this recipe with me. It's become a favorite of our entire family.
—*Kathryn Binder, Pickett, WI*

- - - - - - - - - - - - - - - - - - - - - - - - - - - - - - - - - - - - - - -

**TAKES:** 20 min. • **MAKES:** 10 servings

- ¾ cup mayonnaise
- 3 Tbsp. chili sauce
- 1 can (14 oz.) sauerkraut, rinsed and well drained
- 2 cups shredded Swiss cheese
- 20 slices rye bread
- 12 oz. sliced deli corned beef
- ½ cup butter, softened
  Thousand Island salad dressing, optional

In a large bowl, combine the mayonnaise, chili sauce, sauerkraut and Swiss cheese. Spread over 20 slices of bread, about ¼ cup on each; top half the slices with corned beef and replace to form sandwiches. Lightly butter the outside of sandwiches. Toast on a hot griddle for 4-5 minutes on each side or until golden brown. Serve with Thousand Island dressing if desired.

**1 SANDWICH:** 486 cal., 32g fat (13g sat. fat), 69mg chol., 1308mg sod., 34g carb. (4g sugars, 5g fiber), 17g pro.

**TIP**

Besides the classic Reuben fixings like Swiss cheese and sauerkraut, you can also add caramelized onions, pickles or pickle relish to your sandwiches.

## SPRING PEA SOUP

Truly a soup for the pea lover, this recipe originated with an idea in an old cookbook about eating better to live longer. Sauteed potatoes add body to this easy soup with superb pea flavor.
—*Denise Patterson, Bainbridge, OH*

- - - - - - - - - - - - - - - - - - - - - - - - - - - - - - - - - - - - - -

**PREP:** 10 min. • **COOK:** 30 min. • **MAKES:** 6 servings

- 2 cups cubed peeled potatoes
- 2 Tbsp. butter
- 6 cups chicken broth
- 2 cups fresh or frozen peas, thawed
- 2 Tbsp. minced chives
  Microgreens, optional

1. In a large saucepan, saute potatoes in butter until lightly browned. Stir in broth; bring to a boil. Reduce heat; cover and simmer until potatoes are tender, 10-15 minutes. Add peas; cook until peas are tender, 5-8 minutes. Cool slightly.
2. In a blender, process soup in batches until smooth. Return all to the pan; heat through. Sprinkle with chives and, if desired, microgreens.

**1 CUP:** 133 cal., 5g fat (2g sat. fat), 15mg chol., 1012mg sod., 18g carb. (4g sugars, 3g fiber), 5g pro.

## CANADIAN CHEESE SOUP

My family loves Canadian bacon, but I don't run across a lot of dishes that call for it. Everyone was thrilled the first time I offered this succulent soup.
—*Jolene Roudebush, Troy, MI*

PREP: 15 min. • COOK: 30 min. • MAKES: 8 servings (2 qt.)

3   cups chicken broth
4   medium potatoes, peeled and diced
2   celery ribs, diced
1   medium carrot, diced
1   small onion, diced
6   oz. Canadian bacon, trimmed and diced
2   Tbsp. butter
2   Tbsp. all-purpose flour
1   cup whole milk
2   cups shredded cheddar cheese
⅛   tsp. pepper

1. In a Dutch oven or soup kettle, combine the first 5 ingredients; bring to a boil. Reduce heat; cover and simmer until vegetables are very tender, about 20 minutes. With a potato masher, mash vegetables several times. Add bacon; continue to simmer.
2. Meanwhile, melt butter in a small saucepan; stir in the flour and cook, stirring constantly, for 1 minute. Gradually whisk in milk. Bring to a boil; boil and stir for 2 minutes (mixture will be thick). Add vegetable mixture, stirring constantly. Remove from the heat; add cheese and pepper. Stir just until cheese is melted.
**1 CUP:** 252 cal., 11g fat (0 sat. fat), 33mg chol., 402mg sod., 22g carb. (0 sugars, 0 fiber), 19g pro. **DIABETIC EXCHANGES:** 2 meat, 1 starch, 1 vegetable.

## CHICKEN FLORENTINE PANINI

This grilled sandwich combines chicken with provolone cheese, spinach and red onion.
—*Lee Bremson, Kansas City, MO*

TAKES: 25 min. • MAKES: 4 servings

1   pkg. (5 oz.) fresh baby spinach
2   tsp. olive oil
8   slices sourdough bread
¼   cup creamy Italian salad dressing
8   slices provolone cheese
½   lb. shaved deli chicken
2   slices red onion, separated into rings
¼   cup butter, softened

1. In a large cast-iron or other heavy skillet, saute spinach in oil until wilted, about 2 minutes. Drain; wipe skillet clean.
2. Spread 4 bread slices with salad dressing. Layer with a cheese slice, chicken, spinach, onion and another cheese slice. Top with remaining bread. Butter outsides of sandwiches.
3. Cook in same skillet or a panini maker until bread is golden brown and cheese is melted.
**1 SANDWICH:** 582 cal., 26g fat (10g sat. fat), 62mg chol., 1688mg sod., 63g carb. (4g sugars, 5g fiber), 23g pro.

## BUFFALO CHICKEN CHILI

This Buffalo chicken chili is rich in the best way. Cream cheese, blue cheese and tangy hot sauce join forces for a dinner recipe everyone will love.
—*Peggy Woodward, Shullsburg, WI*

------------------------------------------------

**PREP:** 10 min. • **COOK:** 5½ hours
**MAKES:** 6 servings (2 qt.)

- 1 can (15½ oz.) navy beans, rinsed and drained
- 1 can (14½ oz.) chicken broth
- 1 can (14½ oz.) fire-roasted diced tomatoes
- 1 can (8 oz.) tomato sauce
- ½ cup Buffalo wing sauce
- ½ tsp. onion powder
- ½ tsp. garlic powder
- 1 lb. boneless skinless chicken breast halves
- 1 pkg. (8 oz.) cream cheese, cubed and softened
  Optional: Crumbled blue cheese, chopped celery and chopped green onions

**1.** In a 4- or 5-qt. slow cooker, combine the first 7 ingredients. Add chicken. Cover and cook on low until chicken is tender, 5-6 hours.
**2.** Remove chicken; shred with 2 forks. Return to slow cooker. Stir in cream cheese. Cover and cook on low until cheese is melted, about 30 minutes. Stir until blended. Serve with toppings as desired.

**NOTE:** Leftovers of this chili won't freeze well because of the cream cheese, which can curdle when frozen.

**1¼ CUPS:** 337 cal., 16g fat (8g sat. fat), 80mg chol., 1586mg sod., 25g carb. (5g sugars, 5g fiber), 25g pro.

## GRILLED CHEESE & PEPPERONI SANDWICH

Who doesn't love a good grilled cheese sandwich? This super decadent version comes fully loaded with pepperoni and five types of cheese!
—*Josh Rink, Milwaukee, WI*

------------------------------------------------

**TAKES:** 25 min. • **MAKES:** 4 servings

- 6 Tbsp. butter, softened, divided
- 8 slices sourdough bread
- ½ cup shredded sharp white cheddar cheese
- ½ cup shredded Monterey Jack cheese
- ½ cup shredded Gruyere cheese
- 3 Tbsp. mayonnaise
  3 Tbsp. finely shredded Manchego or Parmesan cheese
- ⅛ tsp. onion powder
- 24 slices pepperoni
- 4 oz. Brie cheese, rind removed and sliced

**1.** Spread 3 Tbsp. butter on 1 side of bread slices. Place bread, butter side down, in a large cast-iron skillet or electric griddle over medium-low heat until golden brown, 2-3 minutes; remove. In a small bowl, combine cheddar, Monterey Jack and Gruyere. In another bowl, mix together remaining 3 Tbsp. butter, mayonnaise, Manchego cheese and onion powder.
**2.** To assemble sandwiches, top toasted side of 4 bread slices with pepperoni; add sliced Brie. Sprinkle cheddar cheese mixture evenly over the Brie. Top with the remaining bread slices, toasted side facing inward. Spread the butter-mayonnaise mixture on the outsides of each sandwich.
**3.** Place sandwiches in the same skillet; cook until bread is golden brown and cheese is melted, 5-6 minutes on each side. Serve immediately.

**1 SANDWICH:** 719 cal., 55g fat (29g sat. fat), 134mg chol., 1207mg sod., 30g carb. (3g sugars, 1g fiber), 27g pro.

Spread **2 Tbsp. creamy peanut butter** over **1 slice of bread.** We like an artisanal bakery kind for exciting texture, but take your pick.
Top with **½ medium banana,** sliced, and **1 bacon strip,** cooked and crumbled.

## - THE ELVIS SANDWICH -
The surprising combo of rich peanut butter, sweet banana and crisp, smoky bacon really is fit for a king.

## CREAMY GARLIC & MUSHROOM SOUP

Cool, crisp winter evenings call for comforting bowls of rich and creamy soup. It's a terrific first course at holiday meals.
—*Mandy Howison, Renfrew, PA*

**PREP:** 15 min. • **COOK:** 30 min. • **MAKES:** 13 servings (3¼ qt.)

- 1 lb. medium fresh mushrooms, sliced
- 1 lb. sliced baby portobello mushrooms
- ½ lb. sliced fresh shiitake mushrooms
- 7 Tbsp. butter
- 12 garlic cloves, minced
- 2 green onions, chopped
- ½ cup all-purpose flour
- 2 cans (14½ oz. each) chicken broth
- 3⅓ cups 2% milk
- 1⅔ cups heavy whipping cream
- 4 tsp. minced fresh thyme or 1½ tsp. dried thyme
- 2 tsp. minced fresh basil or ¾ tsp. dried basil
- 1 tsp. salt
- 1 tsp. pepper
  Minced fresh parsley

**1.** In a Dutch oven, saute mushrooms in butter in batches until tender. Return all to the pan; add garlic and green onions. Cook and stir for 2 minutes. Sprinkle with flour; stir until blended.
**2.** Gradually stir in broth and milk. Bring to a boil; cook and stir until thickened, about 2 minutes. Stir in cream, thyme, basil, salt and pepper; heat through. Sprinkle each serving with parsley.
**1 CUP:** 246 cal., 20g fat (12g sat. fat), 66mg chol., 539mg sod., 13g carb. (5g sugars, 1g fiber), 6g pro.

## 🍎🍲 CHICKEN MUSHROOM STEW

The flavors blend beautifully in this dish of chicken, vegetables and herbs as it simmers in a slow cooker. Folks with busy schedules will love this convenient recipe.
—*Kenny Van Rheenen, Mendota, IL*

**PREP:** 20 min. • **COOK:** 4 hours • **MAKES:** 6 servings (2 qt.)

- 6 boneless skinless chicken breast halves (4 oz. each)
- 2 Tbsp. canola oil, divided
- 8 oz. fresh mushrooms, sliced
- 1 medium onion, diced
- 3 cups diced zucchini
- 1 cup chopped green pepper
- 4 garlic cloves, minced
- 3 medium tomatoes, chopped
- 1 can (6 oz.) tomato paste
- ¾ cup water
- 2 tsp. each dried thyme, oregano, marjoram, and basil
  Chopped fresh thyme, optional

**1.** Cut chicken into 1-in. cubes; brown in 1 Tbsp. oil in a large skillet. Transfer to a 3-qt. slow cooker. In the same skillet, saute the mushrooms, onion, zucchini and green pepper in remaining 1 Tbsp. oil until crisp-tender; add garlic; cook 1 minute longer.
**2.** Place in slow cooker. Add the tomatoes, tomato paste, water and seasonings. Cover and cook on low until the meat is no longer pink and vegetables are tender, 4-5 hours. If desired, top with chopped fresh thyme.
**1⅓ CUPS:** 237 cal., 8g fat (1g sat. fat), 63mg chol., 82mg sod., 15g carb. (7g sugars, 3g fiber), 27g pro. **DIABETIC EXCHANGES:** 3 lean meat, 1 starch, 1 fat.

## DUTCH OVEN BARBECUED PORK SANDWICHES

These fabulous pulled pork sandwiches have a sweet, tangy flavor. If you want a smokier taste, add a little liquid smoke to the pulled pork before returning it to the Dutch oven.
—Taste of Home *Test Kitchen*

**PREP:** 15 min. • **COOK:** 4 hours • **MAKES:** 8 servings

- 1 can (8 oz.) tomato sauce
- 1 large onion, chopped
- 1 cup barbecue sauce
- 3 tsp. chili powder
- 1 tsp. ground cumin
- ½ tsp. ground cinnamon
- 1 boneless pork sirloin roast (2 lbs.)
- 8 seeded hamburger buns, split

**1.** In a Dutch oven, combine the first 6 ingredients; add the pork. Spoon some of the sauce over pork. Bring to a boil; reduce heat and simmer, covered, until meat is tender, 3-4 hours.
**2.** Remove meat; shred with 2 forks. Return to pan and heat through. Spoon ½ cup onto each bun.
**1 SANDWICH:** 357 cal., 9g fat (3g sat. fat), 68mg chol., 771mg sod., 40g carb. (16g sugars, 2g fiber), 28g pro.

## HEARTY BEEF & BARLEY SOUP

Barley soup is a popular menu item in our house throughout the year. Everyone savors the flavor.
—Elizabeth Kendall, Carolina Beach, NC

**PREP:** 20 min. • **COOK:** 1 hour 30 min. • **MAKES:** 9 servings (2¼ qt.)

- 1 Tbsp. canola oil
- 1 lb. beef top round steak, cut into ½-in. cubes
- 3 cans (14½ oz. each) beef broth
- 2 cups water
- ⅓ cup medium pearl barley
- ¾ tsp. salt
- ⅛ tsp. pepper
- 1 cup chopped carrots
- ½ cup chopped celery
- ¼ cup chopped onion
- 3 Tbsp. minced fresh parsley
- 1 cup frozen peas

**1.** In a large saucepan, heat oil over medium heat. Brown beef on all sides; drain. Stir in broth, water, barley, salt and pepper. Bring to a boil. Reduce heat; cover and simmer for 1 hour.
**2.** Add the carrots, celery, onion and parsley; cover and simmer until meat and vegetables are tender, 30-40 minutes. Stir in peas; heat through.
**1 CUP:** 133 cal., 4g fat (1g sat. fat), 28mg chol., 859mg sod., 10g carb. (2g sugars, 2g fiber), 14g pro. **DIABETIC EXCHANGES:** 2 lean meat, ½ starch, ½ fat.

**TIP**

To make this soup in a slow cooker, combine all ingredients in the slow cooker and cook on low until both the beef and barley are tender, 4-5 hours.

## GUACAMOLE CHICKEN SALAD SANDWICHES

This chicken salad recipe is inspired by a truly inventive guacamole I tried at a local restaurant, which was studded with pomegranate seeds. This is an extremely simple recipe to make since rotisserie chicken is used. I serve the salad on homemade tomato bread that is a great contrast in flavor and color. It can also be served on lettuce leaves instead of bread.

*—Debra Keil, Owasso, OK*

--------------------------------------------------------

**TAKES:** 20 min. • **MAKES:** 10 servings

- 1 rotisserie chicken, skin removed, cubed
- 2 medium ripe avocados, peeled and mashed
- ¾ cup pomegranate seeds
- 6 green onions, chopped
- 8 cherry tomatoes, halved
- 1 jalapeno pepper, seeded and minced
- ¼ cup fresh cilantro leaves, chopped
- 3 Tbsp. mayonnaise
- 2 Tbsp. lime juice
- 1 garlic clove, minced
- ½ tsp. salt
- ½ tsp. ground cumin
- ¼ tsp. pepper
- 20 slices multigrain bread, toasted

In a large bowl, combine all ingredients except the toasted bread. Spread over 10 bread slices; top with remaining bread.
**NOTE:** Wear disposable gloves when cutting hot peppers; the oil can burn skin. Avoid touching your face.
**1 SANDWICH:** 295 cal., 12g fat (2g sat. fat), 35mg chol., 370mg sod., 28g carb. (6g sugars, 6g fiber), 19g pro. **DIABETIC EXCHANGES:** 2 starch, 2 lean meat, 2 fat.

## NORTHWEST SALMON CHOWDER

I've lived on a farm in the Yakima Valley all my life. I have a big garden, and by the end of fall, my cellar shelves are full of canned fruits and vegetables. This recipe uses some of the root vegetables I grow—along with the delicious salmon that is so plentiful here.

*—Josephine Parton, Granger, WA*

--------------------------------------------------------

**PREP:** 10 min. • **COOK:** 1 hour • **MAKES:** 8 servings (2 qt.)

- ½ cup each chopped celery, onion and green pepper
- 1 garlic clove, minced
- 3 Tbsp. butter
- 1 can (14½ oz.) chicken broth
- 1 cup uncooked diced peeled potatoes
- 1 cup shredded carrots
- 1½ tsp. salt
- ½ tsp. pepper
- ¼ to ¾ tsp. dill weed
- 1 can (14¾ oz.) cream-style corn
- 2 cups half-and-half cream
- 1¾ to 2 cups fully cooked salmon chunks or 1 can (14¾ oz.) salmon, drained, flaked, bones and skin removed
  Optional: Crumbled cooked bacon, chives and cracked black pepper

**1.** In a large saucepan, saute celery, onion, green pepper and garlic in butter until the vegetables are tender. Add broth, potatoes, carrots, salt, pepper and dill; bring to a boil.
**2.** Reduce heat; cover and simmer for 40 minutes or until the vegetables are nearly tender. Stir in the corn, cream and salmon. Simmer for 15 minutes or until heated through. If desired, garnish with bacon, chives and cracked black pepper.
**1 CUP:** 274 cal., 15g fat (8g sat. fat), 84mg chol., 1095mg sod., 18g carb. (5g sugars, 2g fiber), 16g pro.

## ROASTED MUSHROOM & COUSCOUS SOUP

I love including mushrooms in soup. They add an earthy richness, and roasting them makes them even more flavorful.
—*Robin Haas, Hyde Park, MA*

**PREP:** 15 min. • **COOK:** 30 min. • **MAKES:** 6 servings (2 qt.)

- 1 lb. medium fresh mushrooms, quartered
  Cooking spray
- 2 tsp. dried oregano
- ½ tsp. kosher salt
- 1 Tbsp. butter
- 1 large onion, finely chopped
- 2 medium carrots, diced
- 2 cups diced fennel bulb
- 2 cloves garlic, minced
- 1 cup uncooked pearl (Israeli) couscous
- 6 cups chicken or vegetable broth
- 1 Tbsp. minced fresh parsley
  Lemon wedges, optional

**1.** Preheat oven to 425°. Arrange mushrooms in a greased 15x10x1-in. baking pan. Spritz mushrooms with cooking spray. Sprinkle with oregano and salt; toss to coat. Roast until tender and lightly browned, 15-20 minutes, stirring occasionally.
**2.** Meanwhile, in a large saucepan, heat butter over medium heat; saute onion, carrots and fennel until tender, 4-6 minutes. Add garlic and couscous; cook and stir 2 minutes. Stir in broth and mushrooms; bring to a boil. Reduce heat; simmer, covered, until couscous is tender, 7-8 minutes. Sprinkle with parsley. Serve with lemon wedges if desired.
**1⅓ CUPS:** 182 cal., 4g fat (1g sat. fat), 10mg chol., 1187mg sod., 31g carb. (4g sugars, 2g fiber), 7g pro.

## ROASTED RED PEPPER SOUP

If you like cream of tomato soup, try making it with purchased roasted red peppers instead. Using jarred roasted red peppers makes this recipe extra easy, and pureeing the soup in a blender gives it a nice smooth texture.
—Taste of Home *Test Kitchen*

**PREP:** 10 min. • **COOK:** 25 min. • **MAKES:** 6 servings

- 2 tsp. butter
- 1 large sweet onion, chopped
- 2 garlic cloves, minced
- 2 jars (15½ oz. each) roasted sweet red peppers, drained
- 2 cups vegetable broth
- ½ tsp. dried basil
- ¼ tsp. salt
- 1 cup half-and-half cream
  Optional: Fresh basil leaves and additional half-and-half cream

**1.** In a large saucepan, melt butter over medium heat; add onion. Cook and stir until tender, 3-5 minutes. Add garlic; cook 1 minute longer. Stir in red peppers, broth, basil and salt. Bring to a boil. Reduce heat; cover and simmer 20 minutes. Cool slightly.
**2.** In a blender, cover and process soup in batches until smooth. Remove 1 cup to a small bowl; stir in cream. Return remaining puree to pan. Stir in the cream mixture; heat through (do not boil). If desired, garnish with additional cream and basil.
**1 CUP:** 135 cal., 6g fat (3g sat. fat), 23mg chol., 753mg sod., 21g carb. (9g sugars, 1g fiber), 2g pro.

**TIP**
You can use an immersion blender to puree this soup instead. Be aware, though, that a traditional blender gives the silkiest texture to pureed soups. Is it worth dirtying the extra dishes? That call is up to you.

# SHRIMP PATTY SANDWICHES

Quite often when we eat at a restaurant, my husband will try something and tell me that I could make it better at home. That was the case with this shrimp patty. I made some improvements, and now it's one of my husband's favorites.
—Tina Jacobs, Hurlock, MD

--------------------------------------

**TAKES:** 25 min. • **MAKES:** 8 servings

- 4 large eggs
- 4 cans (6 oz. each) shrimp, rinsed and drained, or 2 cups peeled and deveined cooked shrimp (31-40 per lb.)
- ½ lb. haddock, cooked and flaked
- 1½ cups pancake mix
- 2 Tbsp. cornmeal
- ½ tsp. dried parsley flakes
- ½ tsp. celery salt
- ¼ tsp. ground mustard
- ¼ tsp. paprika
- ½ cup dry bread crumbs
- 3 to 4 Tbsp. canola oil
- 8 hamburger buns
  Optional: Lettuce leaves, tomato slices, onion slices and Sriracha mayonnaise

**1.** In a large bowl, beat the eggs. Add the shrimp, haddock, pancake mix, cornmeal, parsley, celery salt, mustard and paprika; mix well. Shape into 8 patties. Coat with bread crumbs.

**2.** In a large cast-iron or other heavy skillet, cook patties in oil over medium-high heat until golden brown, 2 minutes on each side. Serve on hamburger buns. Top with lettuce, tomato, onion and mayonnaise as desired.

**1 SANDWICH:** 425 cal., 11g fat (2g sat. fat), 324mg chol., 1448mg sod., 45g carb. (4g sugars, 2g fiber), 33g pro.

🕐 🍎
## ROASTED SWEET POTATO & CHICKPEA PITAS

Here's a hearty take on Mediterranean pita pocket sandwiches, this time with sweet potatoes tucked inside.
—*Beth Jacobson, Milwaukee, WI*

**TAKES:** 30 min. • **MAKES:** 6 servings

- 2 medium sweet potatoes (about 1¼ lbs.), peeled and cubed
- 2 cans (15 oz. each) chickpeas or garbanzo beans, rinsed and drained
- 1 medium red onion, chopped
- 3 Tbsp. canola oil, divided
- 2 tsp. garam masala
- ½ tsp. salt, divided
- 2 garlic cloves, minced
- 1 cup plain Greek yogurt
- 1 Tbsp. lemon juice
- 1 tsp. ground cumin
- 2 cups arugula or baby spinach
- 12 whole wheat pita pocket halves, warmed
- ¼ cup minced fresh cilantro

**1.** Preheat oven to 400°. Place potatoes in a large microwave-safe bowl; microwave, covered, on high 5 minutes. Stir in chickpeas and onion; toss with 2 Tbsp. oil, garam masala and ¼ tsp. salt.

**2.** Spread into a 15x10x1-in. pan. Roast until potatoes are tender, about 15 minutes. Cool slightly.

**3.** Place minced garlic and remaining 1 Tbsp. oil in a small microwave-safe bowl; microwave on high until garlic is lightly browned, 1-1½ minutes. Stir in yogurt, lemon juice, cumin and remaining ¼ tsp. salt.

**4.** Toss potato mixture with arugula. Spoon into pitas; top with sauce and cilantro.

**2 FILLED PITA HALVES:** 462 cal., 15g fat (3g sat. fat), 10mg chol., 662mg sod., 72g carb. (13g sugars, 12g fiber), 14g pro.

## STROGANOFF SOUP

My husband and I share a love for all kinds of soup and came up with this delicious recipe together. It really does taste like beef Stoganoff. With a crusty roll, it's a satisfying meal in itself.
—*Karen Shiveley, Springfield, MN*

**PREP:** 15 min. • **COOK:** 40 min. • **MAKES:** 6 servings

- ½ lb. beef top sirloin steak or beef tenderloin, cut into thin strips
- ½ cup chopped onion
- 1 Tbsp. butter
- 2 cups water
- 1½ cups 2% milk
- ¼ cup tomato paste
- 2 tsp. beef bouillon granules
- 1 can (8 oz.) mushroom stems and pieces, drained
- 1 tsp. salt
- ⅛ tsp. pepper
- 1 can (12 oz.) evaporated milk
- ⅓ cup all-purpose flour
- 2 cups cooked wide egg noodles
- ½ cup sour cream
  Minced fresh thyme, optional

**1.** In a 3-qt. saucepan, cook beef and onion in butter over medium heat, until meat is almost cooked through. Stir in water, milk, tomato paste and bouillon. Add mushrooms, salt and pepper; bring to a boil.

**2.** Combine evaporated milk and flour until smooth. Gradually stir into the soup. Bring to a boil; cook and stir until thickened, 1-2 minutes. Add noodles; cook until heated through. Remove from heat; top each serving with sour cream. If desired, garnish with fresh thyme.

**1 CUP:** 314 cal., 13g fat (8g sat. fat), 78mg chol., 935mg sod., 28g carb. (12g sugars, 2g fiber), 17g pro.

 **SIMPLE SHRIMP CHOWDER**

Shrimp fans will be bowled over by this tasty take on chowder. The creamy broth is chock-full of vegetables. Chop up leftover cooked potatoes or use canned ones.
—*Carolyn Schmeling, Brookfield, WI*

- - - - - - - - - - - - - - - - - - - - - - - - - - - - - - - - - - - - - - - - -

**TAKES:** 30 min. • **MAKES:** 5 servings

- ½ cup each chopped onion, celery, carrot and sweet red pepper
- ¼ cup butter, cubed
- ¼ cup all-purpose flour
- 2 cups 2% milk
- ½ lb. cooked small shrimp, peeled and deveined
- 1 can (14½ oz.) diced potatoes, drained
- 1 cup vegetable broth
- 1 cup frozen corn, thawed
- 2 tsp. seafood seasoning
- 1 tsp. minced fresh thyme or ½ tsp. dried thyme

**1.** In a large saucepan, saute the onion, celery, carrot and red pepper in butter until tender, 5 minutes. Stir in flour until blended; gradually add milk. Bring to a boil; cook and stir for 2 minutes or until thickened.
**2.** Add the shrimp, potatoes, broth, corn, seafood seasoning and thyme. Reduce heat; cover and simmer until heated through, about 10 minutes. If desired, top with additional thyme.
**1 CUP:** 268 cal., 12g fat (7g sat. fat), 120mg chol., 901mg sod., 25g carb. (7g sugars, 2g fiber), 16g pro.

## SMASH BURGERS

Now is not the time to cut calories or skimp on salt. Go for ground chuck that's at least 80/20. If you can find a blend with ground brisket or short rib, all the better. The best burger comes from being liberal with kosher salt — it's beef's best friend, trust me.
—*James Schend, Pleasant Prairie, WI*

- - - - - - - - - - - - - - - - - - - - - - - - - - - - - - - - - - - - - - - - -

**TAKES:** 15 min. • **MAKES:** 4 servings

- 1 lb. ground beef (preferably 80% lean)
- 1 tsp. canola oil
- 1 tsp. kosher salt, divided
- 1 tsp. coarsely ground pepper, divided
- 4 hamburger buns, split
  Optional: Mayonnaise, sliced American cheese, sliced tomato, dill pickle slices, lettuce, ketchup and yellow mustard

**1.** Place a 9-in. cast-iron skillet over medium heat. Meanwhile, gently shape beef into 4 balls, shaping just enough to keep together (do not compact).
**2.** Increase burner temperature to medium-high; add oil. Add 2 beef balls. With a heavy metal spatula, flatten each to ¼- to ⅛-in. thickness; sprinkle each with ⅛ tsp. salt and ⅛ tsp. pepper. Cook until the edges start to brown, about 1½ minutes. Turn burgers and sprinkle each with an additional ⅛ tsp. salt and ⅛ tsp. pepper. Cook until well browned and a thermometer reads at least 160°, about 1 minute. Repeat with remaining beef.
**3.** Serve burgers on buns with toppings as desired.
**1 BURGER:** 339 cal., 16g fat (5g sat. fat), 70mg chol., 760mg sod., 22g carb. (3g sugars, 1g fiber), 24g pro.

 REVIEW

> *"This is the first recipe ever for burgers cooked indoors that my guys have devoured and then asked when I'm making them again! I did two patties per person with shredded cheddar, bacon and ketchup and served them on griddled buttered pretzel rolls. A++"*
>
> —**JMARTINELLLI13, TASTEOFHOME.COM**

## BEST EVER GRILLED CHEESE SANDWICHES

Use your imagination to come up with other fillings for your sandwiches, such as chives, Parmesan cheese, Italian seasoning or even a spoonful of salsa.
—*Edie DeSpain, Logan, UT*

- - - - - - - - - - - - - - - - - - - - - - - - - - -

**TAKES:** 20 min. • **MAKES:** 2 servings

- 2 Tbsp. mayonnaise
- 1 tsp. Dijon mustard
- 4 slices sourdough bread
- 2 slices Swiss cheese
- 2 slices cheddar cheese
- 2 slices sweet onion
- 1 medium tomato, sliced
- 6 cooked bacon strips
- 2 Tbsp. butter, softened

1. Combine mayonnaise and mustard; spread over 2 bread slices. Layer with cheeses, onion, tomato and bacon; top with remaining bread. Spread outsides of sandwiches with softened butter.
2. In a small skillet over medium heat, toast sandwiches until cheese is melted, 2-3 minutes on each side.
**1 SANDWICH:** 714 cal., 48g fat (23g sat. fat), 111mg chol., 1291mg sod., 41g carb. (4g sugars, 3g fiber), 29g pro.

HOW-TO

### CLEANING BACON GREASE
Bacon grease is so tasty, it's worth saving for other dishes. Once slightly cooled, strain grease through cheesecloth or a coffee filter. Cover and refrigerate cooled grease up to 6 months. Cook your morning eggs and potato dishes in the bacon grease. Want a real taste surprise? Use the bacon fat for popping your popcorn.

## BASIL TOMATO SOUP WITH ORZO

The soup is so scrumptious that it's worth the little time it takes to chop the fresh onion, garlic and basil. It's even better the next day after the flavors have had a chance to blend together.
—*Tonia Billbe, Elmira, NY*

- - - - - - - - - - - - - - - - - - - - - - - - - - -

**PREP:** 15 min. • **COOK:** 25 min.
**MAKES:** 16 servings (4 qt.)

- 1 large onion, chopped
- ¼ cup butter, cubed
- 2 garlic cloves, minced
- 3 cans (28 oz. each) crushed tomatoes
- 1 carton (32 oz.) chicken broth
- 1 cup loosely packed basil leaves, chopped
- 1 Tbsp. sugar
- ½ tsp. pepper
- 1¼ cups uncooked orzo pasta
- 1 cup heavy whipping cream
- ½ cup grated Romano cheese

1. In a Dutch oven, saute onion in butter for 3 minutes. Add garlic; cook until onion is tender, 1-2 minutes longer. Stir in the tomatoes, broth, basil, sugar and pepper. Bring to a boil. Reduce heat; cover and simmer for 15 minutes.
2. Meanwhile, cook the orzo according to package directions; drain. Add orzo and cream to soup; heat through (do not boil). Sprinkle servings with cheese.
**1 CUP:** 208 cal., 10g fat (6g sat. fat), 27mg chol., 607mg sod., 25g carb. (9g sugars, 3g fiber), 7g pro.

# - 4 -

# SIDES & SALADS

When time is tight, side dishes are often an afterthought...but no longer!
Whether you're looking for a hearty roasted vegetable or a cool refreshing salad,
these recipes hold their own beside any main course.

Strawberry Vinaigrette (p. 91) Corn Stuffing Balls (p. 80) Italian Tomato Cucumber Salad (p. 94)
Garlic & Artichoke Roasted Potatoes (p. 95) Szechuan Sugar Snap Peas (p. 89) Spinach Salad with Hot Bacon Dressing (p. 92)
Radish Cucumber Salad (p. 85) Grapefruit Lettuce Salad (p. 83) Rosemary Sweet Potato Fries (p. 85)

## CLASSIC WILTED LETTUCE SALAD

When we were kids, my sister and I would prepare the freshly picked lettuce for this wilted lettuce recipe, rinsing it several times and carefully drying it. As we did so, we quibbled about the portions we'd each have. Somehow, it seems she always managed to get more! We still can't get enough of this salad.
—Doris Natvig, Jesup, IA

- - - - - - - - - - - - - - - - - - - - - - - - - - - - -

**TAKES:** 15 min. • **MAKES:** 6 servings

- 4 bacon strips, cut up
- ¼ cup white vinegar
- 2 Tbsp. water
- 2 green onions with tops, sliced
- 2 tsp. sugar
- ¼ tsp. salt
- ¼ tsp. pepper
- 8 to 10 cups torn leaf lettuce
- 1 hard-boiled large egg, chopped

**1.** In a large skillet, cook bacon over medium heat until crisp. Using a slotted spoon, remove to paper towels to drain.
**2.** To the hot drippings, add the vinegar, water, onions, sugar, salt and pepper, stirring until sugar is dissolved.
**3.** Place lettuce in a salad bowl; immediately pour dressing over top and toss lightly. Top with egg. Serve immediately.

**1 CUP:** 118 cal., 10g fat (4g sat. fat), 45mg chol., 227mg sod., 5g carb. (3g sugars, 2g fiber), 3g pro.
**WILTED SPINACH SALAD:** Substitute torn fresh spinach for the lettuce.

**TIP**

To make a vegetarian wilted lettuce salad, skip the bacon and make a warm vinaigrette using olive or vegetable oil. Add the vinegar, onions, sugar, salt and pepper to the oil, and heat it at a medium temperature until the sugar dissolves. To get a smoky flavor, add some liquid smoke.

## BALSAMIC BRUSSELS SPROUTS WITH PEARS

One year, I decided to create a new Brussels sprouts recipe for Thanksgiving dinner, and came up a great recipe I can make any time. It uses only a handful of ingredients but still feels special. Apples, fresh figs and pecans are also delicious with this recipe.
—David Ross, Spokane Valley, WA

- - - - - - - - - - - - - - - - - - - - - - - - - - - - -

**PREP:** 20 min. • **BAKE:** 35 min.
**MAKES:** 6 servings

- 1½ lbs. Brussels sprouts, halved
- 3 Tbsp. olive oil
- 1 tsp. kosher salt
- ½ tsp. pepper
- 1 large pear, cut into ½-in.-thick slices
- ½ cup chopped walnuts
- ¾ cup balsamic vinegar
- 1 Tbsp. minced fresh rosemary or 1 tsp. dried rosemary, crushed

**1.** Preheat oven to 400°. Place Brussels sprouts in a 15x10x1-in. baking pan; toss with oil, salt and pepper. Roast for 20 minutes, stirring halfway. Add pear and walnuts to pan. Roast until Brussels sprouts are lightly charred and tender, 15-20 minutes longer.
**2.** Meanwhile, in a small saucepan, bring vinegar to a boil. Reduce heat; simmer, uncovered, until syrupy, 8-10 minutes.
**3.** In a large bowl, combine Brussels sprouts mixture, balsamic syrup and rosemary; toss to combine.
**⅔ CUP:** 220 cal., 13g fat (2g sat. fat), 0 chol., 346mg sod., 24g carb. (14g sugars, 6g fiber), 5g pro. **DIABETIC EXCHANGES:** 2½ fat, 1 starch, 1 vegetable.

## CORN STUFFING BALLS

My mom had many winning recipes, and this was one of our family's favorites. I can still picture these corn stuffing balls encircling the large meat platter piled high with one of her delicious entrees.
—*Audrey Groe, Lake Mills, IA*

------------------------------------------------------------

**PREP:** 20 min. • **BAKE:** 30 min. • **MAKES:** 12 servings

- 6   cups herb-seasoned stuffing croutons
- 1   cup chopped celery
- ½   cup chopped onion
- ¾   cup butter, divided
- 1   can (14¾ oz.) cream-style corn
- 1   cup water
- 1½  tsp. poultry seasoning
- ¾   tsp. salt
- ¼   tsp. pepper
- 3   large eggs yolks, beaten

**1.** Preheat oven to 375°. Place croutons in a large bowl and set aside. In a skillet, saute celery and onion in ½ cup butter. Add the corn, water, poultry seasoning, salt and pepper; bring to a boil. Remove from the heat; cool for 5 minutes. Pour over croutons. Add egg yolks and mix gently.
**2.** Shape ½ cupfuls into balls; flatten slightly. Place in a greased 15x10x1-in. baking pan. Melt remaining ¼ cup butter; drizzle over stuffing balls. Bake, uncovered, until lightly browned, 30 minutes.
**1 STUFFING BALL:** 365 cal., 16g fat (7g sat. fat), 84mg chol., 1233mg sod., 47g carb. (4g sugars, 3g fiber), 10g pro.

## GREEN BEAN, CORN & BUTTERMILK SALAD

I love the crunch of green beans and fresh corn, so I combined them with a buttermilk Caesar dressing. This salad is good served immediately, but it's even better after chilling for a few hours.
—*Arlene Erlbach, Morton Grove, IL*

------------------------------------------------------------

**PREP:** 25 min. • **COOK:** 15 min. + chilling • **MAKES:** 6 servings

- ½   cup reduced-fat mayonnaise
- ½   cup buttermilk
- ½   cup shredded Parmesan cheese
- 1   Tbsp. lemon juice
- 1   tsp. Worcestershire sauce
- ½   tsp. garlic powder
- ½   tsp. salt
- ½   tsp. pepper
- ¾   lb. fresh green beans, trimmed and cut into 1-in. pieces
- 1   Tbsp. olive oil
- 4   medium ears sweet corn

**1.** Whisk mayonnaise, buttermilk, Parmesan, lemon juice, Worcestershire sauce, garlic powder, salt and pepper. Refrigerate, covered, until serving.
**2.** Meanwhile, in a Dutch oven, bring 8 cups water to a boil. Add beans; cook, uncovered, just until crisp-tender, 2-3 minutes. Drain and immediately drop into ice water. Drain and pat dry; transfer to a serving bowl.
**3.** Cut corn from cobs. In a large cast-iron or other heavy skillet, heat 1 Tbsp. oil over medium-high heat. Add corn; cook and stir until tender, 6-8 minutes. Remove from heat and add to beans; refrigerate, covered, until chilled.
**4.** Stir the mayonnaise mixture into the vegetables; toss to coat. If desired, sprinkle with additional Parmesan.
**1 CUP:** 201 cal., 12g fat (3g sat. fat), 13mg chol., 498mg sod., 20g carb. (8g sugars, 3g fiber), 7g pro.

## HEIRLOOM TOMATO SALAD

This simple yet elegant dish always pleases my guests. Not only is it tasty, but it is healthy, too. The more varied the colors of the tomatoes you choose, the prettier the salad will be.
—*Jessie Apfel, Berkeley, CA*

--------------------------------------------------------------------

**PREP:** 20 min. + chilling • **MAKES:** 6 servings

  2   cups cut-up heirloom tomatoes
  1   cup multicolored cherry tomatoes, halved
  2   cups fresh baby spinach
  ½   cup sliced red onion
DRESSING
  3   Tbsp. olive oil
  2   Tbsp. white balsamic vinegar
  1   garlic clove, minced
  ½   tsp. salt
  ¼   tsp. dried basil
  ¼   tsp. dried oregano
  ¼   tsp. dried rosemary, crushed
  ¼   tsp. dried thyme
  ¼   tsp. pepper
  ⅛   tsp. rubbed sage

Place tomatoes, spinach and onion in a large bowl. Whisk together dressing ingredients; toss with salad. Refrigerate, covered, 2 hours. Serve with a slotted spoon.

**⅔ CUP:** 75 cal., 5g fat (1g sat. fat), 0 chol., 161mg sod., 7g carb. (4g sugars, 2g fiber), 1g pro. **DIABETIC EXCHANGES:** 1 vegetable, 1 fat.

## FRENCH POTATO SALAD

French potato salad is vinegar-based instead of creamy, made with Dijon mustard, olive oil, scallions or shallots, and fresh herbs.
—*Denise Cassady, Phoenix, MD*

--------------------------------------------------------------------

**TAKES:** 25 min. • **MAKES:** 6 servings

  1   lb. baby red potatoes
  1   lb. baby yellow potatoes
  1   garlic clove
  ¼   cup olive oil
  2   Tbsp. champagne vinegar or white wine vinegar
  2   tsp. Dijon mustard
  ½   tsp. salt
  ½   tsp. pepper
  1   shallot, finely chopped
  1   Tbsp. each minced fresh chervil, parsley and chives
  1   tsp. minced fresh tarragon

**1.** Place potatoes in a large saucepan; add water to cover. Bring to a boil. Reduce heat; cook, uncovered, 10-15 minutes or until tender. With a slotted spoon, remove potatoes to a colander; cool slightly. Return water to a boil. Add garlic; cook, uncovered, 1 minute. Remove garlic and immediately drop into ice water. Drain and pat dry; mince. Reserve ¼ cup cooking liquid.
**2.** Cut cooled potatoes into ¼-in. slices. Transfer potatoes to a large bowl. In a small bowl, whisk reserved cooking liquid, oil, vinegar, mustard, minced garlic, salt and pepper until blended. Pour over potatoes; toss gently to coat. Gently stir in remaining ingredients. Serve warm or at room temperature.

**1 CUP:** 201 cal., 9g fat (1g sat. fat), 0 chol., 239mg sod., 29g carb. (1g sugars, 2g fiber), 3g pro. **DIABETIC EXCHANGES:** 2 starch, 2 fat.

**TIP**

To add even more zing to this French potato salad, try capers, either finely chopped and added to the dressing or used whole as a garnish. Capers add bold salty flavor, along with some acidity. You can also use more or different herbs—we suggest parsley, rosemary, chives, thyme, tarragon or dill.

## SWEET POTATO PONE

Sweet potatoes are among my favorite vegetables, and this recipe is my absolute favorite way to prepare them. Not only is it an eagerly anticipated side dish for Thanksgiving dinner with family and friends each year, but also I make it to dress up ordinary meals. You can almost serve it as a dessert!
—*Kristine Chayes, Smithtown, NY*

- - - - - - - - - - - - - - - - - - - - - - - - - - - - - - - - -

**PREP:** 15 min. • **BAKE:** 55 min. + standing
**MAKES:** 12 servings

2½ lbs. large sweet potatoes (about 4 large), peeled and shredded
½  cup sugar
½  cup light corn syrup
½  cup butter, melted
1  Tbsp. grated orange zest
¾  cup all-purpose flour
1  tsp. ground nutmeg
1  tsp. ground cinnamon

**1.** Preheat oven to 350°. In a large bowl, combine sweet potatoes, sugar, corn syrup, butter and orange zest. In another bowl, combine the flour, nutmeg and cinnamon. Add to sweet potato mixture; mix well.
**2.** Transfer to a greased 13x9-in. baking dish. Bake until sweet potatoes are bubbly and golden brown, 55-60 minutes. Let stand 10 minutes before serving.
**1 SERVING:** 270 cal., 8g fat (5g sat. fat), 20mg chol., 80mg sod., 49g carb. (29g sugars, 3g fiber), 3g pro.

## GREEN CHILE CORN FRITTERS

This is a crispy side dish, appetizer or snack to add to a Mexican meal. The fritters also go well with chili or soup. I usually have all the ingredients on hand.
—*Johnna Johnson, Scottsdale, AZ*

**PREP:** 20 min. • **COOK:** 5 min./batch • **MAKES:** 2 dozen

- 1 cup yellow cornmeal
- ½ cup all-purpose flour
- 1½ tsp. baking powder
- ¾ tsp. salt
- ½ tsp. garlic powder
- ½ tsp. onion powder
- ½ tsp. paprika
- ½ tsp. pepper
- 1 large egg, room temperature
- ⅔ cup 2% milk
- 1 can (8¾ oz.) whole kernel corn, drained
- 1 can (4 oz.) chopped green chiles, drained
  Oil for deep-fat frying
  Optional: Sriracha mayonnaise or condiment of your choice

**1.** In a large bowl, whisk the first 8 ingredients. In another bowl, whisk egg and milk until blended. Add to the dry ingredients, stirring just until moistened. Let stand 5 minutes. Fold in corn and green chiles.

**2.** In a deep cast-iron or electric skillet, heat oil to 375°. Drop batter by tablespoonfuls, a few at a time, into hot oil. Fry until golden brown, 1-1½ minutes on each side. Drain on paper towels. Serve with desired condiments.

**1 FRITTER:** 74 cal., 4g fat (0 sat. fat), 8mg chol., 159mg sod., 9g carb. (1g sugars, 1g fiber), 1g pro.

## GRAPEFRUIT LETTUCE SALAD

A light vinaigrette flavored with cilantro and grapefruit juice drapes this tangy salad. You can make the dressing ahead of time; it keeps well in the refrigerator.
—*Vivian Haen, Menomonee Falls, WI*

**TAKES:** 15 min. • **MAKES:** 2 servings

- 2 Tbsp. pink grapefruit juice
- 1 Tbsp. olive oil
- 1½ tsp. red wine vinegar
- ½ tsp. honey
- 1½ tsp. minced fresh cilantro
- 2 cups torn Bibb or Boston lettuce
- 1 medium pink grapefruit, peeled and sectioned
  Optional: Sliced fennel bulb, fennel fronds and pistachios

In a small bowl, whisk the grapefruit juice, oil, vinegar and honey; stir in cilantro. In a salad bowl, toss lettuce, grapefruit and, if desired, sliced fennel bulb, fennel fronds and pistachios. Drizzle with dressing; gently toss to coat.

**1 CUP:** 120 cal., 7g fat (1g sat. fat), 0 chol., 5mg sod., 14g carb. (0 sugars, 2g fiber), 1g pro. **DIABETIC EXCHANGES:** 2 vegetable, 1½ fat.

## ROASTED PEAR SALAD

Oven-roasted pears are tossed with crispy greens, dried cranberries and nuts. The creamy dressing adds even more pear flavor, sweetened with a touch of honey.
—Taste of Home *Test Kitchen*

--------------------------------------------------------

**PREP:** 15 min. • **BAKE:** 15 min. + cooling • **MAKES:** 4 servings

- 2 medium pears, halved and cored
- 4 tsp. olive oil, divided
- 2 Tbsp. cider vinegar
- 1 tsp. water
- 1 tsp. honey
- ¼ tsp. salt
- ⅛ tsp. white pepper
- 1 pkg. (10 oz.) mixed baby salad greens
- 1 cup watercress sprigs
- ¼ cup chopped hazelnuts, toasted
- ¼ cup dried cranberries

**1.** Preheat oven to 400°. In a small bowl, toss pears with 1 tsp. oil. Place in a 5x10x1-in. baking pan coated with cooking spray. Bake 10 minutes. Turn pears over; bake until golden and tender, 5-7 minutes longer.

**2.** When cool enough to handle, peel pears. Thinly slice 2 pear halves lengthwise and set aside. Place remaining pear halves in a blender. Add the vinegar, water, honey, salt and white pepper; cover and process until smooth. While processing, gradually add the remaining 3 tsp. oil in a steady stream.

**3.** In a large bowl, toss the salad greens, watercress, hazelnuts and cranberries. Arrange reserved pear slices on top; drizzle with dressing.

**1 SERVING:** 174 cal., 9g fat (1g sat. fat), 0 chol., 178mg sod., 24g carb. (0 sugars, 5g fiber), 3g pro.

## HARVARD BEETS

This pretty side dish's bright, citrusy flavors are an ideal companion for down-to-earth entrees—even for people who usually shy away from beets.
—*Jean Ann Perkins, Newburyport, MA*

--------------------------------------------------------

**TAKES:** 15 min. • **MAKES:** 4 servings

- 1 can (16 oz.) sliced beets
- ¼ cup sugar
- 1½ tsp. cornstarch
- 2 Tbsp. vinegar
- 2 Tbsp. orange juice
- 1 Tbsp. grated orange zest

Drain beets, reserving 2 Tbsp. juice; set beets and juice aside. In a saucepan, combine sugar and cornstarch. Add vinegar, orange juice and beet juice; bring to a boil. Reduce heat and simmer until thickened, 3-4 minutes. Add beets and orange zest; heat through.

**½ CUP:** 93 cal., 0 fat (0 sat. fat), 0 chol., 220mg sod., 23g carb. (19g sugars, 2g fiber), 1g pro.

## RADISH CUCUMBER SALAD

I put this salad together with vegetables I had left in my garden. My family liked it so well, I started bringing it to community suppers and was often asked for the recipe. It's a refreshing side dish for any meat entree.

—*Mildred Sherrer, Fort Worth, TX*

- - - - - - - - - - - - - - - - - - - - - - - - - - - - - - - - - - - - -

**TAKES:** 10 min. • **MAKES:** 2 servings

- ½ medium cucumber, halved and sliced
- 2 radishes, sliced
- 2 Tbsp. chopped red onion
- 1 Tbsp. olive oil
- 1½ tsp. lemon juice
- ⅛ to ¼ tsp. garlic salt
- ⅛ tsp. lemon-pepper seasoning

In a serving bowl, combine the cucumber, radishes and onion. In another bowl, combine the remaining ingredients. Pour over vegetables and toss to coat. Serve immediately.

**1 SERVING:** 77 cal., 7g fat (1g sat. fat), 0 chol., 143mg sod., 4g carb. (2g sugars, 1g fiber), 1g pro. **DIABETIC EXCHANGES:** 1½ fat, 1 vegetable.

> **TIP**
> We recommend serving this summer salad recipe immediately, but you can slice the veggies and prep the lemon juice dressing beforehand to save some extra time.

## ROSEMARY SWEET POTATO FRIES

A local restaurant got me hooked on sweet potato fries. I started experimenting at home, trying to make my recipe taste like theirs, but healthier and baked, not fried. I'm thrilled with these results!

—*Jackie Gregston, Hallsville, TX*

- - - - - - - - - - - - - - - - - - - - - - - - - - - - - - - - - - - - -

**PREP:** 15 min. • **BAKE:** 30 min. • **MAKES:** 4 servings

- 3 Tbsp. olive oil
- 1 Tbsp. minced fresh rosemary
- 1 garlic clove, minced
- 1 tsp. cornstarch
- ¾ tsp. salt
- ⅛ tsp. pepper
- 3 large sweet potatoes, peeled and cut into ¼-in. julienned strips (about 2¼ lbs.)

**1.** Preheat oven to 425°. In a large airtight container, combine the first 6 ingredients. Add sweet potatoes; shake to coat.
**2.** Arrange potatoes in a single layer on two 15x10x1-in. baking pans coated with cooking spray. Bake, uncovered, 30-35 minutes or until tender and lightly browned, turning occasionally.
**1 SERVING:** 256 cal., 10g fat (1g sat. fat), 0 chol., 459mg sod., 39g carb. (16g sugars, 5g fiber), 3g pro.

> **REVIEW**
> *"A winner. They make the house smell as delicious as they taste."*
> —WALLYNBOB, TASTEOFHOME.COM

## STRAWBERRY SHORTCAKE SALAD

This delightful recipe transforms an oldie-but-goodie dessert into a bright, refreshing twist on traditional salad. Springtime strawberries and herbed shortcake croutons provide a pop of sweetness, while spicy arugula and toasted pine nuts bring earthy balance. With creamy Gorgonzola, crispy pancetta and strawberry yogurt dressing, this is a crowd-pleaser at your next potluck and the perfect celebration of spring in a salad bowl.
—*Adrienne Vradenburg, Bakersfield, CA*

- - - - - - - - - - - - - - - - - - - - - - - - - - -

**TAKES:** 25 min. • **MAKES:** 4 servings

- 4   oz. chopped pancetta
- 1   Tbsp. extra virgin olive oil
- 2   individual round shortcakes, cubed
- 3   Tbsp. minced fresh parsley, divided
- ½   tsp. kosher salt, divided
- ½   cup strawberry custard-style yogurt
- 1   Tbsp. fresh lemon juice
- ¼   tsp. coarsely ground pepper
- 4   cups fresh arugula
- 1   cup fresh strawberries, sliced
- ½   cup crumbled Gorgonzola cheese
- ¼   cup pine nuts, toasted

**1.** In a large skillet, cook pancetta over medium-high heat until crispy, about 5 minutes. Remove to paper towels to drain, reserving drippings in pan. Add olive oil to the drippings. Add shortcake cubes; cook, stirring frequently, until golden brown, 3-4 minutes. Transfer to bowl; stir in 2 Tbsp. parsley and ¼ tsp. salt.
**2.** In a small bowl, stir together yogurt, lemon juice, remaining 1 Tbsp. of parsley, ¼ tsp. salt and the pepper. In a salad bowl, toss arugula, strawberries, Gorgonzola, pine nuts, pancetta and the shortcake "croutons." Drizzle with the dressing and serve immediately.
**1 SERVING:** 330 cal., 24g fat (8g sat. fat), 51mg chol., 1074mg sod., 18g carb. (11g sugars, 2g fiber), 12g pro.

## SWISS POTATO PANCAKE

This is the classic Swiss mountain dish called *rösti*. The big potato pancake is cut into wedges and usually served with bratwurst, but I have also prepared this cheese potato dish as a meatless main course. We love the nutty flavor that the Gruyere cheese provides.
—*Sue Jurack, Mequon, WI*

- - - - - - - - - - - - - - - - - - - - - - - - - - -

**TAKES:** 15 min. • **MAKES:** 6 servings

- 2   Tbsp. butter, divided
- 2   Tbsp. canola oil, divided
- 1   pkg. (30 oz.) frozen shredded hash brown potatoes, thawed
- 1   tsp. salt, divided
- ¼   tsp. pepper, divided
- 1½  cups shredded Gruyere or Swiss cheese
     Optional: Sour cream and minced chives

**1.** In a 9-in. nonstick skillet, melt 1 Tbsp. butter with 1 Tbsp. oil over medium-high heat. Spread half the potatoes in an even layer in skillet. Season with ½ tsp. salt and ⅛ tsp. pepper. Sprinkle with cheese, then top with remaining potatoes. Season with remaining ½ tsp. salt and ⅛ tsp. pepper. Press mixture gently into skillet. Cook until bottom is browned, 7 minutes.
**2.** Remove from the heat. Loosen pancake from sides of skillet. Invert onto a plate. Return skillet to heat and heat remaining butter and oil. Slide potato pancake browned side up into skillet. Cook until bottom is browned and cheese is melted, 5-7 minutes.
**3.** Slide pancake onto a plate and cut into wedges. If desired, served with sour cream and chives.
**1 PIECE:** 296 cal., 17g fat (8g sat. fat), 35mg chol., 507mg sod., 27g carb. (2g sugars, 3g fiber), 11g pro.

**TIP** A nonstick skillet is a must for this recipe so the pancake comes out easily.

## - SMOKY CAULIFLOWER BITES -

With a spicy, smoky flavor and an irresistible crunch, these healthy little treats work as a side dish or a fun, bite-sized appetizer.

Break **1 medium head of cauliflower** into florets. Combine **¼ cup olive oil**, **1 tsp. sea salt**, **1 tsp. paprika**, **½ tsp. ground cumin**, **¼ tsp. ground turmeric** and **⅛ tsp. chili powder**. Toss with cauliflower to coat. Transfer to a 15x10x1-in. baking pan. Roast at 450° until tender, 15-20 minutes, stirring halfway.

## SZECHUAN SUGAR SNAP PEAS

Simple seasonings transform crisp, sweet sugar snap peas into an unbeatable side dish your family will love. You can use chopped walnuts in place of the cashews if you prefer.
—*Jeanne Holt, St. Paul, MN*

**TAKES:** 25 min. • **MAKES:** 8 servings

- 6 cups fresh sugar snap peas
- 2 tsp. peanut oil
- 1 tsp. sesame oil
- 3 Tbsp. thinly sliced green onions
- 1 tsp. grated orange zest
- ½ tsp. minced garlic
- ½ tsp. minced fresh gingerroot
- ⅛ tsp. crushed red pepper flakes
- 1 Tbsp. minced fresh cilantro
- ¼ tsp. salt
- ⅛ tsp. pepper
- ⅓ cup salted cashew halves

**1.** In a Dutch oven, saute peas in peanut oil and sesame oil until crisp-tender. Add the onions, orange zest, garlic, ginger and pepper flakes; saute 1 minute longer.
**2.** Remove from the heat; stir in the cilantro, salt and pepper. Sprinkle with cashews just before serving.
**¾ CUP:** 107 cal., 5g fat (1g sat. fat), 0 chol., 121mg sod., 10g carb. (5g sugars, 4g fiber), 5g pro. **DIABETIC EXCHANGES:** 2 vegetable, 1 fat.

## WALNUT CRANBERRY ORZO

I came up with this delightful side dish after being fascinated by the tiny pasta! With red pepper, cranberries, walnuts and Parmesan, the dish is just as colorful as it is flavorful.
—*Judith Comstock, Salado, TX*

**TAKES:** 30 min. • **MAKES:** 6 servings

- 1¼ cups uncooked orzo pasta
- 1 medium sweet red pepper, chopped
- 1 small onion, chopped
- 1½ tsp. olive oil
- ½ cup reduced-sodium chicken broth or vegetable broth
- ½ cup dried cranberries
- ¼ tsp. salt
- ½ cup chopped walnuts, toasted
- ¼ cup grated Parmesan cheese

**1.** Cook orzo according to package directions. Meanwhile, saute red pepper and onion in oil until tender. Stir in the broth, cranberries and salt. Bring to a boil. Reduce heat; simmer, uncovered, for 5 minutes.
**2.** Drain orzo; toss with vegetable mixture. Sprinkle with walnuts and Parmesan cheese.
**⅔ CUP:** 283 cal., 9g fat (1g sat. fat), 3mg chol., 216mg sod., 43g carb. (9g sugars, 3g fiber), 10g pro.

## ZUCCHINI PATTIES

My sister gave me this recipe and I, in turn, have given it to many of my friends. These patties have a nice flavor and are compatible with just about any entree.
—Annabelle Cripe, Goshen, IN

PREP: 15 min. • COOK: 20 min. • MAKES: 4 servings

    2   cups shredded zucchini
    ½   cup shredded cheddar cheese
    ⅓   cup biscuit/baking mix
    2   Tbsp. grated onion
    ½   tsp. salt
    ½   tsp. dried basil
    ¼   tsp. pepper
    2   large eggs, room temperature, lightly beaten
    2   Tbsp. butter

1. In a bowl, combine first 7 ingredients. Stir in eggs; mix well. Shape into 6 patties, using about ¼ cup of zucchini mixture for each patty.
2. In a skillet over medium-high heat, melt butter; cook patties until lightly browned, 4-5 minutes on each side.

2 PATTIES: 195 cal., 14g fat (7g sat. fat), 122mg chol., 577mg sod., 10g carb. (2g sugars, 1g fiber), 8g pro.

> **TIP**
> Excess water in the mixture can cause your zucchini patties to fall apart. Make sure to pat the shredded zucchini dry before adding it to the binding mixture.

## THAI SALAD WITH PEANUT DRESSING

This Thai salad is very fresh and flavorful. The peanut garnish adds a satisfying crunch.
—James Schend, Pleasant Prairie, WI

TAKES: 25 min. • MAKES: 8 servings

    2   cups spring mix salad greens
    ½   cup fresh cilantro leaves
    1   small napa cabbage, shredded
    1   small cucumber, sliced
    1   small red onion, julienned
    2   small carrots, shredded
    2   green onions, sliced
    PEANUT DRESSING
    ¼   cup creamy peanut butter
    3   Tbsp. hot water
    1   Tbsp. lime juice
    1   Tbsp. sesame oil
    1   Tbsp. fish sauce
    1   Tbsp. rice vinegar
    ½   tsp. crushed red pepper flakes
    1   small garlic clove, minced
    ¼   cup dry roasted peanuts
        Jalapeno pepper slices, optional

1. In a large bowl, toss salad greens and next 6 ingredients.
2. For dressing, in a small bowl, whisk the next 8 ingredients. Add to salad and toss to coat. Divide mixture between 4 plates; top with peanuts and, if desired, jalapenos.

NOTE: Wear disposable gloves when cutting hot peppers; the oils can burn skin. Avoid touching your face.

1 CUP: 111 cal., 8g fat (1g sat. fat), 0 chol., 286mg sod., 7g carb. (3g sugars, 2g fiber), 4g pro.

## SYRIAN GREEN BEANS WITH FRESH HERBS

This how my mom always made green beans. She got the recipe from a neighbor when we lived in Turkey. Cook up a double batch, as they make an excellent healthy snack straight from the fridge. Add a thinly sliced onion and red bell pepper if you like. Another idea is to make them ahead to add to a salad.
—Trisha Kruse, Eagle, ID

TAKES: 25 min. • MAKES: 6 servings

- 2 Tbsp. olive oil
- 2 garlic cloves, minced
- 1 lb. fresh green beans, cut into 2-in. pieces
- ½ tsp. salt
- ¼ tsp. pepper
- 2 Tbsp. each minced fresh cilantro, parsley and mint

In a large skillet, heat oil over medium heat. Add garlic; cook for 1 minute. Add green beans, salt and pepper. Cook, covered, until crisp-tender, 8-10 minutes, stirring occasionally. Add herbs; cook and stir just until beans are tender, 1-2 minutes.

**¾ CUP:** 66 cal., 5g fat (1g sat. fat), 0 chol., 203mg sod., 6g carb. (2g sugars, 3g fiber), 2g pro. **DIABETIC EXCHANGES:** 1 vegetable, 1 fat.

## STRAWBERRY VINAIGRETTE

I enjoy using strawberries in a variety of ways, including in this pretty, sweet-tart dressing.
—Carolyn McMunn, San Angelo, TX

TAKES: 10 min. • MAKES: 2½ cups

- 1 pkg. (16 oz.) frozen unsweetened strawberries, thawed
- 6 Tbsp. lemon juice
- ¼ cup sugar
- 2 Tbsp. cider vinegar
- 2 Tbsp. olive oil
- ⅛ tsp. poppy seeds

Place the strawberries in a blender; cover and process until pureed. Add lemon juice and sugar; cover and process until blended. While processing, gradually add vinegar and oil in a steady stream; process until thickened. Stir in poppy seeds. Transfer to a large bowl or jar; cover and store in the refrigerator.

**2 TBSP. VINAIGRETTE:** 31 cal., 1g fat (0 sat. fat), 0 chol., 1mg sod., 5g carb. (4g sugars, 0 fiber), 0 pro.

**BLUEBERRY VINAIGRETTE:** Substitute blueberries for the strawberries.

TIPS
- You can make substitutions to create your own version of this strawberry dressing. Try substituting avocado oil, flaxseed oil or walnut oil for the olive oil, or adding cracked black pepper, fresh basil or Italian seasoning.
- If you want your vinaigrette to be seed-free, use a fine-mesh sieve to strain the strawberries after they've been blended.

## SPINACH SALAD WITH HOT BACON DRESSING

After having a salad like this at a restaurant years ago, I came up with this recipe. It is especially good when the spinach comes right from the garden to the table.
—Wanda Cover, Mediapolis, IA

- - - - - - - - - - - - - - - - - - - - - - - - - - - - - - - - - - - - - - - -

**TAKES:** 25 min. • **MAKES:** 2 servings

- 2 cups fresh baby spinach, torn
- 2 hard-boiled large eggs, sliced
- 4 cherry tomatoes, halved
- 3 medium fresh mushrooms, sliced
- ¼ cup salad croutons
- 6 pitted ripe olives, halved
- 3 slices red onion, halved

DRESSING
- 4 bacon strips, diced
- 1 Tbsp. chopped onion
- 2 Tbsp. sugar
- 2 Tbsp. ketchup
- 1 Tbsp. red wine vinegar
- 1 Tbsp. Worcestershire sauce

**1.** Divide spinach between 2 plates. Arrange the eggs, tomatoes, mushrooms, croutons, olives and red onion over top.
**2.** In a small skillet, cook bacon over medium heat until crisp. Using a slotted spoon, remove to paper towels; drain, reserving 2 Tbsp. drippings in the pan. Saute onion in drippings until tender. Stir in the sugar, ketchup, vinegar and Worcestershire sauce. Bring to a boil. Reduce heat; simmer, uncovered, until thickened, 1-2 minutes. Sprinkle bacon over salads; drizzle with dressing.
**1⅓ CUPS:** 367 cal., 21g fat (6g sat. fat), 238mg chol., 1178mg sod., 29g carb. (21g sugars, 2g fiber), 17g pro.

## SESAME ALMOND SLAW

Crunchy veggies and noodles are coated in a tangy dressing in this pleasant slaw.
—Taste of Home *Test Kitchen*

- - - - - - - - - - - - - - - - - - - - - - - - - - - - - - - - - - - - - - - -

**TAKES:** 20 min. • **MAKES:** 2 servings

- 1 pkg. (3 oz.) ramen noodles
- ¾ cup shredded cabbage
- ¾ cup shredded romaine
- 2 Tbsp. sliced green onion
- 2 tsp. slivered almonds, toasted
- 2 tsp. sesame seeds, toasted

DRESSING
- 1 Tbsp. rice vinegar
- 1½ tsp. sugar
- 1½ tsp. canola oil
- 1 tsp. water
- ½ tsp. sesame oil
- ¼ tsp. reduced-sodium soy sauce
  Dash salt
  Dash pepper

**1.** Split ramen noodles in half. Save the seasoning packet and half the noodles for future use. Break apart the remaining noodles; place in a bowl. Add cabbage, romaine, onion, almonds and sesame seeds.
**2.** For dressing, in a jar with a tight-fitting lid, combine vinegar, sugar, canola oil, water, sesame oil, soy sauce, salt and pepper; shake well. Add to salad and toss to coat. Serve immediately.
**1 CUP:** 187 cal., 10g fat (3g sat. fat), 0 chol., 193mg sod., 20g carb. (4g sugars, 2g fiber), 4g pro. **DIABETIC EXCHANGES:** 1½ fat, 1 starch, 1 vegetable.

# ZUCCHINI FRIES

These aren't anything like potato fries—in a good way! They are air-fried to crispy perfection and so flavorful. Enjoy as an appetizer or a low-carb alternative to French fries. Don't have an air fryer? You can convection bake for the same time.
—*Jen Pahl, West Allis, WI*

------------------------------------------------

**PREP:** 20 min. • **COOK:** 10 min./batch
**MAKES:** 4 servings

- 2 medium zucchini
- 1 cup panko bread crumbs
- 2 tsp. dried basil, divided
- 1½ tsp. seasoned salt
- 1 tsp. garlic powder
- 1 tsp. dried oregano
- ½ cup grated Parmesan cheese plus 2 Tbsp. grated Parmesan cheese
- 2 large eggs, room temperature, lightly beaten
  Cooking spray
  Marinara sauce, warmed

**1.** Preheat air fryer to 375°. Cut each zucchini in half lengthwise and then in half crosswise. Cut each piece lengthwise into ¼-in. slices.
**2.** In a shallow bowl, mix panko, 1 tsp. basil, the seasoned salt, garlic powder, oregano and ½ cup Parmesan cheese. Place eggs and remaining 1 tsp. basil in separate shallow bowls. Dip zucchini slices in egg mixture and then in crumb mixture, patting to help coating adhere.
**3.** In batches, place zucchini in greased air fryer; spritz with cooking spray. Cook until lightly browned, 6-8 minutes. Flip each piece; cook until golden brown, 3-5 minutes longer.
**4.** Sprinkle hot fries with the remaining 2 Tbsp. Parmesan cheese. Serve with marinara sauce.

**1 CUP:** 91 cal., 4g fat (2g sat. fat), 52mg chol., 389mg sod., 9g carb. (2g sugars, 1g fiber), 6g pro. **DIABETIC EXCHANGES:** 1 vegetable, 1 fat.

## SKILLET CABBAGE

I use this dish often when my schedule gets tight and I need a hurry-up vegetable to cook. It adds plenty of substance to a simple meal.
—Charmaine Fricke, St. Charles, IL

TAKES: 25 min. • MAKES: 6 servings

- 2 Tbsp. butter
- 4 cups shredded cabbage
- 1 green pepper, cut into thin strips
- 2 Tbsp. water
- ½ tsp. salt
- ¼ tsp. pepper
- 3 oz. cream cheese, cubed and softened

Melt butter in a large cast-iron or other heavy skillet; add cabbage and green pepper and toss to coat. Stir in water, salt and pepper. Cover; simmer until cabbage is tender, 8-10 minutes. Add cream cheese; stir until melted.

**½ CUP:** 100 cal., 9g fat (5g sat. fat), 26mg chol., 286mg sod., 4g carb. (2g sugars, 1g fiber), 2g pro.

## ITALIAN TOMATO CUCUMBER SALAD

This yummy medley of vegetables is a cool complement to zesty dishes like seasoned fish and barbecued meats and poultry.
—Florine Bruns, Fredericksburg, TX

TAKES: 10 min. • MAKES: 4 servings

- 2 medium cucumbers, sliced
- 1 large tomato, cut into wedges
- 1 small red onion, cut into thin strips
- ¼ cup Italian salad dressing or salad dressing of your choice

In a large bowl, combine the vegetables. Add dressing; toss to coat.

**½ CUP:** 93 cal., 6g fat (1g sat. fat), 0 chol., 257mg sod., 9g carb. (6g sugars, 2g fiber), 2g pro. **DIABETIC EXCHANGES:** 1 vegetable, 1 fat.

## GUACAMOLE TOSSED SALAD

The fresh blend of avocados, tomatoes, red onion and greens in my salad gets additional pizzazz from crumbled bacon and a slightly spicy vinaigrette.
—Lori Fischer, Chino Hills, CA

TAKES: 15 min. • MAKES: 4 servings

- 2 medium tomatoes, seeded and chopped
- ½ small red onion, sliced and separated into rings
- 6 bacon strips, cooked and crumbled
- ⅓ cup canola oil
- 2 Tbsp. cider vinegar
- 1 tsp. salt
- ¼ tsp. pepper
- ¼ tsp. hot pepper sauce
- 2 large ripe avocados, peeled and cubed
- 4 cups torn salad greens

**1.** In a large bowl, combine the tomatoes, onion and bacon; set aside.

**2.** In a small bowl, whisk the oil, vinegar, salt, pepper and hot pepper sauce. Pour over tomato mixture; toss gently. Add avocados.

**3.** Place greens in a large salad bowl; add avocado mixture and toss to coat.

**1 SERVING:** 531 cal., 51g fat (7g sat. fat), 12mg chol., 868mg sod., 17g carb. (3g sugars, 10g fiber), 9g pro.

## GARLIC & ARTICHOKE ROASTED POTATOES

I like to put this side into the oven while I'm baking a main dish. Artichokes give it a gourmet appeal.
—*Marie Rizzio, Interlochen, MI*

**PREP:** 15 min. • **BAKE:** 35 min. • **MAKES:** 10 servings

2½ lbs. medium red potatoes, cut into 1½-in. cubes
2 pkg. (8 oz. each) frozen artichoke hearts
8 garlic cloves, halved
3 Tbsp. olive oil
¾ tsp. salt
¼ tsp. pepper
¼ cup lemon juice
2 Tbsp. minced fresh parsley
1 tsp. grated lemon zest

**1.** Preheat oven to 425°. Place the potatoes, artichokes and garlic in a 15x10x1-in. baking pan coated with cooking spray. Combine the oil, salt and pepper; drizzle over vegetables and toss to coat.
**2.** Bake, uncovered, for 35-40 minutes or until tender, stirring occasionally. Transfer to a large bowl. Add lemon juice, parsley and lemon zest; toss to coat. Serve warm.
**¾ CUP:** 143 cal., 4g fat (1g sat. fat), 0 chol., 209mg sod., 24g carb. (2g sugars, 4g fiber), 4g pro. **DIABETIC EXCHANGES:** 1 starch, 1 vegetable, 1 fat.

## DREAMY POLENTA

I grew up eating polenta, so it's a must at my holiday gatherings. Traditional recipes require constant stirring, but using my handy slow cooker allows me to turn my attention to the lineup of other foods on my spread.
—*Ann Voccola, Milford, CT*

**PREP:** 10 min. • **COOK:** 5 hours • **MAKES:** 12 servings

1 Tbsp. butter
5 cups whole milk
4 cups half-and-half cream
12 Tbsp. butter, cubed, divided
2 cups yellow cornmeal
¾ tsp. salt
½ tsp. minced fresh rosemary
¼ tsp. pepper
2 cups shredded Asiago cheese

**1.** Generously grease a 5-qt. slow cooker with 1 Tbsp. butter. Add milk, cream, 6 Tbsp. cubed butter, cornmeal, salt, rosemary and pepper; stir to combine.
**2.** Cook, covered, on low until polenta is thickened, 5-6 hours, whisking every hour. Just before serving, whisk again; stir in cheese and remaining 6 Tbsp. cubed butter. Garnish with additional rosemary if desired.
**¾ CUP:** 444 cal., 29g fat (18g sat. fat), 100mg chol., 379mg sod., 29g carb. (9g sugars, 1g fiber), 13g pro.

# CREAMED PEAS

I can still taste these wonderful peas in Mama's delicious white sauce. Our food was pretty plain during the week, so I thought this white sauce made the peas "extra fancy" and fitting for a Sunday meal.
—Imogene Hutton, Brownwood, TX

------------------------------------------

**TAKES:** 15 min. • **MAKES:** 4 servings

- 1 pkg. (10 oz.) frozen peas
- 1 Tbsp. butter
- 1 Tbsp. all-purpose flour
- ¼ tsp. salt
- ⅛ tsp. pepper
- ½ cup whole milk
- 1 tsp. sugar

Cook the peas according to the package directions. Meanwhile, melt the butter in a small saucepan. Stir in the flour, salt and pepper until blended; gradually add milk and sugar. Bring to a boil; cook and stir until thickened, 1-2 minutes. Drain peas; stir into the sauce and heat through.

**½ CUP:** 110 cal., 4g fat (2g sat. fat), 12mg chol., 271mg sod., 14g carb. (6g sugars, 3g fiber), 5g pro.

> **TIP**
> To add extra flavor and texture to these creamed peas, try sprinkling on a simple topping like fried onion strips or bacon pieces.

# DIRTY RICE

This is an old Louisiana recipe that I've had longer than I can remember. It's a very popular southern dish. To turn this into a main meal, simply add more sausage and chicken livers.
—Lum Day, Bastrop, LA

------------------------------------------

**TAKES:** 30 min. • **MAKES:** 12 servings

- ½ lb. bulk pork sausage
- ½ lb. chicken livers, chopped
- 3 Tbsp. butter
- 1 large onion, chopped
- 1 celery rib, chopped
- 3 green onions, chopped
- 2 Tbsp. minced fresh parsley
- 1 garlic clove, minced
- 1 can (10½ oz.) condensed chicken broth, undiluted
- ½ tsp. dried basil
- ½ tsp. dried thyme
- ½ tsp. salt
- ¼ tsp. pepper
- ¼ tsp. hot pepper sauce
- 3 cups cooked rice

**1.** In a large cast-iron or other heavy skillet, cook sausage for 2-3 minutes; stir in chicken livers. Cook until sausage and chicken livers are no longer pink, 5-7 minutes; drain and set aside.

**2.** In the same skillet, melt butter over medium heat. Add onion, celery and green onions. Cook and stir until vegetables are tender, 3-5 minutes. Add parsley and garlic; cook 1 minute longer. Add broth, basil, thyme, salt, pepper and hot pepper sauce. Stir in rice and sausage mixture. Heat through, stirring constantly.

**1 CUP:** 148 cal., 7g fat (3g sat. fat), 97mg chol., 325mg sod., 14g carb. (1g sugars, 1g fiber), 6g pro.

# - 5 -

# COOKING FOR TWO

From comforting and casual Tater Tot casserole to elegant merlot-glazed filet mignon for special celebrations, your options are wide open even when you're cooking for a small household. There's even lasagna!

**Slow-Cooked Beef Tips** (p. 106) **Pressure-Cooker Mexican Stuffed Peppers** (p. 114)
**Crab-Stuffed Manicotti** (p. 108) **Salmon with Spinach Sauce** (p. 114) **Fiesta Bean Casserole** (p. 102)
**Oven-Fried Ranch Steak** (p. 116) **Jackfruit Tacos with Green Apple Salsa** (p. 109)
**Spicy Turkey Stir-Fry with Noodles** (p. 105) **Slow-Cooker Veggie Lasagna** (p. 107)

## BEST VEAL SCALLOPINI

I found the original version of this dish in a magazine and adjusted it to suit my family's tastes. Because delicate, fine-textured veal comes with a short cooking time, this simple entree is even more attractive.
—Ruth Lee, Troy, ON

**TAKES:** 25 min. • **MAKES:** 2 servings

- 2 veal cutlets (about 4 oz. each)
- 2 Tbsp. all-purpose flour
- ½ tsp. salt
- ¼ tsp. pepper
- 3 Tbsp. butter, divided
- 1 Tbsp. olive oil
- ¼ lb. fresh mushrooms, thinly sliced
- ⅓ cup chicken broth
- 2 tsp. minced fresh parsley

**1.** Flatten cutlets to ⅛-in. thickness. In a shallow dish, combine flour, salt and pepper. Add veal; turn to coat. In a skillet, heat 2 Tbsp. butter and oil over medium heat. Add veal; cook until juices run clear, about 1 minute on each side. Remove and keep warm.
**2.** Add mushrooms to skillet; cook and stir until tender, 2-3 minutes. Spoon over veal. Stir broth into skillet, stirring to loosen any browned bits. Add parsley and remaining butter; cook and stir until sauce is slightly thickened, 1-2 minutes longer. Pour over veal and mushrooms.
**1 SERVING:** 435 cal., 35g fat (16g sat. fat), 120mg chol., 941mg sod., 8g carb. (0 sugars, 0 fiber), 21g pro.
**WIENER SCHNITZEL:** Omit the oil, mushrooms, chicken broth and parsley. Coat cutlets with flour mixture, then dip in 1 beaten egg and coat with ⅓ cup dry bread crumbs. Cook veal in the entire amount of butter. Serve with lemon slices.

## AIR-FRYER GARLIC-BUTTER STEAK

This quick and easy entree is definitely restaurant-quality and sure to become a staple at your house!
—Lily Julow, Lawrenceville, GA

**TAKES:** 20 min. • **MAKES:** 2 servings

- 1 beef flat iron steak or boneless top sirloin steak (¾ lb.)
- ⅛ tsp. salt
- ⅛ tsp. pepper
- 1 Tbsp. butter, softened
- 1 tsp. minced fresh parsley
- ½ tsp. minced garlic
- ¼ tsp. reduced-sodium soy sauce

**1.** Preheat air fryer to 400°. Sprinkle steak with salt and pepper. Place steak on tray in air-fryer basket. Cook until meat reaches desired doneness (for medium-rare, a thermometer should read 135°; medium, 140°; medium-well, 145°), 8-10 minutes, turning halfway through.
**2.** Meanwhile, combine butter, parsley, garlic and soy sauce. Serve with steak.
**4 OZ. COOKED BEEF WITH 2 TSP. GARLIC BUTTER:** 353 cal., 24g fat (11g sat. fat), 125mg chol., 322mg sod., 0 carb. (0 sugars, 0 fiber), 33g pro.

**TIP**

If you don't have an air fryer, you can make this recipe in a large skillet over medium heat with 1 Tbsp. of butter. Cook until meat reaches desired doneness (for medium-rare, a thermometer should read 135°; medium, 140°; medium-well, 145°), 4-7 minutes per side.

## CHICKEN PAELLA

Turmeric lends flavor and a beautiful golden color to this Spanish-style entree. Haven't tried arborio rice? You'll love its creamy texture.
—Taste of Home *Test Kitchen*

**PREP:** 10 min. • **COOK:** 45 min. • **MAKES:** 2 servings

- 2 boneless skinless chicken thighs (about ½ lb.), cut into 2-in. pieces
- ½ cup cubed fully cooked ham
- ⅓ cup chopped onion
- ⅓ cup julienned sweet red pepper
- 1 Tbsp. olive oil, divided
- ½ cup uncooked arborio rice
- ½ tsp. ground turmeric
- ½ tsp. ground cumin
- ½ tsp. minced garlic
- ⅛ tsp. salt
- 1 cup plus 2 Tbsp. chicken broth
- ¾ cup frozen peas, thawed

**1.** In a large skillet, saute the chicken, ham, onion and red pepper in 2 tsp. oil until chicken is browned on all sides. Remove with a slotted spoon.
**2.** In the same skillet, saute rice in remaining 1 tsp. oil until lightly browned. Stir in the turmeric, cumin, garlic and salt. Return meat and vegetables to pan; toss lightly. Add the broth; bring to a boil. Reduce heat to medium; cover and simmer until rice is tender, 30-35 minutes. Stir in peas.
**1½ CUPS:** 516 cal., 17g fat (4g sat. fat), 99mg chol., 1242mg sod., 52g carb. (5g sugars, 4g fiber), 36g pro.

## FIESTA BEAN CASSEROLE

I don't recall its origin, but I have had this recipe for many years. A Triscuit cracker crust makes it a unique meatless option.
—Karen Tjelmeland, Ely, IA

**PREP:** 20 min. • **BAKE:** 20 min. • **MAKES:** 2 servings

- ¾ cup canned kidney beans, rinsed and drained
- ¼ cup chopped onion
- ¼ cup canned chopped green chiles
- ¼ tsp. ground cumin
- 16 Triscuits or other crackers
- ¾ cup shredded cheddar cheese
- ½ cup 2% milk
- ⅓ cup mayonnaise
- 2 Tbsp. beaten egg
  Optional: Sour cream and sliced ripe olives

**1.** Preheat oven to 350°. In a small bowl, combine the beans, onion, green chiles and cumin. Place 8 crackers in an 8x4-in. loaf pan coated with cooking spray. Top with half of the bean mixture; layer with remaining crackers and bean mixture. Sprinkle with cheese.
**2.** In a small bowl, combine the milk, mayonnaise and egg; pour over cheese. Bake, uncovered, until a thermometer reads 160°, 20-25 minutes. If desired, serve with sour cream and olives.
**1 PIECE:** 561 cal., 31g fat (10g sat. fat), 113mg chol., 1103mg sod., 51g carb. (9g sugars, 9g fiber), 25g pro.

## HERB-STUFFED ROASTED CORNISH HENS

If you're looking for an elegant dinner for two, we suggest these delightful Cornish game hens. As a bonus, the crisp, tasty potatoes cook right alongside.
—Taste of Home *Test Kitchen*

---

**PREP:** 20 min. • **BAKE:** 70 min. • **MAKES:** 2 servings

- 2 Cornish game hens (20 to 24 oz. each)
- 12 fresh sage leaves
- 4 lemon wedges
- 6 green onions, cut into 2-in. lengths, divided
- 2 Tbsp. butter, melted
- 1 Tbsp. olive oil
- 1 Tbsp. lemon juice
- 2 garlic cloves, minced
- 1 tsp. kosher salt or sea salt
- ¼ tsp. coarsely ground pepper
- 6 small red potatoes, halved

**1.** Preheat oven to 375°. Gently lift skin from hen breasts and place sage leaves under skin. Place lemon wedges and a third of the onions in the cavities. Tuck wings under hens; tie legs together. Place in a small greased roasting pan.

**2.** Combine butter, oil, lemon juice and garlic; spoon half of mixture over the hens. Sprinkle with salt and pepper.

**3.** Bake 30 minutes. Add potatoes and remaining onions to pan. Brush hens with remaining butter mixture. Bake until a thermometer inserted in thickest part of thigh reads 170°-175° and potatoes are tender, 40-45 minutes longer.

**4.** Remove hens to a serving platter. Stir potatoes and onions to coat with pan drippings. Serve with hens.

**1 SERVING:** 980 cal., 67 g fat (22 g sat. fat), 379 mg chol., 1,398 mg sod., 29 g carb., 4 g fiber, 63 g pro.

## MERLOT FILET MIGNON

Although this filet is such a simple recipe, you can feel confident serving it to your guests. The rich sauce adds a touch of elegance. Just add a salad and rolls.
—Jauneen Hosking, Waterford, WI

---

**TAKES:** 20 min. • **MAKES:** 2 servings

- 2 beef tenderloin steaks (8 oz. each)
- 3 Tbsp. butter, divided
- 1 Tbsp. olive oil
- 1 cup merlot
- 2 Tbsp. heavy whipping cream
- ⅛ tsp. salt

**1.** In a small skillet, cook steaks in 1 Tbsp. butter and the olive oil over medium heat until meat reaches desired doneness (for medium-rare, a thermometer should read 135°; medium, 140°; medium-well, 145°), 4-6 minutes on each side. Remove and keep warm.

**2.** In the same skillet, add wine, stirring to loosen browned bits from pan. Bring to a boil; cook until liquid is reduced to ¼ cup. Add the cream, salt and remaining butter; bring to a boil. Cook and stir until slightly thickened and butter is melted, 1-2 minutes. Serve with steaks.

**1 STEAK WITH 2 TBSP. SAUCE:** 690 cal., 43g fat (20g sat. fat), 165mg chol., 279mg sod., 4g carb. (1g sugars, 0 fiber), 49g pro

## SHRIMP QUESADILLAS

Switch up your normal quesadilla toppings with this recipe. Serve with salsa on the side and a frosty smoothie if you'd like.
—Tiffany Bryson, San Antonio, TX

------------------------------------------

**TAKES:** 30 min. • **MAKES:** 2 servings

- 4 tsp. canola oil, divided
- ¼ cup chopped onion
- 1 Tbsp. finely chopped jalapeno pepper
- ½ lb. uncooked shrimp, peeled, deveined and chopped
- ¼ tsp. ground cumin
- ⅛ tsp. pepper
- ¼ cup chopped tomato
- 4 flour tortillas (6 in.)
- ½ cup shredded Mexican cheese blend

**1.** Heat 2 tsp. oil in a large nonstick skillet over medium heat; add the onion and jalapeno. Cook and stir until tender, 3-5 minutes. Add shrimp, cumin and pepper; cook and stir until shrimp turn pink, 2-3 minutes. Transfer to a small bowl; stir in tomato.

**2.** Add 1 tsp. oil to the same skillet; add 1 tortilla. Top with half the cheese, half the shrimp mixture and 1 tortilla. Cook over medium heat until lightly browned, 2-3 minutes on each side; remove. Repeat with remaining 1 tsp. oil, tortillas, cheese and shrimp mixture. Cut into wedges.

**NOTE:** Wear disposable gloves when cutting hot peppers; the oils can burn skin. Avoid touching your face.

**1 QUESADILLA:** 523 cal., 27g fat (8g sat. fat), 163mg chol., 707mg sod., 38g carb. (3g sugars, 4g fiber), 30g pro.

**TIP**
Serve these quesadillas with refried beans, rice, a Mexican-inspired salad or street corn.

## SPICY TURKEY STIR-FRY WITH NOODLES

I created this ground turkey stir-fry recipe when I began my journey to get fit. Healthy eating always sounds so bland and boring, so I wanted to bring life to the world of healthy eating. I think I did it with this spicy dish.
—Jermell Clark, Desert Hot Springs, CA

- - - - - - - - - - - - - - - - - - - - - - - - - - - - - - - - - - - - - - - -

**TAKES:** 30 min. • **MAKES:** 2 servings

- 2 oz. thick rice noodles
- ½ lb. lean ground turkey
- 1 small onion, chopped
- ½ cup shredded red cabbage
- ½ cup chopped fresh kale
- ¼ cup packed fresh parsley sprigs, chopped
- 1 tsp. coconut or olive oil
- ½ tsp. pepper
- ¼ tsp. salt
- 3 green onions, thinly sliced
- 1 jalapeno pepper, sliced
- 2 tsp. Sriracha chili sauce
  Thai peanut sauce, optional

**1.** Cook noodles according to package directions. Meanwhile, in a large skillet, cook turkey, onion, cabbage and kale over medium-high heat until turkey is no longer pink and vegetables are tender, 8-10 minutes, breaking up turkey into crumbles.
**2.** Drain noodles; add to skillet. Stir in parsley, coconut oil, pepper and salt. Serve with green onions, jalapeno, chili sauce and, if desired, peanut sauce.
**NOTE:** Wear disposable gloves when cutting hot peppers; the oils can burn skin. Avoid touching your face.
**2 CUPS:** 332 cal., 11g fat (4g sat. fat), 78mg chol., 588mg sod., 32g carb. (4g sugars, 3g fiber), 25g pro. **DIABETIC EXCHANGES:** 3 lean meat, 2 starch, ½ fat.

## SLOW-COOKED BEEF & VEGGIES

My husband and I came up with this soothing slow-cooker recipe. It's simple and filling with lots of flavor.
—LaDonna Reed, Ponca City, OK

- - - - - - - - - - - - - - - - - - - - - - - - - - - - - - - - - - - -

**PREP:** 15 min. + marinating • **COOK:** 8 hours • **MAKES:** 2 servings

- 1 boneless beef top round steak (½ lb.), cut into 2 pieces
  Dash seasoned salt, optional
  Dash pepper
  Dash garlic powder
- 1 cup Italian salad dressing
- ½ cup water
- 1 Tbsp. browning sauce, optional
- 2 medium carrots, cut into 2-in. pieces
- 2 medium red potatoes, cubed
- 1 small onion, sliced
- ½ small green pepper, cut into small chunks

**1.** Sprinkle 1 side of each piece of steak with seasoned salt, if desired, and pepper; sprinkle other side with garlic powder. Cover and refrigerate for 2-3 hours or overnight.
**2.** In a 3-qt. slow cooker, combine the salad dressing, water and, if desired, browning sauce. Add carrots and potatoes; toss to coat. Add steak and coat with sauce. Top with onion and green pepper.
**3.** Cover and cook on low until meat is tender, 8-9 hours.
**1 SERVING:** 505 cal., 22g fat (3g sat. fat), 63mg chol., 1283mg sod., 36g carb. (14g sugars, 5g fiber), 29g pro.

## SPICY TURKEY TENDERLOIN

Here's an easy turkey dish sure to really wake up your taste buds. It's the perfect choice for a weeknight dinner, or you can easily increase the amounts for get-togethers.
—*Sharon Skildum, Maple Grove, MN*

**PREP:** 20 min. • **COOK:** 25 min. • **MAKES:** 2 servings

- ½  tsp. chili powder
- ½  tsp. ground cumin
- ¼ to ½ tsp. salt
- ⅛  tsp. cayenne pepper
- 1  turkey breast tenderloin (½ lb.)
- 3  tsp. olive oil, divided
- ¼  cup chicken broth
- 2  Tbsp. lime juice
- 3  Tbsp. chopped onion
- 2  Tbsp. chopped jalapeno pepper
- 1  cup canned black beans, rinsed and drained
- ½  cup frozen corn, thawed
- 3  Tbsp. chopped fresh tomato
- 4  tsp. picante sauce
- 1  Tbsp. minced fresh cilantro
- 2  lime wedges

**1.** In a small bowl, combine the chili powder, cumin, salt and cayenne. Sprinkle half the spice mixture over turkey. In a skillet, brown turkey in 2 tsp. oil for 3-4 minutes on each side. Add broth and lime juice to skillet. Reduce heat; cover and simmer until turkey juices run clear and thermometer reads 170°, turning once, 15-18 minutes.

**2.** In a small skillet, saute the onion and jalapeno in remaining oil until crisp-tender. Transfer to a bowl. Add the beans, corn, tomato, picante sauce, cilantro and remaining spice mixture. Serve turkey with salsa and lime wedges.

**NOTE:** Wear disposable gloves when cutting hot peppers; the oils can burn skin. Avoid touching your face.

**1 SERVING:** 342 cal., 9g fat (1g sat. fat), 56mg chol., 767mg sod., 32g carb. (4g sugars, 7g fiber), 35g pro. **DIABETIC EXCHANGES:** 3 lean meat, 2 starch, 1½ fat.

## SLOW-COOKED BEEF TIPS

These slow-cooked beef tips remind me of a childhood favorite. I cook them with mushrooms and serve over brown rice, noodles or mashed potatoes.
—*Amy Lents, Grand Forks, ND*

**PREP:** 25 min. • **COOK:** 6¼ hours • **MAKES:** 2 servings

- ¼  lb. sliced baby portobello mushrooms
- ½  small onion, sliced
- 1  beef top sirloin steak (½ lb.), cubed
- ¼  tsp. salt
- ⅛  tsp. pepper
- 1  tsp. olive oil
- 3  Tbsp. dry red wine or beef broth
- 1  cup beef broth
- 1½  tsp. Worcestershire sauce
- 1  Tbsp. cornstarch
- 2  Tbsp. water
  Hot cooked mashed potatoes

**1.** Place mushrooms and onion in a 3-qt. slow cooker. Sprinkle beef with salt and pepper. In a large skillet, heat 1 tsp. oil over medium-high heat; brown meat in batches, adding additional oil as needed. Transfer meat to slow cooker.

**2.** Add wine to skillet, stirring to loosen browned bits from pan. Stir in broth and Worcestershire sauce; pour over meat. Cook, covered, on low 6-8 hours or until meat is tender.

**3.** In a small bowl, mix cornstarch and cold water until smooth; gradually stir into the slow cooker. Cook, covered, on high for 15-30 minutes or until gravy is thickened. Serve with potatoes.

**1 CUP:** 213 cal., 7g fat (2g sat. fat), 46mg chol., 836mg sod., 8g carb. (2g sugars, 1g fiber), 27g pro. **DIABETIC EXCHANGES:** 3 lean meat, 1½ fat, ½ starch.

## SMOKED SAUSAGE DINNER

I treat my wife to this well-seasoned, nourishing meal when she comes home from work. The V8 gives it a unique flavor.
—Raymond Bell, Thornton, CO

- - - - - - - - - - - - - - - - - - - - - - - - - - - - - - - - - - - - - - - -

**TAKES:** 25 min. • **MAKES:** 2 servings

- ½ lb. smoked sausage, sliced
- ⅓ cup chopped green pepper
- ¼ cup chopped onion
- ½ tsp. dried oregano
- ½ tsp. dried basil
- 1 Tbsp. olive oil
- 1 small garlic clove, minced
- ¾ cup V8 juice
- 1½ cups hot cooked rice
    Minced fresh oregano, optional

**1.** In a large skillet, saute the sausage, green pepper, onion, oregano and basil in oil until vegetables are crisp-tender. Add garlic; cook 1 minute longer.

**2.** Stir in V8 juice; bring to a boil. Reduce the heat; simmer, uncovered, until thickened and heated through, 7-8 minutes, stirring occasionally. Serve with rice. If desired, garnish with fresh oregano.

**1⅓ CUPS:** 603 cal., 38g fat (14g sat. fat), 76mg chol., 1518mg sod., 44g carb. (7g sugars, 2g fiber), 21g pro.

## SLOW-COOKER VEGGIE LASAGNA

This veggie-licious alternative to traditional lasagna makes use of slow-cooker convenience. I suggest using chunky spaghetti sauce.
—Laura Davister, Little Suamico, WI

- - - - - - - - - - - - - - - - - - - - - - - - - - - - - - - - - - - - - - - -

**PREP:** 25 min. • **COOK:** 3½ hours • **MAKES:** 2 servings

- ½ cup shredded part-skim mozzarella cheese
- 3 Tbsp. 1% cottage cheese
- 2 Tbsp. grated Parmesan cheese
- 2 Tbsp. egg substitute
- ½ tsp. Italian seasoning
- ⅛ tsp. garlic powder
- ¾ cup meatless spaghetti sauce
- ½ cup sliced zucchini
- 2 no-cook lasagna noodles
- 4 cups fresh baby spinach
- ½ cup sliced fresh mushrooms

**1.** Cut two 18x3-in. strips of heavy-duty foil; crisscross so they resemble an "X." Place strips on bottom and up side of a 1½-qt. slow cooker. Coat strips with cooking spray.

**2.** In a small bowl, combine the first 6 ingredients. Spread 1 Tbsp. spaghetti sauce on the bottom of prepared slow cooker. Top with half of the zucchini and a third of the cheese mixture.

**3.** Break noodles into 1-in. pieces; sprinkle half of the noodles over cheese mixture. Spread with 1 Tbsp. sauce. Top with half of the spinach and half of the mushrooms. Repeat layers. Top with remaining cheese mixture and remaining spaghetti sauce.

**4.** Cover and cook on low for 3½-4 hours or until the noodles are tender.

**1 SERVING:** 259 cal., 8g fat (4g sat. fat), 23mg chol., 859mg sod., 29g carb. (9g sugars, 4g fiber), 19g pro. **DIABETIC EXCHANGES:** 2 lean meat, 2 medium-fat meat, 1½ starch, 1 vegetable, ½ fat.

## CRAB-STUFFED MANICOTTI

I love pasta, and my husband loves seafood. I combined them to create this dish, and he raved that it's the best meal ever.
—Sonya Polfliet, Anza, CA

**PREP:** 25 min. • **BAKE:** 25 min. • **MAKES:** 2 servings

- 4 uncooked manicotti shells
- 1 Tbsp. butter
- 4 tsp. all-purpose flour
- 1 cup fat-free milk
- 1 Tbsp. grated Parmesan cheese
- 1 cup lump crabmeat, drained
- ⅓ cup reduced-fat ricotta cheese
- ¼ cup shredded part-skim mozzarella cheese
- ¼ tsp. lemon-pepper seasoning
- ¼ tsp. pepper
- ⅛ tsp. garlic powder
  Minced fresh parsley

**1.** Preheat oven to 350°. Cook the manicotti shells according to package directions; drain. Meanwhile, in a small saucepan, melt butter. Stir in flour until smooth; gradually add milk. Bring to a boil; cook and stir until thickened, 2 minutes. Remove from the heat; stir in Parmesan cheese.

**2.** In a small bowl, combine crab, ricotta, mozzarella, lemon-pepper seasoning, pepper and garlic powder. Stuff shells with crab mixture. Spread ¼ cup sauce in an 8-in. square baking dish coated with cooking spray. Top with the stuffed manicotti. Pour remaining sauce over top.

**3.** Bake, covered, until heated through, 25-30 minutes. Just before serving, sprinkle with parsley and, if desired, additional grated Parmesan cheese.

**2 SHELLS:** 359 cal., 12g fat (7g sat. fat), 98mg chol., 793mg sod., 38g carb. (11g sugars, 1g fiber), 26g pro. **DIABETIC EXCHANGES:** 2 starch, 2 lean meat, 1 fat, ½ fat-free milk.

## CHICKEN CURRY FOR TWO

I love to try new recipes for my husband and myself, and I actually have cookbooks and recipes from all over the world. When I find a recipe that's well-received, I make a copy and put it in a protective sleeve in a loose-leaf binder. I now have quite a few huge binders!
—Sharon Delaney-Chronis, South Milwaukee, WI

**PREP:** 20 min. • **COOK:** 3 hours • **MAKES:** 2 servings

- 1 small onion, sliced
- 1 Tbsp. plus ⅓ cup water, divided
- ½ lb. boneless skinless chicken breasts, cubed
- 1 small apple, peeled and chopped
- ¼ cup raisins
- 1 garlic clove, minced
- 1 tsp. curry powder
- ¼ tsp. ground ginger
- ⅛ tsp. salt
- 1½ tsp. all-purpose flour
- 1 tsp. chicken bouillon granules
- ½ cup sour cream
- ¾ tsp. cornstarch
- 1 Tbsp. thinly sliced green onion
  Hot cooked rice

**1.** Place onion and 1 Tbsp. water in a microwave-safe bowl. Cover and microwave on high until crisp-tender, 1-1½ minutes.

**2.** In a 1½-qt. slow cooker, combine the chicken, apple, raisins, garlic, curry, ginger, salt and onion. Combine the flour, bouillon and remaining water; pour over chicken mixture. Cover and cook on low until chicken juices run clear, 3-3½ hours.

**3.** Bring sour cream to room temperature. Remove chicken mixture to a bowl; keep warm. Transfer the juices to a small saucepan. Combine cornstarch and sour cream until smooth; add to juices. Cook and stir over medium heat until thickened. Pour over chicken mixture; toss to coat. Sprinkle with green onion and serve with rice.

**1 CUP:** 354 cal., 13g fat (8g sat. fat), 103mg chol., 647mg sod., 30g carb. (19g sugars, 3g fiber), 26g pro.

🍎 **BAKED CRAB CAKES**

Reel in a breezy taste of the seashore with these baked—rather than fried—crab cakes. For a heftier meal, make two larger patties and serve them on buns.
—Amelia Sunderland, Nashville, TN

------------------------------------------------------------

**PREP:** 15 min. + chilling • **BAKE:** 25 min. • **MAKES:** 2 servings

- 1 can (6 oz.) crabmeat, drained, flaked and cartilage removed
- ½ cup soft bread crumbs
- ¼ cup shredded carrot
- 1 large egg, lightly beaten
- 1 Tbsp. butter, melted
- 1 tsp. minced fresh parsley
- 1 tsp. mayonnaise
- ¾ tsp. Worcestershire sauce
- ¼ tsp. ground mustard
- ⅛ tsp. salt
- ⅛ tsp. pepper
  Tartar sauce, optional

**1.** In a large bowl, combine the first 11 ingredients. Shape into 4 patties; cover and refrigerate for at least 30 minutes.
**2.** Place crab cakes on a baking sheet coated with cooking spray. Bake at 350° for 25 minutes or until golden brown. Serve with tartar sauce if desired.
**NOTE:** To make soft bread crumbs, tear the bread into pieces and place in a food processor or blender. Cover and pulse until crumbs form. One slice of bread yields ½-¾ cup crumbs .
**2 CRAB CAKES:** 228 cal., 12g fat (5g sat. fat), 198mg chol., 619mg sod., 8g carb. (2g sugars, 1g fiber), 22g pro. **DIABETIC EXCHANGES:** 3 lean meat, 1½ fat, ½ starch.

## JACKFRUIT TACOS WITH GREEN APPLE SALSA

These easy tacos are flavored with taco seasoning and topped with fresh green apple salsa. Make them vegan by omitting the sour cream sauce or substituting vegan sour cream mixed with a plant-based milk.
—Henrie Marie, Marlboro, NY

------------------------------------------------------------

**PREP:** 25 min. • **COOK:** 10 min. • **MAKES:** 2 servings

- 3 Tbsp. olive oil, divided
- 1 can (20 oz.) jackfruit, rinsed, drained and chopped
- 1 envelope reduced-sodium taco seasoning

GREEN APPLE SALSA
- ½ medium ripe avocado, peeled and cubed
- ½ cup chopped baby cucumber
- ½ cup chopped green apple
- ¼ cup chopped green pepper
- 2 Tbsp. thinly sliced green onions
- ½ jalapeno pepper, seeded and minced
- 4 tsp. lime juice
- 1 Tbsp. chopped fresh cilantro
- ¼ tsp. sea salt

SOUR CREAM SAUCE
- ¼ cup sour cream
- 2 Tbsp. 2% milk
- 6 flour tortillas (6 in.), warmed

**1.** In a large skillet, heat 2 Tbsp. oil over medium-high heat. Add jackfruit; cook and stir until caramelized, 8-10 minutes. Stir in taco seasoning and remaining 1 Tbsp. oil; mix well. Remove from the heat; keep warm.
**2.** In a small bowl, mix all green salsa ingredients. For sour cream sauce, whisk together sour cream and milk until smooth. Serve jackfruit in tortillas with salsa, sour cream sauce and, if desired, lime wedges.
**NOTE:** Wear disposable gloves when cutting hot peppers; the oils can burn skin. Avoid touching your face.
**3 TACOS:** 748 cal., 39g fat (10g sat. fat), 22mg chol., 3603mg sod., 88g carb. (15g sugars, 19g fiber), 15g pro.

## STUFFED PORK TENDERLOIN

My grandmother often prepared this dish for Sunday dinner. She loved to cook and eat, especially when she could share her wonderful food with others.
—*Mary Ann Marino, West Pittsburgh, PA*

------------------------------------------------

**PREP:** 20 min. • **BAKE:** 50 min.
**MAKES:** 2 servings

- 1   pork tenderloin (¾ to 1 lb.)
- ½   cup chopped onion
- 2   Tbsp. butter
- 1   cup soft bread crumbs
- ¼   cup minced fresh parsley
- ¼   tsp. rubbed sage
- ¼   tsp. dried rosemary, crushed
- ¼   tsp. salt
- ⅛   tsp. pepper
- 1   large egg, lightly beaten
- 1   bacon strip

**1.** Make a lengthwise slit about three-fourths of the way through tenderloin; open tenderloin so it lies flat. Flatten to ¼-in. thickness; set aside.

**2.** In a small skillet, saute onion in butter until tender. Add bread crumbs; saute until crumbs are golden brown. Remove from the heat. Stir in parsley, sage, rosemary, salt, pepper and enough egg to moisten the ingredients.

**3.** Spread the stuffing on 1 long side of tenderloin to within ¼ in. of edges. Close the meat and place bacon on top; tie with kitchen string. Place on a rack in a shallow roasting pan.

**4.** Bake tenderloin, uncovered, at 350° for 50-60 minutes or until a thermometer reads 160°. Let meat stand for 5 minutes before slicing.

**NOTE:** To make soft bread crumbs, tear bread into pieces and place in a food processor or blender. Cover and pulse until crumbs form. One slice of bread yields ½-¾ cup crumbs .

**8 OZ. COOKED STUFFED PORK:** 476 cal., 27g fat (12g sat. fat), 239mg chol., 719mg sod., 16g carb. (4g sugars, 2g fiber), 41g pro.

## SEAFOOD FETTUCCINE ALFREDO

I like to serve this lovely pasta with artisan Italian bread. Sprinkled with tomato and parsley, this dish looks as mouthwatering as it tastes.
—*Jimmy Spellings, Oakland, TN*

------------------------------------------------

**TAKES:** 30 min. • **MAKES:** 2 servings

- 4   oz. uncooked fettuccine
- ¼   lb. uncooked medium shrimp, peeled and deveined
- ¼   lb. sea scallops, halved
- 2   Tbsp. olive oil, divided
- 1   small shallot, chopped
- 1   garlic clove, minced
- ¼   cup chicken broth
- ¼   cup white wine or additional chicken broth
- 1   cup heavy whipping cream or half-and-half cream
- ½   cup grated Parmesan cheese
- 1   Roma tomato, diced
- 2   Tbsp. minced fresh parsley

**1.** Cook the fettuccine according to the package directions. Meanwhile, in a large skillet, saute the shrimp and scallops in 1 Tbsp. oil for 3-5 minutes or until shrimp turn pink and scallops are opaque. Remove and keep warm.

**2.** In the same skillet, saute shallot in remaining oil until tender. Add garlic; cook 1 minute longer. Stir in broth and wine. Bring to a boil. Reduce the heat; simmer, uncovered, for 6-8 minutes or until most of the liquid has evaporated. Stir in cream; cook, uncovered, over medium heat for 5 minutes or until thickened.

**3.** Drain fettuccine; stir into cream sauce. Add shrimp, scallops and cheese; toss to coat. Sprinkle with tomato and parsley.

**1¼ CUPS:** 702 cal., 34g fat (14g sat. fat), 179mg chol., 728mg sod., 53g carb. (10g sugars, 3g fiber), 40g pro.

**HOW-TO**

### KEEP PARSLEY FRESH

Trim stems and place in a tumbler of water. Be sure no leaves are in the water. Tie a produce bag around top to trap humidity; refrigerate. Each time you use parsley, change the water and turn the produce bag inside out so any moisture built up inside the bag can escape.

Combine ⅔ cup chopped dill pickles, ½ cup mayonnaise, 3 Tbsp. minced onion and a dash of pepper in a small bowl.

# - CLASSIC TARTAR SAUCE -
Once you taste our rich and puckery homemade version, you'll never want to go back to store-bought.

## AIR-FRYER FISH & CHIPS

Looking for easy air-fryer recipes? Try these simple fish and chips. The fish fillets have a fuss-free coating that's healthier but just as crunchy and golden as the deep-fried kind. Simply seasoned, the crispy fries are perfect on the side.
—Janice Mitchell, Aurora, CO

--------------------------------------

**PREP:** 15 min. • **COOK:** 25 min.
**MAKES:** 2 servings

- 1   medium potato
- 1   Tbsp. olive oil
- ⅛   tsp. pepper
- ⅛   tsp. salt

FISH

- 3   Tbsp. all-purpose flour
- ⅛   tsp. pepper
- 1   large egg
- 2   Tbsp. water
- ⅓   cup crushed cornflakes
- 1½  tsp. grated Parmesan cheese
      Dash cayenne pepper
- ⅛   tsp. salt
- ½   lb. haddock or cod fillets
      Tartar sauce, optional

**1.** Preheat air fryer to 400°. Peel and cut potato lengthwise into ½-in.-thick slices; cut slices into ½-in.-thick sticks.
**2.** In a large bowl, toss potato with oil, pepper and salt. Place potato pieces in a single layer in air-fryer basket; cook until just tender, 5-10 minutes. Toss potatoes in basket to redistribute; continue to cook until lightly browned and crisp, 5-10 minutes longer.
**3.** Meanwhile, in a shallow bowl, mix the flour and pepper. In another shallow bowl, whisk egg with water. In a third bowl, toss the cornflakes with cheese and cayenne. Sprinkle the fish with salt; dip into flour mixture to coat both sides and shake off excess. Dip in egg mixture, then in cornflake mixture, patting to help the coating adhere.
**4.** Remove fries from basket; keep warm. Place fish in a single layer in air-fryer basket. Cook until fish is lightly browned and just beginning to flake easily with a fork, turning halfway through cooking, 8-10 minutes. Do not overcook. Return fries to basket to heat through. Serve immediately. If desired, serve with tartar sauce.

AIR-FRYER FISH & CHIPS

**1 SERVING:** 304 cal., 9g fat (2g sat. fat), 84mg chol., 503mg sod., 33g carb. (3g sugars, 1g fiber), 23g pro. **DIABETIC EXCHANGES:** 3 lean meat, 2 starch, 1½ fat.

## PORK MEATBALLS

This recipe is one of my favorites. My mom used to make the moist, flavorful meatballs often, and they were part of our traditional dinner on Shrove Tuesday, served with homemade gnocchi.
—Joan Newberry, Indiana, PA

--------------------------------------

**PREP:** 15 min. • **COOK:** 30 min.
**MAKES:** 2 servings

- 1   large egg, lightly beaten
- 1   slice bread, crumbled
- 1   garlic clove, minced
- ¼   cup grated Romano
      or Parmesan cheese
- ½   tsp. salt
- ½   tsp. dried parsley flakes
- ¼   tsp. pepper
- ¾   lb. ground pork
- 1   can (14½ oz.) beef broth

**1.** In a bowl, combine first 7 ingredients. Crumble the meat over mixture and mix lightly but thoroughly. Shape into ten 2-in. balls.
**2.** In a saucepan, bring the broth to a boil. Place meatballs in the broth. Reduce heat; cover and simmer for 15 minutes. Turn the meatballs; cook until they are cooked through, about 15 minutes, turning occasionally. Remove balls with a slotted spoon. If desired, sprinkle with additional cheese and parsley.
**FREEZE OPTION:** Freeze cooled meatball mixture in freezer containers. To use, partially thaw in refrigerator overnight. Heat through in a covered saucepan, stirring occasionally; add water or broth if necessary.
**5 MEATBALLS:** 511 cal., 33g fat (14g sat. fat), 235mg chol., 1731mg sod., 8g carb. (2g sugars, 0 fiber), 43g pro.

# PRESSURE-COOKER MEXICAN STUFFED PEPPERS

Traditional stuffed peppers get a southwestern twist! The tasty filling also makes a delicious meat loaf that we even like cold in a sandwich with Mexican blend or cheddar cheese, mayo and salsa.
—*Traci Wynne, Denver, PA*

**PREP:** 20 min. • **COOK:** 15 min. + releasing • **MAKES:** 2 servings

- 2   medium sweet red, orange and/or yellow peppers
- 1   large egg, beaten
- ½   cup crushed tortilla chips
- ½   cup salsa
- ¼   cup finely chopped onion
- 2   Tbsp. minced fresh cilantro
- ½   tsp. ground cumin
- ½   tsp. seeded and finely chopped red chili pepper
- ¼   tsp. minced garlic
- ¼   lb. lean ground beef (90% lean)
- ¼   cup shredded Mexican cheese blend
     Sour cream

**1.** Place trivet insert and 1 cup water in a 3- or 6-qt. electric pressure cooker.
**2.** Cut and discard tops from peppers; remove seeds. In a small bowl, combine the egg, chips, salsa, onion, cilantro, cumin, chili pepper and garlic. Crumble beef over mixture and mix lightly but thoroughly; spoon into peppers. Set peppers on trivet.
**3.** Lock lid; close pressure-release valve. Adjust to pressure-cook on high for 12 minutes. Allow the pressure to release naturally. Sprinkle peppers with cheese. Serve with sour cream and, if desired, additional salsa.
**1 STUFFED PEPPER:** 319 cal., 15g fat (5g sat. fat), 141mg chol., 458mg sod., 25g carb. (8g sugars, 4g fiber), 20g pro. **DIABETIC EXCHANGES:** 3 medium-fat meat, 1 starch, 1 vegetable.

# SALMON WITH SPINACH SAUCE

You won't have to fish for compliments with this tasty recipe. Poaching is a quick and healthy way to prepare an entree as delicate as fish, keeping it moist and tender while cooking. And the flavorful spinach sauce adds a pretty green accent to the pink salmon.
—Taste of Home *Test Kitchen*

**TAKES:** 20 min. • **MAKES:** 2 servings

- 5   oz. frozen chopped spinach, thawed and squeezed dry (about ½ cup)
- ⅓   cup mayonnaise
- 1½ tsp. Dijon mustard
- 1   tsp. lemon juice
- ⅛   tsp. garlic salt
- 2   salmon fillets (6 oz. each)
- ½   tsp. lemon-pepper seasoning
- 4   slices lemon

**1.** In a small bowl, combine spinach, mayonnaise, mustard, lemon juice and garlic salt; cover and refrigerate until serving.
**2.** Place trivet insert and 1 cup water in a 3- or 6-qt. electric pressure cooker. Place salmon on trivet; sprinkle with lemon pepper and top with lemon slices. Lock lid; close pressure-release valve. Adjust to pressure-cook on high for 3 minutes. Quick-release pressure. A thermometer inserted in fish should read at least 145°.
**3.** Discard lemon slices. Serve salmon with spinach sauce.
**1 SERVING:** 533 cal., 43g fat (7g sat. fat), 88mg chol., 617mg sod., 4g carb. (1g sugars, 2g fiber), 32g pro.

# SAUSAGE-STUFFED SHELLS

I wanted to make manicotti one day but was out of the noodles. So I came up with this recipe, using jumbo shells instead. They were much easier to work with.
—*Lori Daniels, Beverly, WV*

**PREP:** 25 min. • **BAKE:** 20 min.
**MAKES:** 2 servings

- ⅓ lb. bulk Italian sausage
- 1 can (8 oz.) tomato sauce
- ¼ cup tomato paste
- 2 Tbsp. water
- 1 tsp. brown sugar
- ½ tsp. Italian seasoning
- ⅓ cup 4% cottage cheese
- ¾ cup shredded part-skim mozzarella cheese, divided
- 2 Tbsp. beaten egg
- ½ tsp. minced fresh parsley
- 6 jumbo pasta shells, cooked and drained
  Grated Parmesan cheese, optional

**1.** Preheat oven to 350°. In a small saucepan, cook sausage over medium heat until no longer pink; drain. Set half of the sausage aside for filling. Add the tomato sauce, tomato paste, water, brown sugar and Italian seasoning to sausage in pan. Bring to a boil. Reduce heat; simmer, uncovered, for 15 minutes, stirring occasionally.

**2.** In a small bowl, combine the cottage cheese, ½ cup mozzarella cheese, egg, parsley and reserved sausage. Stuff into shells. Spread ¼ cup meat sauce in an ungreased 1-qt. shallow baking dish. Place stuffed shells in dish; drizzle with remaining meat sauce.

**3.** Sprinkle with remaining mozzarella cheese and, if desired, Parmesan cheese. Bake, uncovered, until the filling reaches 160°, 20-25 minutes. If desired, garnish with additional parsley.

**3 STUFFED SHELLS:** 437 cal., 14g fat (7g sat. fat), 67mg chol., 1371mg sod., 40g carb. (13g sugars, 4g fiber), 36g pro.

**TIP**

For a little more bite to your shells, opt for spicy Italian sausage. Or for a family-pleasing taste, use ground beef or ground chicken instead of sausage. You could also finely chop some spinach and sneak it into the filling. It's an easy way to get more greens in your meal.

## MEXICAN-STYLE CHICKEN MANICOTTI

Combining an Italian pasta dish with Tex-Mex ingredients created an exceptional dish. This recipe is well liked even here in Cajun country!
—*Larry Phillips, Shreveport, LA*

PREP: 25 min. • BAKE: 25 min. • MAKES: 2 servings

- 4 uncooked manicotti shells
- 1 cup cubed cooked chicken breast
- 1 cup salsa, divided
- ½ cup reduced-fat ricotta cheese
- 2 Tbsp. sliced ripe olives
- 4 tsp. minced fresh parsley
- 1 Tbsp. diced pimientos
- 1 green onion, thinly sliced
- 1 small garlic clove, minced
- ¼ to ½ tsp. hot pepper sauce
- ⅓ cup shredded Monterey Jack cheese

**1.** Cook manicotti according to package directions. In a small bowl, combine the chicken, ¼ cup salsa, ricotta cheese, olives, parsley, pimientos, green onion, garlic and pepper sauce. Drain manicotti; fill with chicken mixture.
**2.** Spread ¼ cup salsa in an 8-in. square baking dish coated with cooking spray. Top with manicotti shells and remaining ½ cup salsa.
**3.** Cover and bake at 400° for 20 minutes. Uncover; sprinkle with Monterey Jack cheese and bake until cheese is melted and filling is heated through, 5-10 minutes longer.
**2 SHELLS:** 352 cal., 10g fat (4g sat. fat), 71mg chol., 708mg sod., 34g carb. (6g sugars, 2g fiber), 30g pro. **DIABETIC EXCHANGES:** 4 lean meat, 2 starch.

## OVEN-FRIED RANCH STEAK

I've made this recipe with chicken instead of beef, and the results were equally good. The combination of ranch salad dressing and Cajun seasoning also is perfect as a dip for fresh veggies.
—*LaDonna Reed, Ponca City, OK*

PREP: 10 min. + marinating • BAKE: 20 min. • MAKES: 2 servings

- 1 cup ranch salad dressing
- 1 tsp. Cajun seasoning
- ¾ lb. beef top sirloin steak
- ⅓ cup cornmeal
- ⅓ cup dry bread crumbs
- ½ tsp. garlic powder

**1.** In a shallow dish, combine salad dressing and seasoning; add the beef and turn to coat. Cover and refrigerate for at least 8 hours or overnight. Drain steak and discard marinade. Using rubber spatula, remove excess ranch coating from steak.
**2.** Place 15x10x1-in. baking sheet into oven; preheat oven to 375°. In a shallow plate, combine the cornmeal, bread crumbs and garlic powder. Coat both sides of beef in cornmeal mixture.
**3.** Carefully remove baking sheet from oven; grease. Quickly place steak on baking sheet and return to oven. Bake until the bottom is golden brown, 8-10 minutes. Carefully flip steak; bake until the meat reaches desired doneness (for medium-rare, a thermometer should read 135°; medium, 140°; medium-well, 145°), 8-10 minutes longer.
**1 SERVING:** 472 cal., 17g fat (4g sat. fat), 77mg chol., 468mg sod., 36g carb. (3g sugars, 2g fiber), 41g pro.

# COWBOY CASSEROLE

This quick and creamy Tater Tot bake is a great homey dinner, especially on a cold night. My family loves this ultimate comfort food.
—*Donna Donhauser, Remsen, NY*

---

**PREP:** 15 min. • **BAKE:** 20 min.
**MAKES:** 2 servings

- ½ lb. lean ground beef (90% lean)
- 1 can (8¾ oz.) whole kernel corn, drained
- ⅔ cup condensed cream of chicken soup, undiluted
- ½ cup shredded cheddar cheese, divided
- ⅓ cup 2% milk
- 2 Tbsp. sour cream
- ¾ tsp. onion powder
- ¼ tsp. pepper
- 2 cups frozen Tater Tots

**1.** Preheat oven to 375°. In a large skillet, cook beef over medium heat until no longer pink. Stir in the corn, soup, ¼ cup cheese, milk, sour cream, onion powder and pepper.

**2.** Place 1 cup Tater Tots in a greased 3-cup baking dish. Layer with the beef mixture and remaining Tater Tots; sprinkle with remaining cheese. Bake, uncovered, until bubbly, 20-25 minutes.

**1 SERVING:** 714 cal., 38g fat (15g sat. fat), 120mg chol., 1675mg sod., 56g carb. (9g sugars, 6g fiber), 37g pro.

**TIP**

This recipe is easily doubled (using a full can of soup) so you can have leftovers for another night. Or prep the doubled recipe in 2 foil loaf pans and give 1 to a friend.

# - 6 -

# 30-MINUTE DINNERS

On the busiest of nights, you need to get supper on the table fast.
Skip the drive-thru or frozen dinners—with these ultra quick recipes,
you'll go from ingredients to finished dish in just a half an hour!

**Apple Cider Pork Chops** (p. 133) **Chicken with Peach-Avocado Salsa** (p. 131) **Garlic Lime Shrimp** (p. 132)
**Salmon with Horseradish Pistachio Crust** (p. 122) **Chicken Thai Pizza** (p. 137) **Classic Crab Cakes** (p. 127)
**Spicy Beef & Pepper Stir-Fry** (p. 126) **Blue Plate Beef Patties** (p. 134) **Pear & Fennel Pork** (p. 123)

## BROILED PARMESAN TILAPIA

Even picky eaters will find a way to love fish when you plate up this toasty Parmesan-coated entree. I serve it with mashed cauliflower and a green salad for a low-calorie meal everyone can enjoy.
—Trisha Kruse, Eagle, ID

------------------------------------------------

**TAKES:** 20 min. • **MAKES:** 6 servings

- 6   tilapia fillets (6 oz. each)
- ¼   cup grated Parmesan cheese
- ¼   cup reduced-fat mayonnaise
- 2   Tbsp. lemon juice
- 1   Tbsp. butter, softened
- 1   garlic clove, minced
- 1   tsp. minced fresh basil or
  ¼ tsp. dried basil
- ½   tsp. seafood seasoning

**1.** Place fillets on a broiler pan coated with cooking spray. In a small bowl, combine the remaining ingredients; spread over fillets.
**2.** Broil 3-4 in. from the heat until fish flakes easily with a fork, 10-12 minutes.
**1 FILLET:** 207 cal., 8g fat (3g sat. fat), 94mg chol., 260mg sod., 2g carb. (1g sugars, 0 fiber), 33g pro. **DIABETIC EXCHANGES:** 5 lean meat, 1 fat.

## PORK SCHNITZEL WITH SAUCE

German-style schnitzel is usually made with veal. I substituted pork to save money without sacrificing flavor. Whenever I serve this dish, I'm asked for the recipe.
—Diane Katzmark, Metamora, MI

------------------------------------------------

**TAKES:** 25 min. • **MAKES:** 2 servings

- 2   pork cutlets (about 5 oz. each)
- 2   Tbsp. all-purpose flour
- ¼   tsp. seasoned salt
- ⅛   tsp. pepper
- 1   large egg
- 2   Tbsp. 2% milk
- ¼   cup dry bread crumbs
- ¼   tsp. paprika
- 1   to 2 Tbsp. vegetable oil

SAUCE
- ⅔   cup chicken broth, divided
- 1½  tsp. all-purpose flour
- 3   Tbsp. sour cream
- ⅛   tsp. dill weed
  Salt and pepper to taste
  Snipped fresh dill, optional

**1.** Flatten meat to ½-in. thickness. In a shallow dish, combine the flour, seasoned salt and pepper. In another shallow bowl, combine egg and milk. Place bread crumbs and paprika in a third shallow dish. Coat meat with flour; dip in egg mixture, then coat with crumb mixture. Let stand for 5 minutes.
**2.** In a large skillet, cook pork in oil for 2 minutes on each side or until browned. Remove and keep warm.
**3.** In the same skillet, stir in ⅓ cup broth, scraping browned bits. In a bowl, combine flour and remaining broth until smooth. Stir into skillet. Bring to a boil; cook and stir for 1-2 minutes or until thickened. Reduce heat; stir in sour cream, dill, salt and pepper; heat through. Serve with cutlets. If desired, garnish with dill.
**1 SERVING:** 341 cal., 19g fat (6g sat. fat), 157mg chol., 687mg sod., 20g carb. (3g sugars, 1g fiber), 21g pro.

**TIP**
Choose a neutral-tasting oil with a high smoke point, such as canola, soybean, corn or many vegetable blends—they are some of the best oils for frying. Add oil to the hot pan and heat it until the oil thins out and coats the bottom. At the perfect temperature, the oil will appear to shimmer with ripples of heat. Be careful not to go higher, or the oil may burn.

## SHRIMP PAD THAI

You can make this yummy Thai classic in no time. Find fish sauce and chili garlic sauce in the Asian foods aisle of your grocery store.
—Elise Ray, Shawnee, KS

------------------------------------------------

**TAKES:** 30 min. • **MAKES:** 4 servings

- 4 oz. uncooked thick rice noodles
- ½ lb. uncooked shrimp (41-50 per lb.), peeled and deveined
- 2 tsp. canola oil
- 1 large onion, chopped
- 1 garlic clove, minced
- 1 large egg, lightly beaten
- 3 cups coleslaw mix
- 4 green onions, thinly sliced
- ⅓ cup rice vinegar
- ¼ cup sugar
- 3 Tbsp. reduced-sodium soy sauce
- 2 Tbsp. fish sauce or additional reduced-sodium soy sauce
- 2 to 3 tsp. chili garlic sauce
- 2 Tbsp. chopped salted peanuts
  Chopped fresh cilantro leaves

**1.** Cook noodles according to package directions. In a large nonstick skillet or wok, stir-fry shrimp in oil until shrimp turn pink; remove and set aside. Add onion and garlic to the pan. Make a well in the center of the onion mixture; add egg. Stir-fry until egg is completely set, 2-3 minutes.

**2.** Add the coleslaw mix, green onions, vinegar, sugar, soy sauce, fish sauce, chili garlic sauce and peanuts; heat through. Return shrimp to the pan and heat through. Drain noodles; toss with shrimp mixture. Garnish with cilantro.

**1¼ CUPS:** 338 cal., 7g fat (1g sat. fat), 115mg chol., 1675mg sod., 52g carb. (23g sugars, 3g fiber), 17g pro.

## SALMON WITH HORSERADISH PISTACHIO CRUST

Impress everyone at your table with this elegant but easy salmon. Feel free to switch up the ingredients to suit your tastes. You can substitute scallions for the shallot or try almonds or pecans instead of pistachios. The nutty coating also plays well with chicken and pork.
—Linda Press Wolfe, Cross River, NY

------------------------------------------------

**TAKES:** 30 min. • **MAKES:** 6 servings

- 6 salmon fillets (4 oz. each)
- ⅓ cup sour cream
- ⅔ cup dry bread crumbs
- ⅔ cup chopped pistachios
- ½ cup minced shallots
- 2 Tbsp. olive oil
- 1 to 2 Tbsp. prepared horseradish
- 1 Tbsp. snipped fresh dill or 1 tsp. dill weed
- ½ tsp. grated lemon or orange zest
- ¼ tsp. crushed red pepper flakes
- 1 garlic clove, minced

Preheat oven to 350°. Place salmon, skin side down, in an ungreased 15x10x1-in. baking pan. Spread sour cream over each fillet. Combine remaining ingredients. Pat crumb-nut mixture onto tops of salmon fillets, pressing to help coating adhere. Bake until fish just begins to flake easily with a fork, 12-15 minutes.

**1 SALMON FILLET:** 376 cal., 25g fat (5g sat. fat), 60mg chol., 219mg sod., 15g carb. (3g sugars, 2g fiber), 24g pro. **DIABETIC EXCHANGES:** 3 lean meat, 2 fat.

TIP

Make sure to use plain horseradish, not horseradish sauce or creamed horseradish. Just 1 Tbsp. of horseradish adds a nice mild flavor, but feel free to increase to 2 or 3 Tbsp. if you like a little more bite.

## PEAR & FENNEL PORK

Fresh fennel has a large bulbous base and pale green stems with wispy foliage. Often mislabeled as sweet anise, it has a sweeter and more delicate flavor than anise, and makes a great match for mild meats like pork and chicken.
—Taste of Home *Test Kitchen*

**TAKES:** 25 min. • **MAKES:** 4 servings

- 4  boneless butterflied pork chops
   (½ in. thick and 6 oz. each)
- ½  tsp. salt
- ¼  tsp. pepper
- 1  Tbsp. olive oil
- 1  cup sliced onion
- 1  cup sliced fennel bulb
- 1  Tbsp. butter
- 2  Tbsp. cornstarch
- 2  cups pear nectar
- 3  Tbsp. maple syrup
- ½  to 1 tsp. ground nutmeg

**1.** Sprinkle pork chops with salt and pepper. In a large skillet, cook chops in oil over medium-high heat until juices run clear, 4-5 minutes on each side; drain. Set chops aside and keep warm.
**2.** In same skillet, saute onion and fennel in butter until crisp-tender. In a small bowl, combine cornstarch, pear nectar, syrup and nutmeg until smooth; add to the skillet. Bring to a boil; cook and stir until thickened, about 2 minutes. Serve over pork chops.
**1 SERVING:** 431 cal., 16g fat (6g sat. fat), 90mg chol., 390mg sod., 38g carb. (30g sugars, 2g fiber), 33g pro.

## TAPENADE-STUFFED CHICKEN BREASTS

I created this recipe for my husband, who absolutely loves olives. I usually make a larger batch of the olive tapenade and serve it with bread or crackers as a snack or appetizer.
—Jessica Levinson, Nyack, NY

**TAKES:** 30 min. • **MAKES:** 4 servings

- 4  oil-packed sun-dried tomatoes
- 4  pitted Greek olives
- 4  pitted Spanish olives
- 4  pitted ripe olives
- ¼  cup roasted sweet red peppers, drained
- 4  garlic cloves, minced
- 1  Tbsp. olive oil
- 2  tsp. balsamic vinegar
- 4  boneless skinless chicken breast halves (6 oz. each)
   Grated Parmesan cheese

**1.** Place the first 8 ingredients in a food processor; pulse until the tomatoes and olives are coarsely chopped. Cut a pocket horizontally in the thickest part of each chicken breast. Fill with olive mixture; secure with toothpicks.
**2.** Lightly coat grill rack with cooking oil. Grill chicken, covered, over medium heat or broil 4 in. from heat 8-10 minutes on each side or until a thermometer inserted in stuffing reads 165°. Sprinkle with cheese. Discard toothpicks before serving.
**1 STUFFED CHICKEN BREAST HALF:** 264 cal., 11g fat (2g sat. fat), 94mg chol., 367mg sod., 5g carb. (1g sugars, 1g fiber), 35g pro.
**DIABETIC EXCHANGES:** 5 lean meat, 1 fat.

# EASY SHRIMP TACOS

I love preparing these easy-to-make shrimp tacos. Hatch chiles are a staple ingredient in my home state of Texas, and this was the very first recipe that I conquered with them. Mix and match your favorite toppings—salsa and avocado would be perfect additions.
—Deborah Jamison, Austin, TX

- - - - - - - - - - - - - - - - - - - - - - - - - - - - - - - - -

**TAKES:** 25 min. • **MAKES:** 4 servings

- 1   cup plain Greek yogurt or sour cream
- ¼   cup minced fresh cilantro
- 3   Tbsp. lemon juice
- 2   Tbsp. lime juice
- ⅛   tsp. plus ¼ tsp. salt , divided
- 2   Tbsp. olive oil
- 2   medium green pepper, chopped
- 4   fresh green chiles, such as Hatch or Anaheim, seeded and chopped
- ½   cup chopped red onion
- 1   lb. uncooked shrimp (31-40 per lb.), peeled and deveined
- 4   garlic cloves, minced
- 1   tsp. ground cumin
- 8   corn tortillas (6 in.), warmed
- 2   cups torn lettuce

**1.** In a small bowl, combine yogurt, cilantro, lemon juice, lime juice and ⅛ tsp. salt; set aside.

**2.** In a large skillet, heat oil over medium-high heat. Add peppers and onion; cook and stir until crisp-tender, 4-5 minutes. Add shrimp, garlic, cumin and remaining ¼ tsp. salt. Cook and stir until shrimp turn pink, 2-3 minutes. Remove from the heat. Serve in tortillas with lettuce, yogurt sauce and, if desired, lime wedges.

**NOTE:** This would work on the grill as well. Grill the shrimp on skewers and grill the peppers and chiles whole before cutting.

**2 TACOS:** 359 cal., 16g fat (5g sat. fat), 153mg chol., 422mg sod., 32g carb. (6g sugars, 5g fiber), 24g pro. **DIABETIC EXCHANGES:** 3 lean meat, 3 fat, 2 starch.

**TIPS**
Try chopped red onion, lettuce, and Cotija cheese as toppings. Also, *elote*, or Mexican street corn, makes a fabulous side to any taco, as does a tropical salsa or a bed of rice and beans.

## SUPER QUICK SHRIMP & GREEN CHILE QUESADILLAS

If I am really short on time, I head to the grocery store for prepared guacamole for this recipe. Use shredded rotisserie chicken instead of shrimp for another fun option.

—Angie Ressa, Cheney, WA

- - - - - - - - - - - - - - - - - - - - - - - - - - - - - - - - - - - - - - - - - - - - - - - -

**TAKES:** 10 min. • **MAKES:** 4 servings (½ cup guacamole)

  1¾ cups shredded cheddar cheese
    1 cup peeled and deveined cooked small shrimp
    1 can (4 oz.) chopped green chiles, drained
    2 green onions, thinly sliced
    8 flour tortillas (8 in.)
    1 medium ripe avocado, peeled and pitted
    2 Tbsp. salsa
    ¼ tsp. garlic salt

**1.** In a bowl, combine the cheese, shrimp, green chiles and green onions. Place half of the tortillas on a greased griddle; sprinkle with cheese mixture. Top with remaining tortillas. Cook over medium heat for 1-2 minutes on each side or until golden brown and cheese is melted.

**2.** Meanwhile, in a small bowl, mash avocado with salsa and garlic salt. Serve with quesadillas.

**1 QUESADILLA WITH 2 TBSP. GUACAMOLE:** 676 cal., 30g fat (12 g sat fat), 178mg chol., 1186mg sod., 62g carb. (1g sugars, 6g fiber), 38g pro.

## QUICK FETTUCCINE ALFREDO

This simple recipe combines heavy whipping cream, Parmesan and Romano cheese for a creamy, cheesy sauce that comes together in minutes.

—Jo Gray, Park City, MT

- - - - - - - - - - - - - - - - - - - - - - - - - - - - - - - - - - - - - - - - - - - - - - - -

**TAKES:** 20 min. • **MAKES:** 4 servings

    8 oz. uncooked fettuccine
    6 Tbsp. butter, cubed
    2 cups heavy whipping cream
    ¾ cup grated Parmesan cheese, divided
    ½ cup grated Romano cheese
    2 large egg yolks, lightly beaten
    ¼ tsp. salt
    ⅛ tsp. pepper
    ⅛ tsp. ground nutmeg

**1.** Cook fettuccine according to package directions. Meanwhile, in a saucepan, melt butter over medium-low heat. Stir in cream, ½ cup Parmesan cheese, Romano cheese, egg yolks, salt, pepper and nutmeg. Cook and stir sauce over medium-low heat until a thermometer reads 160° (do not boil).

**2.** Drain fettuccine; serve with Alfredo sauce and the remaining ¼ cup Parmesan cheese.

**1 CUP:** 908 cal., 73g fat (45g sat. fat), 339mg chol., 821mg sod., 44g carb. (2g sugars, 2g fiber), 23g pro.

## SPINACH SHRIMP FETTUCCINE

I experimented for a couple of years before perfecting this colorful dish, and now everyone raves about it. This dish is easy and light, and it fits into my busy schedule.
—Kirstin Walker, Suffolk, VA

-------------------------------------------------------------

**TAKES:** 20 min. • **MAKES:** 8 servings

- 1 lb. uncooked fettuccine
- 1 pkg. (6 oz.) baby spinach
- 2 Tbsp. olive oil
- 4 garlic cloves, minced
- 1 lb. uncooked shrimp (31-40 per lb.), peeled and deveined
- 2 medium plum tomatoes, seeded and chopped
- ½ tsp. Italian seasoning
- ¼ tsp. salt
- ¼ cup shredded Parmesan cheese

**1.** Cook fettuccine according to package directions. Meanwhile, in a large skillet, saute spinach in oil for 2 minutes or until leaves begins to wilt. Add garlic; cook 1 minute longer.

**2.** Add the shrimp, tomatoes, Italian seasoning and salt; saute 2-3 minutes or until shrimp turn pink. Drain fettuccine and add to skillet; toss to coat. Sprinkle with cheese.

**1¼ CUPS:** 283 cal., 5g fat (1g sat. fat), 85mg chol., 209mg sod., 41g carb. (2g sugars, 3g fiber), 17g pro. **DIABETIC EXCHANGES:** 2 starch, 2 vegetable, 1½ lean meat.

## SPICY BEEF & PEPPER STIR-FRY

Think of this stir-fry as your chance to play with heat and spice. I balance the savory beef with coconut milk and a spritz of lime.
—Joy Zacharia, Clearwater, FL

-------------------------------------------------------------

**PREP:** 20 min. + standing • **COOK:** 10 min. • **MAKES:** 4 servings

- 1 lb. beef top sirloin steak, cut into thin strips
- 1 Tbsp. minced fresh gingerroot
- 3 garlic cloves, minced, divided
- ¼ tsp. pepper
- ¾ tsp. salt, divided
- 1 cup light coconut milk
- 2 Tbsp. sugar
- 1 Tbsp. Sriracha chili sauce
- ½ tsp. grated lime zest
- 2 Tbsp. lime juice
- 2 Tbsp. canola oil, divided
- 1 large sweet red pepper, cut into thin strips
- ½ medium red onion, thinly sliced
- 1 jalapeno pepper, seeded and thinly sliced
- 4 cups fresh baby spinach
- 2 green onions, thinly sliced
- 2 Tbsp. chopped fresh cilantro

**1.** In a large bowl, toss beef with ginger, 2 garlic cloves, pepper and ½ tsp. salt; let stand 15 minutes. Meanwhile, in a small bowl, whisk coconut milk, sugar, chili sauce, lime zest, lime juice and remaining ¼ tsp. salt until blended.

**2.** In a large skillet, heat 1 Tbsp. oil over medium-high heat. Add beef; stir-fry until no longer pink, 2-3 minutes. Remove from pan.

**3.** Stir-fry red pepper, red onion, jalapeno and remaining clove of garlic in remaining 1 Tbsp. oil just until vegetables are crisp-tender, 2-3 minutes. Stir in coconut milk mixture; heat through. Add spinach and beef; cook until spinach is wilted and beef is heated through, stirring occasionally. Sprinkle with green onions and cilantro.

**¾ CUP:** 312 cal., 16g fat (5g sat. fat), 46mg chol., 641mg sod., 15g carb. (10g sugars, 2g fiber), 26g pro.

## FRIED CHICKEN STRIPS

I recently made this recipe of Mom's for my in-laws and they said it was the best fried chicken ever. Slicing the chicken breasts into strips cuts down on cooking time and ensures every piece is crunchy and evenly coated.

—Genny Monchamp, Redding, CA

------------------------------------------------------------

**TAKES:** 20 min. • **MAKES:** 6 servings

2⅔ cups crushed saltines (about 80 crackers)
1 tsp. garlic salt
½ tsp. dried basil
½ tsp. paprika
⅛ tsp. pepper
1 large egg
1 cup 2% milk
1½ lbs. boneless skinless chicken breasts, cut into ½-in. strips
Oil for frying

**1.** In a shallow bowl, combine the first 5 ingredients. In another shallow bowl, beat egg and milk. Dip chicken into egg mixture, then cracker mixture.
**2.** In an electric skillet or deep-fat fryer, heat oil to 375°. Fry chicken, a few strips at a time, for 2-3 minutes on each side or until golden brown. Drain on paper towels.

**4 OZ. COOKED CHICKEN:** 388 cal., 19g fat (3g sat. fat), 98mg chol., 704mg sod., 25g carb. (2g sugars, 1g fiber), 28g pro.

> **TIP**
> To prepare in air fryer: Preheat to 375°. Coat chicken by dipping in egg mixture, then in cracker mixture. Working in batches, add chicken to air fryer basket in a single layer. Cook until a thermometer reads 170°, turning halfway, about 20 minutes. Repeat with remaining chicken. When the last batch of chicken is cooked, return all chicken to basket and cook 2-3 minutes longer to heat through.

## CLASSIC CRAB CAKES

Our region is known for good seafood, and crab cakes are a traditional favorite. I learned to make them from a chef in a restaurant where the cakes were a bestseller. The crabmeat's sweet and mild flavor gets a spark from the other ingredients.

—Debbie Terenzini, Lusby, MD

------------------------------------------------------------

**TAKES:** 20 min. • **MAKES:** 8 servings

1 lb. fresh or canned crabmeat, drained, flaked and cartilage removed
2 to 2½ cups soft bread crumbs
1 large egg, beaten
¾ cup mayonnaise
⅓ cup each chopped celery, green pepper and onion
2 tsp. lemon juice
1 Tbsp. seafood seasoning
1 Tbsp. minced fresh parsley
1 tsp. Worcestershire sauce
1 tsp. prepared mustard
¼ tsp. pepper
⅛ tsp. hot pepper sauce
Optional: 2 to 4 Tbsp. vegetable oil and lemon wedges

In a large bowl, combine the crab, bread crumbs, egg, mayonnaise, vegetables, juice and seasonings. Shape into 8 patties. Broil or cook patties in a cast-iron or other ovenproof skillet in oil; cook for 4 minutes on each side or until golden brown. If desired, serve with lemon.

**FREEZE OPTION:** Freeze cooled crab cakes in freezer containers, separating layers with waxed paper. To use, reheat crab cakes on a baking sheet in a preheated 325° oven until heated through.

**1 SERVING:** 282 cal., 22g fat (3g sat. fat), 85mg chol., 638mg sod., 7g carb. (1g sugars, 1g fiber), 14g pro.

# EASY MEDITERRANEAN CHICKEN

Friends and family love this special chicken recipe. I changed a few things to make it healthier, but it tastes just as good.
—*Kara Zilis, Oak Forest, IL*

-------------------------------------------

**TAKES:** 30 min. • **MAKES:** 4 servings

- 4 boneless skinless chicken breast halves (4 oz. each)
- 1 Tbsp. olive oil
- 1 can (14½ oz.) no-salt-added stewed tomatoes
- 1 cup water
- 1 tsp. dried oregano
- ¼ tsp. garlic powder
- 1½ cups instant brown rice
- 1 pkg. (12 oz.) frozen cut green beans
- 12 pitted Greek olives, halved
- ½ cup crumbled feta cheese

**1.** In a large nonstick skillet, brown chicken in oil on each side. Stir in the tomatoes, water, oregano and garlic powder. Bring to a boil; reduce heat. Cover and simmer 10 minutes.

**2.** Stir in rice and green beans. Return to a boil. Cover and simmer until a thermometer reads 165° and rice is tender, 8-10 minutes longer. Stir in olives; sprinkle with cheese.

**1 SERVING:** 417 cal., 12g fat (3g sat. fat), 70mg chol., 386mg sod., 44g carb. (6g sugars, 6g fiber), 31g pro. **DIABETIC EXCHANGES:** 3 lean meat, 2 starch, 2 vegetable, 1 fat.

> **TIP**
> To make this recipe your own, use ingredients or seasonings you love. Use minced garlic, try fresh tomatoes instead of canned, and add any fresh vegetable instead of frozen green beans. We suggest chopped asparagus, fresh green beans or even broccoli florets. You can also add a squeeze of fresh lemon juice at the end for some brightness and flavor!

# FAJITA-STYLE SHRIMP & GRITS

I combined two of my favorite dishes—shrimp with cheesy grits, and fajitas—into this spicy one-dish meal. For more heat, use pepper jack cheese instead of Mexican cheese blend.
—*Arlene Erlbach, Morton Grove, IL*

-------------------------------------------

**TAKES:** 30 min. • **MAKES:** 4 servings

- 1 lb. uncooked shrimp (16-20 per lb.), peeled and deveined
- 2 Tbsp. fajita seasoning mix
- 1 cup quick-cooking grits
- 4 cups boiling water
- 1½ cups shredded Mexican cheese blend
- 3 Tbsp. 2% milk
- 2 Tbsp. canola oil
- 3 medium sweet peppers, seeded and cut into 1-in. strips
- 1 medium sweet onion, cut into 1-in. strips
- 1 jar (15½ to 16 oz.) chunky medium salsa
- ¼ cup orange juice
- ¼ cup plus 1 Tbsp. fresh cilantro leaves, divided

**1.** Sprinkle shrimp with fajita seasoning; toss to coat. Set aside.

**2.** Slowly stir grits into boiling water. Reduce heat to medium; cook, covered, stirring occasionally, until thickened, 5-7 minutes. Remove from heat. Stir in cheese until melted; stir in milk. Keep warm.

**3.** In a large skillet, heat oil over medium-high heat. Add peppers and onion; cook and stir until tender and pepper edges are slightly charred. Add salsa, orange juice and shrimp. Cook, stirring constantly, until shrimp turn pink, 4-6 minutes. Stir in ¼ cup cilantro. Remove from heat.

**4.** Spoon grits into serving bowls; top with shrimp mixture. Sprinkle with the remaining 1 Tbsp. cilantro.

**1 SERVING:** 561 cal., 23g fat (8g sat. fat), 176mg chol., 1324mg sod., 55g carb. (12g sugars, 4g fiber), 33g pro.

For each serving, place a **haddock fillet** (about ⅓ lb.) on a 12-in. square of parchment. Drizzle with **1 Tbsp. dry white wine**; sprinkle with **½ tsp. fresh dill** and **½ tsp. lemon zest**. Top with **2 Tbsp. each julienned carrot** and **zucchini**. Sprinkle with **1 Tbsp. almonds**; dot with **1 Tbsp. butter**. Fold parchment around fish, sealing tightly. Bake on a baking sheet at 375° until fish just begins to flake easily with a fork, 10-12 minutes. Open carefully.

# - HADDOCK EN PAPILLOTE-

Impress your guests with this elegant, showstopping entree.
Your own little secret? It couldn't be easier to prepare!

## ROSEMARY GARLIC SHRIMP

Delicate shrimp take on fabulous flavor when simmered in a chicken broth mixed with garlic and ripe olives.
—Taste of Home *Test Kitchen*

**TAKES:** 20 min. • **MAKES:** 8 servings

1¼ cups chicken or vegetable broth
3 Tbsp. chopped ripe olives
1 small cayenne or other fresh red chili pepper, finely chopped
2 Tbsp. lemon juice
1 Tbsp. minced fresh rosemary or 1 tsp. dried rosemary, crushed
4 garlic cloves, minced
2 tsp. Worcestershire sauce
1 tsp. paprika
½ tsp. salt
¼ to ½ tsp. pepper
2 lbs. uncooked shrimp (31-40 per lb.), peeled and deveined

In a large skillet, combine all ingredients except shrimp; bring to a boil. Cook, uncovered, until liquid is reduced by half. Stir in shrimp; return just to a boil. Reduce heat; simmer, uncovered, until shrimp turn pink, 3-4 minutes, stirring occasionally.

**½ CUP:** 110 cal., 2g fat (0 sat. fat), 139mg chol., 473mg sod., 3g carb. (1g sugars, 0 fiber), 19g pro. **DIABETIC EXCHANGES:** 3 lean meat.

## CHICKEN WITH PEACH-AVOCADO SALSA

This super-fresh dinner is pure summer—juicy peaches, creamy avocado, grilled chicken and a kick of hot sauce and lime. To get it on the table even quicker, make the salsa ahead.
—Shannon Norris, Cudahy, WI

**TAKES:** 30 min. • **MAKES:** 4 servings

1 medium peach, peeled and chopped
1 medium ripe avocado, peeled and cubed
½ cup chopped sweet red pepper
3 Tbsp. finely chopped red onion
1 Tbsp. minced fresh basil
1 Tbsp. lime juice
1 tsp. hot pepper sauce
½ tsp. grated lime zest
¾ tsp. salt, divided
½ tsp. pepper, divided
4 boneless skinless chicken breast halves (6 oz. each)

**1.** For salsa, in a small bowl, combine peach, avocado, red pepper, onion, basil, lime juice, hot sauce, lime zest, ¼ tsp. salt and ¼ tsp. pepper.

**2.** Sprinkle chicken with remaining ½ tsp. salt and ¼ tsp. pepper. On a lightly greased grill rack, grill chicken, covered, over medium heat 5 minutes. Turn; grill until a thermometer reads 165°, 7-9 minutes longer. Serve with salsa.

**1 CHICKEN BREAST HALF WITH ½ CUP SALSA:** 265 cal., 9g fat (2g sat. fat), 94mg chol., 536mg sod., 9g carb. (4g sugars, 3g fiber), 36g pro. **DIABETIC EXCHANGES:** 5 lean meat, 1 fat, ½ starch.

## GARLIC LIME SHRIMP

Our son, a restaurant owner, showed me how to make this quick shrimp and noodle dish zipped up with garlic and cayenne. It's also tasty served over rice.
—*Gertraud Casbarro, Summerville, SC*

**TAKES:** 20 min. • **MAKES:** 4 servings

- 1 lb. uncooked shrimp (31-40 per lb.), peeled and deveined
- 5 garlic cloves, minced
- ½ tsp. salt
- ¼ to ½ tsp. cayenne pepper
- ½ cup butter
- 3 Tbsp. lime juice
- 1 Tbsp. minced fresh parsley
  Hot cooked pasta

In a large skillet, saute the shrimp, garlic, salt and cayenne in butter until the shrimp turn pink, about 5 minutes. Stir in lime juice and parsley. Serve with pasta.

**1 CUP:** 309 cal., 25g fat (15g sat. fat), 199mg chol., 613mg sod., 3g carb. (0 sugars, 0 fiber), 19g pro.

**REVIEW**

*"This is a great dish! I added more cayenne and fresh Italian parsley from my garden and yummy, yummy, yummy! Fabulous!"*

SUSIEQ6969, TASTEOFHOME.COM

## CHICKEN PARMESAN BURGERS

A restaurant-quality burger topped with marinara and loaded with cheese—what's not to love? Add fresh basil for even more flavor if you'd like.
—*Brooke Petras, Alpine, CA*

**TAKES:** 30 min. • **MAKES:** 4 servings

- 3 Tbsp. olive oil, divided
- 1 small onion, finely chopped
- 2 garlic cloves, minced
- ¾ cup marinara sauce, divided
- ½ cup finely chopped or shredded part-skim mozzarella cheese
- ½ cup dry bread crumbs
- 1 tsp. Italian seasoning
- 1 tsp. dried oregano
- ½ tsp. salt
- ½ tsp. pepper
- 1 lb. ground chicken
- 4 slices part-skim mozzarella cheese
- 4 hamburger buns, split and toasted
- ¼ cup shredded Parmesan cheese
  Fresh basil leaves, optional

**1.** In a large skillet, heat 1 Tbsp. oil over medium-high heat. Add onion; cook and stir until tender, about 3 minutes. Add garlic; cook 1 minute longer. Remove from heat; cool slightly.
**2.** In a large bowl, combine ¼ cup marinara sauce with the chopped mozzarella cheese, bread crumbs, seasonings and onion mixture. Add chicken; mix lightly but thoroughly. With wet hands, shape into four ½-in.-thick patties.
**3.** In the same skillet, heat remaining 2 Tbsp. oil over medium heat. Cook burgers until a thermometer reads 165°, 4-5 minutes on each side. Top with sliced mozzarella cheese; cook, covered, until cheese is melted, 1-2 minutes.
**4.** Serve in buns; top with remaining ½ cup marinara sauce, Parmesan cheese and, if desired, basil leaves.

**1 BURGER:** 603 cal., 33g fat (10g sat. fat), 108mg chol., 1275mg sod., 41g carb. (8g sugars, 3g fiber), 38g pro.

# GRAPEFRUIT GREMOLATA SALMON

If you're looking for a simple fish dish, make this Italian-inspired recipe that combines salmon, broiled grapefruit and a fragrant gremolata. You can use halibut instead of salmon if you prefer.
—*Gilda Lester, Millsboro, DE*

**TAKES:** 30 min. • **MAKES:** 4 servings

- 2 medium grapefruit
- ¼ cup minced fresh parsley
- 1 garlic clove, minced
- 1 Tbsp. plus 1 tsp. brown sugar, divided
- 4 salmon fillets (6 oz. each)
- 1 Tbsp. cumin seeds, crushed
- ½ tsp. salt
- ½ tsp. coarsely ground pepper

1. Preheat broiler. Finely grate enough zest from grapefruit to measure 2 Tbsp. In a small bowl, mix parsley, garlic and grapefruit zest. Set aside.
2. Cut a thin slice from the top and bottom of each grapefruit; stand grapefruit upright on a cutting board. With a knife, cut off peel and outer membrane from grapefruit. Cut along the membrane of each segment to remove fruit. Arrange sections in a single layer on half of a foil-lined 15x10x1-in. baking pan. Sprinkle with 1 Tbsp. brown sugar.
3. Place salmon on other half of pan. Mix cumin seeds, salt, pepper and remaining 1 tsp. brown sugar; sprinkle over salmon.
4. Broil 3-4 in. from heat 8-10 minutes or until fish just begins to flake easily with a fork and grapefruit is lightly browned. Sprinkle salmon with parsley mixture; serve with grapefruit.

**1 SERVING:** 332 cal., 16g fat (3g sat. fat), 85mg chol., 387mg sod., 16g carb. (13g sugars, 2g fiber), 30g pro. **DIABETIC EXCHANGES:** 4 lean meat, 1 starch.

# APPLE CIDER PORK CHOPS

With cider gravy, these pork chops are a must for fall family dinners. I serve them with buttered egg noodles to soak up more of that delicious sauce. The recipe is easy to double when company pops in.
—*Debiana Casterline, Egg Harbor Township, NJ*

**TAKES:** 25 min. • **MAKES:** 6 servings

- 2 Tbsp. olive oil
- 6 boneless pork loin chops (6 to 8 oz. each), about ¾ in. thick
- 1 garlic clove, minced
- 1 Tbsp. Dijon mustard
- 1 tsp. honey
- ½ tsp. apple pie spice
- ½ tsp. coarsely ground pepper
- ¼ tsp. dried thyme
- ¼ tsp. salt
- 1 cup apple cider
- 1 Tbsp. plus 1 tsp. cornstarch
- 2 Tbsp. water
  Minced fresh parsley

1. In a large skillet, heat olive oil over medium heat. Brown pork chops on both sides.
2. Meanwhile, in a small bowl, combine next 7 ingredients; stir in apple cider. Pour over pork chops. Reduce heat to medium-low; cook, covered, until a thermometer inserted into chops reads 145°, 4-5 minutes. Remove chops from skillet; let stand for 5 minutes.
3. In a small bowl, mix cornstarch and water until smooth; stir into cider mixture in skillet. Return to a boil, stirring constantly; cook and stir until thickened, 1-2 minutes. Pour over chops; sprinkle with fresh parsley.

**1 PORK CHOP:** 301 cal., 14g fat (4g sat. fat), 82mg chol., 210mg sod., 8g carb. (5g sugars, 0 fiber), 33g pro. **DIABETIC EXCHANGES:** 4 lean meat, 1 fat, ½ starch.

## ASPARAGUS & SHRIMP WITH ANGEL HAIR

We've all heard that the way to a man's heart is through his stomach, so when I plan a romantic dinner, this is one dish I like to serve. It's easy on the budget and turns out perfectly for two.
—*Shari Neff, Takoma Park, MD*

**TAKES:** 30 min. • **MAKES:** 2 servings

- 3 oz. uncooked angel hair pasta
- ½ lb. uncooked shrimp (16-20 per lb.), peeled and deveined
- ¼ tsp. salt
- ⅛ tsp. crushed red pepper flakes
- 2 Tbsp. olive oil, divided
- 8 fresh asparagus spears, trimmed and cut into 2-in. pieces
- ½ cup sliced fresh mushrooms
- ¼ cup chopped seeded tomato, peeled
- 4 garlic cloves, minced
- 2 tsp. chopped green onion
- ½ cup white wine or chicken broth
- 1½ tsp. minced fresh basil
- 1½ tsp. minced fresh oregano
- 1½ tsp. minced fresh parsley
- 1½ tsp. minced fresh thyme
- ¼ cup grated Parmesan cheese
  Lemon wedges

1. Cook pasta according to package directions. Meanwhile, sprinkle shrimp with salt and pepper flakes. In a large skillet or wok, heat 1 Tbsp. oil over medium-high heat. Add shrimp; stir-fry until pink, 2-3 minutes. Remove; keep warm.
2. In same skillet, stir-fry the next 5 ingredients in remaining 1 Tbsp. oil until vegetables are crisp-tender, about 5 minutes. Add wine and seasonings. Return shrimp to pan.
3. Drain pasta; add to shrimp mixture and toss gently. Cook and stir until heated through, 1-2 minutes. Sprinkle with Parmesan cheese. Serve with lemon wedges.
**1¾ CUPS:** 488 cal., 19g fat (4g sat. fat), 132mg chol., 584mg sod., 41g carb. (4g sugars, 3g fiber), 29g pro.

## BLUE PLATE BEEF PATTIES

A friend and I discovered this recipe together and now we both consider it a staple menu item. I fix the moist, mild-tasting patties often for family and friends. We love them with mashed potatoes, rice or noodles and the gravy, which gets great flavor from fresh mushrooms.
—*Phyllis Miller, Danville, IN*

**TAKES:** 20 min. • **MAKES:** 4 servings

- 1 large egg
- 2 green onions with tops, sliced
- ¼ cup seasoned bread crumbs
- 1 Tbsp. prepared mustard
- 1½ lbs. ground beef
- 1 jar (12 oz.) beef gravy
- ½ cup water
- 2 to 3 tsp. prepared horseradish
- ½ lb. fresh mushrooms, sliced
  Minced fresh parsley, optional

1. In a large bowl, beat the egg; stir in the onions, bread crumbs and mustard. Add beef and mix lightly but thoroughly. Shape into four ½-in.-thick patties.
2. In an ungreased skillet, cook patties until meat is no longer pink, 4-5 minutes on each side; drain.
3. In a small bowl, combine gravy, water and horseradish; add mushrooms. Pour over patties. Cook, uncovered, until mushrooms are tender and heated through, about 5 minutes. If desired, sprinkle with parsley.
**1 SERVING:** 438 cal., 24g fat (9g sat. fat), 170mg chol., 825mg sod., 14g carb. (2g sugars, 1g fiber), 41g pro.

**TIP**
Adding an egg to ground beef helps patties, meat loaf and meatballs hold together without overworking the meat, which can make it tough.

# BROCCOLI BEEF BRAIDS

Each slice of this fast-to-fix, golden bread is like a hot sandwich packed with beef, broccoli and mozzarella.
—*Penny Lapp, North Royalton, OH*

-------------------------------------------

**TAKES:** 30 min.
**MAKES:** 2 loaves (4 servings each)

- 1  lb. ground beef
- ½  cup chopped onion
- 3  cups frozen chopped broccoli
- 1  cup shredded part-skim mozzarella cheese
- ½  cup sour cream
- ¼  tsp. salt
- ¼  tsp. pepper
- 2  tubes (8 oz. each) refrigerated crescent rolls

1. Preheat oven to 350°. In a large skillet, cook beef and onion over medium heat 6-8 minutes or until beef is no longer pink, breaking meat into crumbles; drain. Stir in broccoli, cheese, sour cream, salt and pepper; heat through.
2. Unroll 1 tube of crescent dough onto a greased baking sheet; form into a 12x8-in. rectangle, pressing perforations to seal. Spoon half the beef mixture lengthwise down the center of the dough.
3. On each long side, cut 1-in.-wide strips at an angle, about 3 in. into the center. Fold 1 strip from each side over filling and pinch ends together; repeat.
4. Repeat with remaining ingredients to make a second braid. Bake until golden brown, 15-20 minutes.

**1 PIECE:** 396 cal., 23g fat (6g sat. fat), 48mg chol., 644mg sod., 29g carb. (8g sugars, 2g fiber), 20g pro.

## CHICKEN CHILES RELLENOS ALFREDO

This recipe combines my daughter's love of chiles rellenos and my love of chicken Alfredo! To cut down on the spice level you could substitute plain Monterey Jack cheese for the pepper jack.

—Jennifer Stowell, Deep River, IA

--------------------------------------------------

**TAKES:** 30 min. • **MAKES:** 8 servings

- 1 pkg. (16 oz.) angel hair pasta
- 1½ to 2 lbs. boneless skinless chicken breasts, cubed
- 1 Tbsp. garlic powder
- 1 Tbsp. dried cilantro
- 1 tsp. ground cumin
- ½ cup butter
- 2 cups heavy whipping cream
- ½ cup cream cheese, softened
- 1½ tsp. grated lime zest
- ½ cup pepper jack cheese
- 2 cans (4 oz. each) chopped green chiles
- 2 Tbsp. lime juice

1. Cook angel hair according to package directions. Drain.
2. Meanwhile, sprinkle chicken with garlic powder, cilantro and cumin. In a large nonstick skillet, cook and stir chicken over medium heat until no longer pink, 6-8 minutes. Remove.
3. In same skillet, melt butter. Stir in heavy cream, cream cheese and lime zest until combined, 4-6 minutes. Stir in pepper jack until melted. Add chiles and lime juice. Return chicken to skillet; heat through. Toss chicken mixture with pasta.

**1 CUP:** 698 cal., 43g fat (26g sat. fat), 167mg chol., 354mg sod., 48g carb. (4g sugars, 3g fiber), 30g pro.

## MEATBALL SUBMARINE CASSEROLE

We were hosting a bunch of friends, and after a comedy of errors, I had to come up with a plan B for dinner. Much-loved meatball subs are even better as a hearty casserole—so delicious!

—Rick Friedman, Palm Springs, CA

--------------------------------------------------

**TAKES:** 30 min. • **MAKES:** 4 servings

- 1 pkg. (12 oz.) frozen fully cooked Italian meatballs
- 4 slices sourdough bread
- 1½ tsp. olive oil
- 1 garlic clove, halved
- 1½ cups pasta sauce with mushrooms
- ½ cup shredded part-skim mozzarella cheese, divided
- ½ cup grated Parmesan cheese, divided

1. Preheat broiler. Microwave meatballs, covered, on high until heated through, 4-6 minutes. Meanwhile, place bread on an ungreased baking sheet; brush 1 side of bread with oil. Broil 4-6 in. from heat until golden brown, 1-2 minutes. Rub bread with cut surface of garlic; discard garlic. Tear bread into bite-sized pieces; transfer to a greased 11x7-in. baking dish. Reduce oven setting to 350°.
2. Add pasta sauce, ¼ cup mozzarella cheese and ¼ cup Parmesan cheese to meatballs; toss to combine. Pour mixture over bread pieces; sprinkle with remaining cheeses. Bake, uncovered, until cheeses are melted, 15-18 minutes.

**1 SERVING:** 417 cal., 28g fat (13g sat. fat), 59mg chol., 1243mg sod., 22g carb. (8g sugars, 3g fiber), 23g pro.

## PEPPER RICOTTA PRIMAVERA

Garlic, peppers and herbs top creamy ricotta cheese in this meatless skillet meal you can make in just 20 minutes.
—*Janet Boulger, Botwood, NL*

- - - - - - - - - - - - - - - - - - - - - - - - - - - - - - - - - - - - -

**TAKES:** 20 min. • **MAKES:** 6 servings

- 1 cup part-skim ricotta cheese
- ½ cup fat-free milk
- 4 tsp. olive oil
- 1 garlic clove, minced
- ½ tsp. crushed red pepper flakes
- 1 medium green pepper, julienned
- 1 medium sweet red pepper, julienned
- 1 medium sweet yellow pepper, julienned
- 1 medium zucchini, sliced
- 1 cup frozen peas, thawed
- ¼ tsp. dried oregano
- ¼ tsp. dried basil
- 6 oz. fettuccine, cooked and drained

**1.** Whisk together ricotta cheese and milk; set aside. In a large skillet, heat oil over medium heat. Add garlic and pepper flakes; saute 1 minute. Add next 7 ingredients. Cook and stir over medium heat until vegetables are crisp-tender, about 5 minutes.
**2.** Add cheese mixture to fettuccine; top with vegetables. Toss to coat. Serve immediately.
**1 CUP:** 229 cal., 7g fat (3g sat. fat), 13mg chol., 88mg sod., 31g carb. (6g sugars, 4g fiber), 11g pro. **DIABETIC EXCHANGES:** 2 starch, 1 medium-fat meat, ½ fat.

**TIP**
This is a mostly mild dish with a bit of a spicy kick. To punch up the flavor use fresh herbs in place of dried and sprinkle with Parmesan cheese before serving.

## CHICKEN THAI PIZZA

This is a recipe I make for my friends for a girls' night that's filled with fun and laughter. It is simple to make but is full of flavor.
—*Kimberly Knuppenburg, Menomonee Falls, WI*

- - - - - - - - - - - - - - - - - - - - - - - - - - - - - - - - - - - - -

**TAKES:** 25 min. • **MAKES:** 6 servings

- 1 prebaked 12-in. pizza crust
- ⅔ cup Thai peanut sauce
- 2 Tbsp. reduced-sodium soy sauce
- 2 Tbsp. creamy peanut butter
- 1 cup shredded cooked chicken breast
- 1 cup shredded part-skim mozzarella cheese
- 3 green onions, chopped
- ½ cup bean sprouts
- ½ cup shredded carrot

**1.** Preheat oven to 400°. Place crust on an ungreased 12-in. pizza pan or baking sheet. In a small bowl, combine peanut sauce, soy sauce and peanut butter. Add chicken; toss to coat. Spread over crust; sprinkle with cheese and onions.
**2.** Bake until cheese is melted, 10-12 minutes. Top with bean sprouts and carrot.
**1 PIECE:** 361 cal., 15g fat (4g sat. fat), 29mg chol., 1183mg sod., 35g carb. (4g sugars, 3g fiber), 23g pro.

# - 7 -

# GIVE ME
# 5 OR FEWER

Turning out an amazing meal doesn't require a long list of ingredients!
Save on time, money and energy with these recipes that require no more than
five items (not including salt & pepper, oil, water and optional extras). From
casual family night to showstopping feasts, these are your new go-to dishes.

**Habanero Raspberry Ribs** (p. 142) **Mom's Roast Chicken** (p. 152)
**Grilled Ribeye with Garlic Blue Cheese Mustard Sauce** (p. 147)
**Spicy Chicken Nuggets** (p. 154) **Spinach Ravioli Bake** (p. 161) **BBQ Meat Loaf Minis** (p. 145)
**Rosemary-Apricot Pork Tenderloin** (p. 157) **Chicken Provolone** (p. 153) **Ranch Pork Roast** (p. 154)

## FETTUCCINE WITH SAUSAGE & FRESH TOMATO SAUCE

Fresh homemade sauce doesn't take much more time than using jarred—and the results are so good!
—Taste of Home *Test Kitchen*

**PREP:** 15 min. • **COOK:** 30 min.
**MAKES:** 4 servings

- 2 Tbsp. olive oil
- 1 pkg. (12 oz.) fully cooked Italian chicken sausage links, cut into ½-in. slices
- 1 large onion, finely chopped
- 2 lbs. plum tomatoes, chopped (about 5 cups)
- ½ tsp. salt
- ¼ tsp. pepper
- 8 oz. uncooked fettuccine
- ¼ cup thinly sliced fresh basil
- 1 tsp. sugar, optional
  Optional toppings: Grated Romano cheese and additional basil

**1.** In a 6-qt. stockpot, heat 1 Tbsp. oil over medium heat. Brown sausage slices; remove. In remaining 1 Tbsp. oil, saute onion until tender, 3-5 minutes. Stir in sausage, tomatoes, salt and pepper; bring to a boil. Reduce heat; simmer, uncovered, until thickened, 20-25 minutes.

**2.** Meanwhile, cook fettuccine according to package directions; drain.

**3.** Stir basil and, if desired, sugar into sauce. Serve over fettuccine. If desired, top with grated Romano cheese and additional basil.

**FREEZE OPTION:** Freeze cooled sauce in freezer containers. To use, partially thaw in refrigerator overnight. Heat through in a saucepan, stirring occasionally.

**1 CUP PASTA WITH 1 CUP SAUCE:** 457 cal., 15g fat (3g sat. fat), 65mg chol., 792mg sod., 56g carb. (9g sugars, 5g fiber), 25g pro.

## CILANTRO-TOPPED SALMON

This has been a favorite with everyone who has tried it. A tongue-tingling cilantro-lime sauce complements tender salmon fillets in this pleasing entree.
—Nancy Culbert, Whitehorn, CA

**TAKES:** 30 min. • **MAKES:** 6 servings

- 1½ lbs. salmon fillets
- ¼ cup lime juice, divided
- ½ cup minced fresh cilantro
- 3 Tbsp. thinly sliced green onions
- 1 Tbsp. finely chopped jalapeno pepper
- 1 Tbsp. olive oil
- ¼ tsp. salt
- ⅛ tsp. pepper
  Optional: Lime wedges, sliced jalapeno and cilantro sprigs

**1.** Preheat oven to 350°. Place salmon skin side down in a 13x9-in. baking dish coated with cooking spray. Drizzle with 1½ tsp. lime juice.

**2.** In a small bowl, combine the cilantro, onions, jalapeno, oil, salt, pepper and remaining lime juice. Spread over salmon. Bake, uncovered, until fish just begins to flakes easily with a fork, 20-25 minutes. If desired, serve with lime wedges, sliced jalapeno and cilantro sprigs.

**NOTE:** Wear disposable gloves when cutting hot peppers; the oils can burn skin. Avoid touching your face.

**3 OZ. COOKED SALMON:** 232 cal., 15g fat (3g sat. fat), 67mg chol., 166mg sod., 1g carb. (0 sugars, 0 fiber), 23g pro. **DIABETIC EXCHANGES:** 3 lean meat, 1 fat.

**TIP**
If you prefer skinless salmon fillets, you can certainly use them. However, skin-on fillets work best for this recipe because the skin creates a barrier between the salmon meat and the bottom of the dish. That way, if the salmon sticks to the bottom of the dish, it's the skin that sticks—and not the meat.

## HABANERO RASPBERRY RIBS

Roasting these tender, tangy ribs in the oven means you can enjoy them any time of year—no waiting for grilling season. The heat from the habanero and the sweetness of the jam complement each other perfectly.
—Yvonne Roat, Linden, MI

**PREP:** 10 min. • **BAKE:** 3 hours and 10 min. • **MAKES:** 5 servings

- 2 racks pork baby back ribs (about 4½ lbs.)
- 2½ cups barbecue sauce, divided
- 2 cups seedless raspberry jam
- 1 habanero pepper, finely chopped
  Additional barbecue sauce, optional

**1.** Place each rack of ribs on a double thickness of heavy-duty foil (about 28x18 in.). Combine 2 cups barbecue sauce, the jam and habanero; pour over ribs. Wrap foil tightly around ribs.
**2.** Place in a shallow roasting pan. Bake at 325° for 3 hours or until meat is tender.
**3.** Carefully unwrap ribs. Place on baking sheets. Brush with the remaining ½ cup barbecue sauce. Broil 4 in. from the heat 8-10 minutes or until bubbly. If desired, serve with additional barbecue sauce.
**NOTE:** Wear disposable gloves when cutting hot peppers; the oils can burn skin. Avoid touching your face.
**1 SERVING:** 1067 cal., 38g fat (14g sat. fat), 147mg chol., 1562mg sod., 139g carb. (122g sugars, 1g fiber), 41g pro.

## HONEY-MUSTARD GLAZED SALMON

You won't need to fish for compliments from your dinner guests when you serve this spectacular salmon!
—Taste of Home *Test Kitchen*

**TAKES:** 20 min. • **MAKES:** 10 servings

- 10 salmon fillets (5 oz. each)
- ⅔ cup packed brown sugar
- 2 Tbsp. Dijon mustard
- 2 Tbsp. honey
- ½ tsp. salt

**1.** Place fillets, skin side down, on a greased baking sheet. In a small bowl, combine brown sugar, mustard, honey and salt; spoon over salmon.
**2.** Broil 3-4 in. from the heat until fish just begins to flake easily with a fork, 8-12 minutes.
**1 FILLET:** 292 cal., 13g fat (3g sat. fat), 71mg chol., 265mg sod., 18g carb. (18g sugars, 0 fiber), 24g pro.

**TIPS**

- How can you tell when salmon is done? Cooked salmon should be opaque and a little firm, and flake easily with a fork. Still not sure? Use a thermometer to make sure the salmon has reached an internal temperature of 145°.
- If you'd like to add a little heat to this recipe, stir 1 tsp. of chili-garlic sauce into your glaze—a generous pinch of red pepper flakes or cayenne will do the trick too! For extra flavor, try adding minced garlic or smoked paprika.

## GLAZED CORNISH HENS

If you're looking to add a touch of elegance to your dinner table, our home economists suggest these Cornish game hens topped with a sweet apricot glaze.
—Taste of Home *Test Kitchen*

------------------------------------------------------------

**PREP:** 5 min. • **BAKE:** 1 hour • **MAKES:** 4 servings

- 2 Cornish game hens (20 to 24 oz. each), split lengthwise
- ¼ tsp. salt
- ⅛ tsp. white pepper
- ⅓ cup apricot spreadable fruit
- 1 Tbsp. orange juice

**1.** Preheat oven to 350°. Place hens, breast side up, on a rack in a shallow roasting pan. Sprinkle with salt and pepper. Bake, uncovered, 30 minutes.

**2.** In a small bowl, combine spreadable fruit and orange juice. Spoon some of the apricot mixture over the hens. Bake until golden brown and juices run clear, 30-35 minutes longer, basting several times with remaining apricot mixture. Let stand 5 minutes before serving.

**½ HEN:** 402 cal., 24g fat (7g sat. fat), 175mg chol., 233mg sod., 14g carb. (11g sugars, 0 fiber), 30g pro.

> *"I served this on Christmas Eve. It was so easy to fix and I was out of the kitchen in no time flat! The family raved about it!!"*
> **—JO-SUE, TASTEOFHOME.COM**

## COCOA-CRUSTED BEEF TENDERLOIN

My family and I have cooking competitions with secret ingredients and a 30-minute time limit. This tenderloin recipe earned me a sweet victory.
—Gina Myers, Spokane, WA

------------------------------------------------------------

**TAKES:** 30 min. • **MAKES:** 4 servings

- 4 beef tenderloin steaks (1½ in. thick and 6 oz. each)
- ½ tsp. salt
- ½ tsp. coarsely ground pepper
- 3 Tbsp. baking cocoa
- 3 Tbsp. finely ground coffee

**1.** Preheat broiler. Sprinkle steaks with salt and pepper. In a shallow bowl, mix cocoa and coffee. Dip steaks in cocoa mixture to coat all sides; shake off excess.

**2.** Place steaks on a rack of a broiler pan. Broil 3-4 in. from heat 9-11 minutes on each side or until meat reaches desired doneness (for medium-rare, a thermometer should read 135°; medium, 140°; medium-well, 145°).

**1 STEAK:** 252 cal., 10g fat (4g sat. fat), 75mg chol., 296mg sod., 1g carb. (0 sugars, 0 fiber), 37g pro. **DIABETIC EXCHANGES:** 5 lean meat.

## AIR-FRYER BACON-WRAPPED SCALLOPS WITH PINEAPPLE QUINOA

Bacon-wrapped scallops seem so decadent and fancy that I often forget how easy they are to prepare. Paired with a pineapple quinoa, this elegant dinner can be ready in under 30 minutes.
—*Laura Greenberg, Lake Balboa, CA*

-------------------------------------------

**TAKES:** 30 min. • **MAKES:** 4 servings

- 1  can (14½ oz.) vegetable broth
- 1  cup quinoa, rinsed
- ¼  tsp. salt
- ⅛  tsp. plus ¼ tsp. pepper, divided
- 10  bacon strips
- 16  sea scallops (about 2 lbs.), side muscles removed
- 1  cup drained canned pineapple tidbits

**1.** In a small saucepan, bring broth to a boil. Add quinoa, salt and ⅛ tsp. pepper. Reduce heat; simmer, covered, until liquid is absorbed, 12-15 minutes.

**2.** Meanwhile, preheat air fryer to 400°. Arrange 8 strips of bacon in a single layer on tray in air-fryer basket. Cook for 3 minutes or until partially cooked but not crisp. Remove and set aside. Add the remaining 2 bacon strips; cook until crisp, 5-6 minutes. Finely chop the crisp bacon strips. Cut the partially cooked bacon strips lengthwise in half.

**3.** Wrap a halved bacon strip around each scallop; secure with a toothpick. Sprinkle with remaining ¼ tsp. pepper.

**4.** Arrange scallops in a single layer on greased tray in air-fryer basket. Cook until firm and opaque, 8-10 minutes.

**5.** Remove quinoa from heat; fluff with a fork. Stir in pineapple and chopped bacon. Serve with scallops.

**4 SCALLOPS WITH ¾ CUP QUINOA:** 455 cal., 12g fat (3g sat. fat), 75mg chol., 1717mg sod., 45g carb. (10g sugars, 3g fiber), 41g pro.

**TIP**

You shouldn't need to flip the scallops halfway through the cooking time, but every air fryer is different. If you notice the bottoms seem to be browning more quickly than the tops, feel free to flip!

## 🕐 5i ❄ BBQ MEAT LOAF MINIS

Kids can have fun helping to prepare these mini meat loaves in muffin cups. If we're in the mood for extra spice, we add 2 teaspoons chili powder and 1 cup of salsa to the meat mixture.
—*Linda Call, Falun, KS*

**TAKES:** 30 min. • **MAKES:** 6 servings

- 1 pkg. (6 oz.) stuffing mix
- 1 cup water
- 2 Tbsp. hickory smoke-flavored barbecue sauce
- 1 lb. ground beef
- 1 cup shredded cheddar cheese
  Additional hickory smoke-flavored barbecue sauce, optional

1. Preheat oven to 375°. In a large bowl, combine stuffing mix, water and 2 Tbsp. barbecue sauce. Add beef; mix lightly but thoroughly. Press ⅓ cup mixture into each of 12 ungreased muffin cups.
2. Bake, uncovered, until a thermometer reads 160°, 18-22 minutes. Sprinkle tops with cheese; bake until the cheese is melted, 2-4 minutes longer. If desired, serve with additional barbecue sauce.

**FREEZE OPTION:** Securely wrap and freeze cooled meat loaves in foil. To use, partially thaw in refrigerator overnight. Place meat loaves on a greased shallow baking pan. Bake in a preheated 350° oven until heated through. Top with cheese as directed.

**2 MINI MEAT LOAVES:** 330 cal., 17g fat (7g sat. fat), 67mg chol., 668mg sod., 21g carb. (4g sugars, 1g fiber), 21g pro.

## 🕐 5i 🍎 CARIBBEAN CHICKEN STIR-FRY

Fruit in stir-fry? You might be surprised by how good this dish is. It's a promising go-to option when time's tight.
—*Jeanne Holt, St. Paul, MN*

**TAKES:** 25 min. • **MAKES:** 4 servings

- 2 tsp. cornstarch
- ¼ cup water
- 1 lb. boneless skinless chicken breasts, cut into ½-in. strips
- 2 tsp. Caribbean jerk seasoning
- 1 can (15 oz.) mixed tropical fruit, drained and coarsely chopped
- 2 pkg. (8.8 oz. each) ready-to-serve brown rice

1. In a small bowl, mix cornstarch and water until smooth.
2. Heat a large skillet coated with cooking spray over medium-high heat. Add chicken; sprinkle with jerk seasoning. Stir-fry until no longer pink, 3-5 minutes. Stir cornstarch mixture and add to pan. Add fruit. Bring to a boil; cook and stir until sauce is thickened, 1-2 minutes.
3. Meanwhile, heat rice according to package directions. Serve with chicken.

**¾ CUP STIR-FRY WITH 1 CUP RICE:** 419 cal., 5g fat (1g sat. fat), 63mg chol., 208mg sod., 54g carb. (17g sugars, 3g fiber), 27g pro.

## CHICKEN & VEGETABLE CURRY COUSCOUS

For my busy family, a semi-homemade one-pot meal is the best way to get dinner done in a hurry. Use your favorite blend of frozen veggies and serve with toasted pita bread for smiles all around.
—*Elizabeth Hokanson, Arborg, MB*

**TAKES:** 25 min. • **MAKES:** 6 servings

- 1 Tbsp. butter
- 1 lb. boneless skinless chicken breasts, cut into strips
- 1 pkg. (16 oz.) frozen vegetable blend of your choice
- 1¼ cups water
- 1 pkg. (5.7 oz.) curry-flavored couscous mix
- ½ cup raisins

**1.** In a cast-iron or other heavy skillet, heat butter over medium-high heat. Add chicken; cook and stir until no longer pink.
**2.** Add vegetable blend, water and the contents of the couscous seasoning packet. Bring to a boil; stir in couscous and raisins. Remove from heat; let stand, covered, until water is absorbed, about 5 minutes. Fluff with a fork.

**1 CUP:** 273 cal., 4g fat (2g sat. fat), 47mg chol., 311mg sod., 39g carb. (9g sugars, 4g fiber), 21g pro. **DIABETIC EXCHANGES:** 2 starch, 2 lean meat, 1 vegetable, ½ fat.

## BBQ COUNTRY-STYLE RIBS

Quick to prep for the slow cooker, this dinner is terrific with a salad and a fresh side. My family practically cheers whenever I make it!
—*Cheryl Mann, Winside, NE*

**PREP:** 10 min. • **COOK:** 6 hours • **MAKES:** 6 servings

- 3 lbs. boneless country-style pork ribs
- ½ tsp. salt
- ½ tsp. pepper
- 1 large onion, cut into ½-in. rings
- 1 bottle (18 oz.) hickory smoke–flavored barbecue sauce
- ⅓ cup maple syrup
- ¼ cup spicy brown mustard
  Thinly sliced green onions, optional

**1.** Sprinkle ribs with salt and pepper. Place onion in a 6-qt. slow cooker. Top with ribs. In a large bowl, combine barbecue sauce, maple syrup and mustard; pour over ribs. Cook, covered, on low until meat is tender, 6-8 hours.
**2.** Transfer meat to a serving platter; keep warm. Pour cooking liquid into a large saucepan; bring to a boil. Reduce heat; simmer, uncovered, 10 minutes or until sauce is thickened. Serve with pork. If desired, sprinkle with onions.

**6 OZ. COOKED PORK WITH ⅓ CUP SAUCE:** 598 cal., 21g fat (8g sat. fat), 131mg chol., 1443mg sod., 56g carb. (46g sugars, 1g fiber), 41g pro.

## GRILLED RIBEYE WITH GARLIC BLUE CHEESE MUSTARD SAUCE

This simple steak gets a big flavor boost from two of my favorites: mustard and blue cheese. My husband and I make this recipe to celebrate our anniversary each year!
—*Ashley Lecker, Green Bay, WI*

------------------------------------------------

**PREP:** 20 min. • **GRILL:** 10 min. + standing • **MAKES:** 4 servings

- 1 cup half-and-half cream
- ½ cup Dijon mustard
- ¼ cup plus 2 tsp. crumbled blue cheese, divided
- 1 garlic clove, minced
- 2 beef ribeye steaks (1½ in. thick and 12 oz. each)
- 1 Tbsp. olive oil
- ¼ tsp. salt
- ¼ tsp. pepper

**1.** In a small saucepan over medium heat, whisk together cream, mustard, ¼ cup blue cheese and the garlic. Bring to a simmer. Reduce heat to low; whisk occasionally.

**2.** Meanwhile, rub meat with olive oil; sprinkle with salt and pepper. Grill steaks, covered, on a greased rack over high direct heat 4-6 minutes on each side until meat reaches desired doneness (for medium-rare, a thermometer should read 135°; medium, 140°; medium-well, 145°). Remove from grill; let stand 10 minutes while sauce finishes cooking.

**3.** When sauce is reduced by half, pour over steaks; top with remaining 2 tsp. blue cheese.

**½ STEAK WITH 3 TBSP. SAUCE:** 547 cal., 39g fat (17g sat. fat), 138mg chol., 1088mg sod., 3g carb. (2g sugars, 0 fiber), 34g pro.

## JALAPENO POPPER STUFFED CHICKEN BREASTS

One of my husband's favorite snacks are jalapeno poppers, so I created this recipe. He loves chicken cooked this way and best of all is the quick cooking with little cleanup!
—*Donna Gribbins, Shelbyville, KY*

------------------------------------------------

**PREP:** 15 min. • **COOK:** 15 min./batch • **MAKES:** 4 servings

- 4 oz. cream cheese, softened
- 1 cup shredded cheddar cheese
- 1 jalapeno pepper, seeded and finely chopped
- 4 boneless skinless chicken breast halves (6 oz. each)
- ½ tsp. salt
- ½ tsp. pepper
- 8 thick-sliced bacon strips

**1.** Preheat air fryer to 375°. In a small bowl, mix cream cheese, cheddar cheese and jalapeno. Cut a pocket horizontally in the thickest part of each chicken breast. Fill with cheese mixture. Sprinkle chicken with salt and pepper. Wrap 2 bacon strips around each chicken breast; secure with toothpicks.

**2.** In batches, place chicken in greased air fryer, seam side down. Cook until a thermometer inserted into chicken reads 165°, 14-16 minutes, turning once. Let stand 5 minutes. Discard toothpicks before serving.

**NOTE:** Wear disposable gloves when cutting hot peppers; the oils can burn skin. Avoid touching your face.

**1 STUFFED CHICKEN BREAST:** 518 cal., 33g fat (15g sat. fat), 171mg chol., 1150mg sod., 3g carb. (1g sugars, 0 fiber), 51g pro.

## OLD-FASHIONED POOR MAN'S STEAK

These flavorful steaks fit into everybody's budget. A special friend shared the recipe, and I think of her each time I make this.
—*Susan Wright, Mineral Wells, WV*

------------------------------------------

**PREP:** 25 min. + chilling • **COOK:** 4 hours
**MAKES:** 9 servings

- 1 cup crushed saltine crackers (about 30 crackers)
- ⅓ cup water
  Salt and pepper to taste
- 2 lbs. ground beef
- ¼ cup all-purpose flour
- 2 Tbsp. canola oil
- 2 cans (10¾ oz. each) condensed cream of mushroom soup, undiluted
  Hot mashed potatoes or noodles
  Minced fresh parsley, optional

**1.** In a large bowl, combine cracker crumbs, water, salt and pepper. Crumble beef over mixture and mix lightly but thoroughly. Press into an ungreased 9-in. square pan. Cover and refrigerate for at least 3 hours.
**2.** Cut into 3-in. squares; dredge in flour. In a large skillet, heat oil over medium heat; add beef and cook until browned on both sides, 2-3 minutes on each side.
**3.** Transfer to a 3-qt. slow cooker with a slotted spatula or spoon. Add soup.
**4.** Cover and cook on high until meat is no longer pink, 4 hours. Serve with mashed potatoes or noodles. If desired, top with minced parsley.
**1 SERVING:** 292 cal., 18g fat (6g sat. fat), 68mg chol., 372mg sod., 10g carb. (1g sugars, 1g fiber), 22g pro.

**TIPS**

- You can also make this recipe using ground turkey. If you're all out of saltine crackers, try using dried breadcrumbs instead.
- Salisbury steak can also be made in the oven or on the stovetop. To use the oven, swap the slow-cooker step for 1 hour in the oven at 325°F, or until meat reaches an internal temperature of 160°F. To make on the stovetop, sear steaks as directed, then let them simmer in the soup uncovered until cooked through.

## CHICKEN WITH SHALLOT SAUCE

Even though it doesn't take long to put together, this flavorful chicken tastes like it simmered all day. It's wonderful with mashed potatoes and a green vegetable.
—*Kathy Anderson, Rockford, IL*

------------------------------------------

**PREP:** 10 min. • **COOK:** 50 min.
**MAKES:** 6 servings

- 6 bacon strips, chopped
- 1 broiler/fryer chicken (3 to 4 lbs.), cut up
- ½ tsp. salt
- ½ tsp. pepper
- 10 shallots, thinly sliced
- 1 cup water
- 1 whole garlic bulb, cloves separated and peeled
- ½ cup balsamic vinegar

**1.** In a large skillet, cook the bacon over medium heat until crisp. Remove to paper towels with a slotted spoon; drain, reserving 2 Tbsp. drippings in pan.
**2.** Sprinkle chicken with salt and pepper; brown in drippings. Remove and keep warm. Add shallots; cook and stir until tender. Stir in water and garlic. Return chicken to pan. Bring to a boil. Reduce heat; cover and simmer 30-35 minutes or until a thermometer inserted in thigh reads 170°-175°.
**3.** Remove chicken to a serving platter; keep warm. Skim fat from cooking juices. Mash garlic; add vinegar. Bring liquid to a boil; cook until slightly thickened. Spoon sauce over chicken; sprinkle with the reserved bacon.
**7 OZ. COOKED CHICKEN WITH ¼ CUP SAUCE:** 456 cal., 24g fat (7g sat. fat), 117mg chol., 448mg sod., 20g carb. (8g sugars, 1g fiber), 38g pro.

## - EGGS BENEDICT BAKED POTATOES -

This baked potato dish would be eggs-cellent for a breakfast-for-dinner evening! Whip it up as a quick meal for one or make multiples to feed the whole family.

Scrub **1 large baking potato**; pierce several times with a fork. Bake at 400° until tender, 50-75 minutes. Cut an "X" in the potato; fluff the pulp with a fork and season with **salt** and **pepper**. Top with **2 slices Canadian bacon** and **1 poached egg**, then drizzle with **2 Tbsp. prepared hollandaise** and sprinkle with **minced parsley**.

## AIR-FRYER BEEF TURNOVERS

My mom's recipe for these flavorful pockets called for dough made from scratch, but I streamlined it by using refrigerated crescent rolls and an air fryer. My children love the turnovers plain or dipped in ketchup, and they're also great with mustard.
—Claudia Bodeker, Ash Flat, AR

- - - - - - - - - - - - - - - - - - - - - - - - - - - - - - - - - - -

**TAKES:** 30 min. • **MAKES:** 1 dozen

1 lb. ground beef
1 medium onion, chopped
1 jar (16 oz.) sauerkraut, rinsed, drained and chopped
1 cup shredded Swiss cheese
3 tubes (8 oz. each) refrigerated crescent rolls

**1.** In a large skillet, cook beef and onion over medium heat until meat is no longer pink, 5-7 minutes; crumble meat; drain. Add sauerkraut and cheese.
**2.** Preheat air fryer to 350°. Unroll crescent roll dough and separate into rectangles; pinch seams to seal. Place ½ cup beef mixture in the center of each rectangle. Bring corners to the center and pinch to seal. In batches, place turnovers in a single layer in greased air fryer. Cook until golden brown, 12-15 minutes.
**2 TURNOVERS:** 634 cal., 35g fat (7g sat. fat), 63mg chol., 1426mg sod., 54g carb. (14g sugars, 2g fiber), 27g pro.

## CAESAR SALMON WITH ROASTED TOMATOES & ARTICHOKES

This is my go-to recipe for quick dinners, either for family or guests. This dish is colorful, healthy, easy to prepare and absolutely delicious. Hard to believe it only has five ingredients!
—Mary Hawkes, Prescott, AZ

- - - - - - - - - - - - - - - - - - - - - - - - - - - - - - - - - - -

**TAKES:** 25 min. • **MAKES:** 4 servings

4 salmon fillets (5 oz. each)
5 Tbsp. reduced-fat Caesar vinaigrette, divided
¼ tsp. pepper, divided
2 cups grape tomatoes
1 can (14 oz.) water-packed artichoke hearts, drained and quartered
1 medium sweet orange or yellow pepper, cut into 1-in. pieces

**1.** Preheat oven to 425°. Place salmon on half of a 15x10x1-in. baking pan coated with cooking spray. Brush with 2 Tbsp. vinaigrette; sprinkle with ⅛ tsp. pepper.
**2.** In a large bowl, combine tomatoes, artichoke hearts and sweet pepper. Add the remaining 3 Tbsp. vinaigrette and ⅛ tsp. pepper; toss to coat. Place tomato mixture on the remaining half of the pan. Roast until fish just begins to flake easily with a fork and the vegetables are tender, 12-15 minutes.
**1 FILLET WITH ¾ CUP TOMATO MIXTURE:** 318 cal., 16g fat (3g sat. fat), 73mg chol., 674mg sod., 12g carb. (4g sugars, 2g fiber), 28g pro.
**DIABETIC EXCHANGES:** 4 lean meat, 1 vegetable, 1 fat.

## COD & ASPARAGUS BAKE

The lemon pulls this flavorful and healthy dish together. You can use grated Parmesan cheese instead of Romano.
—*Thomas Faglon, Somerset, NJ*

**TAKES:** 30 min. • **MAKES:** 4 servings

- 4   cod fillets (4 oz. each)
- 1   lb. fresh thin asparagus, trimmed
- 1   pint cherry tomatoes, halved
- 2   Tbsp. lemon juice
- 1½  tsp. grated lemon zest
- ¼   cup grated Romano cheese

**1.** Preheat oven to 375°. Place cod and asparagus in a 15x10x1-in. baking pan brushed with oil. Add tomatoes, cut sides down. Brush fish with lemon juice; sprinkle with lemon zest. Sprinkle fish and vegetables with Romano cheese. Bake until fish just begins to flake easily with a fork, about 12 minutes.
**2.** Remove pan from oven; preheat broiler. Broil mixture 3-4 in. from heat until vegetables are lightly browned, 2-3 minutes.
**1 SERVING:** 141 cal., 3g fat (2g sat. fat), 45mg chol., 184mg sod., 6g carb. (3g sugars, 2g fiber), 23g pro. **DIABETIC EXCHANGES:** 3 lean meat, 1 vegetable.

> **TIP**
> If asparagus isn't in season, fresh green beans make a fine substitute and will cook in about the same amount of time. We tested cod fillets that were about ¾ in. thick. You'll need to adjust the bake time up or down if your fillets are thicker or thinner.

## MOM'S ROAST CHICKEN

This is the best way to cook a whole chicken that roasts up super juicy with crisp, golden skin. It's simply seasoned, but it packs in so much flavor.
—*James Schend, Pleasant Prairie, WI*

**PREP:** 15 min. + chilling • **BAKE:** 35 min. + standing
**MAKES:** 6 servings

- 1   broiler/fryer chicken (4 to 5 lbs.)
- 2   tsp. kosher salt
- 1   tsp. coarsely ground pepper
- 2   tsp. olive oil
     Optional: Minced fresh thyme or rosemary

**1.** Rub outside of chicken with salt and pepper. Transfer the chicken to a rack on a rimmed baking sheet. Refrigerate, uncovered, overnight.
**2.** Preheat oven to 450°. Remove chicken from refrigerator while oven heats. Heat a 12-in. cast-iron or ovenproof skillet in the oven for 15 minutes.
**3.** Place chicken on a work surface, neck side down. Cut through skin where legs connect to body. Press thighs down so joints pop and legs lie flat.
**4.** Carefully place chicken, breast side up, into hot skillet; press legs down so they lie flat on bottom of pan. Brush with oil. Roast until a thermometer inserted in thickest part of thigh reads 170°-175°, 35-40 minutes. Remove chicken from oven; let stand 10 minutes before carving. If desired, top with herbs before serving.
**5 OZ. COOKED CHICKEN:** 405 cal., 24g fat (6g sat. fat), 139mg chol., 760mg sod., 0 carb. (0 sugars, 0 fiber), 44g pro.

# CHICKEN PROVOLONE

Though this is one of my simplest dishes, it's one of my husband's favorites. It is easy to prepare and looks fancy served on a dark plate with a garnish of fresh parsley or basil. Add some buttered noodles for an easy side dish.
—*Dawn E. Bryant, Thedford, NE*

------------------------------------------------

**TAKES:** 25 min. • **MAKES:** 4 servings

- 4 boneless skinless chicken breast halves (4 oz. each)
- ¼ tsp. pepper
- 8 fresh basil leaves
- 4 thin slices prosciutto or deli ham
- 4 slices provolone cheese

**1.** Sprinkle chicken with pepper. In a large skillet coated with cooking spray, cook chicken over medium heat until a thermometer reads 165°, 4-5 minutes on each side.
**2.** Transfer chicken to an ungreased baking sheet; top with the basil, prosciutto and cheese. Broil 6-8 in. from the heat until the cheese is melted, 1-2 minutes.

**1 CHICKEN BREAST HALF:** 236 cal., 11g fat (6g sat. fat), 89mg chol., 435mg sod., 1g carb. (0 sugars, 0 fiber), 33g pro. **DIABETIC EXCHANGES:** 4 lean meat.

# LEMON CHICKEN WITH BASIL

No matter when I eat it, this tangy slow-cooked chicken reminds me of summer meals with friends and family.
—*Deborah Posey, Virginia Beach, VA*

------------------------------------------------

**PREP:** 5 min. • **COOK:** 3 hours • **MAKES:** 4 servings

- 4 boneless skinless chicken breast halves (6 oz. each)
- 2 medium lemons
- 1 bunch fresh basil leaves (¾ oz.)
- 2 cups chicken stock
  Optional: Additional grated lemon zest and chopped basil

**1.** Place chicken breasts in a 3-qt. slow cooker. Finely grate enough zest from lemons to measure 4 tsp. Cut lemons in half; squeeze juice. Add zest and juice to slow cooker.
**2.** Tear basil leaves directly into slow cooker. Add chicken stock. Cook, covered, on low until meat is tender, 3-4 hours. When cool enough to handle, shred meat with 2 forks. If desired, stir in additional lemon zest and chopped basil.
**FREEZE OPTION:** Freeze cooled chicken mixture in freezer containers. To use, partially thaw in refrigerator overnight. Heat through in a saucepan, stirring occasionally; add broth or water if necessary.
**5 OZ. COOKED CHICKEN:** 200 cal., 4g fat (1g sat. fat), 94mg chol., 337mg sod., 3g carb. (1g sugars, 0 fiber), 37g pro. **DIABETIC EXCHANGES:** 5 lean meat.

**TIP** For a sweet and savory treat, layer chicken, butter lettuce leaves and apple slices on toasted raisin bread.

## SPICY CHICKEN NUGGETS

We devour these golden brown chicken nuggets at least once a week. If you want to tone down the heat, skip the chipotle pepper.
—*Cheryl Cook, Palmyra, VA*

**TAKES:** 30 min. • **MAKES:** 6 servings

- 1½ cups panko bread crumbs
- 1½ cups grated Parmesan cheese
- ½ tsp. ground chipotle pepper, optional
- ¼ cup butter, melted
- 1½ lbs. boneless skinless chicken thighs, cut into 1½-in. pieces

**1.** Preheat oven to 400°. In a shallow bowl, mix bread crumbs, cheese and, if desired, chipotle pepper. Place butter in a separate shallow bowl. Dip chicken pieces in butter, then in crumb mixture, patting to help coating adhere.

**2.** Place chicken in a greased 15x10x1-in. baking pan; sprinkle with remaining crumb mixture. Bake until no longer pink, 20-25 minutes.

**1 SERVING:** 371 cal., 22g fat (10g sat. fat), 113mg chol., 527mg sod., 13g carb. (1g sugars, 1g fiber), 29g pro.

**TIPS**

- If you want to make these chicken nuggets spicier, you can increase the ground chipotle pepper in the recipe or add ¼ tsp. cayenne. Or, lightly sprinkle the chicken thighs with hot sauce before coating them. You can also add some heat to your dipping sauce.
- Honey, honey mustard, ranch dressing, marinara, BBQ sauce—your options are endless for dipping.

## RANCH PORK ROAST

This simple pork roast with a mild rub is perfect for new cooks. The leftover meat is tender and flavorful, and can be used in countless recipes calling for cooked pork.
—Taste of Home *Test Kitchen*

**PREP:** 10 min. • **BAKE:** 50 min. + standing • **MAKES:** 8 servings

- 1 boneless pork loin roast (2½ lbs.)
- 2 Tbsp. olive oil
- 1 Tbsp. ranch salad dressing mix
- 2 tsp. Dijon mustard
- 1 garlic clove, minced
- ½ tsp. pepper

**1.** Preheat oven to 350°. If desired, tie pork with kitchen string at 2-in. intervals to help roast hold its shape. Combine the next 5 ingredients; rub over roast. Place on a rack in a shallow roasting pan. Pour 1 cup water into pan.

**2.** Bake, uncovered, until a thermometer reads 145°, 50-55 minutes. Let stand for 10-15 minutes before slicing.

**FREEZE OPTION:** Freeze cooled sliced pork in freezer containers. To use, partially thaw in refrigerator overnight. Heat through in a covered saucepan, gently stirring; add a little broth or water if necessary.

**4 OZ. COOKED PORK:** 212 cal., 10g fat (3g sat. fat), 70mg chol., 248mg sod., 2g carb. (0 sugars, 0 fiber), 27g pro. **DIABETIC EXCHANGES:** 4 lean meat, ½ fat.

# PANCETTA & MUSHROOM-STUFFED CHICKEN BREAST

I was inspired by a stuffed chicken Marsala dish I had at a restaurant and wanted to come up with my own version using a different flavor profile.
—Ashley Laymon, Lititz, PA

-------------------------------------------

**PREP:** 15 min. • **BAKE:** 30 min.
**MAKES:** 4 servings

- 4 slices pancetta
- 1 Tbsp. olive oil
- 1 shallot, finely chopped
- ¾ cup chopped fresh mushrooms
- ¼ tsp. salt, divided
- ¼ tsp. pepper, divided
- 4 boneless skinless chicken breast halves (6 oz. each)
- ½ cup prepared pesto

1. Preheat oven to 350°. In a large skillet, cook pancetta over medium heat until partially cooked but not crisp; drain on paper towels.
2. In same skillet, heat oil over medium-high heat. Add shallot; cook and stir until lightly browned, 1-2 minutes. Stir in mushrooms; cook until tender, 1-2 minutes. Add ⅛ tsp. salt and ⅛ tsp. pepper.
3. Pound chicken breasts with a meat mallet to ¼-in. thickness. Spread each with 2 Tbsp. pesto; layer with 1 slice pancetta and a fourth of the mushroom mixture. Fold chicken in half, enclosing filling; secure with toothpicks. Sprinkle with remaining salt and pepper.
4. Transfer to a greased 13x9-in. baking dish. Bake until a thermometer inserted in chicken reads 165°, 30-35 minutes. Discard toothpicks before serving.

**1 STUFFED CHICKEN BREAST HALF:** 420 cal., 25g fat (6g sat. fat), 112mg chol., 1013mg sod., 5g carb. (2g sugars, 1g fiber), 41g pro.

**TIP**
Serve over pasta tossed with pesto. For those who don't like mushrooms, substitute 1 cup baby spinach and saute it with the shallots.

## SPAGHETTI WITH EGGS & BACON

Most people are surprised to see this combination of ingredients. Then they taste it—and it's gone in a flash!
—*Gail Jenner, Etna, CA*

-----------------------------------------------------

**TAKES:** 25 min. • **MAKES:** 4 servings

- 8  oz. uncooked spaghetti
- 4  large eggs
- ¾  cup half-and-half cream
- ½  cup grated Parmesan cheese
- ½  lb. bacon strips, cooked and crumbled

**1.** Cook spaghetti according to package directions in a 6-qt. stockpot. In a small saucepan, whisk eggs and cream until blended. Cook over low heat until a thermometer reads 160°, stirring constantly (do not allow to simmer). Remove from heat; stir in Parmesan cheese.

**2.** Drain spaghetti; return to stockpot. Add sauce and bacon; toss to combine. Serve immediately. If desired, sprinkle with additional Parmesan cheese.

**1 SERVING :** 486 cal., 21g fat (9g sat. fat), 238mg chol., 611mg sod., 45g carb. (3g sugars, 2g fiber), 26g pro.

## SWEET & SPICY CHIPOTLE CHICKEN

My husband and I have created many wonderful memories by sharing this meal with our friends. In the winter, we bake it indoors; in the summer, it works well on the grill too! Either way, the chicken pretty much cooks itself, leaving you plenty of time to visit with friends and family.
—*Ashlie Delshad, West Lafayette, IN*

-----------------------------------------------------

**PREP:** 15 min. + marinating • **BAKE:** 1 hour 50 min. + standing
**MAKES:** 8 servings

- 2  chipotle peppers in adobo sauce plus 3 Tbsp. adobo sauce
- ¼  cup tomato paste
- 3  Tbsp. honey
- 2  Tbsp. olive oil
- 1  tsp. sea salt
- 1  roasting chicken (6 to 7 lbs.)

**1.** Pulse chipotle peppers, adobo sauce, tomato paste, honey, olive oil and sea salt in a food processor or blender until smooth. Spread mixture evenly over chicken. Refrigerate, covered, at least 1 hour or overnight.

**2.** Preheat oven to 400°. Place chicken on a rack in a shallow roasting pan, breast side up. Tuck wings under chicken; tie drumsticks together.

**3.** Roast for 20 minutes. Reduce oven setting to 350°. Roast 1½-1¾ hours longer or until a thermometer inserted in the thickest part of thigh reads 170°-175°. (Cover loosely with foil if chicken browns too quickly.)

**4.** Remove chicken from oven; tent with foil. Let stand 15 minutes before carving. If desired, skim fat and thicken pan drippings for gravy. Serve with chicken.

**6 OZ. COOKED CHICKEN:** 462 cal., 27g fat (7g sat. fat), 134mg chol., 437mg sod., 9g carb. (8g sugars, 1g fiber), 43g pro.

## 🕐 🈯 SUPER QUICK CHICKEN FRIED RICE

After my first child was born, I needed meals that were satisfying and fast. This fried rice is now part of our routine dinners.

—Alicia Gower, Auburn, NY

- - - - - - - - - - - - - - - - - - - - - - - - - - - - - - - - - - - - - - - - - -

**TAKES:** 30 min. • **MAKES:** 6 servings

- 1  pkg. (12 oz.) frozen mixed vegetables
- 2  Tbsp. olive oil, divided
- 2  large eggs, lightly beaten
- 4  Tbsp. sesame oil, divided
- 3  pkg. (8.8 oz. each) ready-to-serve garden vegetable rice
- 1  rotisserie chicken, skin removed, shredded
- ¼  tsp. salt
- ¼  tsp. pepper

**1.** Prepare frozen vegetables according to package directions. Meanwhile, in a large skillet, heat 1 Tbsp. olive oil over medium-high heat. Pour in eggs; cook and stir until eggs are thickened and no liquid egg remains. Remove from pan.

**2.** In same skillet, heat 2 Tbsp. sesame oil and remaining 1 Tbsp. olive oil over medium-high heat. Add rice; cook and stir until rice begins to brown, 10-12 minutes.

**3.** Stir in chicken, salt and pepper. Add eggs and vegetables; heat through, breaking eggs into small pieces and stirring to combine. Drizzle with remaining 2 Tbsp. sesame oil.

**1½ CUPS:** 548 cal., 25g fat (5g sat. fat), 163mg chol., 934mg sod., 43g carb. (3g sugars, 3g fiber), 38g pro.

## 🈯 🍎 ROSEMARY-APRICOT PORK TENDERLOIN

You'll be surprised at how quickly this dish comes together for an easy weeknight meal. And with very little effort, you'll have tender and juicy meat that begs to be added to a salad or sandwich the next day.

—Marie Rizzio, Interlochen, MI

- - - - - - - - - - - - - - - - - - - - - - - - - - - - - - - - - - - - - - - - - -

**PREP:** 15 min. • **BAKE:** 25 min. • **MAKES:** 8 servings

- 3  Tbsp. minced fresh rosemary or
   1  Tbsp. dried rosemary, crushed
- 3  Tbsp. olive oil, divided
- 4  garlic cloves, minced
- 1  tsp. salt
- ½  tsp. pepper
- 2  pork tenderloins (1 lb. each)

GLAZE
- 1  cup apricot preserves
- 3  Tbsp. lemon juice
- 2  garlic cloves, minced

**1.** Preheat oven to 425°. In a small bowl, combine rosemary, 1 Tbsp. oil, garlic, salt and pepper; brush over pork.

**2.** In a large cast-iron or other ovenproof skillet, brown pork in remaining 2 Tbsp. oil on all sides. Bake for 15 minutes.

**3.** In a small bowl, combine the glaze ingredients; brush over pork. Bake until a thermometer reads 145°, 10-15 minutes longer, basting occasionally with pan juices. Let stand for 5 minutes before slicing.

**3 OZ. COOKED PORK:** 280 cal., 9g fat (2g sat. fat), 63mg chol., 357mg sod., 27g carb. (15g sugars, 0 fiber), 23g pro.

## ROAST LEG OF LAMB WITH ROSEMARY

Rubbing rosemary, garlic and onion into this delectable roast lamb takes it to a whole new level of deliciousness!
—*Suzy Horvath, Milwaukie, OR*

**PREP:** 10 min. • **BAKE:** 2 hours + standing
**MAKES:** 8 servings

- ⅓  cup olive oil
- ¼  cup minced fresh rosemary
- ¼  cup finely chopped onion
- 4  garlic cloves, minced
- ½  tsp. salt
- ¼  tsp. pepper
- 1  bone-in leg of lamb (5 to 6 lbs.), trimmed

1. Preheat oven to 325°. Combine the oil, rosemary, onion, garlic, salt and pepper; rub over lamb. Place fat side up on a rack in a shallow roasting pan.
2. Bake, uncovered, for 2-2½ hours or until meat reaches desired doneness (for medium-rare, a thermometer should read 135°; medium, 140°; medium-well, 145°), basting occasionally with pan juices. Let stand 15 minutes before slicing.

**5 OZ. COOKED LAMB:** 316 cal., 18g fat (5g sat. fat), 128mg chol., 206mg sod., 1g carb. (0 sugars, 0 fiber), 36g pro.

**TIPS**

- Although we prefer cooking with fresh herbs whenever possible, you can use dried rosemary instead of fresh in this leg of lamb recipe. Instead of ¼ cup fresh rosemary leaves, use 4 tsp. dried. To release the flavor from the dried leaves, rub them between your hands before combining with the other ingredients.

- This leg of lamb can be marinated ahead of time. In fact, the longer it marinates (up to 24 hours), the more flavorful it will be!

## SPINACH-ARTICHOKE RIGATONI

I love pasta, and so does my family. However, they are not so keen on their veggies. This one-pot meal that gets us all eating our spinach.
—*Yvonne Starlin, Westmoreland, TN*

**TAKES:** 30 min. • **MAKES:** 4 servings

- 3  cups uncooked rigatoni or large tube pasta
- 1  pkg. (10 oz.) frozen creamed spinach
- 1  can (14 oz.) water-packed artichoke hearts, rinsed, drained and quartered
- 2  cups shredded part-skim mozzarella cheese, divided
- ¼  cup grated Parmesan cheese
- ½  tsp. salt
- ¼  tsp. pepper

1. Preheat broiler. Prepare rigatoni and spinach according to package directions.
2. Drain pasta, reserving ½ cup pasta water; return pasta to pan. Add artichoke hearts, ½ cup mozzarella cheese, Parmesan cheese, salt, pepper and creamed spinach; toss to combine, adding some of the reserved pasta water to thin, if desired.
3. Transfer to a greased 2-qt. broiler-safe baking dish; sprinkle with the remaining 1½ cups mozzarella cheese. Broil 4-6 in. from heat until the cheese is melted, 2-3 minutes.

**1½ CUPS:** 448 cal., 14g fat (8g sat. fat), 37mg chol., 1224mg sod., 54g carb. (6g sugars, 3g fiber), 28g pro.

## TASTY ONION CHICKEN

French-fried onions are the secret to a yummy, crunchy coating that keeps the chicken juicy and tender. This entree is perfect with green beans and buttermilk biscuits.
—*Jennifer Hoeft, Thorndale, TX*

**TAKES:** 30 min. • **MAKES:** 4 servings

- ½ cup butter, melted
- 1 Tbsp. Worcestershire sauce
- 1 tsp. ground mustard
- 1 can (2.8 oz.) French-fried onions, crushed
- 4 boneless skinless chicken breast halves (4 oz. each)

**1.** In a shallow bowl, combine butter, Worcestershire sauce and mustard. Place onions in another shallow bowl. Dip chicken in butter mixture, then coat with onions.
**2.** Place in a greased 11x7-in. baking dish; drizzle with the remaining butter mixture. Bake, uncovered, at 400° for 20-25 minutes or until a thermometer reads 165°.
**1 CHICKEN BREAST HALF:** 460 cal., 36g fat (18g sat. fat), 124mg chol., 449mg sod., 10g carb. (0 sugars, 0 fiber), 23g pro.

## SLOW-COOKED CHERRY PORK CHOPS

I mixed and matched several recipes to come up with this one. I'm always happy to adapt recipes for my slow cooker. It's so easy to prepare a meal that way.
—*Mildred Sherrer, Fort Worth, TX*

**PREP:** 10 min. • **COOK:** 3 hours • **MAKES:** 6 servings

- 6 bone-in pork loin chops (8 oz. each)
- ⅛ tsp. salt
  Dash pepper
- 1 cup canned cherry pie filling
- 2 tsp. lemon juice
- ½ tsp. chicken bouillon granules
- ⅛ tsp. ground mace
  Additional cherry pie filling, warmed, optional

**1.** In a large skillet coated with cooking spray, brown pork chops over medium heat on both sides. Season with salt and pepper.
**2.** In a 3-qt. slow cooker, combine pie filling, lemon juice, bouillon and mace. Add the pork chops. Cook, covered, on low until the meat is no longer pink, 3-4 hours. Serve with additional pie filling if desired.
**1 SERVING:** 371 cal., 18g fat (7g sat. fat), 111mg chol., 203mg sod., 13g carb. (0 sugars, 0 fiber), 36g pro.

## MOM'S SLOPPY TACOS

No matter how hectic the weeknight, there's always time to serve your family a healthy meal with recipes this easy and delicious!
—*Kami Jones, Avondale, AZ*

**TAKES:** 30 min. • **MAKES:** 6 servings

1½ lbs. extra-lean ground beef (95% lean)
1 can (15 oz.) tomato sauce
¾ tsp. garlic powder
½ tsp. salt
¼ tsp. pepper
¼ tsp. cayenne pepper
12 taco shells, warmed
   Optional: Shredded lettuce, shredded cheese, chopped tomatoes, avocado and olives

**1.** In a large skillet, cook beef over medium heat until no longer pink, 6-8 minutes, crumbling beef. Stir in tomato sauce, garlic powder, salt, pepper and cayenne. Bring to a boil. Reduce heat; simmer, uncovered, for 10 minutes.
**2.** Fill each taco shell with ¼ cup beef mixture and toppings of your choice.

**2 TACOS:** 264 cal., 10g fat (4g sat. fat), 65mg chol., 669mg sod., 17g carb. (1g sugars, 1g fiber), 25g pro. **DIABETIC EXCHANGES:** 3 lean meat, 1 starch, 1 fat.

## SPINACH RAVIOLI BAKE

This entree is unbelievably simple to prepare yet tastes delicious. Because you use frozen ravioli—straight from the bag without cooking it first—you save so much time.
—*Susan Kehl, Pembroke Pines, FL*

**PREP:** 5 min. • **BAKE:** 40 min. • **MAKES:** 6 servings

2 cups spaghetti sauce
1 pkg. (25 oz.) frozen sausage ravioli or ravioli of your choice
2 cups shredded part-skim mozzarella cheese
1 pkg. (10 oz.) frozen chopped spinach, thawed and squeezed dry
¼ cup grated Parmesan cheese

**1.** Place 1 cup spaghetti sauce in a greased shallow 2-qt. baking dish. Top with half of each: ravioli, mozzarella cheese, spinach and Parmesan cheese. Repeat layers.
**2.** Bake, uncovered, at 350° until heated through and cheese is melted, 40-45 minutes.

**1 CUP:** 470 cal., 17g fat (7g sat. fat), 67mg chol., 1441mg sod., 54g carb. (7g sugars, 7g fiber), 27g pro.

# - 8 -

# INSTANT POT®
# & AIR FRYER

What would we do without our kitchen gadgets? Today's tools make creating homemade meals easier than ever. These recipes take advantage of two of the most popular kitchen devices to make healthy, delicious recipes, from appetizers to dessert and everything in between.

**Air-Fryer Black Bean Chimichangas** (p. 175) **Air-Fryer Lime & Gin Coconut Macaroons** (p. 181)
**Air-Fryer Buffalo Chicken Wings** (p. 176) **Pressure-Cooker Balsamic Pork Tenderloin** (p. 166)
**Air-Fryer Spinach Feta Turnovers** (p. 170) **Pressure-Cooker Lava Cake** (p. 169)
**Air-Fryer Pretzel-Crusted Catfish** (p. 177) **Pressure-Cooker Steamed Mussels with Peppers** (p. 167)
**Pressure-Cooker Red Beans & Rice** (p. 180)

## PRESSURE-COOKER HERBED CHICKEN & SHRIMP

Tender chicken and shrimp make a flavorful combination that's easy to prepare, yet elegant enough to serve at a dinner party. I serve it over hot cooked rice with crusty bread and a green salad.
—*Diana Knight, Reno, NV*

**PREP:** 15 min. • **COOK:** 30 min. + releasing
**MAKES:** 4 servings

- 1 tsp. salt
- 1 tsp. pepper
- 1 broiler/fryer chicken (3 to 4 lbs.), cut up and skin removed
- 1 Tbsp. canola oil
- 1 large onion, chopped
- 1 can (8 oz.) tomato sauce
- ½ cup white wine or chicken broth
- 1 garlic clove, minced
- 1 tsp. dried basil
- ¼ cup butter, softened
- 1 lb. uncooked shrimp (31-40 per lb.), peeled and deveined
  Hot cooked pasta, optional

**1.** Combine salt and pepper; rub over the chicken pieces. Select saute setting on a 6-qt. electric pressure cooker. Adjust for medium heat; add oil. When oil is hot, working in batches, brown chicken on all sides.
**2.** Combine next 5 ingredients and pour over chicken. Dot with butter. Lock lid; close pressure-release valve. Adjust to pressure-cook on high for 15 minutes. Let pressure release naturally for 10 minutes; quick-release any remaining pressure. A thermometer inserted in chicken should read at least 165°.
**3.** Select saute setting; adjust for medium heat. Stir in shrimp. Cook until shrimp turn pink, about 5 minutes. Serve over egg noodles, if desired.
**1 SERVING:** 606 cal., 34g fat (13g sat. fat), 330mg chol., 1275mg sod., 7g carb. (3g sugars, 1g fiber), 61g pro.

## AIR-FRYER SOUTHWESTERN CHICKEN ENCHILADAS

These quick and easy enchiladas are a perfect dinner for Taco Tuesday or any day of the week. Use rotisserie chicken for a quick source of cooked chicken.
—*Joan Hallford, North Richland Hills, TX*

**PREP:** 20 min. • **COOK:** 10 min./batch
**MAKES:** 6 servings

- 2 cups shredded cooked chicken
- 1¼ cups shredded Monterey Jack cheese or pepper jack cheese, divided
- 1¼ cups shredded sharp cheddar cheese, divided
- ½ cup hominy or whole kernel corn, rinsed and drained
- ½ cup canned black beans, rinsed and drained
- 1 can (4 oz.) chopped green chiles
- 1 Tbsp. chili seasoning mix
- ¼ tsp. salt
- ¼ tsp. pepper
- 12 flour tortillas (6 in.), warmed
- 1 cup enchilada sauce
  Optional: Sour cream, guacamole, salsa and limes

**1.** Do not preheat air fryer. In a large bowl, combine chicken, ½ cup Monterey Jack cheese, ½ cup cheddar cheese, hominy, beans, chiles and seasonings. Line air fryer basket with foil, letting ends extend up sides; grease foil. Place ¼ cup chicken mixture off center on each tortilla; roll up. In 2 batches, place in air fryer, seam side down. Top with half the enchilada sauce; sprinkle with half the remaining Monterey Jack and cheddar cheeses.
**2.** Cook until heated through and cheeses are melted, 10-12 minutes. Repeat with remaining ingredients. Serve with the toppings of your choice.
**2 ENCHILADAS:** 525 cal., 24g fat (12g sat. fat), 86mg chol., 1564mg sod., 43g carb. (3g sugars, 3g fiber), 33g pro.

---

### AIR FRYER COOK TIMES

In our testing, we find cook times vary dramatically between brands of air fryers. As a result, we give wider than normal ranges on suggested cook times. Begin checking at the first time listed and adjust as needed.

## PRESSURE-COOKER
## BALSAMIC PORK TENDERLOIN

This pork tenderloin with a sweet brown sugar and balsamic glaze will become a go-to dinner your whole family will love. It's perfect for busy weeknights, but also special enough for company.
—*Karen Kelly, Germantown, MD*

----------------------------------------

**TAKES:** 30 min. • **MAKES:** 8 servings

¼ cup packed brown sugar
¼ cup plus 2 Tbsp. water, divided
¼ cup balsamic vinegar
1 Tbsp. minced fresh rosemary
3 garlic cloves, minced
1 Tbsp. soy sauce
2 pork tenderloins (1 lb. each), halved widthwise
1 Tbsp. olive oil
1 Tbsp. cornstarch

**1.** In a small bowl, whisk brown sugar, ¼ cup water, vinegar, rosemary, garlic and soy sauce; set aside.
**2.** Select saute or browning setting on a 6-qt. electric pressure cooker. Adjust for medium heat; add oil. When oil is hot, brown the pork in batches. Press cancel. Return all pork and the vinegar mixture to pressure cooker.
**3.** Lock lid; close pressure-release valve. Adjust to pressure-cook on high for 20 minutes. Let pressure release naturally. Remove pork to a serving platter. In a small bowl, whisk cornstarch and remaining 2 Tbsp. water until smooth; stir into pressure cooker. Select saute setting and adjust for low heat. Simmer, stirring constantly, until thickened, 3-5 minutes. Drizzle over pork. If desired, sprinkle with additional rosemary.
**1 SERVING:** 188 cal., 6g fat (2g sat. fat), 64mg chol., 162mg sod., 10g carb. (9g sugars, 0 fiber), 23g pro.

**TIP**

To make this gluten-free, substitute tamari for soy sauce.

## PRESSURE-COOKER
## SPICY LIME CHICKEN

This tender chicken with light lime flavor is a natural filling for tacos, but my son Austin also loves it spooned over cooked rice and sprinkled with his favorite taco toppings.
—*Christine Hair, Odessa, FL*

----------------------------------------

**TAKES:** 20 min. • **MAKES:** 6 servings

4 boneless skinless chicken breast halves (6 oz. each)
2 cups chicken broth
3 Tbsp. lime juice
1 Tbsp. chili powder
1 tsp. grated lime zest
Fresh cilantro leaves, optional

**1.** Place chicken in a 6-qt. electric pressure cooker. Combine broth, lime juice and chili powder; pour over chicken. Lock lid; close pressure-release valve. Adjust to pressure-cook on high for 6 minutes.
**2.** Quick-release pressure. A thermometer inserted in chicken should read at least 165°.
**3.** Remove chicken. When cool enough to handle, shred meat with 2 forks; return to pressure cooker. Stir in lime zest. If desired, serve with cilantro.
**FREEZE OPTION:** Freeze cooled meat mixture in freezer containers. To use, partially thaw in refrigerator overnight. Microwave, covered, on high until heated through, stirring occasionally; add a little broth if necessary.
**1 SERVING:** 132 cal., 3g fat (1g sat. fat), 64mg chol., 420mg sod., 2g carb. (1g sugars, 1g fiber), 23g pro. **DIABETIC EXCHANGES:** 3 lean meat.

## AIR-FRYER APPLE DANISH

I came up with this quick and tasty treat when my daughter had a sleepover. I whipped these together in no time, and the girls devoured them!
—*Jennifer Stowell, Deep River, IA*

- - - - - - - - - - - - - - - - - - - - - - - - - - - - - - - - - - - - - - - - -

**PREP:** 20 min. • **COOK:** 10 min./batch • **MAKES:** 8 servings

- 1 tube (8 oz.) refrigerated crescent rolls
- ½ cup chunky applesauce
- 4 tsp. apple cider or juice, divided
- 1½ tsp. sugar
- ½ tsp. ground cinnamon
- ½ cup confectioners' sugar

**1.** Preheat air fryer to 300°. Unroll crescent dough; separate into 8 triangles. Place 1 Tbsp. applesauce at the wide end of each triangle; carefully roll up. Brush tops with 2 tsp. cider. Combine sugar and cinnamon; sprinkle over rolls.
**2.** In batches, arrange rolls, point side down, in a single layer in greased air fryer. Curve to form crescents. Cook until golden brown, 7-9 minutes. Cool slightly. Combine confectioners' sugar and remaining 2 tsp. cider; drizzle over rolls. Serve warm.
**1 DANISH:** 146 cal., 5g fat (2g sat. fat), 0 chol., 213mg sod., 24g carb. (14g sugars, 0 fiber), 2g pro.

> **REVIEW**
> *"What a great recipe! Our grandkids recently spent the weekend with us and I thought this would be fun to make with them. They loved rolling up the little triangles and sprinkling on the cinnamon sugar!"*
> **—SGRONHOLZ, TASTEOFHOME.COM**

## PRESSURE-COOKER STEAMED MUSSELS WITH PEPPERS

Here's a worthy way to use your one-pot cooker. Serve French bread along with the mussels to soak up the deliciously seasoned broth. If you like your food spicy, add the jalapeno's seeds.
—*Taste of Home Test Kitchen*

- - - - - - - - - - - - - - - - - - - - - - - - - - - - - - - - - - - - - - - - -

**PREP:** 30 min. • **COOK:** 5 min. • **MAKES:** 4 servings

- 2 lbs. fresh mussels, scrubbed and beards removed
- 2 Tbsp. olive oil
- 1 jalapeno pepper, seeded and chopped
- 3 garlic cloves, minced
- 1 bottle (8 oz.) clam juice
- ½ cup white wine or additional clam juice
- ⅓ cup chopped sweet red pepper
- 3 green onions, sliced
- ½ tsp. dried oregano
- 1 bay leaf
- 2 Tbsp. minced fresh parsley
- ¼ tsp. salt
- ¼ tsp. pepper
  French bread baguette, sliced, optional

**1.** Tap mussels; discard any that do not close. Select saute setting on a 6-qt. electric pressure cooker. Adjust for medium heat; add oil. When oil is hot, cook and stir jalapeno until crisp-tender, 2-3 minutes. Add garlic; cook 1 minute longer. Press cancel. Stir in mussels, clam juice, wine, red pepper, green onions, oregano and bay leaf. Lock lid; close pressure-release valve. Adjust to pressure-cook on high 2 minutes. Quick-release pressure.
**2.** Discard bay leaf and any unopened mussels. Sprinkle with parsley, salt and pepper. If desired, serve with baguette slices.
**NOTE:** Wear disposable gloves when cutting hot peppers; the oils can burn skin. Avoid touching your face.
**12 MUSSELS:** 293 cal., 12g fat (2g sat. fat), 65mg chol., 931mg sod., 12g carb. (1g sugars, 1g fiber), 28g pro.

# AIR-FRYER FISH TACOS

These crispy tacos are good enough to challenge the best food truck. I love that the fish is deliciously guilt-free because it's air-fried instead of deep-fried.
—Lena Lim, Seattle, WA

---------------------------------------

**PREP:** 30 min. • **COOK:** 10 min./batch
**MAKES:** 8 servings

| | |
|---|---|
| ¾ | cup reduced-fat sour cream |
| 1 | can (4 oz.) chopped green chiles |
| 1 | Tbsp. fresh cilantro leaves |
| 1 | Tbsp. lime juice |
| 4 | tilapia fillets (4 oz. each) |
| ½ | cup all-purpose flour |
| 1 | large egg white, beaten |
| ½ | cup panko bread crumbs |
| | Cooking spray |
| ½ | tsp. salt |
| ½ | tsp. each white pepper, cayenne pepper and paprika |
| 8 | corn tortillas (6 in.), warmed |
| 1 | large tomato, finely chopped |

**1.** Place sour cream, chiles, cilantro and lime juice in a food processor; cover and process until blended. Set aside.
**2.** Cut each tilapia fillet lengthwise into 2 portions. Place the flour, egg white and bread crumbs in separate shallow bowls. Dip tilapia in flour, then egg white, then crumbs.
**3.** Preheat air fryer to 400°. In batches, arrange fillets in a single layer on greased tray in air-fryer basket; spritz with cooking spray. Cook until fish flakes easily with a fork, 10-12 minutes, turning once.
**4.** Combine seasonings; sprinkle over fish. Place a portion of fish on each tortilla; top with about 2 Tbsp. sour cream mixture. Sprinkle with tomato. If desired, top with additional cilantro.
**1 TACO:** 178 cal., 3g fat (1g sat. fat), 30mg chol., 269mg sod., 22g carb. (2g sugars, 2g fiber), 16g pro. **DIABETIC EXCHANGES:** 2 lean meat, 1½ starch, ½ fat.

**TIPS**
- A mild whitefish like tilapia works best for fish tacos. Other options include snapper, mahi mahi, grouper, flounder, halibut or cod.
- The USDA recommends cooking fish to 145°F (62.8°C). Visually, the fish should be opaque and the flesh should flake easily.

## PRESSURE-COOKER AUTUMN APPLE CHICKEN

Fill the whole house with the aroma of chicken with apples and barbecue sauce. This is a meal you won't want to wait to dig into.
—Caitlyn Hauser, Brookline, NH

PREP: 25 min. • COOK: 20 min. • MAKES: 4 servings

- 4  bone-in chicken thighs (about 1½ lbs.), skin removed
- ¼  tsp. salt
- ¼  tsp. pepper
- 1  Tbsp. canola oil
- ½  cup apple cider or juice
- 1  medium onion, chopped
- ⅓  cup barbecue sauce
- 1  Tbsp. honey
- 1  garlic clove, minced
- 2  medium Fuji or Gala apples, coarsely chopped

1. Sprinkle chicken with salt and pepper. Select saute or browning setting on a 6-qt. electric pressure cooker. Adjust for medium heat; add oil. When oil is hot, brown chicken; remove and keep warm.
2. Add cider, stirring to loosen browned bits from pan. Stir in onion, barbecue sauce, honey, garlic and chicken. Press cancel. Lock lid; close pressure-release valve. Adjust to pressure-cook on high for 10 minutes. Let pressure release naturally for 5 minutes; quick-release any remaining pressure. Press cancel. A thermometer inserted in chicken should read at least 170°.
3. Remove chicken; keep warm. Select saute setting and adjust for low heat. Add apples; simmer, stirring constantly, until apples are tender, about 10 minutes. Serve with chicken.

**1 CHICKEN THIGH WITH ½ CUP APPLE MIXTURE:** 340 cal., 13g fat (3g sat. fat), 87mg chol., 458mg sod., 31g carb. (24g sugars, 3g fiber), 25g pro. **DIABETIC EXCHANGES:** 4 lean meat, 1½ starch, ½ fruit.

## PRESSURE-COOKER LAVA CAKE

Because I love chocolate, this decadent cake has long been a family favorite. It's even great cold the next day—assuming you have any leftovers!
—Elizabeth Farrell, Hamilton, MT

PREP: 15 min. • COOK: 20 min. + standing • MAKES: 8 servings

- 1  cup all-purpose flour
- 1  cup packed brown sugar, divided
- 5  Tbsp. baking cocoa, divided
- 2  tsp. baking powder
- ¼  tsp. salt
- ½  cup 2% milk
- 2  Tbsp. canola oil
- ½  tsp. vanilla extract
- ⅛  tsp. ground cinnamon
- 1¼  cups hot water
   Optional: Fresh raspberries and vanilla ice cream

1. In a large bowl, whisk flour, ½ cup brown sugar, 3 Tbsp. cocoa, baking powder and salt. In another bowl, whisk milk, oil and vanilla until blended. Add to flour mixture; stir just until moistened.
2. Spread into a 1½-qt. baking dish coated with cooking spray. In a small bowl, mix cinnamon and remaining ½ cup brown sugar and 2 Tbsp. cocoa; stir in hot water. Pour over batter (do not stir).
3. Place trivet insert and 1 cup water in a 6-qt. electric pressure cooker. Cover baking dish with foil. Fold an 18x12-in. piece of foil lengthwise into thirds, making a sling. Use the sling to lower the dish onto the trivet. Lock lid; close pressure-release valve. Adjust to pressure-cook on high for 20 minutes. Quick-release pressure.
4. Using foil sling, carefully remove baking dish. Let stand for 15 minutes. A toothpick inserted in cake portion should come out clean. If desired, serve with raspberries and ice cream.

**1 SERVING:** 208 cal., 4g fat (0 sat. fat), 0 chol., 208mg sod., 42g carb. (28g sugars, 1g fiber), 3g pro.

## PRESSURE-COOKER CRANBERRY STUFFED APPLES

Cinnamon, nutmeg and walnuts add a homey autumn flavor to these stuffed apples. What a lovely old-fashioned treat!
—*Grace Sandvigen, Rochester, NY*

- - - - - - - - - - - - - - - - - - - - - - - - - - - - - - - - - - - - - - - - - -

**TAKES:** 15 min. • **MAKES:** 5 servings

- 5 medium apples
- ⅓ cup fresh or frozen cranberries, thawed and chopped
- ¼ cup packed brown sugar
- 2 Tbsp. chopped walnuts
- ¼ tsp. ground cinnamon
- ⅛ tsp. ground nutmeg
  Optional: Whipped cream or vanilla ice cream

**1.** Core apples, leaving bottoms intact. Peel top third of each apple. Place trivet insert and 1 cup water in a 6-qt. electric pressure cooker. Combine cranberries, brown sugar, walnuts, cinnamon and nutmeg; spoon into apples. Place apples on trivet.
**2.** Lock lid; close pressure-release valve. Adjust to pressure-cook on high for 3 minutes. Quick-release pressure. If desired, serve with whipped cream or ice cream.

**1 STUFFED APPLE:** 142 cal., 2g fat (0 sat. fat), 0 chol., 5mg sod., 33g carb. (27g sugars, 4g fiber), 1g pro. **DIABETIC EXCHANGES:** 1 starch, 1 fruit.

## AIR-FRYER SPINACH FETA TURNOVERS

These quick and easy turnovers are one of my wife's favorite entrees. The refrigerated pizza dough makes preparation a snap!
—*David Baruch, Weston, FL*

- - - - - - - - - - - - - - - - - - - - - - - - - - - - - - - - - - - - - - - - - -

**TAKES:** 30 min. • **MAKES:** 4 servings

- 2 large eggs
- 1 pkg. (10 oz.) frozen spinach, thawed, squeezed dry and chopped
- ¾ cup crumbled feta cheese
- 2 garlic cloves, minced
- ¼ tsp. pepper
- 1 tube (13.8 oz.) refrigerated pizza crust
  Refrigerated tzatziki sauce, optional

**1.** Preheat air fryer to 425°. In a bowl, whisk eggs; set aside 1 Tbsp. of eggs. Combine the spinach, feta cheese, garlic, pepper and remaining beaten eggs.
**2.** Unroll pizza crust; roll into a 12-in. square. Cut into four 6-in. squares. Top each square with about ⅓ cup spinach mixture. Fold into a triangle and pinch edges to seal. Cut slits in top; brush with reserved egg.
**3.** In batches if necessary, place triangles in a single layer on greased tray in air-fryer basket. Cook until golden brown, 10-12 minutes. If desired, serve with tzatziki sauce.

**1 TURNOVER:** 361 cal., 9g fat (4g sat. fat), 104mg chol., 936mg sod., 51g carb. (7g sugars, 4g fiber), 17g pro.

## PRESSURE-COOKER PINEAPPLE CHICKEN

We love Hawaiian-style chicken in a slow cooker, but sometimes we need something that comes together fast! We tweaked our favorite recipe to work in a pressure cooker for a quick and easy weeknight dinner. Add a side salad for a complete meal.
—*Courtney Stultz, Weir, KS*

- - - - - - - - - - - - - - - - - - - - - - - - - - - - - - - - - - - - - - - - - -

**PREP:** 10 min. • **COOK:** 20 min. + releasing • **MAKES:** 6 servings

| | |
|---|---|
| 1½ | lbs. boneless skinless chicken breasts |
| 1 | can (20 oz.) unsweetened pineapple chunks, undrained |
| ¼ | cup barbecue sauce |
| 1 | cup chicken broth |
| 1 | cup uncooked long grain brown rice |
| ½ | tsp. salt |
| | Optional: Minced fresh cilantro and sliced green onions |

**1.** Combine the first 6 ingredients in a 6-qt. electric pressure cooker. Lock lid; close pressure-release valve. Adjust to pressure-cook on high for 20 minutes.

**2.** Let pressure release naturally. Remove chicken to a cutting board and shred with 2 forks. Add shredded chicken back to pot and stir until combined. If desired, sprinkle with cilantro and green onions.

**1 CUP:** 313 cal., 4g fat (1g sat. fat), 63mg chol., 536mg sod., 41g carb. (16g sugars, 3g fiber), 27g pro. **DIABETIC EXCHANGES:** 3 lean meat, 2½ starch.

> **REVIEW**
> "The flavor was great, and the leftovers were even better the next day."
> —SHANNONDOBOS126, TASTEOFHOME.COM

## AIR-FRYER PARMESAN BREADED SQUASH

This yellow squash is beautifully crisp. You don't have to turn the pieces, but do keep an eye on them. If you don't have an air fryer, you can make this recipe in the oven.
—*Debi Mitchell, Flower Mound, TX*

- - - - - - - - - - - - - - - - - - - - - - - - - - - - - - - - - - - - - - - - - -

**PREP:** 15 min. • **COOK:** 10 min./batch • **MAKES:** 4 servings

| | |
|---|---|
| 4 | cups thinly sliced yellow summer squash (3 medium) |
| 3 | Tbsp. olive oil |
| ½ | tsp. salt |
| ½ | tsp. pepper |
| ⅛ | tsp. cayenne pepper |
| ¾ | cup panko bread crumbs |
| ¾ | cup grated Parmesan cheese |

**1.** Preheat air fryer to 350°. Place squash in a large bowl. Add oil and seasonings; toss to coat.

**2.** In a shallow bowl, mix bread crumbs and cheese. Dip squash in crumb mixture to coat both sides, patting to help coating adhere. In batches, arrange squash in a single layer on tray in air-fryer basket. Cook until squash is tender and coating is golden brown, about 10 minutes.

**½ CUP:** 203 cal., 14g fat (3g sat. fat), 11mg chol., 554mg sod., 13g carb. (4g sugars, 2g fiber), 6g pro. **DIABETIC EXCHANGES:** 3 fat, 1 vegetable, ½ starch.

# PRESSURE-COOKER MEAT LOAF

I used to make this recipe a lot when my kids were growing up and I was working. It's easy to make and a family favorite. You can make several loaves ahead and freeze them. Thaw a loaf in the refrigerator overnight, and it's ready to cook.
—Kallee Krong-McCreery, Escondido, CA

**PREP:** 15 min. + standing
**COOK:** 45 min. + releasing
**MAKES:** 8 servings

- 1 cup soft bread crumbs
- 2 large eggs, lightly beaten
- ⅓ cup 2% milk
- ¼ cup finely chopped onion
- 2 Tbsp. ketchup
- 1 tsp. seasoned salt
- 1 tsp. dried parsley flakes
- 1½ lbs. lean ground beef (90% lean)
- 1 lb. bulk pork sausage
- ¼ cup barbecue sauce

1. In a large bowl, combine the first 7 ingredients. Add beef and pork; mix lightly but thoroughly. On a 12x8 piece of foil, shape into a 8x5-in. loaf. Bring foil up around sides of loaf, but do not cover top of loaf.
2. Place trivet insert and 1 cup water in a 6-qt. electric pressure cooker. Place foil-wrapped loaf on trivet. Lock lid; close pressure-release valve. Adjust to pressure-cook on high for 45 minutes.
3. Let pressure release naturally for 10 minutes; quick-release any remaining pressure. A thermometer inserted in meat loaf should read at least 160°. Remove meat loaf from pressure cooker and top with barbecue sauce. Let stand 10 minutes before removing from foil and slicing.
**1 PIECE:** 315 cal., 21g fat (7g sat. fat), 131mg chol., 678mg sod., 6g carb. (2g sugars, 0 fiber), 25g pro.

> **TIP**
> Because this recipe cooks the ground beef quickly, it's best to work with a higher-fat blend of beef. This will keep your meat loaf from drying out. Ask your butcher for a 60/40 or 70/30 blend (this is the ratio of lean meat to fat).

# PRESSURE-COOKER SMOKED SAUSAGE & WHITE BEANS

My husband grew up in the South, where sausage and beans were on the menu weekly. I quickly became a fan. The pressure cooker eliminates the lengthy process of soaking the beans overnight and then slow-cooking them. Serve the dish over white rice and use crusty bread to soak up the broth. I used gourmet smoked sausage flavored with Gouda and pear for this dish, but you can use any smoked sausage you like.
—Debbie Glasscock, Conway, AR

**PREP:** 20 min. • **COOK:** 25 min.
**MAKES:** 8 servings

- 10 cups water
- 1 lb. dried great northern beans
- 1 lb. smoked sausage, sliced
- 1 smoked ham hock (about ½ lb.)
- 1 large onion, chopped
- 5 garlic cloves, minced
- 1 tsp. kosher salt
- 1 tsp. sugar
- 1 tsp. each dried parsley flakes, oregano and basil
- ¼ tsp. pepper
  Hot cooked rice and minced fresh parsley
  Sriracha chili sauce, optional

1. Place water, beans, sausage, ham hock, onion, garlic, salt, sugar and seasonings in a 6-qt. electric pressure cooker. Lock lid; close pressure-release valve. Adjust to pressure-cook on high for 22 minutes.
2. Quick-release pressure. Remove ham hock. Serve bean mixture with rice, parsley and desired amount of cooking liquid. If desired, serve with chili sauce.
**1¼ CUPS BEAN MIXTURE:** 382 cal., 16g fat (7g sat. fat), 38mg chol., 909mg sod., 40g carb. (4g sugars, 12g fiber), 21g pro.

# - EASY BOILED EGGS -

Eat them straight, or use them in salads, sandwiches and many more recipes. Modern gadgets make it a snap to always have some boiled eggs ready and waiting in the fridge!

**For air fryer:**
Preheat air fryer to 275°. Place eggs in a single layer on tray in air fryer. Cook 15 minutes. Remove eggs; rinse in cold water and then place in ice water until completely cooled. Drain and refrigerate.

**For pressure cooker:**
Pressure-cook the eggs on high for 5 minutes, wait 5 minutes before releasing pressure and then plunge the eggs into an ice water bath for 5 minutes. For extra large or jumbo eggs, increase the cooking time to 7 or 8 minutes, respectively.

## PRESSURE-COOKER GERMAN GOULASH

Goulash reminds me of living in Germany when my father was in the Army there. We had a German friend who didn't speak English, but she would always bring us her traditional dishes to try, and this was one of my favorites. I'm sure she cooked it in the oven or on top of the stove for hours, but having a pressure cooker speeds up the time so it's ready in less than an hour.
—*Johnna Johnson, Scottsdale, AZ*

- - - - - - - - - - - - - - - - - - - - - - - - - - - - - - - - - - - - - - - - -

**PREP:** 20 min. • **COOK:** 25 min. + releasing • **MAKES:** 8 servings

- 3  Tbsp. olive oil
- 1  boneless beef chuck roast (2½ lbs.), cut into 2-in. cubes
- 4  small onions, thinly sliced
- 1  cup beer or beef broth
- ½  cup dry red wine or beef broth
- 3  Tbsp. tomato paste
- 2  Tbsp. sweet Hungarian paprika
- 1  Tbsp. beef base
- 1  tsp. caraway seeds
- 1  tsp. dried marjoram
- ½  tsp. salt
- ¼  tsp. pepper
- 2  bay leaves
   Hot cooked pasta

**1.** Select saute or browning setting on a 6-qt. electric pressure cooker. Adjust for medium heat; add oil. When oil is hot, brown meat in batches. Remove and keep warm. Cook onions in drippings until tender, 4-5 minutes. Press cancel. Combine the next 10 ingredients; add to cooker. Return beef to cooker.
**2.** Lock lid; close pressure-release valve. Adjust to pressure-cook on high for 25 minutes. Let pressure release naturally for 10 minutes; quick-release any remaining pressure.
**3.** Select saute setting and adjust for medium heat; bring liquid to a boil. Cook until sauce reaches desired thickness, about 20 minutes. Remove bay leaves. Serve with pasta.
**FREEZE OPTION:** Freeze cooled meat mixture in freezer containers. To use, partially thaw in refrigerator overnight. Heat through in a saucepan, stirring occasionally; add broth if necessary.
**¾ CUP:** 326 cal., 19g fat (6g sat. fat), 92mg chol., 468mg sod., 7g carb. (3g sugars, 2g fiber), 29g pro.

## AIR-FRYER BLACK BEAN CHIMICHANGAS

These chimichangas get a little love from the air fryer, so they're healthier than their deep-fried counterparts. Black beans provide protein, and the recipe is a smart way to use up leftover rice.
—*Kimberly Hammond, Kingwood, TX*

- - - - - - - - - - - - - - - - - - - - - - - - - - - - - - - - - - - - - - - - -

**PREP:** 20 min. • **COOK:** 5 min./batch • **MAKES:** 6 servings

- 2  cans (15 oz. each) black beans, rinsed and drained
- 1  pkg. (8.8 oz.) ready-to-serve brown rice
- ⅔  cup frozen corn
- ⅔  cup minced fresh cilantro
- ⅔  cup chopped green onions
- ½  tsp. salt
- 6  whole wheat tortillas (8 in.), warmed if necessary
- 4  tsp. olive oil
   Optional: Guacamole and salsa

**1.** Preheat air fryer to 400°. In a large microwave-safe bowl, mix beans, rice and corn; microwave, covered, until heated through, 4-5 minutes, stirring halfway. Stir in cilantro, green onions and salt.
**2.** To assemble, spoon ¾ cup bean mixture across the center of each tortilla. Fold bottom and sides of tortilla over filling and roll up. Brush with olive oil.
**3.** In batches, place chimichangas seam side down on greased tray in air-fryer basket. Cook until golden brown and crispy, 2-3 minutes. If desired, serve with guacamole and salsa.
**1 CHIMICHANGA:** 337 cal., 5g fat (0 sat. fat), 0 chol., 602mg sod., 58g carb. (2g sugars, 10g fiber), 13g pro.

## AIR-FRYER BUFFALO CHICKEN WINGS

Cayenne, red sauce and spices keep these tangy wings good and hot, just like the originals. And the air fryer keeps them healthier than a fried version.
—*Nancy Chapman, Center Harbor, NH*

- - - - - - - - - - - - - - - - - - - - - - - - - - - - - - - - - - - - - - -

**PREP:** 10 min. • **COOK:** 25 min./batch • **MAKES:** about 4 dozen

- 25  whole chicken wings (about 5 lbs.)
- 1  cup butter, cubed
- ¼  cup Louisiana-style hot sauce
- ¾  tsp. cayenne pepper
- ¾  tsp. celery salt
- ½  tsp. onion powder
- ½  tsp. garlic powder
     Optional: Celery ribs, crumbled blue cheese and ranch salad dressing

**1.** Preheat air fryer to 300°. Cut chicken wings into 3 sections; discard wing tip sections. In batches, arrange wings in a single layer on greased tray in air-fryer basket. Cook 10 minutes. Increase temperature to 400°; cook until chicken juices run clear and wings are golden brown, 15-20 minutes longer.
**2.** Meanwhile, in a small saucepan, melt butter. Stir in hot sauce and spices. Place chicken in a large bowl; add sauce and toss to coat. Remove to a serving plate with a slotted spoon. Serve with celery, crumbled blue cheese and ranch dressing if desired.
**1 PIECE:** 83 cal., 7g fat (3g sat. fat), 24mg chol., 106mg sod., 0 carb. (0 sugars, 0 fiber), 5g pro.

**TIPS**

- With air fryers you want the least amount of moisture possible, so be sure to pat your chicken dry before cooking. The drier the skin, the crispier and more delicious it will be once cooked.
- While many air fryers have nonstick cooking baskets and trays, some recipes (like these wings) benefit from added grease. A light coating of cooking spray gives an added layer of protection. Be sure to check with your air fryer's manual—some recommend avoiding nonstick sprays.

## PRESSURE-COOKER CLAM SAUCE

I serve this bright and fresh clam sauce often, usually with pasta. But it's also delectable as a hot dip for special get-togethers.
—*Frances Pietsch, Flower Mound, TX*

- - - - - - - - - - - - - - - - - - - - - - - - - - - - - - - - - - - - - - -

**TAKES:** 15 min. • **MAKES:** 4 cups

- 4  Tbsp. butter
- 2  Tbsp. olive oil
- ½  cup finely chopped onion
- 8  oz. fresh mushrooms, chopped
- 2  garlic cloves, minced
- 2  cans (10 oz. each) whole baby clams
- ½  cup water
- ¼  cup sherry
- 2  tsp. lemon juice
- 1  bay leaf
- ¾  tsp. dried oregano
- ½  tsp. garlic salt
- ¼  tsp. white pepper
- ¼  tsp. Italian seasoning
- ¼  tsp. pepper
- 2  Tbsp. chopped fresh parsley
     Hot cooked pasta
     Grated Parmesan cheese, optional

**1.** Select saute setting on a 6-qt. electric pressure cooker. Adjust for medium heat; add butter and oil. When hot, add onion; cook and stir 2 minutes. Add mushrooms and garlic; cook 1 minute longer. Press cancel.
**2.** Drain clams, reserving liquid; coarsely chop. Add clams, reserved clam juice and the next 9 ingredients to pressure cooker. Lock lid; close pressure-release valve. Adjust to pressure-cook on high 2 minutes. Quick-release pressure.
**3.** Discard bay leaf; stir in parsley. Serve with pasta. If desired, serve with grated Parmesan cheese and additional lemon juice and parsley.
**½ CUP:** 138 cal., 10g fat (4g sat. fat), 40mg chol., 580mg sod., 5g carb. (1g sugars, 0 fiber), 7g pro.

## AIR-FRYER ROSEMARY-LEMON CHICKEN THIGHS

These chicken thighs always remind me of Sunday dinner. The lemon-and-herb butter really makes the chicken flavorful and juicy! If you don't have an air fryer, the chicken can be baked in the oven at 400° for about 45 minutes.
—*Alyssa Lang, North Scituate, RI*

- - - - - - - - - - - - - - - - - - - - - - - - - - - - - - - - - - - - - - - - - - -

**PREP:** 10 min. • **COOK:** 25 min. • **MAKES:** 4 servings

- ¼ cup butter, softened
- 3 garlic cloves, minced
- 2 tsp. minced fresh rosemary or ½ tsp. dried rosemary, crushed
- 1 tsp. minced fresh thyme or ¼ tsp. dried thyme
- 1 tsp. grated lemon zest
- 1 Tbsp. lemon juice
- 4 bone-in chicken thighs (about 1½ lbs.)
- ⅛ tsp. salt
- ⅛ tsp. pepper

**1.** Preheat air fryer to 400°. In a small bowl, combine butter, garlic, rosemary, thyme, lemon zest and lemon juice. Spread 1 tsp. butter mixture under the skin of each chicken thigh. Spread remaining butter over the skin of each thigh. Sprinkle with salt and pepper.
**2.** Place chicken, skin side up, on greased tray in air-fryer basket. Cook for 20 minutes, turning once. Turn chicken again (skin side up) and cook until a thermometer reads 170°-175°, about 5 minutes longer.
**1 CHICKEN THIGH:** 329 cal., 26g fat (11g sat. fat), 111mg chol., 234mg sod., 1g carb. (0 sugars, 0 fiber), 23g pro.

## AIR-FRYER PRETZEL-CRUSTED CATFISH

I love the flavor of this catfish recipe. I'm not a big fish lover, so any concoction that has me loving fish is a keeper in my book. It's wonderful served with classic southern sides like corn muffins, greens, herbed rice pilaf or macaroni and cheese.
—*Kelly Williams, Forked River, NJ*

- - - - - - - - - - - - - - - - - - - - - - - - - - - - - - - - - - - - - - - - - - -

**PREP:** 15 min. • **COOK:** 10 min./batch • **MAKES:** 4 servings

- 4 catfish fillets (6 oz. each)
- ½ tsp. salt
- ½ tsp. pepper
- 2 large eggs
- ⅓ cup Dijon mustard
- 2 Tbsp. 2% milk
- ½ cup all-purpose flour
- 4 cups honey mustard miniature pretzels, coarsely crushed
  Cooking spray
  Lemon slices, optional

**1.** Preheat air fryer to 325°. Sprinkle catfish with salt and pepper. Whisk eggs, mustard and milk in a shallow bowl. Place flour and pretzels in separate shallow bowls. Coat fillets with flour, then dip in egg mixture and coat with crushed pretzels.
**2.** In batches, place fillets in a single layer on greased tray in air-fryer basket; spritz with cooking spray. Cook until the fish flakes easily with a fork, 10-12 minutes. If desired, serve with lemon slices.
**1 FILLET:** 466 cal., 14g fat (3g sat. fat), 164mg chol., 1580mg sod., 45g carb. (2g sugars, 2g fiber), 33g pro.

**TIP** If you don't have an air fryer, you can make this recipe in a deep fryer, an electric skillet or on the stovetop.

## AIR-FRYER STEAK FAJITAS

Zesty salsa and tender strips of steak make these traditional fajitas extra special.
—*Rebecca Baird, Salt Lake City, UT*

- - - - - - - - - - - - - - - - - - - - - - - - - - - - - - - - - - -

**TAKES:** 30 min. • **MAKES:** 6 servings

2   large tomatoes, seeded and chopped
½   cup diced red onion
¼   cup lime juice
1   pepper, seeded and minced
3   Tbsp. minced fresh cilantro
2   tsp. ground cumin, divided
¾   tsp. salt, divided
1   beef flank steak (about 1½ lbs.)
1   large onion, halved and sliced
6   whole wheat tortillas (8 in.), warmed
     Optional: Sliced avocado and lime wedges

**1.** For salsa, place first 5 ingredients in a small bowl; stir in 1 tsp. cumin and ¼ tsp. salt. Let stand until serving.
**2.** Preheat air fryer to 400°. Sprinkle steak with the remaining 1 tsp. cumin and ½ tsp. salt. Place on greased tray in air-fryer basket. Cook until meat reaches desired doneness (for medium-rare, a thermometer should read 135°; medium, 140°; medium-well, 145°), 6-8 minutes per side. Remove from basket and let stand 5 minutes.
**3.** Meanwhile, place onion on tray in air-fryer basket. Cook until crisp-tender, 2-3 minutes, stirring once. Slice steak thinly across the grain; serve in tortillas with onion and salsa. If desired, serve with avocado and lime wedges.
**1 FAJITA:** 309 cal., 9g fat (4g sat. fat), 54mg chol., 498mg sod., 29g carb. (3g sugars, 5g fiber), 27g pro. **DIABETIC EXCHANGES:** 4 lean meat, 2 starch.

## PRESSURE-COOKER SALSA LONDON BROIL

I love using my pressure cooker for this recipe because it comes together so quickly but still has that long, slow-cooked flavor. The veggies semi-melt into the sauce to give it an added savory taste and the lime gives it a pleasant finish.
—*Ann Sheehy, Lawrence, MA*

- - - - - - - - - - - - - - - - - - - - - - - - - - - - - - - - - - -

**TAKES:** 25 min. • **MAKES:** 4 servings

1   to 1½ lbs. beef top round steak
1   jar (16 oz.) salsa
1   medium sweet potato, peeled and chopped
1   large carrot, thinly sliced
1   garlic clove, minced
     Lime wedges
     Chopped fresh cilantro, optional

**1.** Cut steak into thirds; place in a 6-qt. electric pressure cooker. Add the salsa, sweet potato, carrot and garlic. Lock lid; close pressure-release valve. Adjust to pressure-cook on high for 10 minutes. Let pressure release naturally.
**2.** Slice roast. Serve with vegetables. Garnish with lime wedges and, if desired, chopped cilantro.
**1 SERVING:** 239 cal., 4g fat (1g sat. fat), 63mg chol., 503mg sod., 23g carb. (10g sugars, 2g fiber), 27g pro. **DIABETIC EXCHANGES:** 4 lean meat, 1½ starch.

TIP

To make in a stovetop pressure cooker, close cover according to manufacturer's directions; place pressure regulator on vent pipe. Bring cooker to full pressure over high heat. Reduce to medium-high; cook 10 minutes. (Regulator should maintain a slow steady rocking motion or release of steam; adjust heat if needed.) Remove from heat. Allow pressure to drop on its own.

# AIR-FRYER NACHO DOGS

Adults and kids alike will love these yummy Southwest-inspired hot dogs. This dish is not only budget-friendly, but it's hot, cheesy and delicious too.

—Joan Hallford, North Richland Hills, TX

------------------------------------------

**PREP:** 20 min. • **COOK:** 15 min.
**MAKES:** 6 servings

- 6 hot dogs
- 3 cheddar cheese sticks, halved lengthwise
- 1¼ cups self-rising flour
- 1 cup plain Greek yogurt
- ¼ cup salsa
- ¼ tsp. chili powder
- 3 Tbsp. chopped seeded jalapeno pepper
- 1 cup crushed nacho-flavored tortilla chips, divided
  Optional: Guacamole and sour cream

**1.** Cut a slit down the length of each hot dog without cutting through; insert a halved cheese stick into the slit. Set aside.
**2.** Preheat air fryer to 350°. In a large bowl, stir together flour, yogurt, salsa, chili powder, jalapenos and ¼ cup crushed tortilla chips to form a soft dough. Place dough on a lightly floured surface; divide into 6 pieces. Roll a piece of dough into a 15-in. long strip and wrap it in a spiral around a cheese-stuffed hot dog. Repeat with remaining dough and hot dogs. Spray wrapped dogs with cooking spray and gently roll in remaining crushed chips. Spray air fryer basket with cooking spray; place dogs in basket not touching each other, leaving room to expand.
**3.** In batches, cook until the dough is slightly browned and the cheese starts to melt, 8-10 minutes. If desired, serve with additional salsa, guacamole and sour cream.

**NOTE:** Wear disposable gloves when cutting hot peppers; the oils can burn skin. Avoid touching your face.

**1 NACHO DOG:** 216 cal., 9g fat (5g sat. fat), 23mg chol., 513mg sod., 26g carb. (3g sugars, 1g fiber), 9g pro.

# PRESSURE-COOKER RED BEANS & RICE

My family loves New Orleans–style cooking, so I make this dish often. I appreciate how simple it is, and the smoky ham flavor is scrumptious.
—*Celinda Dahlgren, Napa, CA*

**PREP:** 20 min. • **COOK:** 45 min. • **MAKES:** 6 servings

- 3 cups water
- 2 smoked ham hocks (about 1 lb.)
- 1 cup dried red beans
- 1 medium onion, chopped
- 1½ tsp. minced garlic
- 1 tsp. ground cumin
- 1 medium tomato, chopped
- 1 medium green pepper, chopped
- 1 tsp. salt
- 4 cups hot cooked rice

**1.** Place the first 6 ingredients in a 6-qt. electric pressure cooker. Lock lid; close pressure-release valve. Adjust to pressure-cook on high for 35 minutes. Let pressure release naturally.

**2.** Remove ham hocks; cool slightly. Remove meat from bones. Finely chop meat and return to pressure cooker; discard bones. Stir in tomato, green pepper and salt. Select saute setting and adjust for low heat. Simmer, stirring constantly, until chopped pepper is tender, 8-10 minutes. Serve with rice.

**FREEZE OPTION:** Freeze cooled bean mixture in freezer containers. To use, partially thaw in refrigerator overnight. Microwave, covered, on high in a microwave-safe dish until heated through, gently stirring; add water if necessary.

**⅓ CUP BEAN MIXTURE WITH ⅔ CUP RICE:** 216 cal., 2g fat (0 sat. fat), 9mg chol., 671mg sod., 49g carb. (3g sugars, 12g fiber), 12g pro.

# PRESSURE-COOKER SPICY PORK & SQUASH RAGU

This recipe is a marvelously spicy combo perfect for cooler fall weather—so satisfying after a day spent outdoors.
—*Monica Osterhaus, Paducah, KY*

**PREP:** 20 min. • **COOK:** 15 min. + releasing • **MAKES:** 10 servings

- 2 cans (14½ oz. each) stewed tomatoes, undrained
- 1 pkg. (12 oz.) frozen cooked winter squash, thawed
- 1 large sweet onion, cut into ½-in. pieces
- 1 medium sweet red pepper, cut into ½-in. pieces
- ¾ cup reduced-sodium chicken broth
- 1½ tsp. crushed red pepper flakes
- 2 lbs. boneless country-style pork ribs
- 1 tsp. salt
- ¼ tsp. garlic powder
- ¼ tsp. pepper
  Hot cooked pasta
  Shaved Parmesan cheese, optional

**1.** Combine the first 6 ingredients in a 6-qt. electric pressure cooker. Sprinkle ribs with salt, garlic powder and pepper; place in pressure cooker. Lock lid; close pressure-release valve. Adjust to pressure-cook on high for 15 minutes. Let pressure release naturally for 10 minutes; quick-release any remaining pressure.

**2.** Remove cover; stir to break pork into smaller pieces. Serve with pasta. If desired, top with Parmesan cheese.

**FREEZE OPTION:** Freeze cooled ragu in freezer containers. To use, partially thaw in refrigerator overnight. Heat through in a saucepan, stirring occasionally.

**1 CUP RAGU:** 196 cal., 8g fat (3g sat. fat), 52mg chol., 469mg sod., 13g carb. (6g sugars, 2g fiber), 18g pro. **DIABETIC EXCHANGES:** 2 lean meat, 1 starch.

🕐 5️⃣ 🍎 📋
## AIR-FRYER OKRA WITH SMOKED PAPRIKA

When you want to cook okra without frying it, roast it with lemon juice for a lighter version—you can use an air fryer or a traditional oven. Smoked paprika gives the dish even more roasty oomph.
—*Lee Evans, Queen Creek, AZ*

- - - - - - - - - - - - - - - - - - - - - - - - - - - - - - - - - - - -

**TAKES:** 20 min. • **MAKES:** 4 servings

- 1 lb. fresh okra pods
- 1 Tbsp. olive oil
- 1 Tbsp. lemon juice
- ½ tsp. smoked paprika
- ¼ tsp. salt
- ⅛ tsp. garlic powder
- ⅛ tsp. pepper

Preheat air fryer to 375°. Toss together all ingredients. Place okra on greased tray in air-fryer basket. Cook until tender and lightly browned, 15-20 minutes, stirring occasionally.

**⅔ CUP:** 57 cal., 4g fat (1g sat. fat), 0 chol., 155mg sod., 6g carb. (3g sugars, 3g fiber), 2g pro. **DIABETIC EXCHANGES:** 1 vegetable, 1 fat.

📋
## AIR-FRYER LIME & GIN COCONUT MACAROONS

I took these macaroons to our annual cookie exchange, where we always name a queen. I won the crown!
—*Milissa Kirkpatrick, Palestine, TX*

- - - - - - - - - - - - - - - - - - - - - - - - - - - - - - - - - - - -

**PREP:** 20 min. • **COOK:** 5 min./batch • **MAKES:** about 2½ dozen

- 4 large egg whites, room temperature
- ⅔ cup sugar
- 3 Tbsp. gin
- 1½ tsp. grated lime zest
- ¼ tsp. salt
- ¼ tsp. almond extract
- 1 pkg. (14 oz.) sweetened shredded coconut
- ½ cup all-purpose flour
- 8 oz. white baking chocolate, melted

**1.** Preheat air fryer to 350°. Whisk the first 6 ingredients until blended. In another bowl, toss coconut with flour; stir in the egg white mixture.
**2.** In batches, place by tablespoonfuls 1 in. apart on greased tray in air-fryer basket. Cook until browned, 4-5 minutes. Remove to wire racks to cool.
**3.** Dip bottoms of macaroons into melted chocolate, allowing excess to drip off. Place on waxed paper; let stand until set. Store in an airtight container.

**1 COOKIE:** 133 cal., 7g fat (6g sat. fat), 0 chol., 67mg sod., 17g carb. (15g sugars, 1g fiber), 2g pro.

**TIP**

> If you don't have an air fryer, you can make this recipe in an oven. These are also great dipped in melted dark chocolate!

# AIR-FRYER TURKEY CLUB ROULADES

Weeknights turn elegant when these quick-prep roulades with familiar ingredients are on the menu. Not a fan of turkey? Substitute lightly pounded chicken breasts. You can also make this recipe on the stovetop, if you don't have an air fryer.
—Taste of Home *Test Kitchen*

- - - - - - - - - - - - - - - - - - - - - - - - - - -

**PREP:** 20 min. • **COOK:** 10 min./batch
**MAKES:** 8 servings

- ¾ lb. fresh asparagus, trimmed
- 8 turkey breast cutlets (about 1 lb.)
- 1½ tsp. Dijon mustard
- 1½ tsp. mayonnaise
- 8 slices deli ham
- 8 slices provolone cheese
- ½ tsp. poultry seasoning
- ½ tsp. pepper
- 8 bacon strips

SAUCE
- ⅓ cup Dijon mustard
- ⅓ cup mayonnaise
- 4 tsp. 2% milk
- ¼ tsp. poultry seasoning

**1.** Preheat air fryer to 375°. Place the asparagus on greased tray in air-fryer basket. Cook until crisp-tender, 4-5 minutes, tossing halfway through cooking time. Set aside.
**2.** Mix together 1½ tsp. each mustard and mayonnaise; spread over the turkey cutlets. Layer with ham, cheese and asparagus. Sprinkle with poultry seasoning and pepper. Roll up tightly and wrap with bacon.
**3.** In batches, arrange roulades in a single layer on greased tray in air-fryer basket. Cook until bacon is crisp and turkey is no longer pink, 8-10 minutes, turning occasionally. Combine sauce ingredients; serve with roulades.
**1 ROULADE WITH 1 TBSP. SAUCE:** 224 cal., 11g fat (5g sat. fat), 64mg chol., 1075mg sod., 2g carb. (1g sugars, 0 fiber), 25g pro.

# AIR-FRYER GARLIC & WINE LAMB CHOPS

This recipe is special to me because the flavor reminds me of my mother's lamb roast that cooks all day. It's a special meal that doesn't take much time or effort, so you can have it all year.
—Dorice Winston, Concord, NC

- - - - - - - - - - - - - - - - - - - - - - - - - - -

**PREP:** 15 min. + marinating
**COOK:** 10 min./batch
**MAKES:** 4 servings

- 1 cup dry white wine or chicken broth
- ⅓ cup olive oil
- 5 garlic cloves, crushed
- 1 fresh rosemary sprig or
  1 Tbsp. dried rosemary, crushed
- 1 fresh thyme sprig or
  1 Tbsp. dried thyme
- 1 Tbsp. herbes de Provence
- 1 Tbsp. Worcestershire sauce
- 1 tsp. salt
- 1 tsp. dried minced onion
- 1 tsp. pepper
- 8 lamb rib chops (about 1 in. thick
  and 3 oz. each)

**1.** In a large bowl or shallow dish, combine all ingredients but lamb. Add lamb; turn to coat. Refrigerate 6 hours or overnight.
**2.** Drain lamb, discarding marinade. Preheat air fryer to 390°. In batches, arrange chops in greased air fryer. Cook until meat reaches desired doneness (for medium-rare, a thermometer should read 135°; medium, 140°; medium-well, 145°), 4-5 minutes on each side. Let stand for 5 minutes before serving.
**2 LAMB CHOPS:** 228 cal., 13g fat (3g sat. fat), 68mg chol., 272mg sod., 2g carb. (0 sugars, 0 fiber), 22g pro. **DIABETIC EXCHANGES:** 3 lean meat, 1 fat.

# - 9 -

# MAKE-AHEAD MARVELS

With today's busy schedules, it helps to work ahead. All the recipes in this chapter let you get a jump on your meals—whether it's a slow-cooked dish, a freezer-friendly recipe, or a meal that's assembled ahead of time and popped in the oven when you're ready.

**Feta Chicken Burgers** (p. 189) **Overnight Yeast Waffles** (p. 193) **Almond Broccoli Salad** (p. 188)
**Avocado Salsa** (p. 202) **Freezer Mashed Potatoes** (p. 198) **Thai Chicken Thighs** (p. 191)
**Slow-Cooker Cassoulet with Crumb Topping** (p. 192) **Mushroom & Olive Bruschetta** (p. 197) **Lemon Olive Oil Cake** (p. 200)

## BEEF OSSO BUCCO

Our beef osso bucco boasts a thick, savory sauce complemented by the addition of gremolata, a chopped herb condiment made with lemon zest, garlic and parsley.
—Taste of Home *Test Kitchen*

------------------------------------------------

**PREP:** 30 min. • **COOK:** 7 hours
**MAKES:** 6 servings

- ½ cup all-purpose flour
- ¾ tsp. salt, divided
- ½ tsp. pepper
- 6 beef shanks (14 oz. each)
- 2 Tbsp. butter
- 1 Tbsp. olive oil
- ½ cup white wine or beef broth
- 1 can (14½ oz.) diced tomatoes, undrained
- 1½ cups beef broth
- 2 medium carrots, chopped
- 1 medium onion, chopped
- 1 celery rib, sliced
- 1 Tbsp. dried thyme
- 1 Tbsp. dried oregano
- 2 bay leaves
- 3 Tbsp. cornstarch
- ¼ cup cold water

GREMOLATA
- ⅓ cup minced fresh parsley
- 1 Tbsp. grated lemon zest
- 1 Tbsp. grated orange zest
- 2 garlic cloves, minced
  Polenta, optional

1. In a large resealable container, combine flour, ½ tsp. salt and the pepper. Add beef, a few pieces at a time, and shake to coat.
2. In a large skillet, brown beef in butter and oil. Transfer meat and drippings to a 6-qt. slow cooker. Add wine to skillet, stirring to loosen browned bits from pan; pour over meat. Add the tomatoes, broth, carrots, onion, celery, thyme, oregano, bay leaves and remaining ¼ tsp. salt.
3. Cook, covered, on low until meat is tender, 7-9 hours. Discard bay leaves.
4. Skim fat from cooking juices; transfer juices to a large saucepan. Bring to a boil. Combine cornstarch and water until smooth; gradually stir into the pan. Bring to a boil; cook and stir until thickened, 2 minutes.
5. Combine the gremolata ingredients. Serve beef with sauce and gremolata. If desired, serve over polenta.
**1 SHANK WITH 1 CUP SAUCE AND 4 TSP. GREMOLATA:** 398 cal., 15g fat (6g sat. fat), 112mg chol., 640mg sod., 17g carb. (5g sugars, 4g fiber), 47g pro.

> **TIP**
> Pair with French bread or serve over polenta, mashed potatoes or pasta. This dish reheats well, so you can make it ahead.

## CANDIED BACON PALMIERS

You only need three ingredients to make this beautiful and delicious appetizer! I also like to serve them as a breakfast pastry when I make a brunch buffet. They are special and just a little different from what's usually served.
—Jolene Martinelli, Fremont, NH

------------------------------------------------

**PREP:** 20 min. + chilling • **BAKE:** 15 min.
**MAKES:** 3 dozen

- 6 bacon strips
- 1 pkg. (17.30 oz.) frozen puff pastry, thawed
- ¾ cup packed light brown sugar

1. In a large skillet, cook bacon over medium heat until crisp. Remove to paper towels to drain; crumble. Unfold 1 sheet of puff pastry. Sprinkle with half the brown sugar and half the bacon.
2. Roll up the left and right sides toward the center, jelly-roll style, until the rolls meet in the middle. Repeat with the remaining pastry sheet and ingredients. Refrigerate until firm enough to slice, about 30 minutes.
3. Preheat oven to 400°. Cut each roll crosswise into ½-in. slices. Place slices 2 in. apart on parchment-lined baking sheets. Bake until golden and crisp, 15-20 minutes. Cool on pans 2 minutes. Remove to wire racks to cool.
**FREEZE OPTION:** Cover and freeze sliced, unbaked palmiers on waxed paper–lined baking sheets until firm. Transfer to freezer containers; close tightly and return to freezer. To use, thaw and bake palmiers as directed.
**1 PALMIER:** 91 cal., 4g fat (1g sat. fat), 1mg chol., 70mg sod., 12g carb. (4g sugars, 1g fiber), 1g pro.

## CHICKEN & RICE CASSEROLE

Everyone loves this casserole because it's a tasty combination of hearty and crunchy ingredients mixed in a creamy sauce. You can assemble the casserole ahead of time and keep it in the fridge; just wait to add the chips until you're ready to bake it.
—*Myrtle Matthews, Marietta, GA*

PREP: 15 min. • BAKE: 1 hour • MAKES: 12 servings

- 4 cups cooked white rice or a combination of wild and white rice
- 4 cups diced cooked chicken
- ½ cup slivered almonds
- 1 small onion, chopped
- 1 can (8 oz.) sliced water chestnuts, drained
- 1 pkg. (10 oz.) frozen peas, thawed
- ¾ cup chopped celery
- 1 can (10¾ oz.) condensed cream of celery soup, undiluted
- 1 can (10¾ oz.) condensed cream of chicken soup, undiluted
- 1 cup mayonnaise
- 2 tsp. lemon juice
- 1 tsp. salt
- 2 cups crushed potato chips
  Paprika

**1.** Preheat oven to 350°. In a greased 13x9-in. baking dish, combine the first 7 ingredients. In a large bowl, combine soups, mayonnaise, lemon juice and salt. Pour over the chicken mixture and toss to coat.

**2.** Sprinkle with potato chips and paprika. Bake until heated through, about 1 hour.

**1 CUP:** 439 cal., 26g fat (5g sat. fat), 51mg chol., 804mg sod., 31g carb. (3g sugars, 3g fiber), 19g pro.

## ALMOND BROCCOLI SALAD

This colorful salad is easy to make, and I like that it can be prepared ahead of time. Add the almonds and bacon just before serving so they stay nice and crunchy.
—*Margaret Garbade, Tulsa, OK*

TAKES: 25 min. • MAKES: 12 servings

- 1 bunch broccoli (about 1½ lbs.)
- 1 cup mayonnaise
- ¼ cup red wine vinegar
- 2 Tbsp. sugar
- ¼ tsp. salt
- ½ tsp. freshly ground pepper
- 1 pkg. (7 oz.) mixed dried fruit
- ¼ cup finely chopped red onion
- 1 pkg. (2¼ oz.) slivered almonds, toasted
- 4 bacon strips, cooked and crumbled

**1.** Cut florets from broccoli, reserving stalks; cut florets into 1-in. pieces. Using a paring knife, remove peel from thick stalks; cut stalks into ½-in. pieces.

**2.** In a small bowl, mix mayonnaise, vinegar, sugar, salt and pepper. In a large bowl, combine broccoli, dried fruit and onion. Add mayonnaise mixture; toss to coat. Refrigerate until serving.

**3.** Just before serving, sprinkle with almonds and bacon.

**¾ CUP:** 236 cal., 17g fat (3g sat. fat), 1mg chol., 180mg sod., 21g carb. (15g sugars, 3g fiber), 3g pro.

## BARBECUED MEATBALLS

Grape jelly and chili sauce are the secrets that make these meatballs so fantastic. If I'm serving them at a party, I prepare the meatballs and sauce in advance and reheat them right before my guests arrive.
—*Irma Schnuelle, Manitowoc, WI*

PREP: 20 min. • COOK: 15 min. • MAKES: about 3 dozen

- ½ cup dry bread crumbs
- ⅓ cup finely chopped onion
- ¼ cup 2% milk
- 1 large egg, lightly beaten
- 1 Tbsp. minced fresh parsley
- 1 tsp. salt
- 1 tsp. Worcestershire sauce
- ½ tsp. pepper
- 1 lb. lean ground beef (90% lean)
- ¼ cup canola oil
- 1 bottle (12 oz.) chili sauce
- 1 jar (10 oz.) grape jelly

1. In a large bowl, combine the first 8 ingredients. Crumble beef over mixture and mix lightly but thoroughly. Shape into 1-in. balls. In a large skillet, brown meatballs in oil on all sides.
2. Remove meatballs and drain. In the same skillet, combine chili sauce and jelly; cook and stir over medium heat until jelly has melted. Return meatballs to pan; heat through.
**1 MEATBALL:** 71 cal., 3g fat (1g sat. fat), 13mg chol., 215mg sod., 9g carb. (7g sugars, 0 fiber), 3g pro.

## FETA CHICKEN BURGERS

My friends always request these tasty chicken burgers on the grill. I sometimes add olives to punch up the flavor. Try them with the mayo topping.
—*Angela Robinson, Findlay, OH*

TAKES: 30 min. • MAKES: 6 servings

- ¼ cup finely chopped cucumber
- ¼ cup reduced-fat mayonnaise

BURGERS
- ½ cup chopped roasted sweet red pepper
- 1 tsp. garlic powder
- ½ tsp. Greek seasoning
- ¼ tsp. pepper
- 1½ lbs. lean ground chicken
- 1 cup crumbled feta cheese
- 6 whole wheat hamburger buns, split and toasted
  Optional: Lettuce leaves and tomato slices

1. Preheat broiler. Mix cucumber and mayonnaise.
2. In a separate bowl, mix roasted red pepper and seasonings. Add ground chicken and feta cheese; mix lightly but thoroughly (mixture will be sticky). Shape into six ½-in.-thick patties.
3. Broil burgers 4 in. from heat until a thermometer reads 165°, 3-4 minutes per side. Serve on buns with cucumber sauce. If desired, top with lettuce and tomato.
**FREEZE OPTION:** Place uncooked patties on a waxed paper–lined baking sheet; cover and freeze until firm. Remove from pan and transfer to an airtight freezer container; return to freezer. To use, broil frozen patties as directed, increasing time as necessary.
**1 BURGER WITH 1 TBSP. SAUCE:** 356 cal., 14g fat (5g sat. fat), 95mg chol., 703mg sod., 25g carb. (5g sugars, 4g fiber), 31g pro. **DIABETIC EXCHANGES:** 5 lean meat, 2 starch, ½ fat.

## ❄ FLAKY CHICKEN WELLINGTON

This cozy and flavorful entree takes a classic recipe and makes it super easy! I like to cook the chicken a day or so ahead of time to make it even simpler to throw together on busy nights.
—*Kerry Dingwall, Wilmington, NC*

------------------------------------------

**PREP:** 30 min. • **BAKE:** 15 min.
**MAKES:** 2 pastries (3 servings each)

- 2 cups cubed cooked chicken
- 1 pkg. (10 oz.) frozen chopped spinach, thawed and squeezed dry
- 3 hard-boiled large eggs, chopped
- ½ cup finely chopped dill pickles
- ⅓ cup finely chopped celery
- 2 tubes (8 oz. each) refrigerated crescent rolls
- 2 tsp. prepared mustard, divided
- 1 cup sour cream
- 2 Tbsp. dill pickle juice

**1.** Preheat oven to 350°. In a large bowl, combine the first 5 ingredients. Unroll 1 tube of crescent dough into 1 long rectangle; press perforations to seal.
**2.** Spread half the mustard over dough; top with half the chicken mixture to within ¼ in. of edges. Roll up jelly-roll style, starting with a long side; pinch seam to seal. Place seam side down on a parchment-lined baking sheet. Cut slits in top. Repeat with remaining crescent dough, mustard and chicken mixture.
**3.** Bake until golden brown, 15-20 minutes. Meanwhile, combine sour cream and pickle juice; serve with pastries.
**FREEZE OPTION:** Cover and freeze unbaked pastries on a parchment-lined baking sheet until firm. Transfer to a freezer container; return to freezer. To use, bake pastries on a parchment-lined baking sheet in a preheated 350° oven until golden brown, 30-35 minutes. Prepare sauce as directed.
**⅓ PASTRY WITH ABOUT 3 TBSP. SAUCE:** 495 cal., 28g fat (6g sat. fat), 144mg chol., 830mg sod., 37g carb. (10g sugars, 2g fiber), 25g pro.

## PORTOBELLO MUSHROOM & CREAM CHEESE TAQUITOS

This party appetizer was inspired by a dish I saw on an episode of *Top Chef*. I simplified it a little and tweaked the flavors a bit. The taquitos can be made ahead and reheated in a 250° oven for 10 minutes.

—*Lily Julow, Lawrenceville, GA*

- - - - - - - - - - - - - - - - - - - - - - - - - - - - - - - - - - - - - - -

**PREP:** 30 min. • **COOK:** 15 min. • **MAKES:** 10 servings

- 2  Tbsp. extra virgin olive oil
- 8  oz. large portobello mushrooms, gills discarded, finely chopped
- 1  tsp. dried oregano
- 1  tsp. dried thyme
- ½  tsp. crushed red pepper flakes
- ¼  tsp. salt
- 1  pkg. (8 oz.) cream cheese, softened
- 4  oz. whole-milk ricotta cheese
- 10  flour tortillas (8 in.)
   Oil for deep-fat frying
   Major Grey's chutney

**1.** In a cast-iron or other heavy skillet, heat olive oil to 350°. Add mushrooms; saute 4 minutes. Add oregano, thyme, pepper flakes and salt; saute until mushrooms are browned, 4-6 minutes. Cool. Wipe out skillet.

**2.** Combine cheeses; fold in mushrooms, mixing well. Spread 3 Tbsp. mushroom mixture on bottom half of each tortilla. Roll up tightly, making sure filling isn't seeping from either end. Secure rolls with toothpicks.

**3.** In same skillet, heat oil to 375°. Fry taquitos, a few at a time, until golden brown, 2-4 minutes. Drain on paper towels. When taquitos are cool enough to handle, discard toothpicks. Serve with chutney.

**1 TAQUITO:** 375 cal., 25g fat (7g sat. fat), 27mg chol., 380mg sod., 30g carb. (2g sugars, 2g fiber), 8g pro.

## THAI CHICKEN THIGHS

With the slow cooker, a traditional Thai dish with peanut butter, jalapeno peppers and chili sauce becomes incredibly easy to make. To crank up the spice, just use more jalapeno peppers.
—Taste of Home *Test Kitchen*

- - - - - - - - - - - - - - - - - - - - - - - - - - - - - - - - - - - - - - -

**PREP:** 25 min. • **COOK:** 5 hours • **MAKES:** 8 servings

- 8  bone-in chicken thighs (about 3 lbs.), skin removed
- ½  cup salsa
- ¼  cup creamy peanut butter
- 2  Tbsp. lemon juice
- 2  Tbsp. reduced-sodium soy sauce
- 1  Tbsp. chopped seeded jalapeno pepper
- 2  tsp. Thai chili sauce
- 1  garlic clove, minced
- 1  tsp. minced fresh gingerroot
- 2  green onions, sliced
- 2  Tbsp. sesame seeds, toasted
   Hot cooked basmati rice, optional

Place chicken in a 3-qt. slow cooker. Combine the salsa, peanut butter, lemon juice, soy sauce, jalapeno, Thai chili sauce, garlic and ginger; pour over chicken. Cook, covered, on low until chicken is tender, 5-6 hours. Sprinkle with green onions and sesame seeds. Serve with rice if desired.

**NOTE:** Wear disposable gloves when cutting hot peppers; the oils can burn skin. Avoid touching your face.

**1 CHICKEN THIGH WITH ¼ CUP SAUCE:** 261 cal., 15g fat (4g sat. fat), 87mg chol., 350mg sod., 5g carb. (2g sugars, 1g fiber), 27g pro.

**DIABETIC EXCHANGES:** 4 lean meat, 1 fat, ½ starch.

## VEGGIE DILL DIP

I like to keep this good-for-you dip and a variety of cut-up veggies on hand for an easy snack.
—Hazel Baber, Yuma, AZ

------------------------------------------------

**PREP:** 10 min. + chilling • **MAKES:** 2½ cups

- 2 cups 1% cottage cheese
- 3 Tbsp. fat-free milk
- ¾ cup fat-free mayonnaise
- 1 Tbsp. dried minced onion
- 1 Tbsp. dried parsley flakes
- 1 tsp. dill weed
- 1 tsp. seasoned salt
- ¼ tsp. garlic powder

In a blender, blend cottage cheese and milk until smooth. Stir in remaining ingredients and mix well. Chill overnight. Serve with raw vegetables.

**2 TBSP. DIP:** 37 cal., 0 fat (0 sat. fat), 2mg chol., 303mg sod., 3g carb. (2g sugars, 0 fiber), 5g pro.

## SLOW-COOKER CASSOULET WITH CRUMB TOPPING

Classically inspired, this dish is loaded with chicken thighs, pork and smoked sausage. Tomatoes, beans and wine round out the hearty French stew, and bread crumbs thicken it slightly.
—Marie Rizzio, Interlochen, MI

------------------------------------------------

**PREP:** 20 min. • **COOK:** 7 hours • **MAKES:** 8 servings

- 1 cup soft bread crumbs
- 2 lbs. boneless skinless chicken thighs
- 1 lb. boneless pork shoulder, trimmed and cut into 1-in. pieces
- 8 oz. kielbasa, halved lengthwise and cut into ½-in. slices
- 2 cans (15 oz. each ) cannellini beans, rinsed and drained
- 1 can (14½ oz.) petite diced tomatoes, drained
- 1 cup chopped onion
- 1 cup chicken broth
- ¾ cup white wine
- 1 Tbsp. tomato paste
- ½ tsp. salt
- ½ tsp. pepper
- 2 garlic cloves, crushed
- 2 fresh thyme sprigs
- 1 bay leaf
  Minced fresh parsley, optional

1. Preheat oven to 350°. Place bread crumbs in a 15x10x1-in. baking pan. Bake, uncovered until crumbs are lightly browned, stirring occasionally, 8-12 minutes. Set aside.
2. Combine the remaining ingredients in a 5- or 6-qt. slow cooker. Cover and cook on low until meat is tender, about 7 hours. Remove and discard thyme sprigs and bay leaf. Stir in ¾ cup toasted bread crumbs. Top individual servings with remaining toasted bread crumbs. If desired, sprinkle with chopped parsley.

**1¼ CUPS:** 482 cal., 22g fat (7g sat. fat), 129mg chol., 802mg sod., 24g carb. (4g sugars, 6g fiber), 40g pro.

**TIP**
Traditional French cassoulet is a dish of white beans, duck, pork and sausage topped with a rich breadcrumb crust and slow-cooked for a long period of time. It takes its name from the vessel it's cooked in, the *cassole d'Issel*.

## OVERNIGHT YEAST WAFFLES

You might not think you'd have time to cook up waffles for breakfast, but this batter is made the night before so it's ready to go. These easy, fluffy waffles are so good that I freeze them to have some handy for busy mornings.
—Mary Balcomb, Florence, OR

- - - - - - - - - - - - - - - - - - - - - - - - - - - - - - - - - - - - - - -

**PREP:** 15 min. + chilling • **COOK:** 5 min./batch • **MAKES:** 10 servings

- 1 pkg. (¼ oz.) active dry yeast
- ½ cup warm water (110° to 115°)
- 1 tsp. sugar
- 2 cups warm 2% milk (110° to 115°)
- ½ cup butter, melted
- 2 large eggs, room temperature, lightly beaten
- 2¾ cups all-purpose flour
- 1 tsp. salt
- ½ tsp. baking soda

**1.** In a large bowl, dissolve yeast in warm water. Add sugar; let stand for 5 minutes. Add milk, butter and eggs; mix well. Combine flour and salt; stir into milk mixture. Cover and refrigerate overnight.

**2.** Stir batter; sift in baking soda and stir well. Bake waffles in a preheated waffle iron according to manufacturer's directions until golden brown.

**2 WAFFLES:** 220 cal., 12g fat (7g sat. fat), 74mg chol., 366mg sod., 22g carb. (3g sugars, 1g fiber), 6g pro.

> **REVIEW**
> "My very picky 7-year-old ate five and told me not to lose the recipe!"
> **—DJ-SPOI, TASTEOFHOME.COM**

## LISA'S ALL-DAY SUGAR & SALT PORK ROAST

My family loves this tender and juicy roast, so we eat it a lot. The sweet and salty crust is so delicious mixed into the pulled pork.
—Lisa Allen, Joppa, AL

- - - - - - - - - - - - - - - - - - - - - - - - - - - - - - - - - - - - - - -

**PREP:** 15 min. + marinating • **COOK:** 6¼ hours • **MAKES:** 12 servings

- 1 cup plus 1 Tbsp. sea salt, divided
- 1 cup sugar
- 1 bone-in pork shoulder butt roast (6 to 8 lbs.)
- ¼ cup barbecue seasoning
- ½ tsp. pepper
- ½ cup packed brown sugar
- 12 hamburger buns or kaiser rolls, split

**1.** Combine 1 cup sea salt and the granulated sugar; rub onto all sides of the roast. Place roast in a shallow dish; refrigerate, covered, overnight.

**2.** Preheat oven to 300°. Using a kitchen knife, scrape salt and sugar coating from roast; discard any accumulated juices. Transfer pork to a large shallow roasting pan. Rub with barbecue seasoning; sprinkle with pepper. Roast until tender, 6-8 hours.

**3.** Increase oven temperature to 500°. Combine brown sugar and remaining 1 Tbsp. sea salt; sprinkle over cooked pork. Return pork to oven and roast until a crisp crust forms, 10-15 minutes. Remove; when cool enough to handle, shred meat with 2 forks. Serve warm on fresh buns or rolls.

**FREEZE OPTION:** Freeze cooled meat with some of the juices in freezer containers. To use, partially thaw in refrigerator overnight. Heat through in a saucepan, stirring occasionally; add water if necessary.

**1 SANDWICH:** 534 cal., 24g fat (9g sat. fat), 135mg chol., 2240mg sod., 33g carb. (14g sugars, 1g fiber), 43g pro.

## CHICKEN CHILES RELLENOS STRATA

This versatile bake can be made as an entree, a brunch option or a potluck dish. It's one of the easiest meals to assemble on a busy weeknight.
—*Kallee Krong-McCreery, Escondido, CA*

**PREP:** 20 min. + chilling
**BAKE:** 35 min. + standing
**MAKES:** 10 servings

- 6 cups cubed French bread (about 6 oz.)
- 2 cans (4 oz. each) chopped green chiles
- 2 cups shredded Monterey Jack cheese
- 2 cups shredded cooked chicken
- 12 large eggs
- 1½ cups 2% milk
- 2 tsp. baking powder
- 1 tsp. garlic salt
- 1 cup shredded cheddar cheese
  Salsa

**1.** In a greased 13x9-in. baking dish, layer half of each of the following: bread cubes, chiles, Monterey Jack cheese and chicken. Repeat layers.
**2.** In a large bowl, whisk eggs, milk, baking powder and garlic salt until blended. Pour over layers. Sprinkle with cheddar cheese. Refrigerate, covered, overnight.
**3.** Preheat oven to 350°. Remove strata from refrigerator while the oven heats. Bake, uncovered, until puffed and golden at edges, 35-40 minutes. Let stand for about 10 minutes before serving. Serve with salsa.
**1 PIECE:** 338 cal., 20g fat (9g sat. fat), 282mg chol., 820mg sod., 13g carb. (3g sugars, 1g fiber), 27g pro.

## BANANA CRUMB PUDDING

Friends and family ask me to make my thick and creamy banana pudding for all occasions. They can't get enough of the flavor combination of the bananas and the vanilla wafer crumbs. You can top this with meringue instead of whipped cream.
—*Yvonnia Butner, Pinnacle, NC*

**PREP:** 15 min. • **COOK:** 20 min. + chilling
**MAKES:** 15 servings

- 1 cup sugar
- ½ cup cornstarch
- 6 cups 2% milk
- 5 large egg yolks
- ¼ cup butter, cubed
- 2 tsp. vanilla extract
- 1 tsp. kosher salt
- 2 pkg. (11 oz. each) vanilla wafers
- 7 medium bananas, sliced

**TOPPING**
- 2 cups heavy whipping cream
- 6 Tbsp. sugar

**1.** In a large heavy saucepan, mix sugar and cornstarch. Whisk in milk. Cook and stir over medium heat until thickened and bubbly. Reduce heat to low; cook and stir 2 minutes longer. Remove from heat.

**2.** In a bowl, whisk a small amount of the hot mixture into the egg yolks; return all to pan, whisking constantly. Bring to a gentle boil; cook and stir 2 minutes. Remove from heat. Stir in butter, vanilla and salt. Cool for 15 minutes, stirring occasionally.
**3.** Reserve 1 cup whole wafers and 1 banana for topping. Crush 2 cups wafers and set aside. In a 13x9-in. baking dish, place a single layer of whole wafers, filling gaps with crushed wafers. Layer with a third each of the bananas and pudding. Repeat layers twice. Press waxed paper onto surface of pudding. Refrigerate, covered, overnight.
**4.** In a bowl, beat heavy cream until it begins to thicken. Add sugar; beat until soft peaks form (do not overmix). Just before serving, remove paper and spread whipped cream over pudding; top with reserved banana, sliced, and wafers.
**¾ CUP:** 535 cal., 27g fat (13g sat. fat), 121mg chol., 370mg sod., 70g carb. (46g sugars, 1g fiber), 7g pro.

**TIP**
Want to change things up? Add 2 Tbsp. spiced rum at the same time as the vanilla extract for an additional, rich flavor note.

## - NO-FRY FRIED ICE CREAM -
This ice cream has a crispy cinnamon coating just like fried ice cream, minus the oily mess. Make ahead of time and freeze until serving.

Using a ½-cup ice cream scoop, place **8 scoops of ice cream** on a baking sheet. Freeze until firm, about 1 hour. Meanwhile, combine **¼ cup brown sugar**, **1 Tbsp. melted butter** and **1 tsp. cinnamon**. Stir in **2 cups crushed cornflakes**. Transfer mixture to an ungreased 15x10x1-in. baking pan. Bake at 350° until lightly browned, 4-6 minutes. Cool completely. Roll ice cream balls in crumb mixture. Cover and freeze until firm, at least 1 hour. Serve with **whipped cream** and **caramel ice cream topping**.

## MUSHROOM & OLIVE BRUSCHETTA

I tried this delicious bruschetta toast at a party and knew I had to make it myself. Since I couldn't find the person who brought the dish, I began trying to duplicate it on my own. The original was made on an English muffin, but party rye or baguette slices work as well.
—*Lynne German, Buford, GA*

- - - - - - - - - - - - - - - - - - - - - - - - - - - - - - - - - - - - - - - - - - - - - - - - - - - - -

**PREP:** 15 min. • **BAKE:** 10 min. • **MAKES:** 4 dozen

- 1½  cups finely shredded cheddar cheese
- ½  cup canned mushroom stems and pieces, drained and chopped
- ½  cup chopped green onions
- ½  cup chopped pitted green olives
- ½  cup chopped ripe olives
- ½  cup mayonnaise
- ¼  tsp. curry powder
- 2  French bread baguettes (10½ oz. each), cut into ½-in. slices
Julienned green onions, optional

1. Preheat oven to 400°. Combine first 7 ingredients. Cut each baguette into 24 slices; place on ungreased baking sheets. Bake until lightly toasted, about 5 minutes.
2. Top baguette slices with cheese mixture. Bake until cheese is melted, 4-5 minutes. If desired, top with julienned green onions.
**FREEZE OPTION:** Cover and freeze unbaked topped baguette slices on a parchment-lined baking sheet until firm. Transfer to a freezer container; return to freezer. To use, bake baguette slices on ungreased baking sheets in a preheated 400° oven until heated through, 8-10 minutes.
**1 PIECE:** 66 cal., 3g fat (1g sat. fat), 4mg chol., 161mg sod., 7g carb. (0 sugars, 0 fiber), 2g pro.

**PM**

## LEMONY CHICKEN & RICE

I couldn't say who loves this recipe best, because every time I serve it, it gets raves! Occasionally I even get a phone call or email from a friend requesting the recipe, and it's certainly a favorite for my grown children and 15 grandchildren.
—*Maryalice Wood, Langley, BC*

- - - - - - - - - - - - - - - - - - - - - - - - - - - - - - - - - - - - - - - - - - - - - - - - - - - - -

**PREP:** 15 min. + marinating • **BAKE:** 55 min.
**MAKES:** 2 casseroles (4 servings each)

- 2  cups water
- ½  cup reduced-sodium soy sauce
- ¼  cup lemon juice
- ¼  cup olive oil
- 2  garlic cloves, minced
- 2  tsp. ground ginger
- 2  tsp. pepper
- 16  bone-in chicken thighs, skin removed (about 6 lbs.)
- 2  cups uncooked long grain rice
- 4  Tbsp. grated lemon zest, divided
- 2  medium lemons, sliced

1. In a large shallow dish, combine the first 7 ingredients. Add chicken; turn to coat and cover. Refrigerate 4 hours or overnight.
2. Preheat oven to 325°. Spread 1 cup rice into each of 2 greased 13x9-in. baking dishes. Top each with 1 Tbsp. lemon zest, 8 chicken thighs and half the marinade. Top with sliced lemons.
3. Bake, covered, 40 minutes. Uncover, and continue baking until a thermometer inserted in chicken reads 170°-175°, 15-20 minutes longer. Sprinkle with remaining lemon zest.
**2 CHICKEN THIGHS WITH ¾ CUP RICE MIXTURE:** 624 cal., 26g fat (6g sat. fat), 173mg chol., 754mg sod., 41g carb. (1g sugars, 1g fiber), 53g pro.

## 5i ❄ FREEZER MASHED POTATOES

Can you freeze mashed potatoes? You bet you can! I always make these potatoes and give them to my kids when they go away to school. All they have to do is keep it in a freezer until it's mashed potato time!

—Jessie Fortune, Pocahontas, AR

**PREP:** 30 min. + freezing • **BAKE:** 30 min. • **MAKES:** 14 servings

- 5 lbs. potatoes (about 9 large), peeled and cut into chunks
- 2 Tbsp. butter, softened
- 1 cup sour cream
- 6 oz. cream cheese, cubed
- ½ tsp. onion powder
- ½ tsp. salt
- ¼ tsp. pepper

1. Place potatoes in a large saucepan and cover with water. Bring to a boil. Reduce heat; cover and cook for 10-15 minutes or until tender. Drain.
2. In a large bowl, mash potatoes with butter. Beat in sour cream, cream cheese, onion powder, salt and pepper. Transfer to a greased 13x9-in. baking dish. Bake, uncovered, at 350° until heated through, 30-35 minutes. Or, transfer 1½ cup portions to greased 2-cup baking dishes. Cover and freeze up to 6 months.
**NOTE:** To use frozen potatoes, thaw in the refrigerator overnight. Bake at 350° until heated through, 30-35 minutes.
**¾ CUP:** 195 cal., 6g fat (4g sat. fat), 19mg chol., 173mg sod., 31g carb. (4g sugars, 3g fiber), 6g pro.

**TIP**

If stored in an airtight container, these mashed potatoes can last up to 2 months in the freezer. Ideally, you should allow frozen mashed potatoes to thaw overnight in the refrigerator before baking. However, if you're in a pinch, you can thaw them on the stovetop over low heat; stir occasionally so they don't scorch.

## ⏱ ❄ FIESTA TURKEY TORTILLA SOUP

I'm always amazed when I can pull together such a delicious soup in less than half an hour!

—Amy McFadden, Chelsea, AL

**TAKES:** 25 min. • **MAKES:** 8 servings

- 4 cans (14½ oz. each) chicken broth
- 3 cups shredded cooked turkey or rotisserie chicken
- 1 can (15 oz.) black beans, rinsed and drained
- 1 can (15¼ oz.) whole kernel corn, drained
- ½ cup medium salsa
- 5 corn tortillas (6 in.), cut into ¼-in. strips
- ¼ cup chopped fresh cilantro

1. In a Dutch oven, combine the first 5 ingredients; bring to a boil. Reduce heat; simmer for 10 minutes, stirring occasionally.
2. Meanwhile, spread tortilla strips in a single layer on a baking sheet. Bake at 400° until golden brown and crisp, 4-6 minutes.
3. Stir cilantro into soup. Top individual servings with tortilla strips. If desired, serve with additional salsa.
**FREEZE OPTION:** Freeze cooled soup in freezer containers. To use, partially thaw in refrigerator overnight. Heat through in a saucepan, stirring occasionally and adding a little broth or water if necessary. Meanwhile, bake tortillas as directed and sprinkle over each serving. Serve with additional salsa if desired.
**1⅓ CUPS:** 203 cal., 3g fat (1g sat. fat), 58mg chol., 1264mg sod., 21g carb. (5g sugars, 4g fiber), 20g pro.

## ❄ 🍲 EASY ROPA VIEJA STEW

Use your slow cooker for this meaty Cuban classic, which offers bold flavors without a lot of hands-on time.
—*Denise Nyland, Panama City, FL*

**PREP:** 25 min. • **COOK:** 6 hours • **MAKES:** 8 servings

- 1 boneless beef chuck roast (2 lbs.), cut in half
- 2 Tbsp. olive oil
- 2 large onions, coarsely chopped
- 2 large green peppers, coarsely chopped
- 4 jalapeno peppers, seeded and minced
- 1 habanero pepper, seeded and minced
- 3 cans (14½ oz. each) diced tomatoes, undrained
- ½ cup water
- 6 garlic cloves, minced
- 2 Tbsp. minced fresh cilantro
- 4 tsp. beef bouillon granules
- 2 tsp. pepper
- 1½ tsp. ground cumin
- 1 tsp. dried oregano
- ½ cup pimiento-stuffed olives, coarsely chopped
  Hot cooked rice, optional

**1.** In a large skillet, brown beef in oil on all sides. Transfer to a 5-qt. slow cooker. Add onions and peppers. Combine tomatoes, water, garlic, cilantro, beef bouillon, pepper, cumin and oregano; pour over vegetables.

**2.** Cook, covered, on low until meat is tender, 6-8 hours. Remove beef; cool slightly. Skim fat from cooking juices; stir in olives. Shred beef with 2 forks and return to slow cooker; heat through. Serve with rice if desired.

**NOTE:** Wear disposable gloves when cutting hot peppers; the oils can burn skin. Avoid touching your face.

**FREEZE OPTION:** Freeze individual portions in freezer containers. To use, partially thaw in refrigerator overnight. Heat through in a saucepan; stir occasionally and add a little water if necessary.

**1⅓ CUPS:** 306 cal., 16g fat (5g sat. fat), 74mg chol., 821mg sod., 16g carb. (8g sugars, 4g fiber), 25g pro.

## EASY EGG ROLLS

I've always loved egg rolls, but every recipe I saw seemed too complicated. So I decided to start with a packaged coleslaw mix. Now I can make these yummy treats at a moment's notice.
—*Samantha Dunn, Leesville, LA*

**PREP:** 30 min. • **COOK:** 30 min. • **MAKES:** 28 servings

- 1 lb. ground beef
- 1 pkg. (14 oz.) coleslaw mix
- 2 Tbsp. soy sauce
- ½ tsp. garlic powder
- ¼ tsp. ground ginger
- ⅛ tsp. onion powder
- 1 Tbsp. all-purpose flour
- 28 egg roll wrappers
  Vegetable oil for frying

**1.** In a large skillet, cook beef over medium heat until no longer pink, 5-7 minutes, breaking into crumbles; drain and cool slightly. In a bowl, combine beef, coleslaw mix, soy sauce, garlic powder, ginger and onion powder. In a small bowl, combine flour and enough water to make a paste.

**2.** With 1 corner of an egg roll wrapper facing you, place ¼ cup filling just below center of wrapper. (Cover remaining wrappers with a damp paper towel until ready to use.) Fold bottom corner over filling; moisten remaining wrapper edges with flour paste. Fold side corners toward center over filling. Roll egg roll up tightly, pressing at tip to seal. Repeat.

**3.** In an electric skillet or deep-fat fryer, heat oil to 375°. Fry egg rolls, a few at a time, until golden brown, 3-4 minutes, turning occasionally. Drain on paper towels.

**1 EGG ROLL:** 185 cal., 9g fat (1g sat. fat), 13mg chol., 261mg sod., 20g carb. (1g sugars, 1g fiber), 6g pro.

**TIP** To make ahead of time, refrigerate fried egg rolls in a single layer on a tray lined with paper towels. Reheat in a low oven for 10 minutes on each side.

## CORN PUDDING WITH BACON & CHEDDAR

This cheddar corn pudding can be prepared ahead and refrigerated overnight. Remove from the refrigerator for 30 minutes before baking.
—*Lynn Albright, Fremont, NE*

**PREP:** 25 min. • **BAKE:** 40 min. + standing • **MAKES:** 6 servings

- 1 Tbsp. olive oil
- ¾ cup chopped sweet onion
- ¾ cup chopped sweet red pepper
- 4 large eggs, room temperature
- 1 cup heavy whipping cream
- 1 tsp. baking soda
- 1 tsp. hot pepper sauce
- ½ tsp. salt
- 2 cups fresh or frozen corn
- 2 cups crushed cornbread stuffing
- ½ lb. bacon strips, cooked and crumbled
- 1½ cups shredded sharp cheddar cheese, divided

1. Preheat oven to 350°. In a 10-in. cast-iron or other ovenproof skillet, heat oil over medium heat. Add onion and red pepper; cook and stir until crisp-tender, 6-8 minutes. Remove from skillet; set aside.
2. Whisk eggs, cream, baking soda, hot pepper sauce and salt. Stir in corn, stuffing, bacon, 1 cup cheese and the onion mixture. Transfer to skillet.
3. Bake, uncovered, 35 minutes. Sprinkle with remaining ½ cup cheese. Bake until puffed and golden brown, 5-10 minutes longer. Let stand 10 minutes before serving.

**¾ CUP:** 516 cal., 36g fat (18g sat. fat), 211mg chol., 1117mg sod., 29g carb. (7g sugars, 3g fiber), 20g pro.

## LEMON OLIVE OIL CAKE

Olive oil cakes are tender and moist, and stay that way longer than butter-based cakes, so they are wonderful if you need to make dessert ahead of time. Serve this recipe with fresh berries when your favorites are in season.
—*Nicole Gackowski, Antioch, CA*

**PREP:** 15 min. • **BAKE:** 30 min. + cooling • **MAKES:** 8 servings

- 2 large eggs, room temperature
- ⅔ cup sugar
- ½ cup extra virgin olive oil
- ⅓ cup 2% milk
- 1 Tbsp. grated lemon zest
- 3 Tbsp. lemon juice
- 1 cup all-purpose flour
- 1 tsp. baking powder
- ¼ tsp. salt
  Confectioners' sugar

1. Preheat oven to 350°. Line a greased 8-in. round baking pan with parchment. In a large bowl, beat eggs on high speed for 3 minutes. Gradually add sugar, beating until thickened. Gradually beat in oil. Beat in milk, lemon zest and lemon juice.
2. In another bowl, whisk flour, baking powder and salt; fold into egg mixture. Transfer batter to prepared pan, spreading evenly.
3. Bake until a toothpick inserted near the center comes out clean, 30-35 minutes. Cool in pan 15 minutes before removing to a wire rack; remove parchment. Cool completely. Dust with confectioners' sugar.

**1 PIECE:** 266 cal., 15g fat (2g sat. fat), 47mg chol., 157mg sod., 30g carb. (18g sugars, 1g fiber), 4g pro.

**TIP**
This cake keeps amazingly well for up to a week in an airtight container. It does not need to be refrigerated and is actually better the day after it's baked— perfect to prepare ahead for a party or potluck.

# EGGPLANT CASSEROLE

With lots of vegetables, this good-for-you dish is low in calories, but full of flavor. I make it often in summer when fresh produce is abundant.

—*Marelyn Baugher, Holdredge, NE*

-----

**PREP:** 20 min. • **BAKE:** 30 min.
**MAKES:** 6 servings

1   medium eggplant, peeled and cubed
1½  lbs. ground beef
1   medium onion, chopped
1   medium green pepper, chopped
3   medium tomatoes, chopped
    Salt and pepper to taste
½   cup 2% milk
1   large egg, beaten
½   cup dry bread crumbs
2   Tbsp. butter, melted

**1.** Preheat oven to 375°. In a saucepan, bring 4 cups water to a boil; add eggplant. Boil until tender, 5-8 minutes. Drain and set aside.

**2.** In a large skillet, cook beef, onion and green pepper over medium heat until beef is no longer pink, 6-8 minutes, breaking meat into crumbles; drain. Add tomatoes, salt and pepper. Cook and stir until tomatoes are tender, about 5 minutes. Remove from the heat. Stir in milk, egg and eggplant; mix well.

**3.** Transfer to a greased 13x9-in. baking dish. In a small bowl, combine bread crumbs and butter; sprinkle over top. Bake, uncovered, until heated through, 30-35 minutes.

**1⅓ CUPS:** 342 cal., 19g fat (8g sat. fat), 113mg chol., 186mg sod., 18g carb. (7g sugars, 4g fiber), 25g pro.

**TIPS**

- Because the eggplant and beef are cooked, this casserole can be frozen before or after baking. If you plan to bake it to save for a later date, skip the topping—it won't hold up well in the freezer.

- While it's fine to leave the skin on eggplant in some dishes, the texture and flavor won't work well here, so this recipe calls for peeled eggplant.

## BANG BANG SHRIMP CAKE SLIDERS

My family loves these shrimp sliders. The bang bang slaw dressing and shrimp cake patties can be made ahead. When ready to serve, toss the cabbage slaw and sear the shrimp cakes, then assemble and enjoy.
—Kim Banick, Turner, OR

PREP: 30 min. + chilling • COOK: 10 min./batch • MAKES: 12 sliders

- 1 lb. uncooked shrimp (41-50 per lb.), peeled and deveined
- 1 large egg, lightly beaten
- ½ cup finely chopped sweet red pepper
- 6 green onions, divided and chopped
- 1 Tbsp. minced fresh gingerroot
- ¼ tsp. salt
- 1 cup panko bread crumbs
- ¼ cup mayonnaise
- 1 Tbsp. Sriracha chili sauce
- 1 Tbsp. sweet chili sauce
- 5 cups shredded Chinese or napa cabbage
- 12 mini buns or dinner rolls
- 3 Tbsp. canola oil

1. Place shrimp in a food processor; pulse until chopped. In a large bowl, combine egg, red pepper, 4 green onions, ginger and salt. Add shrimp and bread crumbs; mix lightly but thoroughly. Shape into twelve ½-in.-thick patties. Refrigerate 20 minutes.
2. Meanwhile, in a large bowl, combine mayonnaise and the chili sauces; stir in cabbage and remaining 2 green onions. Place buns on a baking sheet, cut sides up. Broil 3-4 in. from heat until golden brown, 2-3 minutes.
3. In a large cast-iron or other heavy skillet, heat the oil over medium heat. Add shrimp cakes in batches; cook until golden brown on both sides, 4-5 minutes per side. Serve on toasted buns with slaw. If desired, secure each slider with a toothpick. Serve with additional Sriracha chili sauce if desired.
**1 SLIDER:** 210 cal., 10g fat (1g sat. fat), 63mg chol., 321mg sod., 20g carb. (3g sugars, 1g fiber), 11g pro.

## AVOCADO SALSA

I first made this recipe for a party, and it was an absolute success. People love the combination of flavors. Scoop it up with chips, spoon it over chicken or steak, or eat it on its own!
—Susan Vandermeer, Ogden, UT

PREP: 20 min. + chilling • MAKES: about 7 cups

- 1⅔ cups (about 8¼ oz.) frozen corn, thawed
- 2 cans (2¼ oz. each) sliced ripe olives, drained
- 1 medium sweet red pepper, chopped
- 1 small onion, chopped
- 5 garlic cloves, minced
- ⅓ cup olive oil
- ¼ cup lemon juice
- 3 Tbsp. cider vinegar
- 1 tsp. dried oregano
- ½ tsp. salt
- ½ tsp. pepper
- 4 medium ripe avocados, peeled
  Tortilla chips

1. Combine corn, olives, red pepper and onion. In another bowl, mix the next 7 ingredients. Pour over corn mixture; toss to coat. Refrigerate, covered, overnight.
2. Just before serving, chop avocados and stir into salsa. Serve with tortilla chips.
**¼ CUP:** 82 cal., 7g fat (1g sat. fat), 0 chol., 85mg sod., 5g carb. (1g sugars, 2g fiber), 1g pro. **DIABETIC EXCHANGES:** 1½ fat.

## OPEN-FACED PIZZA BURGERS

I'm not sure where I first saw this recipe, but I'm glad I did! My family requests these burgers often. A dash of oregano livens up canned pizza sauce.
—*Sharon Schwartz, Burlington, WI*

------------------------------------------------------------

**TAKES:** 30 min. • **MAKES:** 12 servings

1½ lbs. ground beef
¼ cup chopped onion
1 can (15 oz.) pizza sauce
1 can (4 oz.) mushroom stems and pieces, drained
1 Tbsp. sugar
½ tsp. dried oregano
6 hamburger buns, split and toasted
1½ cups shredded part-skim mozzarella cheese

**1.** In a large cast-iron or other heavy skillet, cook beef and onion over medium heat until the meat is no longer pink, 3-5 minutes, breaking beef into crumbles. Drain. Stir in pizza sauce, mushrooms, sugar and oregano; mix well. Spoon onto buns; sprinkle with mozzarella cheese.

**2.** Place on ungreased baking sheets. Broil 4 in. from the heat until cheese is melted, 2 minutes.

**FREEZE OPTION:** Place the split and toasted buns on a baking sheet. Spoon the meat mixture onto buns; freeze for 1 hour. Transfer to freezer-safe airtight containers. To use, thaw completely in the refrigerator. Sprinkle with cheese. Broil 4 in. from the heat until heated through and cheese is melted, 2 minutes.

**1 PIZZA BURGER:** 205 cal., 8g fat (4g sat. fat), 36mg chol., 357mg sod., 15g carb. (4g sugars, 1g fiber), 16g pro.

## SO-TENDER SWISS STEAK

When I was little, my mother's Swiss steak was the dinner I requested the most. Now it's a favorite in my house, too.
—*Linda McGinty, Parma, OH*

------------------------------------------------------------

**PREP:** 30 min. • **BAKE:** 2 hours • **MAKES:** 8 servings

¼ cup all-purpose flour
½ tsp. salt
¼ tsp. pepper
2 lbs. beef top round steak, cut into serving-size pieces
2 Tbsp. canola oil
1 medium onion, thinly sliced
2 cups water
2 Tbsp. Worcestershire sauce

**GRAVY**

¼ cup all-purpose flour
¼ tsp. salt
⅛ tsp. pepper
1¼ cups beef broth or water
Optional: Hot cooked noodles or mashed potatoes

**1.** Preheat oven to 325°. In a large shallow dish, combine flour, salt and pepper. Pound steak with a mallet to tenderize. Add meat, a few pieces at a time, and toss to coat.

**2.** In an ovenproof Dutch oven, brown steak in oil on both sides. Arrange onion slices between layers of meat. Add water and Worcestershire sauce.

**3.** Cover and bake 2-2½ hours or until meat is very tender. Remove meat to a serving platter and keep warm.

**4.** For gravy, in a small bowl, combine flour, salt, pepper and broth until smooth; stir into the pan juices. Bring to a boil over medium heat; cook and stir 2 minutes or until thickened. Serve steak and gravy with noodles or mashed potatoes, if desired.

**FREEZE OPTION:** Freeze cooled beef mixture in freezer containers. To use, partially thaw in refrigerator overnight. Heat through in a covered saucepan, stirring occasionally; add a little broth or water if necessary.

**4 OZ. COOKED BEEF:** 213 cal., 7g fat (2g sat. fat), 64mg chol., 424mg sod., 9g carb. (1g sugars, 1g fiber), 27g pro.

## FALAFEL

A common street food in the Middle East, falafel are gluten free, crunchy on the outside, tender on the inside, and full of flavor from cilantro, mint, coriander and nutty sesame seeds. The classic version is deep-fried, but they can also be pan-fried, baked or cooked in an air fryer. Serve in or alongside pita bread with cucumbers, tomatoes, olives and tahini sauce.
—*Nithya Narasimhan, Chennai, India*

**PREP:** 10 min. + chilling • **COOK:** 15 min.
**MAKES:** 16 pieces

- 1 cup dried chickpeas
- ½ tsp. baking soda
- 1 cup fresh cilantro leaves
- ½ cup fresh mint leaves
- 5 garlic cloves
- 1 tsp. ground coriander
- 1 tsp. chili powder
- 1 tsp. salt
- ½ tsp. pepper, optional
- 1 tsp. sesame seeds
- 1 tsp. baking powder
  Oil for deep-fat frying

**1.** In a large bowl, cover chickpeas with water. Stir in ½ tsp. baking soda. Cover and let stand overnight. Drain chickpeas; rinse and pat dry.
**2.** In a food processor, pulse cilantro and mint until finely chopped. Add chickpeas, garlic, coriander, chili powder, salt and, if desired, pepper. Pulse until mixture is blended and the texture of coarse meal. Transfer to a large bowl. Cover; refrigerate for at least 1 hour.
**3.** Stir in sesame seeds and baking powder. Shape into sixteen 2-in. balls. In an electric skillet or a deep-fat fryer, heat oil to 375°. Fry chickpea balls, a few at a time, until golden brown, about 2 minutes, turning occasionally. Drain on paper towels.
**4 PIECES:** 224 cal., 13g fat (1g sat. fat), 0 chol., 760mg sod., 32g carb. (1g sugars, 16g fiber), 9g pro.

> **TIP**
> Chilling the falafel mixture makes it easier to shape, so make sure you don't skip that step! You can chill it for longer, to make in advance, but don't add the baking powder until you're ready to shape and cook the mixture.

## OLD-TIME CAKE DOUGHNUTS

This tender cake doughnut is a little piece of heaven at breakfast. For a variation, add a little rum extract or 1 tablespoon of dark rum.
—*Alissa Stehr, Gau-Odernheim, Germany*

**PREP:** 30 min. + chilling
**COOK:** 5 min./batch
**MAKES:** about 2 dozen

- 2 Tbsp. unsalted butter, softened
- 1½ cups sugar, divided
- 3 large eggs, room temperature
- 4 cups all-purpose flour
- 1 Tbsp. baking powder
- 3 tsp. ground cinnamon, divided
- ½ tsp. salt
- ⅛ tsp. ground nutmeg
- ¾ cup 2% milk
  Oil for deep-fat frying

**1.** In a large bowl, beat butter and 1 cup sugar until crumbly, about 2 minutes. Add eggs, 1 at a time, beating well after each addition.
**2.** Combine the flour, baking powder, 1 tsp. cinnamon, the salt and nutmeg; add to butter mixture alternately with milk, beating well after each addition. Cover and refrigerate for 2 hours.
**3.** Turn dough onto a heavily floured surface; pat to ¼-in. thickness. Cut with a floured 2½-in. doughnut cutter. In an electric skillet or deep fryer, heat oil to 375°.
**4.** Fry doughnuts, a few at a time, about 2 minutes per side or until golden brown on both sides. Drain on paper towels.
**5.** Combine remaining ½ cup sugar and 2 tsp. cinnamon; roll warm doughnuts in mixture.

**FREEZE OPTION:** After frying, wrap doughnuts in foil; transfer to a resealable freezer container. May be frozen for up to 3 months. To use, remove foil. Thaw doughnuts at room temperature. Warm if desired. Combine ½ cup sugar and 2 tsp. cinnamon; roll warm doughnuts in mixture.
**1 DOUGHNUT:** 198 cal., 8g fat (1g sat. fat), 30mg chol., 112mg sod., 29g carb. (13g sugars, 1g fiber), 3g pro.
**GLAZED CAKE DOUGHNUTS:** Omit the cinnamon-sugar mixture. Combine 2 cups confectioners' sugar, 1-2 Tbsp. orange juice and 1 tsp. grated orange peel. Spread over cooled doughnuts.

# - 10 -

# HOT OFF THE GRILL

Whether you break out the grill for special get-togethers or you cook out as long as the weather holds (and longer!), these recipes will give you tons of ideas for delectable grilled goodies. Appetizers, mains, sides and desserts—you really can grill anything!

**Grilled Pound Cake with Berries** (p. 221) **German Brat Seafood Boil** (p. 214) **Grilled Campfire Trout Dinner** (p. 220) **Elote (Mexican Street Corn)** (p. 211) **Provolone-Stuffed Pork Chops with Tarragon Vinaigrette** (p. 224) **Cuban Sandwich Burgers** (p. 219) **Grilled Pork Tenderloin with Cherry Salsa Mole** (p. 215) **Smoky Grilled Shrimp Appetizers** (p. 210) **Chicken Yakitori** (p. 222)

## STEAK & PROSCIUTTO SKEWERS WITH CREAMY BASIL-TARRAGON SAUCE

These flavorful bites of marinated steak layered with prosciutto can be cooked on the grill or under the broiler, so they're ideal for holiday parties no matter what climate you live in! The thick sauce is lovely and creamy—use it as a dip, or smear it on a plate and set the skewers over top.
—*Elizabeth Nutt, Alpharetta, GA*

--------------------------------------------

**PREP:** 25 min. + marinating • **GRILL:** 10 min.
**MAKES:** 7 kabobs (1 cup sauce)

- ½ cup minced fresh gingerroot
- ½ cup Worcestershire sauce
- ¼ cup cider vinegar
- ¼ cup dry red wine or beef broth
- 2 garlic cloves, minced
- 1 beef flank steak (1¼ lbs.), cut into ½-in. strips
- 1 pkg. (3 oz.) thinly sliced prosciutto, cut into ½-in. strips
- 2 Tbsp. olive oil
- ¼ tsp. salt
- ¼ tsp. pepper

**SAUCE**

- ⅔ cup cream cheese, softened
- ¼ cup heavy whipping cream
- 2 Tbsp. lemon juice
- 2 Tbsp. minced fresh basil
- 2 Tbsp. minced fresh tarragon
- 1 Tbsp. minced fresh parsley

**1.** In a bowl or shallow dish, combine the first 5 ingredients. Add beef and turn to coat. Refrigerate at least 4 hours.
**2.** Drain beef, discarding marinade. Layer 1 slice steak and 1 slice prosciutto; roll up. Repeat with remaining slices of meat.
**3.** Thread rolls onto metal or soaked wooden skewers. Brush with oil; sprinkle with salt and pepper. Grill, covered, over medium-high heat or broil 4 in. from heat until the beef reaches desired doneness, 10-12 minutes, turning occasionally.
**4.** In a small bowl, beat cream cheese and cream until blended. Stir in lemon juice and herbs. Serve with kabobs.
**1 KABOB WITH ABOUT 2 TBSP. SAUCE:** 298 cal., 22g fat (10g sat. fat), 81mg chol., 502mg sod., 4g carb. (2g sugars, 0 fiber), 21g pro.

## FOIL-PACKET POTATOES & SAUSAGE

My family enjoys camping and cooking over a fire. These hearty foil-packet meals turn out beautifully over a campfire, on the grill or in the oven at home.
—*Julie Koets, Elkhart, IN*

--------------------------------------------

**PREP:** 20 min. • **COOK:** 30 min.
**MAKES:** 8 servings

- 3 lbs. red potatoes, cut into ½-in. cubes
- 2 pkg. (12 oz. each) smoked sausage links, cut into ½-in. slices
- 4 bacon strips, cooked and crumbled
- 1 medium onion, chopped
- 2 Tbsp. chopped fresh parsley
- ¼ tsp. salt
- ¼ tsp. garlic salt
- ¼ tsp. pepper

**1.** Prepare campfire or grill for medium heat. In a large bowl, toss the potatoes with sausage, bacon, onion, parsley, salts and pepper.
**2.** Divide mixture among eight 18x12-in. pieces of heavy-duty nonstick foil, placing food on the dull side of the foil. Fold foil around potato mixture, sealing tightly.
**3.** Place packets over campfire or grill; cook 15 minutes on each side or until potatoes are tender. Open packets carefully to allow steam to escape. If desired, sprinkle with additional parsley.
**1 PACKET:** 414 cal., 25g fat (10g sat. fat), 61mg chol., 1181mg sod., 31g carb. (4g sugars, 3g fiber), 17g pro.

**TIPS**

- Change up the flavor of this dish with other types of fully cooked sausage, like spinach-and-feta chicken sausage.
- If you don't have heavy-duty foil on hand, use a double thickness of regular foil.

## SMOKY GRILLED SHRIMP APPETIZERS

Grill up these bacon-wrapped hors d'oeuvres and watch them disappear! They taste just as scrumptious as they look, and the reserved sauce is wonderful for dipping.
—*Debbie Taylor, White Bluff, TN*

- - - - - - - - - - - - - - - - - - - - - - - - - - - - - - - - - - - - -

**TAKES:** 20 min. • **MAKES:** 1 dozen (⅓ cup sauce)

- ½ lb. bacon strips
- ⅔ cup honey Dijon salad dressing
- 2 tsp. prepared horseradish
- 1 small garlic clove, minced
- 12 uncooked large shrimp, peeled and deveined

**1.** Cut bacon strips in half widthwise. In a large skillet, cook bacon over medium heat until partially cooked but not crisp. Remove to paper towels to drain.
**2.** In a small bowl, combine the salad dressing, horseradish and garlic; set aside ⅓ cup. Brush remaining mixture over both sides of shrimp. Wrap a piece of bacon around each shrimp; thread onto 2 metal or soaked wooden skewers.
**3.** On a lightly oiled grill rack, grill shrimp, covered, over medium heat or broil 4 in. from the heat for 5-8 minutes or until shrimp turn pink, turning once. Serve with reserved sauce.
**1 SHRIMP WITH 1¼ TSP. SAUCE:** 133 cal., 10g fat (3g sat. fat), 32mg chol., 268mg sod., 4g carb. (3g sugars, 0 fiber), 5g pro.

## ULTIMATE GRILLED PORK CHOPS

A little brining and a special dry rub go a long way to making the perfect pork chop. Once you've mastered the techniques, you'll be enjoying them all summer long.
—*Matthew Hass, Ellison Bay, WI*

- - - - - - - - - - - - - - - - - - - - - - - - - - - - - - - - - - - - -

**PREP:** 20 min. + brining • **GRILL:** 10 min. • **MAKES:** 4 servings

- ¼ cup kosher salt
- ¼ cup sugar
- 2 cups water
- 2 cups ice water
- 4 center-cut pork rib chops (1 in. thick and 8 oz. each)
- 2 Tbsp. canola oil

**BASIC RUB**

- 3 Tbsp. paprika
- 1 tsp. each garlic powder, onion powder, ground cumin and ground mustard
- 1 tsp. coarsely ground pepper
- ½ tsp. ground chipotle pepper

**1.** In a large saucepan, combine salt, sugar and 2 cups water; cook and stir over medium heat until salt and sugar are dissolved. Remove from heat. Add 2 cups ice water to cool brine to room temperature.
**2.** Place pork chops in a 13x9-in. baking dish; add the cooled brine. Turn pork chops to coat. Cover and refrigerate for 8-12 hours.
**3.** Remove chops from brine; rinse and pat dry. Discard brine. Brush both sides of chops with oil. In a small bowl, mix rub ingredients; rub over pork chops. Let stand at room temperature for 30 minutes.
**4.** Grill chops on an oiled rack, covered, over medium heat for 4-6 minutes on each side or until a thermometer reads 145°. Let stand 5 minutes before serving.
**1 PORK CHOP:** 300 cal., 18g fat (4g sat. fat), 72mg chol., 130mg sod., 5g carb. (1g sugars, 2g fiber), 30g pro.
**SMOKY PORK RUB:** Prepare rub as directed, using smoked paprika in place of regular paprika.
**SPICY PORK RUB:** Add ½ tsp. cayenne pepper to rub mixture.
**SWEET PORK RUB:** Add 3 Tbsp. brown sugar to rub mixture.

**TIP**
Do not brine your pork chops longer than 12 hours; the proteins in the meat will break down too much and the chops will taste too salty. If you're not ready to cook after 12 hours, remove the meat from the brine, pat it dry and keep it in the refrigerator.

🍎
## STUFFED GRILLED ZUCCHINI

Pair these zucchini boats with charred pork chops, smoked fish or other grilled greats.
—*Nancy Zimmerman, Cape May Court House, NJ*

PREP: 25 min. • GRILL: 10 min. • MAKES: 4 servings

- 4 medium zucchini
- 5 tsp. olive oil, divided
- 2 Tbsp. finely chopped red onion
- ¼ tsp. minced garlic
- ½ cup dry bread crumbs
- ½ cup shredded part-skim mozzarella cheese
- 1 Tbsp. minced fresh mint
- ½ tsp. salt
- 3 Tbsp. grated Parmesan cheese

1. Cut zucchini in half lengthwise; scoop out flesh, leaving ¼-in. shells. Brush shells with 2 tsp. oil; set aside. Chop zucchini flesh.
2. In a large skillet, saute flesh and onion in remaining 1 Tbsp. oil. Add garlic; cook 1 minute longer. Add bread crumbs; cook and stir until golden brown, about 2 minutes.
3. Remove from the heat. Stir in the mozzarella cheese, mint and salt. Spoon into zucchini shells. Sprinkle with Parmesan cheese.
4. Grill, covered, over medium heat until zucchini is tender, 8-10 minutes.

**2 STUFFED ZUCCHINI HALVES:** 186 cal., 10g fat (3g sat. fat), 11mg chol., 553mg sod., 17g carb. (4g sugars, 3g fiber), 9g pro. **DIABETIC EXCHANGES:** 1 vegetable, 1 lean meat, 1 fat, ½ starch.

## ELOTE (MEXICAN STREET CORN)

Elote, otherwise known as Mexican street corn, is grilled, covered in mayo, and then sprinkled with chili powder, Cotija and cilantro. A squeeze of lime juice is the perfect finishing touch. This makes a great side dish with tacos, fajitas or pork carnitas. Make it a Mexican night!
—Taste of Home *Test Kitchen*

PREP: 15 min. + soaking • GRILL: 25 min. • MAKES: 6 servings

- 6 medium ears sweet corn
- 2 Tbsp. olive oil
- ½ cup mayonnaise
- 2 to 3 tsp. chili powder
- 6 Tbsp. Cotija cheese
- ½ cup fresh cilantro leaves
  Lime wedges

1. Carefully peel back corn husks to within 1 in. of bottoms; remove silk. Brush corn with oil. Rewrap corn in husks; secure with kitchen string. Place in a Dutch oven; cover with cold water. Soak 20 minutes; drain.
2. Grill corn, covered, over medium heat 25-30 minutes or until tender, turning often. Peel back husks. Spread mayonnaise over each ear; sprinkle with chili powder, cojita cheese and cilantro. Squeeze lime wedges over corn before serving.

**1 EAR:** 278 cal., 22g fat (4g sat. fat), 14mg chol., 245mg sod., 20g carb. (6g sugars, 2g fiber), 5g pro.

TIP

Mexican street corn is pretty versatile—so don't be afraid to experiment. Try Mexican *crema* instead of mayo, or sprinkle with Tajin seasoning, garlic powder, smoked paprika or any of your favorite spices. If you don't have Cotija, try Parmesan, Romano, queso fresco or feta.

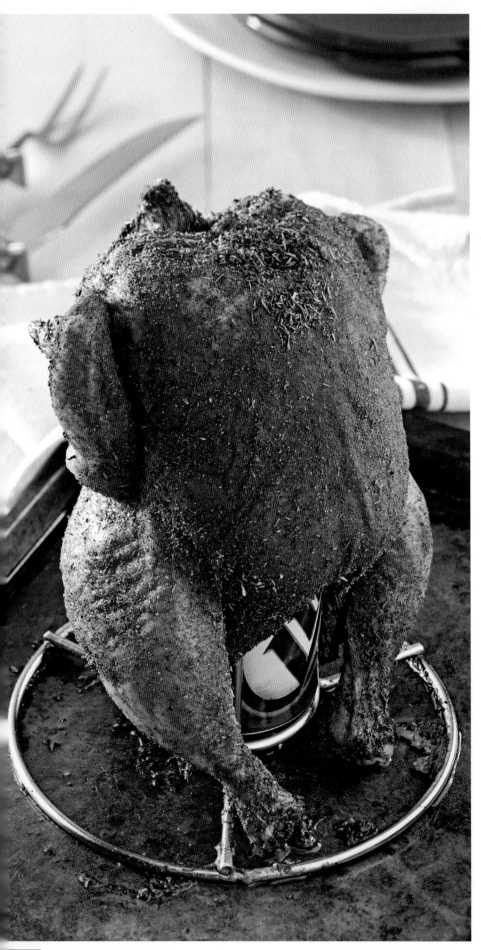

## AT-ATTENTION GRILLED CHICKEN

After years of making this recipe, I have yet to find a better grilled chicken. The cooking technique makes it so juicy and tender, you won't want to fix chicken any other way at your next summer cookout.
—*Shirley Hodge, Bangor, PA*

- - - - - - - - - - - - - - - - - - - - - - - - - - - - - - - -

**PREP:** 15 min. + marinating
**GRILL:** 1¼ hours + standing
**MAKES:** 6 servings

- 3 Tbsp. minced fresh thyme or
  1 Tbsp. dried thyme
- 1 Tbsp. grated lemon zest
- 1 Tbsp. ground cumin
- 1 tsp. salt
- 1 tsp. ground allspice
- 1 tsp. chili powder
- 1 tsp. pepper
- ½ tsp. ground nutmeg
- 1 broiler/fryer chicken (3 to 4 lbs.)
- 1 Tbsp. olive oil
- 1 can (12 oz.) beer or nonalcoholic beer

**1.** In a small bowl, mix first 8 ingredients. Place chicken on a large plate; tuck under wings. With fingers, carefully loosen skin from chicken breast; rub oil and 2 Tbsp. thyme mixture under skin. Rub remaining mixture over skin. Refrigerate, covered, at least 1 hour or overnight.
**2.** Prepare grill for indirect heat, using a drip pan. Remove a third of the beer from can. Using a can opener, make additional large holes in top of can. Cover bottom and sides of can with heavy-duty foil, wrapping tightly. Carefully slide chicken over foil, neck end up.
**3.** Stand chicken over drip pan, spreading the legs slightly to secure. Grill chicken, covered, over indirect medium heat for 1¼-1½ hours or until a thermometer inserted in thickest part of thigh reads 170°-175°.
**4.** Carefully remove chicken from grill; tent with foil. Let stand for 15 minutes before carving.
**4 OZ. COOKED CHICKEN:** 322 cal., 19g fat (5g sat. fat), 104mg chol., 498mg sod., 2g carb. (0 sugars, 1g fiber), 33g pro.

## CRAB & SHRIMP STUFFED SOLE

Even the most casual cookout will seem elegant when it features this delicate fish combined with seafood stuffing and a lemony sauce. Just add a salad and baguette.
—*Bryn Namavari, Chicago, IL*

------------------------------------------------------------

**PREP:** 25 min. • **GRILL:** 15 min. • **MAKES:** 4 servings

- 1   can (6 oz.) crabmeat, drained, flaked and cartilage removed
- ½   cup chopped cooked peeled shrimp
- ¼   cup soft bread crumbs
- ¼   cup butter, melted, divided
- 2   Tbsp. whipped cream cheese
- 2   tsp. minced chives
- 1   garlic clove, minced
- 1   tsp. grated lemon zest
- 1   tsp. minced fresh parsley
- 4   sole fillets (6 oz. each)
- 1½   cups cherry tomatoes
- 2   Tbsp. dry white wine or chicken broth
- 2   Tbsp. lemon juice
- ½   tsp. salt
- ½   tsp. pepper

**1.** Combine crab, shrimp, bread crumbs, 2 Tbsp. butter, cream cheese, chives, garlic, lemon zest and parsley. Spoon about ¼ cup stuffing onto each fillet; roll up and secure with toothpicks.
**2.** Place each fillet on a double thickness of heavy-duty foil (about 18x12 in.). Combine tomatoes, wine, lemon juice, salt, pepper and remaining 2 Tbsp. butter; spoon over fillets. Fold foil around fish and seal tightly.
**3.** Grill, covered, over medium heat until fish flakes easily with a fork, 12-15 minutes. Open foil carefully to allow steam to escape.
**NOTE:** To make soft bread crumbs, tear bread into pieces and place in a food processor or blender. Cover and pulse until crumbs form. One slice of bread yields ½-¾ cup crumbs.
**1 PACKET:** 363 cal., 16g fat (9g sat. fat), 184mg chol., 728mg sod., 6g carb. (2g sugars, 1g fiber), 46g pro.

## GRILLED BROCCOLI

I started using this recipe in 1987, when I began cooking light, and it's been a favorite side dish ever since. With its lemon and Parmesan flavors, it once took second place in a cooking contest.
—*Alice Nulle, Woodstock, IL*

------------------------------------------------------------

**PREP:** 5 min. + standing • **GRILL:** 20 min. • **MAKES:** 6 servings

- 6   cups fresh broccoli spears
- 2   Tbsp. plus 1½ tsp. lemon juice
- 2   Tbsp. olive oil
- ¼   tsp. salt
- ¼   tsp. pepper
- ¾   cup grated Parmesan cheese
    Optional: Grilled lemon slices and red pepper flakes

**1.** Place broccoli in a large bowl. Combine lemon juice, oil, salt and pepper; drizzle over broccoli and toss to coat. Let stand for 30 minutes.
**2.** Toss broccoli and drain, discarding marinade. Place cheese in a small shallow bowl. Add broccoli, a few pieces at a time; toss to coat.
**3.** Prepare grill for indirect heat using a drip pan. Place broccoli over drip pan on an oiled grill rack. Grill, covered, over indirect medium heat for 8-10 minutes on each side or until crisp-tender. If desired, garnish with grilled lemon slices and red pepper flakes.
**1 CUP:** 107 cal., 8g fat (3g sat. fat), 8mg chol., 304mg sod., 5g carb. (2g sugars, 2g fiber), 6g pro. **DIABETIC EXCHANGES:** 1½ fat, 1 vegetable.

## GERMAN BRAT SEAFOOD BOIL

Grilled bratwurst and onion add a smoky flavor to corn, potatoes and fish for a hearty meal that's always a hit.
—Trisha Kruse, Eagle, ID

PREP: 25 min. • COOK: 30 min. • MAKES: 6 servings

- 1 pkg. (19 oz.) uncooked bratwurst links
- 1 medium onion, quartered
- 2 bottles (12 oz. each) beer or 3 cups reduced-sodium chicken broth
- ½ cup seafood seasoning
- 5 medium ears sweet corn, cut into 2-in. pieces
- 2 lbs. small red potatoes
- 1 medium lemon, halved
- 1 lb. cod fillet, cut into 1-in. pieces
  Coarsely ground pepper

1. Grill bratwurst, covered, over medium heat, turning frequently, until meat is no longer pink, 15-20 minutes. Grill onion, covered, until lightly browned, 3-4 minutes on each side. Cut grilled bratwurst into 2-in. pieces.
2. In a stockpot, combine 2 qt. water, beer and seafood seasoning; add corn, potatoes, lemon, bratwurst and onion. Bring to a boil. Reduce heat; simmer, uncovered, until the potatoes are tender, 15-20 minutes. Stir in cod; cook until the fish flakes easily with a fork, 4-6 minutes. Drain; transfer to a large serving bowl. Sprinkle with pepper.
**1 SERVING:** 553 cal., 28g fat (9g sat. fat), 95mg chol., 1620mg sod., 46g carb. (8g sugars, 5g fiber), 30g pro.

## GRILLED NECTARINE & CHEESE CROSTINI

At our house, we love the summer tastes of sweet grilled nectarines and fresh basil over goat cheese. I can usually find all the ingredients at the farmers market.
—Brandy Hollingshead, Grass Valley, CA

TAKES: 25 min. • MAKES: 1 dozen

- ½ cup balsamic vinegar
- 1 Tbsp. olive oil
- 12 slices French bread baguette (¼ in. thick)
- 2 medium nectarines, halved
- ¼ cup fresh goat cheese, softened
- ¼ cup loosely packed basil leaves, thinly sliced

1. In a small saucepan, bring vinegar to a boil; cook until liquid is reduced to 3 Tbsp., 10-15 minutes. Remove from heat.
2. Brush oil over both sides of baguette slices. Grill, uncovered, over medium heat until golden brown on both sides. Grill nectarines until tender and lightly browned, 45-60 seconds on each side. Cool slightly.
3. Spread goat cheese over toasts. Cut nectarines into thick slices; arrange over cheese. Drizzle with balsamic syrup; sprinkle with basil. Serve immediately.
**1 APPETIZER:** 48 cal., 2g fat (1g sat. fat), 5mg chol., 55mg sod., 6g carb. (3g sugars, 0 fiber), 1g pro. **DIABETIC EXCHANGES:** ½ starch.

# GRILLED PISTACHIO-LEMON PESTO SHRIMP

Not your ordinary pesto, this one is made with arugula and pistachios. It's excellent on more than shrimp too. Try spreading it on crostini or tossing it with pasta.
—*Amy Dale, Long Beach, CA*

**PREP:** 15 min. + chilling • **GRILL:** 5 min. • **MAKES:** 8 servings

- ¾ cup fresh arugula
- ½ cup minced fresh parsley
- ⅓ cup shelled pistachios
- 2 Tbsp. lemon juice
- 1 garlic clove, peeled
- ¼ tsp. grated lemon zest
- ½ cup olive oil
- ¼ cup shredded Parmesan cheese
- ¼ tsp. salt
- ⅛ tsp. pepper
- 1½ lbs. uncooked jumbo shrimp, peeled and deveined

**1.** Place the first 6 ingredients in a food processor; pulse until finely chopped. Continue processing while gradually adding oil in a steady stream. Add Parmesan cheese, salt and pepper; pulse just until combined. Transfer ⅓ cup pesto to a large bowl. Add shrimp; toss to coat. Refrigerate, covered, 30 minutes.

**2.** Thread shrimp onto 8 metal or soaked wooden skewers; place on greased grill rack. Cook, covered, over medium heat until shrimp turn pink, 5-6 minutes, turning once. Serve with the remaining pesto.

**1 SKEWER WITH ABOUT 1 TBSP. PESTO:** 236 cal., 18g fat (3g sat. fat), 105mg chol., 241mg sod., 3g carb. (1g sugars, 1g fiber), 16g pro.

# GRILLED PORK TENDERLOIN WITH CHERRY SALSA MOLE

The combination of pork and cherries has long been a favorite of mine. The hint of spice and chocolate in the salsa mole makes the combination even more special.
—*Roxanne Chan, Albany, CA*

**PREP:** 25 min. • **GRILL:** 15 min. + standing • **MAKES:** 6 servings

- 2 pork tenderloins (¾ lb. each)
- 1 Tbsp. canola oil
- ½ tsp. salt
- ¼ tsp. ground cumin
- ¼ tsp. chili powder
- 1 cup pitted fresh or frozen dark sweet cherries, thawed and chopped
- 1 jalapeno pepper, seeded and minced
- ½ cup finely chopped peeled jicama
- 1 oz. semisweet chocolate, grated
- 2 Tbsp. minced fresh cilantro
- 1 green onion, thinly sliced
- 1 Tbsp. lime juice
- 1 tsp. honey
  Salted pumpkin seeds or pepitas

**1.** Brush pork with oil; sprinkle with salt, cumin and chili powder. Grill, covered, over medium heat until a thermometer reads 145°, 15-20 minutes, turning occasionally. Let stand 10-15 minutes.

**2.** Meanwhile, combine cherries, jalapeno, jicama, chocolate, cilantro, green onion, lime juice and honey. Slice pork; serve with cherry salsa and pumpkin seeds.

**NOTE:** Wear disposable gloves when cutting hot peppers; the oils can burn skin. Avoid touching your face.

**3 OZ. COOKED PORK WITH ¼ CUP SALSA:** 218 cal., 8g fat (3g sat. fat), 64mg chol., 248mg sod., 11g carb. (9g sugars, 2g fiber), 23g pro.
**DIABETIC EXCHANGES:** 3 lean meat, ½ starch, ½ fat.

## KEY WEST FLANK STEAK

My husband, Jason, is the cook in our family. This is his recipe, inspired by his Colombian roots and our visits to Key West. Serve with sides of rice and fried plantains.
—*Gretchen Ospina, Columbia Heights, MN*

- - - - - - - - - - - - - - - - - - - - - - - - - - - - - -

**PREP:** 20 min. + marinating
**GRILL:** 15 min. + standing
**MAKES:** 4 servings

- 1  **large red onion, sliced**
- 1  **cup minced fresh cilantro**
- ¼  **cup white wine vinegar**
- ¼  **cup Key lime juice**
- 3  **Tbsp. extra virgin olive oil, divided**
- 6  **Key limes, halved**
- 1  **beef flank steak (1 lb.)**
- 1  **tsp. kosher salt**
- ⅛  **tsp. pepper**

**1.** In a small bowl, combine the onion, cilantro, vinegar, lime juice and 2 Tbsp. oil until blended. Pour 1 cup marinade into a large bowl or shallow dish; add lime halves. Cover and refrigerate remaining marinade. Rub steak with remaining 1 Tbsp. oil; sprinkle with salt and pepper. Add steak to bowl with marinade; turn to coat. Refrigerate 8 hours or overnight.
**2.** Drain steak, discarding marinade and limes in bowl. Place reserved marinade in a food processor; process until chopped.
**3.** Grill steak, covered, over medium heat or broil 4 in. from heat until meat reaches desired doneness (for medium-rare, a thermometer should read 135°; medium, 140°), 6-8 minutes per side. Baste occasionally with reserved marinade. Let stand 10 minutes before thinly slicing steak across the grain. If desired, serve with additional grilled onions, grilled lime halves and fresh cilantro.
**3 OZ. COOKED STEAK:** 271 cal., 16g fat (5g sat. fat), 54mg chol., 431mg sod., 12g carb. (3g sugars, 3g fiber), 23g pro. **DIABETIC EXCHANGES:** 3 lean meat, 1½ fat.

## GRILLED SALMON FILLET

Growing up on a family-owned resort, I was expected to help around the kitchen. Grilling salmon became my specialty.
—*Paul Noetzel, Grafton, WI*

- - - - - - - - - - - - - - - - - - - - - - - - - - - - - -

**TAKES:** 25 min. • **MAKES:** 4 servings

- 1  **salmon fillet (about 1 lb.)**
- 2  **Tbsp. lemon juice**
- 2  **Tbsp. red wine vinegar**
- 2  **tsp. grated lemon zest**
- 1½  **tsp. dried basil**
- 1  **tsp. garlic powder**
- 1  **tsp. soy sauce**
- 4½  **tsp. grated Parmesan cheese**
  **Dash pepper**
  **Lemon wedges, optional**

**1.** Place fish, skin side down, in disposable foil pan. Combine the lemon juice, vinegar, lemon zest, basil, garlic powder and soy sauce; pour over fish. Sprinkle with Parmesan cheese and pepper.
**2.** Place pan on grill. Cover grill and cook over medium heat until the fish flakes easily with a fork, 15-20 minutes. Top with pepper and, if desired, additional grated Parmesan cheese. Serve with lemon wedges if desired.
**3 OZ. COOKED SALMON:** 193 cal., 11g fat (2g sat. fat), 59mg chol., 163mg sod., 2g carb. (0 sugars, 0 fiber), 20g pro. **DIABETIC EXCHANGES:** 3 lean meat.

**TIPS**
- Be careful not to overcook the salmon. Follow the recipe and cook just until the fish flakes into pieces when you gently poke the fillet with a fork.
- When grilling salmon, always start skin-side down. This recipe uses a foil pan for ease of use, but some recipes start with an oiled grill grate and flip the salmon. If you keep the lid on the grill, however, you don't have to flip it.

# - GRILLING MARINADES -

Prepare to become a pit master! Mix up your sauce in a shallow dish, toss in the main ingredient and rest it in the fridge for up to the max marinating time (see "Match the Marinade," below).

### 1 Huli Huli

1 cup packed brown sugar,
¾ cup ketchup, ¾ cup reduced-sodium
soy sauce, ⅓ cup sherry or chicken broth,
2½ tsp. minced fresh gingerroot
and 1½ tsp. minced garlic.
—Sharon Boling, San Diego, CA

### 2 Northwoods

6 Tbsp. maple syrup,
6 Tbsp. balsamic vinegar, ¾ tsp. salt
and ¾ tsp. coarsely ground pepper.
—Nicholas King, Duluth, MN

### 3 Honey-Garlic

¼ cup lemon juice, ¼ cup honey,
2 Tbsp. soy sauce and
2 minced garlic cloves.
—Helen Carpenter, Albuquerque, NM

### 4 Orange-Spice

½ cup thawed orange juice concentrate,
¼ cup honey, ¼ cup soy sauce,
1 tsp. Chinese five-spice powder
and ½ tsp. garlic powder.
—Debra Stevens, Lutz, FL

### 5 Ranch

2 cups sour cream, 1 envelope ranch
salad dressing mix, 4 tsp. lemon juice,
4 tsp. Worcestershire sauce, 2 tsp. celery
salt, 2 tsp. paprika, 1 tsp. garlic salt
and 1 tsp. pepper.
—Barbee Decker, Whispering Pines, NC

### 6 Heavenly Greek

⅓ cup lemon juice, 2 Tbsp. olive oil,
4 tsp. grated lemon zest, 2 minced garlic
cloves, 1 tsp. dried oregano, ¼ tsp. salt
and ¼ tsp. pepper.
—Meagan Jensen, Reno, NV

### 7 Southwest Chili

2 Tbsp. olive oil, 1 Tbsp. chili powder,
1 tsp. garlic salt, 1 tsp. ground coriander,
1 tsp. dried oregano, ½ tsp. ground cumin
and ½ tsp. pepper.
—Lindsay Matuszak, Reno, NV

### 8 Balsamic Mustard

1¼ cups balsamic vinaigrette, 4 tsp.
ground mustard, 2¼ tsp. Worcestershire
sauce and 2 minced garlic cloves.
—Gail Garcelon, Beaverton, OR

### 9 Ginger-Peach

¼ cup peach preserves, 1 Tbsp. lemon
juice, 1 Tbsp. finely chopped crystallized
ginger, 2 tsp. grated lemon zest and
⅛ tsp. ground cloves.
—Jacqueline Correa, Landing, NJ

### 10 Tangy Barbecue

1 cup barbecue sauce, ½ cup burgundy
wine or beef broth and ¼ cup lemon juice.
—Beverly Dietz, Surprise, AZ

**MATCH THE MARINADE**

| | |
|---|---|
| **Beef:** 8 hrs | |
| **Pork:** 6 hrs | |
| **Chicken:** 4 hrs | |
| **Fruit:** 1 hr | |
| **Seafood:** 30 min | |

## CUBAN SANDWICH BURGERS

My mom would make these Cuban burgers when we would visit her in Florida. They are a take on the real Cuban sandwich. My kids love them. My boys could eat two of these monsters in one sitting!
—*Marina Castle-Kelley, Canyon Country, CA*

**PREP:** 20 min. • **GRILL:** 15 min. • **MAKES:** 4 servings

- ½ lb. ground beef
- ½ lb. ground pork
- 1 Tbsp. lemon juice
- 1 tsp. garlic salt, divided
- ½ tsp. pepper, divided
- ½ cup mayonnaise
- ¼ cup Dijon mustard
- 4 hamburger buns, split
- 8 thin slices Swiss cheese
- 4 thin slices deli ham
- 4 thin sandwich pickle slices

**1.** Prepare grill for medium heat. Place a large cast-iron skillet on the grill grates.
**2.** In a large bowl, combine beef, pork, lemon juice, ½ tsp. garlic salt and ¼ tsp. pepper, mixing lightly but thoroughly. Shape into four ½-in.-thick patties. Grill burgers, covered, over medium heat until a thermometer reads 160°, 5-7 minutes on each side.
**3.** Combine mayonnaise, mustard, remaining ½ tsp. garlic salt and ¼ tsp. pepper; spread over cut sides of buns. Place burgers on bun bottoms; top with Swiss cheese, ham, pickles and bun tops. Using oven mitts, carefully place preheated skillet on top of sandwiches. Grill sandwiches, covered, until buns are browned and cheese is melted, 5-8 minutes.
**1 BURGER:** 690 cal., 44g fat (12g sat. fat), 104mg chol., 1706mg sod., 32g carb. (2g sugars, 1g fiber), 36g pro.

## GRILLED MAHI MAHI

Instead of grilling the usual hamburgers or chicken breasts, prepare this grilled mahi mahi and reel in raves!
—Taste of Home *Test Kitchen*

**PREP:** 20 min. + marinating • **GRILL:** 10 min. • **MAKES:** 8 servings

- ¾ cup reduced-sodium teriyaki sauce
- 2 Tbsp. sherry or pineapple juice
- 2 garlic cloves
- 8 mahi mahi fillets (6 oz. each)

**TROPICAL FRUIT SALSA**
- 1 medium mango, peeled and diced
- 1 cup chopped seeded peeled papaya
- ¾ cup chopped green pepper
- ½ cup cubed fresh pineapple
- ½ medium red onion, chopped
- ¼ cup minced fresh cilantro
- ¼ cup minced fresh mint
- 1 Tbsp. chopped seeded jalapeno pepper
- 1 Tbsp. lime juice
- 1 Tbsp. lemon juice
- ½ tsp. crushed red pepper flakes

**1.** In a shallow dish, combine teriyaki sauce, sherry and garlic; add the mahi mahi. Turn to coat; refrigerate for 30 minutes.
**2.** In a large bowl, combine the salsa ingredients. Cover and refrigerate until serving.
**3.** Drain and discard marinade. Place mahi mahi on an oiled grill rack. Grill, covered, over medium heat or broil 4 in. from the heat for 4-5 minutes on each side or until fish flakes easily with a fork. Serve with salsa.
**NOTE:** Wear disposable gloves when cutting hot peppers; the oils can burn skin. Avoid touching your face.
**1 FILLET WITH ¼ CUP SALSA:** 195 cal., 2g fat (0 sat. fat), 124mg chol., 204mg sod., 12g carb. (9g sugars, 2g fiber), 32g pro. **DIABETIC EXCHANGES:** 5 lean meat, 1 fruit.

**GRILLED FLANK STEAK**

This recipe is from my sister and it's a favorite of mine for serving company. The meat and vegetables can be prepared ahead of time. When the company arrives, I just fire up the grill and serve a meaty main meal in minutes!
—*Jenny Reece, Farwell, MN*

------------------------------------------------------------

**PREP:** 20 min. + marinating • **GRILL:** 15 min. • **MAKES:** 5 servings

- ¼ cup soy sauce
- 2 Tbsp. white vinegar
- 1 green onion, sliced
- 1½ tsp. garlic powder
- 1½ tsp. ground ginger
- 3 Tbsp. honey
- ¾ cup vegetable oil
- 1 beef flank steak (about 1½ lbs.)
- 1 lb. fresh mushrooms, sliced
- 1 green pepper, cut into thin strips
- 1 yellow or sweet red pepper, cut into thin strips
- 3 carrots, cut into julienned strips

**1.** Combine first 7 ingredients. Pour ¾ cup marinade into a shallow dish; add beef. Turn to coat; refrigerate, covered, up to 24 hours, turning once. Cover and refrigerate remaining marinade.

**2.** Drain beef and discard marinade. Grill flank steak, uncovered, over medium heat for 6-8 minutes on each side or until meat reaches desired doneness (for medium-rare, a thermometer should read 135°; medium, 140°; medium-well, 145°).

**3.** In a skillet, cook vegetables in reserved marinade until crisp-tender. Thinly slice steak across the grain. Serve with vegetables.

**3 OZ. COOKED BEEF WITH ⅔ CUP VEGETABLES:** 265 cal., 12g fat, 65mg chol., 173mg sod., 11g carb., 28g pro. **DIABETIC EXCHANGES:** 3 lean meat, 2 vegetable, 1 fat.

**GRILLED CAMPFIRE TROUT DINNER**

Your fresh catch will taste even better with this simple treatment that keeps the fish moist. Carrots are an excellent accompaniment; cook them up in a separate foil packet.
—*Wendy McGowan, Fontana, CA*

------------------------------------------------------------

**PREP:** 20 min. • **GRILL:** 30 min. • **MAKES:** 4 servings

- 4 bacon strips
- 2 dressed trout (1 lb. each)
- 4 lemon slices
- 1 small onion, halved and sliced
- ¼ tsp. salt
- ⅛ tsp. pepper

CARROTS
- 4 medium carrots, thinly sliced
- ⅛ tsp. salt
-   Dash pepper
- 1 Tbsp. butter
-   Lemon wedges

**1.** Cook bacon until partially cooked but not crisp; drain. Place each trout on a double thickness of heavy-duty foil (about 20x18 in.). Place lemon and onion in the trout cavities; sprinkle with salt and pepper. Wrap trout with bacon. Fold foil around trout and seal tightly.

**2.** Place carrots on a double thickness of heavy-duty foil (about 20x18 in.); sprinkle with salt and pepper. Dot with butter. Fold foil around carrots and seal tightly.

**3.** Grill carrots, covered, over medium heat for 10 minutes. Add trout packets to the grill; cook until the fish flakes easily with a fork and carrots are tender, 20-25 minutes longer. Serve with lemon wedges.

**1 SERVING:** 362 cal., 16g fat (6g sat. fat), 136mg chol., 530mg sod., 8g carb. (4g sugars, 2g fiber), 44g pro.

## GRILLED JERK CHICKEN

Jerk refers to a dry seasoning blend that originated in the Caribbean and that includes spices like allspice, ginger, cinnamon and a blend of peppers. It'll have your taste buds feeling warm all over.
—Taste of Home *Test Kitchen*

**PREP:** 10 min. + marinating • **GRILL:** 30 min. • **MAKES:** 4 servings

- 4 tsp. curry powder
- 4 tsp. ground cumin
- 4 tsp. paprika
- 3 tsp. ground ginger
- 3 tsp. ground allspice
- 1 tsp. salt
- 1 tsp. cayenne pepper
- 1 tsp. coarsely ground pepper
- 4 bone-in chicken breast halves with skin (8 oz. each)
- 4 bone-in chicken thighs (about 1½ lbs.)

In a small bowl, combine the first 8 ingredients; rub over the chicken pieces. Cover and refrigerate for 1 hour. Grill chicken, covered, over indirect medium heat for 30-40 minutes or until a thermometer reaches 165° for chicken breasts and 170°-175° for thighs.

**1 CHICKEN BREAST HALF AND 1 THIGH:** 444 cal., 21g fat (6g sat. fat), 167mg chol., 741mg sod., 6g carb. (0 sugars, 3g fiber), 56g pro.

## GRILLED POUND CAKE WITH BERRIES

The toasty flavor of lightly grilled pound cake makes it the perfect accompaniment for summertime berries, with a dollop of delightful lemon-kissed whipping cream as a finishing touch.
—Taste of Home *Test Kitchen*

**TAKES:** 25 min. • **MAKES:** 6 servings

- 1 cup sliced fresh strawberries
- 1 cup fresh raspberries
- 1 cup fresh blueberries
- 5 Tbsp. sugar, divided
- 1 Tbsp. minced fresh mint
- 1 cup heavy whipping cream
- 1 Tbsp. lemon juice
- 1 tsp. grated lemon zest
- 3 Tbsp. butter, softened
- 6 slices pound cake (about 1 in. thick)

**1.** In a large bowl, combine the strawberries, raspberries, blueberries, 2 Tbsp. sugar and the mint; set aside.
**2.** In a small bowl, beat cream until it begins to thicken. Beat in remaining 3 Tbsp. sugar. Add lemon juice and zest; beat until soft peaks form. Cover and refrigerate until serving.
**3.** Spread butter over both sides of each cake slice. Grill, uncovered, over indirect medium heat for 1-2 minutes on each side or until light golden brown. Serve with berry mixture and whipped cream.

**1 PIECE:** 377 cal., 27g fat (16g sat. fat), 136mg chol., 193mg sod., 34g carb. (24g sugars, 3g fiber), 3g pro.

## GRILLED PORK WITH PEAR SALSA

My husband, Dave, and I have been in a dinner group with three other couples for a few years. We often share our recipes. This grilled pork was served by one of the couples, and I decided to pair it with this fabulous salsa.

—*Suzan Ward, Coeur d'Alene, ID*

- - - - - - - - - - - - - - - - - - - - - - - - - - - - - - - - - - - - - - - - - - - - - - - - -

**PREP:** 15 min. + marinating • **GRILL:** 10 min. • **MAKES:** 8 servings

- ¼ cup lime juice
- 2 Tbsp. olive oil
- 2 garlic cloves, minced
- 1½ tsp. ground cumin
- 1½ tsp. dried oregano
- ½ tsp. pepper
- 2 lbs. pork tenderloin, cut into ¾-in. slices

**PEAR SALSA**

- 4 cups chopped peeled pears (about 4 medium)
- ⅓ cup chopped red onion
- 2 Tbsp. chopped fresh mint or 2 tsp. dried mint
- 2 Tbsp. lime juice
- 1 Tbsp. grated lime zest
- 1 jalapeno pepper, seeded and chopped
- 1 tsp. sugar
- ½ tsp. pepper

**1.** In a large bowl, combine lime juice, oil, garlic, cumin, oregano and pepper; add pork. Turn to coat; cover and refrigerate overnight. Drain pork, discarding marinade.

**2.** Grill pork, uncovered, over medium heat for 4-6 minutes on each side or until juices run clear.

**3.** Combine the salsa ingredients. Serve with the pork.

**NOTE:** Wear disposable gloves when cutting hot peppers; the oils can burn skin. Avoid touching your face.

**3 OZ. COOKED PORK WITH ½ CUP SALSA:** 214 cal., 7g fat (2g sat. fat), 64mg chol., 47mg sod., 14g carb. (8g sugars, 3g fiber), 23g pro. **DIABETIC EXCHANGES:** 3 lean meat, 1 fruit, ½ fat.

## CHICKEN YAKITORI

I grew up in Tokyo, and some of my favorite memories include eating street food like this with my friends. Although we now live thousands of miles apart, we still reminisce about our nights sharing secrets and bonding over delicious meals. This one is easy to re-create at home, which makes it perfect for when I'm feeling homesick. I like to serve it with rice.

—*Lindsay Howerton-Hastings, Greenville, SC*

- - - - - - - - - - - - - - - - - - - - - - - - - - - - - - - - - - - - - - - - - - - - - - - - -

**TAKES:** 30 min. • **MAKES:** 6 servings

- ½ cup mirin (sweet rice wine)
- ½ cup sake
- ½ cup soy sauce
- 1 Tbsp. sugar
- 2 large sweet red peppers, cut into 2-in. pieces
- 2 lbs. boneless skinless chicken thighs, cut into 1½-in. pieces
- 1 bunch green onions

**1.** In a small saucepan, combine the first 4 ingredients. Bring to a boil over medium-high heat. Remove from heat; set aside half the mixture for serving.

**2.** Thread peppers onto 2 metal or soaked wooden skewers. Thread chicken onto 6 metal or soaked wooden skewers. Grill chicken, covered, over medium heat until meat is cooked through, 10-12 minutes, turning occasionally and basting frequently with soy sauce mixture during the last 3 minutes. Grill peppers, covered, until tender, 4-5 minutes, turning occasionally. Grill onions, covered, until lightly charred, 1-2 minutes, turning occasionally. Serve chicken and vegetables with reserved sauce for dipping.

**1 SERVING:** 332 cal., 11g fat (3g sat. fat), 101mg chol., 1316mg sod., 14g carb. (11g sugars, 1g fiber), 32g pro.

# GRILLED LOBSTER TAILS

I had never made lobster at home until I tried this convenient and deliciously different grilled recipe. It turned out amazing, and has left me with little reason to ever order lobster at a restaurant again.
—*Katie Rush, Kansas City, MO*

**PREP:** 15 min. + marinating
**GRILL:** 10 min. • **MAKES:** 6 servings

- 6 frozen lobster tails (8 to 10 oz. each), thawed
- ¾ cup olive oil
- 3 Tbsp. minced fresh chives
- 3 garlic cloves, minced
- ½ tsp. salt
- ½ tsp. pepper

**1.** Using scissors, cut 3 or 4 lengthwise slits in underside of tail to loosen shell slightly. Cut top of lobster shell lengthwise down the center, leaving tail fin intact. Cut shell at an angle away from the center of the tail at base of tail fin. Loosen meat from shell, keeping the fin end attached; lift meat and lay over shell.

**2.** In a small bowl, combine the remaining ingredients; spoon over lobster meat. Cover and refrigerate for 20 minutes.

**3.** Place lobster tails, meat side up, on grill rack. Grill, covered, over medium heat until meat is opaque, 10-12 minutes.

**1 LOBSTER TAIL:** 446 cal., 29g fat (4g sat. fat), 215mg chol., 869mg sod., 2g carb. (0 sugars, 0 fiber), 43g pro.

**BAKED LOBSTER TAILS:** Prepare the lobster tails as recipe directs. Preheat oven to 375°. Place on a baking sheet. Bake, uncovered, 15-20 minutes or until meat is firm and opaque.

**BROILED LOBSTER TAILS:** Prepare lobster tails as recipe directs. Preheat broiler. Place on a foil-lined 15x10x1-in. pan. Broil 5-6 in. from heat until meat is opaque, 5-8 minutes.

**TIP**
To remove the vein from a lobster tail, hold the fleshy end of the tail (where it connected to the body), locate the vein and gently pull until it detaches from the tail. You can use a sharp paring knife to get the vein started before completely loosening it with your fingers.

## PROVOLONE-STUFFED PORK CHOPS WITH TARRAGON VINAIGRETTE

A fresh tarragon vinaigrette on these stuffed pork chops gives you the savory feel of dining in Provence.
—*Barbara Pletzke, Herndon, VA*

**TAKES:** 25 min. • **MAKES:** 4 servings

- ½ cup olive oil
- ¼ cup white balsamic vinegar
- 2 Tbsp. minced fresh tarragon or 2 tsp. dried tarragon
- 2 garlic cloves, minced
- ¼ tsp. salt
- ¼ tsp. pepper

PORK CHOPS

- 4 bone-in pork loin chops (8 oz. each and ¾ in. thick)
- 4 slices provolone cheese, cut into eighths
- 2 Tbsp. olive oil
- 2 tsp. minced fresh tarragon or ½ tsp. dried tarragon
- ¼ tsp. salt
- ¼ tsp. pepper
- 2 large tomatoes, each cut into 6 wedges

**1.** In a small bowl, whisk the first 6 ingredients. Set aside ¼ cup vinaigrette for serving.
**2.** For pork chops, cut a pocket in each chop by slicing almost to the bone; fill pockets with cheese. Combine the oil, tarragon, salt and pepper; brush onto both sides of chops.
**3.** Brush tomato wedges with some of the remaining vinaigrette. Grill, uncovered, on a lightly oiled grill over medium heat or broil 4 in. from the heat for 1-3 minutes on each side or until lightly browned. Set aside.
**4.** Grill chops, covered, over medium heat or broil 4-5 in. from the heat 4-5 minutes on each side or until a thermometer reads 145°. Baste frequently with the remaining vinaigrette during the last 3 minutes of cooking. Let stand for 5 minutes. Serve with the grilled tomatoes and reserved vinaigrette.

**1 PORK CHOP WITH 3 TOMATO WEDGES AND 1 TBSP. VINAIGRETTE:** 702 cal., 58g fat (15g sat. fat), 126mg chol., 517mg sod., 3g carb. (2g sugars, 0 fiber), 41g pro.

## GRILLED POTATOES

Need a simple sidekick for steaks or chops? Try these potatoes, which are bursting with fresh flavor. I make this recipe for picnics and potlucks. The potatoes turn out tender and well-seasoned. Plus, there's one less pot to wash!
—*Jena Coffey, Rock Hill, MO*

**PREP:** 10 min. • **GRILL:** 30 min. • **MAKES:** 4 servings

- 1 Tbsp. olive oil
- 2 garlic cloves, minced
- ½ tsp. dried basil
- ¼ tsp. salt
- ⅛ tsp. pepper
- 3 medium potatoes, peeled and cut into 1-in. cubes

**1.** In a large bowl, combine the first 5 ingredients. Add potatoes; toss to coat. Spoon onto a greased double thickness of heavy-duty foil (about 18 in. square).
**2.** Fold foil around the potato mixture and seal tightly. Grill, covered, over medium heat until potatoes are tender, turning once, 30-35 minutes. Open foil carefully to allow steam to escape.
**¾ CUP:** 125 cal., 3g fat (1g sat. fat), 0 chol., 151mg sod., 22g carb. (2g sugars, 2g fiber), 2g pro. **DIABETIC EXCHANGES:** 1½ starch, ½ fat.

TIPS

- The best potatoes to grill are Yukon Golds, but sweet potatoes or Idaho potatoes could do the job too.
- You can tell that your potatoes are done grilling if you can pierce them without any resistance. You should be able to slide a fork or wooden skewer smoothly into the flesh.
- This recipe is a great base for different seasoning ideas. If you're looking for something classic, try garlic powder or a mixed herb seasoning. Want a little spice? Try chili powder or cayenne.

## LEMON-BASIL GRILLED SHRIMP & COUSCOUS

The basil and lemon flavors in this dish complement each other so nicely. Make sure to use fresh basil and fresh lemon juice and zest—they really make a big difference.
—*Trisha Kruse, Eagle, ID*

- - - - - - - - - - - - - - - - - - - - - - - - - - - - - - - - - - - - - - - - -

**TAKES:** 25 min. • **MAKES:** 6 servings

- 1½ **cups uncooked pearl (Israeli) couscous**
- ⅓ **cup lemon juice**
- ¼ **cup olive oil**
- 2 **Tbsp. Dijon mustard**
- 3 **garlic cloves, minced**
- ½ **tsp. salt**
- ¼ **tsp. pepper**
- ½ **cup minced fresh basil, divided**
- 2 **lbs. uncooked large shrimp, peeled and deveined**
- 2 **tsp. grated lemon zest**

**1.** Cook couscous according to package directions; remove from heat. Meanwhile, in a large bowl, whisk lemon juice, oil, mustard, garlic, salt and pepper until blended; stir in ¼ cup basil. Stir ¼ cup dressing into the cooked couscous; reserve remaining dressing.
**2.** Thread shrimp onto metal or soaked wooden skewers. Grill shrimp, covered, on an oiled rack over medium-high heat until pink, 2-3 minutes on each side.
**3.** Remove shrimp from skewers; toss with reserved dressing. Serve with couscous. Sprinkle with lemon zest and remaining ¼ cup basil.
**8 SHRIMP WITH ½ CUP COUSCOUS:** 363 cal., 12g fat (2g sat. fat), 184mg chol., 497mg sod., 34g carb. (0 sugars, 0 fiber), 29g pro.
**DIABETIC EXCHANGES:** 3 lean meat, 2 starch, 2 fat.

## GRILLED BURGERS

Sour cream makes these burgers delightfully moist, and thyme and black pepper give them zip. They're a terrific taste of summer.
—*Jesse and Anne Foust, Bluefield, WV*

- - - - - - - - - - - - - - - - - - - - - - - - - - - - - - - - - - - - - - - - -

**TAKES:** 20 min. • **MAKES:** 10 servings

- ¼ **cup sour cream**
- 2 **tsp. dried parsley flakes**
- 1 **tsp. dried thyme**
- 1 **tsp. salt**
- ½ **tsp. pepper**
- 2½ **lbs. ground beef**
- 10 **hamburger buns, split**
  **Optional: Cheese, lettuce leaves, sliced tomato, pickles, sliced onion, ketchup and mayonnaise**

**1.** In a large bowl, combine the first 5 ingredients; add beef and mix lightly but thoroughly. Shape into 10 patties.
**2.** Grill, uncovered, over medium heat for 4-5 minutes on each side or until the meat is no longer pink. Serve on buns with desired toppings.
**1 BURGER:** 358 cal., 17g fat (7g sat. fat), 79mg chol., 534mg sod., 22g carb. (3g sugars, 1g fiber), 26g pro.

> **TIP**
> To make the best hamburgers, we recommend going for chuck, round or brisket cuts of beef. Choosing the right ratio of lean meat to fat can be tricky—for a classic, medium-rare burger, go for an 80% lean product.

## SOURDOUGH BREAD BOWL SANDWICH

I created this recipe for when my husband and I go to the lake. I don't like to spend a lot of time hovering over a stove or grill, especially in the hot Oklahoma summer months, and this filling sourdough bread bowl sandwich is ready in minutes. For extra flavor, brush melted garlic and herb butter over the top prior to cooking.
—*Shawna Welsh-Garrison, Owasso, OK*

------------------------------------------

**PREP:** 15 min. • **COOK:** 25 min. + standing
**MAKES:** 8 servings

- 1 round loaf sourdough bread (1½ lbs.)
- ½ cup honey mustard salad dressing
- 4 slices sharp cheddar cheese
- ⅓ lb. thinly sliced deli ham
- 4 slices smoked provolone cheese
- ⅓ lb. thinly sliced deli smoked turkey
- 1 Tbsp. butter, melted

**1.** Prepare campfire or grill for low heat. Cut a thin slice off top of bread loaf. Hollow out bottom of loaf, leaving a ½-in.-thick shell (save removed bread for another use). Spread dressing on the inside of the hollowed loaf and under the bread top. Layer inside with cheddar, ham, provolone and turkey. Replace top. Place on a piece of heavy-duty foil (about 24x18 in.). Brush loaf with butter. Fold foil edges over top, crimping to seal.

**2.** Cook over campfire or grill until heated through, 25-30 minutes. Let stand for 15 minutes before removing foil. Cut into wedges.

**1 WEDGE:** 346 cal., 17g fat (6g sat. fat), 46mg chol., 865mg sod., 30g carb. (5g sugars, 1g fiber), 19g pro.

> **TIP**
> This giant sandwich can be tricky to slice. Cut it with a serrated knife using a sawing motion. Consider inserting kabob skewers through each piece prior to cutting to hold the layers together.

## SPICED GRILLED CHICKEN WITH CILANTRO LIME BUTTER

This grilled chicken gets a lovely pop of color and flavor from the lime butter—don't skip it!
—*Diane Halferty, Corpus Christi, TX*

------------------------------------------

**PREP:** 20 min. • **GRILL:** 35 min.
**MAKES:** 6 servings

- 1 Tbsp. chili powder
- 1 Tbsp. brown sugar
- 2 tsp. ground cinnamon
- 1 tsp. baking cocoa
- ½ tsp. salt
- ½ tsp. pepper
- 3 Tbsp. olive oil
- 1 Tbsp. balsamic vinegar
- 6 bone-in chicken breast halves (8 oz. each)

**CILANTRO LIME BUTTER**
- ⅓ cup butter, melted
- ¼ cup minced fresh cilantro
- 2 Tbsp. finely chopped red onion
- 1 Tbsp. lime juice
- 1 serrano pepper, finely chopped
- ⅛ tsp. pepper

**1.** In a small bowl, combine the first 8 ingredients. Brush over chicken.

**2.** Place chicken skin side down on grill rack. Grill, covered, over indirect medium heat for 15 minutes. Turn; grill 20-25 minutes longer or until a thermometer reads 165°.

**3.** Meanwhile, in a small bowl, combine the butter ingredients. Drizzle over the chicken before serving.

**NOTE:** Wear disposable gloves when cutting hot peppers; the oils can burn skin. Avoid touching your face.

**1 CHICKEN BREAST HALF WITH 1 TBSP. LIME BUTTER:** 430 cal., 27g fat (10g sat. fat), 138mg chol., 411mg sod., 5g carb. (3g sugars, 1g fiber), 40g pro.

> **DID YOU KNOW?**
> This recipe gives you a hint of classic mole flavor. Mole is a Mexican sauce that can be made in many ways, but often includes the standout flavors of cumin, cinnamon and cocoa.

# - 11 -

# ONE-DISH RECIPES

Easy, efficient prep and ultra-fast cleanup—all that and hearty, delicious flavor, too!
Sheet pans, Dutch ovens, slow cookers, cast-iron skillets and casserole dishes
all get their turn to produce these one-dish wonders your family will adore.

**Southwestern Rice** (p. 235) **Favorite Company Casserole** (p. 244)
**Taco Skillet Pizza with Cornbread Crust** (p. 244)
**One-Pot Dutch Oven Pasta Bake** (p. 247) **Heirloom Tomato Tart** (p. 233)
**Sausage, Pear & Sweet Potato Sheet-Pan Dinner** (p. 237) **One-Dish Turkey Dinner** (p. 241)
**Sunshine Chicken** (p. 236) **Rotisserie-Style Chicken** (p. 242)

## ONE-SKILLET PASTA

This recipe was given to me 25 years ago and remains a family favorite. It's a simple dish with a great twist on traditional spaghetti. Cooking everything in one pot saves time on prep and cleanup.
—*Susan Spence, Lawrenceville, VA*

------------------------------------------

**PREP:** 20 min. • **COOK:** 1¼ hours
**MAKES:** 5 servings

- 1½ lbs. ground turkey
- 1 medium onion, finely chopped
- 1 medium sweet red pepper, finely chopped
- 1 can (28 oz.) diced tomatoes, undrained
- 1 can (14½ oz.) fire-roasted diced tomatoes, undrained
- 1 can (14½ oz.) reduced-sodium beef broth
- 1 can (4 oz.) sliced mushrooms, drained
- 1 Tbsp. packed brown sugar
- 1 Tbsp. chili powder
- 8 oz. uncooked angel hair pasta
- 1 cup shredded cheddar cheese

**1.** In a large cast-iron or other heavy skillet, cook the turkey, onion and red pepper over medium heat, breaking turkey into crumbles, until meat is no longer pink; drain.

**2.** Add the tomatoes, broth, mushrooms, brown sugar and chili powder. Bring to a boil. Reduce heat; simmer, uncovered, for 30 minutes.

**3.** Add pasta; return to a boil. Reduce heat; simmer, covered, until the pasta is tender, 30-35 minutes. Sprinkle with cheese. Cover and cook until cheese is melted, 2-3 minutes longer.

**1⅔ CUPS:** 553 cal., 19g fat (7g sat. fat), 114mg chol., 994mg sod., 55g carb. (14g sugars, 7g fiber), 41g pro.

**TIP**
You can use a different meat in this recipe—ground chicken or beef would work.If you use a lean meat, you don't need to drain the fat after browning.

## SLOW-COOKED MOROCCAN CHICKEN

Spices work their magic on plain chicken in this exciting dish. Dried fruit and couscous add an exotic touch.
—*Kathy Morgan, Ridgefield, WA*

------------------------------------------

**PREP:** 20 min. • **COOK:** 6 hours
**MAKES:** 4 servings

- 4 medium carrots, sliced
- 2 large onions, halved and sliced
- 1 broiler/fryer chicken (3 to 4 lbs.), cut up, skin removed
- ½ tsp. salt
- ½ cup chopped dried apricots
- ½ cup raisins
- 1 can (14½ oz.) reduced-sodium chicken broth
- ¼ cup tomato paste
- 2 Tbsp. all-purpose flour
- 2 Tbsp. lemon juice
- 2 garlic cloves, minced
- 1½ tsp. ground ginger
- 1½ tsp. ground cumin
- 1 tsp. ground cinnamon
- ¾ tsp. pepper
  Hot cooked couscous

**1.** Place carrots and onions in a greased 5-qt. slow cooker. Sprinkle chicken with salt; add to slow cooker. Top with apricots and raisins. In a small bowl, whisk broth, tomato paste, flour, lemon juice, garlic and seasonings until blended; add to slow cooker.

**2.** Cook, covered, on low until the chicken is tender, 6-7 hours. Serve with hot cooked couscous.

**1 SERVING:** 435 cal., 9g fat (3g sat. fat), 110mg chol., 755mg sod., 47g carb. (27g sugars, 6g fiber), 42g pro.

## BACON & ASPARAGUS FRITTATA

This makes a nice light meal. When I prepare it for guests, I serve it with fruit and bread. It's quick and easy, but it always wins me many compliments!
—Gwen Clemon, Soldier, IA

PREP: 10 min. • COOK: 25 min. • MAKES: 6 servings

- 12 oz. bacon
- 2 cups sliced fresh asparagus (cut in ½-in. pieces)
- 1 cup chopped onion
- 2 garlic cloves, minced
- 10 large eggs, beaten
- ¼ cup minced parsley
- ½ tsp. seasoned salt
- ¼ tsp. pepper
- 1 large tomato, thinly sliced
- 1 cup shredded cheddar cheese

1. In a 9- or 10-in. ovenproof skillet, cook bacon until crisp. Drain, reserving 1 Tbsp. drippings. Heat reserved drippings on medium-high. Add asparagus, onion and garlic; saute until onion is tender. Chop bacon; set aside a third. In a large bowl, combine remaining bacon, eggs, parsley, salt and pepper.
2. Pour egg mixture into skillet; stir. Top with tomato, cheese and reserved bacon. Cover and cook over medium-low until eggs are nearly set, 10-15 minutes. Preheat broiler; place skillet 6 in. from heat. Broil until lightly browned, about 2 minutes. Serve immediately.

1 PIECE: 344 cal., 24g fat (10g sat. fat), 351mg chol., 738mg sod., 7g carb. (3g sugars, 2g fiber), 23g pro.

> **TIP**
> Looking to feed a larger crowd? You can make this in a 12-in. skillet by increasing each ingredient by 50% and baking the frittata for 20-25 minutes.

## CAROLINA CRAB BOIL

This is a fun way to feed a crowd for a tailgate. You can serve it two ways: Drain the cooking liquid and pour out the pot on a paper-lined table so folks can dig in, or serve it as a stew in its liquid over hot rice.
—Melissa Pelkey Hass, Waleska, GA

PREP: 15 min. • COOK: 35 min. • MAKES: 4 servings

- 2 tsp. canola oil
- 1 pkg. (14 oz.) smoked turkey sausage, cut into ½-in. slices
- 2 cartons (32 oz. each) reduced-sodium chicken broth
- 4 cups water
- 1 bottle (12 oz.) light beer or 1½ cups additional reduced-sodium chicken broth
- ¼ cup seafood seasoning
- 5 bay leaves
- 4 medium ears sweet corn, cut into 2-in. pieces
- 1 lb. fingerling potatoes
- 1 medium red onion, quartered
- 2 lbs. cooked snow crab legs
  Pepper to taste

1. In a stockpot, heat oil over medium-high heat; brown sausage. Stir in broth, water, beer, seafood seasoning and bay leaves. Add corn, potatoes and onion; bring to a boil. Reduce heat; simmer, uncovered, 20-25 minutes or until potatoes are tender.
2. Add crab; heat through. Drain; remove bay leaves. Transfer to a serving bowl; season with pepper.

1 SERVING: 420 cal., 12g fat (3g sat. fat), 143mg chol., 2206mg sod., 37g carb. (7g sugars, 5g fiber), 40g pro.

## HEIRLOOM TOMATO TART

Here's a delicious way to use the tomato bounty from your garden or the great buys from the local farmers market. If you don't have heirloom tomatoes, try regular tomatoes mixed with grape or plum tomatoes.
—*Kathryn Conrad, Milwaukee, WI*

PREP: 20 min. • BAKE: 10 min. • MAKES: 6 servings

- 2  tsp. cornmeal, divided
- 1  refrigerated pie pastry
   Cooking spray
- 3  Tbsp. shredded Asiago cheese
- 3  large heirloom tomatoes, cut into ¼-in. slices
- 3  small heirloom tomatoes, cut into ¼-in. slices
- 1  Tbsp. extra virgin olive oil
- ½  tsp. coarsely ground pepper
- ¼  tsp. salt
- ¼  cup crumbled goat or feta cheese
   Fresh basil leaves, optional

1. Preheat oven to 450°. Sprinkle a large baking sheet with 1 tsp. cornmeal.
2. On a lightly floured surface, roll pastry into a 12-in. circle; transfer to prepared sheet. Spritz dough with cooking spray. Sprinkle with remaining 1 tsp. cornmeal, pressing cornmeal gently into dough. Prick thoroughly with a fork. Sprinkle with Asiago cheese.
3. Bake for 10 minutes or until lightly browned. Cool on a wire rack.
4. Layer with tomatoes. Drizzle with olive oil; sprinkle with pepper and salt. Top with goat cheese; garnish with basil if desired. Serve immediately.

**1 PIECE:** 236 cal., 14g fat (6g sat. fat), 16mg chol., 270mg sod., 24g carb. (5g sugars, 2g fiber), 4g pro.

## ONE-POT CHILI MAC

This hearty entree is low in fat and full of flavor. I love that you can cook the dried pasta right in the chili. One less pot to wash! This also reheats perfectly in the microwave.
—*Dawn Forsberg, Country Club, MO*

PREP: 25 min. • COOK: 15 min. • MAKES: 6 servings (2 qt.)

- 1  lb. lean ground turkey
- 1  small onion, chopped
- ¼  cup chopped green pepper
- 1  tsp. olive oil
- 2  cups water
- 1  can (15 oz.) pinto beans, rinsed and drained
- 1  can (14½ oz.) reduced-sodium beef broth
- 1  can (14½ oz.) diced tomatoes with mild green chilies, undrained
- 1  can (8 oz.) no-salt-added tomato sauce
- 2  tsp. chili powder
- 1  tsp. ground cumin
- ½  tsp. dried oregano
- 2  cups uncooked multigrain penne pasta
- ¼  cup reduced-fat sour cream
- ¼  cup minced fresh cilantro

1. In a large saucepan coated with cooking spray, cook the turkey, onion and pepper in oil over medium heat, breaking turkey into crumbles, until meat is no longer pink; drain.
2. Stir in the water, beans, broth, tomatoes, tomato sauce, chili powder, cumin and oregano. Bring to a boil. Add pasta; cook for 15-20 minutes or until tender, stirring occasionally. Serve with sour cream; sprinkle with cilantro.

**1⅓ CUPS:** 384 cal., 10g fat (2g sat. fat), 64mg chol., 598mg sod., 47g carb. (10g sugars, 8g fiber), 25g pro. **DIABETIC EXCHANGES:** 3 starch, 2 lean meat, 1 vegetable.

## NORTH AFRICAN CHICKEN & RICE

I'm always looking to try recipes from different cultures, and this one is a huge favorite. We love the spice combinations. This cooks equally well in a slow cooker or a pressure cooker.
—*Courtney Stultz, Weir, KS*

------------------------------------------

**PREP:** 10 min. • **COOK:** 4 hours
**MAKES:** 8 servings

- 1 medium onion, diced
- 1 Tbsp. olive oil
- 8 boneless skinless chicken thighs (about 2 lbs.)
- 1 Tbsp. minced fresh cilantro
- 1 tsp. ground turmeric
- 1 tsp. paprika
- 1 tsp. sea salt
- ½ tsp. pepper
- ½ tsp. ground cinnamon
- ½ tsp. chili powder
- 1 cup golden raisins
- ½ to 1 cup chopped pitted green olives
- 1 medium lemon, sliced
- 2 garlic cloves, minced
- ½ cup chicken broth or water
- 4 cups hot cooked brown rice

In a 3- or 4-qt. slow cooker, combine onion and oil. Place chicken thighs on top of onion; sprinkle with next 7 ingredients. Top with raisins, olives, lemon and garlic. Add broth. Cook, covered, on low until chicken is tender, 4-5 hours. Serve with hot cooked rice.

**1 SERVING:** 386 cal., 13g fat (3g sat. fat), 76mg chol., 556mg sod., 44g carb. (12g sugars, 3g fiber), 25g pro.

**TIP**

Heavily spiced, with a mixture of interesting ingredients, the cuisine from North Africa may be a bit unfamiliar, but we know you'll fall in love with the delicous combination of flavors. If olives aren't your favorite, don't leave them out entirely, but go with ½ cup. They add a nice underlying flavor as well as a little saltiness to the dish.

## SOUTHWESTERN RICE

I created this colorful side dish after eating something similar at a restaurant. It complements any Tex-Mex meal wonderfully. Sometimes I add cubes of grilled chicken breast to the rice to make it a meal in itself.
—*Michelle Dennis, Clarks Hill, IN*

**TAKES:** 30 min. • **MAKES:** 8 servings

- 1 Tbsp. olive oil
- 1 medium green pepper, diced
- 1 medium onion, chopped
- 2 garlic cloves, minced
- 1 cup uncooked long grain rice
- ½ tsp. ground cumin
- ⅛ tsp. ground turmeric
- 1 can (14½ oz.) reduced-sodium chicken broth
- 2 cups frozen corn (about 10 oz.), thawed
- 1 can (15 oz.) black beans, rinsed and drained
- 1 can (10 oz.) diced tomatoes and green chiles, undrained

**1.** In a large nonstick skillet, heat oil over medium-high heat; saute pepper and onion 3 minutes. Add garlic; cook and stir 1 minute.

**2.** Stir in rice, spices and broth; bring to a boil. Reduce heat; simmer, covered, until rice is tender, about 15 minutes. Stir in remaining ingredients; cook, covered, until heated through.

**¾ CUP:** 198 cal., 3g fat (1g sat. fat), 1mg chol., 339mg sod., 37g carb. (0 sugars, 5g fiber), 7g pro.

## SAUCY BEEF & CABBAGE DINNER

Using cabbage is a great way to bulk up a meal without adding extra fat and calories. The cabbage in this dish is tender but still has a nice crunch.
—*Marcia Doyle, Pompano, FL*

**PREP:** 15 min. • **COOK:** 25 min. • **MAKES:** 8 servings

- 1 lb. lean ground beef (90% lean)
- 1 large onion, chopped
- 1 cup sliced fresh mushrooms
  Optional: Fresh thyme and fresh parsley, chopped
- 1 medium head cabbage, chopped
- 1 can (46 oz.) reduced-sodium tomato juice
- 1 cup instant brown rice
- 1 can (6 oz.) tomato paste
- ¼ cup packed brown sugar
- 2 Tbsp. lemon juice
- 1 tsp. dried thyme
- 1 tsp. dried parsley flakes
- ½ tsp. pepper

**1.** In a Dutch oven, cook the beef, onion and mushrooms over medium heat until meat is no longer pink, breaking beef into crumbles; drain. If desired, sprinkle with thyme and parsley.

**2.** Add remaining ingredients. Bring to a boil. Reduce heat; cover and simmer until cabbage and rice are tender, 15-20 minutes.

**1⅓ CUPS:** 253 cal., 5g fat (2g sat. fat), 35mg chol., 170mg sod., 36g carb. (19g sugars, 5g fiber), 17g pro. **DIABETIC EXCHANGES:** 2 vegetable, 2 lean meat, 1½ starch.

## SUNSHINE CHICKEN

Since it can be easily doubled and takes little time or effort to prepare, this recipe is ideal to serve for large groups. Even my husband, who usually doesn't enjoy cooking, likes to make this dish.

—*Karen Gardiner, Eutaw, AL*

**PREP:** 15 min. • **COOK:** 20 min. • **MAKES:** 6 servings

- 2 to 3 tsp. curry powder
- 1¼ tsp. salt, divided
- ¼ tsp. pepper
- 6 boneless skinless chicken breast halves (5 oz. each)
- 1½ cups orange juice
- 1 cup uncooked long grain rice
- ¾ cup water
- 1 Tbsp. brown sugar
- 1 tsp. ground mustard
- Chopped fresh parsley

**1.** Combine curry powder, ½ tsp. salt and the pepper; rub over both sides of chicken. In a skillet, combine orange juice, rice, water, brown sugar, mustard and remaining ¾ tsp. salt. Add chicken pieces; bring to a boil. Reduce heat; cover and simmer until chicken juices run clear, 20-25 minutes.
**2.** Remove from the heat and let stand, covered, until all liquid is absorbed, about 5 minutes. Sprinkle with parsley.
**1 SERVING:** 317 cal., 4g fat (1g sat. fat), 78mg chol., 562mg sod., 36g carb. (8g sugars, 1g fiber), 32g pro. **DIABETIC EXCHANGES:** 4 lean meat, 2 starch.

## VEG JAMBALAYA

The flavorful vegetarian entree won't leave you hungry, since it uses convenient canned beans in place of meat.
—*Crystal Jo Bruns, Iliff, CO*

**PREP:** 10 min. • **COOK:** 30 min. • **MAKES:** 6 servings

- 1 Tbsp. canola oil
- 1 medium green pepper, chopped
- 1 medium onion, chopped
- 1 celery rib, chopped
- 3 garlic cloves, minced
- 2 cups water
- 1 can (14½ oz.) diced tomatoes, undrained
- 1 can (8 oz.) tomato sauce
- ½ tsp. Italian seasoning
- ¼ tsp. salt
- ¼ tsp. crushed red pepper flakes
- ⅛ tsp. fennel seed, crushed
- 1 cup uncooked long grain rice
- 1 can (16 oz.) butter beans, rinsed and drained
- 1 can (16 oz.) red beans, rinsed and drained

**1.** In a Dutch oven, heat oil over medium-high heat. Add the green pepper, onion and celery; cook and stir until tender. Add garlic; cook 1 minute longer.
**2.** Add the water, tomatoes, tomato sauce and seasonings. Bring to a boil; stir in rice. Reduce heat; cover and simmer until liquid is absorbed and rice is tender, 15-18 minutes. Stir in the beans; heat through.
**1⅓ CUPS:** 281 cal., 3g fat (0 sat. fat), 0 chol., 796mg sod., 56g carb. (6g sugars, 9g fiber), 11g pro.

## SHEET-PAN TANDOORI CHICKEN

This tandoori chicken recipe is easy for weeknights since it uses just one pan, but it's also special enough for company. The best part is there isn't much to clean up when dinner is over! Put the chicken in the marinade in the morning, and everything will come together in record time for dinner!
—*Anwar Khan, Iriving, TX*

PREP: 20 min. + marinating • BAKE: 25 min. • MAKES: 4 servings

- 1  cup plain Greek yogurt
- 3  Tbsp. tandoori masala seasoning
- ⅛  to ¼ tsp. crushed red pepper flakes, optional
- 8  bone-in chicken thighs (about 3 lbs.), skin removed
- 2  medium sweet potatoes, peeled and cut into ½-in. wedges
- 1  Tbsp. olive oil
- 16  cherry tomatoes
     Lemon slices
     Optional: Minced fresh cilantro and naan flatbread

1. In a large bowl, whisk yogurt, tandoori seasoning and, if desired, pepper flakes until blended. Add chicken and turn to coat. Cover and refrigerate 6-8 hours, turning occasionally.
2. Preheat oven to 450°. Drain chicken, discarding marinade in bowl. Place chicken in a greased 15x10x1-in. baking pan. Add sweet potatoes; drizzle with oil. Bake 15 minutes. Add tomatoes and lemon slices. Bake until a thermometer inserted into chicken reads 170°-175°, 10-15 minutes longer. Broil 4-5 in. from the heat until browned, 4-5 minutes. If desired, serve with cilantro and naan.

**2 CHICKEN THIGHS WITH 1 CUP SWEET POTATOES AND 4 TOMATOES:** 589 cal., 27g fat (9g sat. fat), 186mg chol., 187mg sod., 29g carb. (13g sugars, 6g fiber), 52g pro.

## SAUSAGE, PEAR & SWEET POTATO SHEET-PAN DINNER

This foolproof weeknight dinner is naturally gluten free, uses one pan and is on your table in no time! The recipe is also easily adaptable to seasonal fruits or veggies.
—*Melissa Erdelac, Valparaiso, IN*

PREP: 15 min. • BAKE: 45 min. • MAKES: 5 servings

- 2  large sweet potatoes, peeled and cut into ½-in. cubes
- 1  large sweet onion, cut into wedges
- 2  Tbsp. olive oil
- 1  Tbsp. brown sugar
- ½  tsp. salt
- ½  tsp. ground allspice
- ¼  tsp. ground cinnamon
- ⅛  tsp. pepper
- 3  small pears, quartered
- 1  pkg. (19 oz.) Italian sausage links

1. Preheat oven to 425°. Place sweet potatoes and onion in a 15x10x1-in. baking pan; drizzle with oil. Sprinkle with brown sugar and seasonings; toss to coat. Bake 15 minutes. Gently stir in pears; top with sausages.
2. Bake 20 minutes longer, stirring once. Increase oven temperature to 450°. Bake until sausages are golden brown and a thermometer inserted in sausage reads at least 160°, 8-10 minutes longer, turning once.

**1 SERVING:** 533 cal., 29g fat (8g sat. fat), 58mg chol., 912mg sod., 56g carb. (28g sugars, 8g fiber), 15g pro.

TIP

If you like to get creative, this is a perfect recipe for you. The easiest thing to swap is the sausage—try using Polish sausage, bratwurst or other link sausages. Switch in peeled butternut squash for the sweet potatoes. Another easy swap is using apples instead of pears.

## BEAN & BURGER POCKETS

This recipe started out as an alternative to baked beans—just for a change of taste. One day, I decided to add ground beef and other ingredients. Now it's a main dish we enjoy often.
—Gwen Parsons, Boring, OR

- - - - - - - - - - - - - - - - - - - - - - - - - - - - - - -

**PREP:** 5 min. • **COOK:** 65 min.
**MAKES:** 6 servings

- 1¼ lbs. ground beef
- 1 can (14½ oz.) diced tomatoes, undrained
- 1 can (8 oz.) tomato sauce
- ½ cup chopped onion
- 1 garlic clove, minced
- 1 Tbsp. brown sugar
- 1 tsp. seasoned salt
- 1 tsp. chili powder
- ½ tsp. ground cumin
- ⅛ tsp. each dried thyme, savory, marjoram, oregano and parsley flakes
- 1 can (16 oz.) navy beans, rinsed and drained
- 1 can (16 oz.) kidney beans, rinsed and drained
- 1 can (8½ oz.) lima beans
- 12 pita pocket halves
  Shredded cheddar cheese, optional

**1.** In a heavy saucepan or Dutch oven, cook the beef over medium heat until no longer pink, 5-7 minutes, crumbling meat; drain.

**2.** Add tomatoes, tomato sauce, onion, garlic, brown sugar and seasonings. Simmer, covered, for 1 hour, stirring occasionally.

**3.** Stir in beans; heat through. Spoon about ½ cup into each pita half. If desired, top with cheese.

**2 FILLED PITA HALVES:** 516 cal., 12g fat (4g sat. fat), 58mg chol., 1227mg sod., 68g carb. (8g sugars, 11g fiber), 34g pro.

## ONE-POT SPAGHETTI DINNER

All you need is one pot to make this meal that features a simple homemade sauce. Allspice adds its unique taste, but you can substitute Italian seasoning if you prefer.
—Carol Benzel-Schmidt, Stanwood, WA

- - - - - - - - - - - - - - - - - - - - - - - - - - - - - - -

**PREP:** 10 min. • **COOK:** 25 min.
**MAKES:** 4 servings

- 1 lb. lean ground beef (90% lean)
- 1¾ cups sliced fresh mushrooms
- 3 cups tomato juice
- 1 can (14½ oz.) no-salt-added diced tomatoes, drained
- 1 can (8 oz.) no-salt-added tomato sauce
- 1 Tbsp. dried minced onion
- ½ tsp. salt
- ½ tsp. garlic powder
- ½ tsp. ground mustard
- ¼ tsp. pepper
- ⅛ tsp. ground allspice
- ⅛ tsp. ground mace, optional
- 6 oz. uncooked multigrain spaghetti, broken into pieces
  Optional: Fresh mozzarella cheese pearls or shaved Parmesan cheese

**1.** In a Dutch oven, cook beef and mushrooms over medium heat until meat is no longer pink, 5-7 minutes, crumbling meat; drain. Add tomato juice, tomatoes, tomato sauce, onion and seasonings.

**2.** Bring to a boil. Stir in spaghetti. Simmer, covered, until spaghetti is tender, 12-15 minutes. If desired, serve with cheese.

**1½ CUPS:** 414 cal., 10g fat (4g sat. fat), 71mg chol., 925mg sod., 48g carb. (15g sugars, 6g fiber), 33g pro.

**TIP**

This easy technique lets you skip the cumbersome task of boiling the pasta in water and draining separately. The tomato juice in this recipe gives the sauce enough liquid to cook the dried pasta. While the ingredients are simmering, stir occasionally to prevent sticking.

Cut **1 red pepper** and **1 green pepper** into 1-in. pieces. In a Dutch oven over medium heat, cook in **1 Tbsp. olive oil** until tender. Add **1 large sweet potato** (peeled, quartered and sliced) and **½ tsp. minced fresh rosemary**; cook 4-5 minutes. Add **3 cloves garlic** (minced); cook 1 minute. Stir in **½ cup water** and **¼ tsp. pepper**. Bring to a boil. Reduce heat; cover and simmer until sweet potato is tender, 5-7 minutes. Stir in **2 cans cannellini beans** (rinsed and drained), **1 can diced tomatoes** and **¼ tsp. salt**; heat through.

# - WHITE BEAN, SWEET POTATO & PEPPER RAGOUT -
Hearty and healthy, this rich and flavorful comfort food is the perfect option for meatless Monday—or any night of the week!

## SHEET-PAN CHICKEN CURRY DINNER

My husband loves anything curry and will even eat veggies when they have a curry sauce. This is a quick one-pan way to get a whole meal on the table with minimal fuss. Everyone loves it, and it is healthy to boot. Serve it with a side of jasmine rice.
—*Trisha Kruse, Eagle, ID*

-------------------------------------------------------------

**PREP:** 20 min. • **BAKE:** 40 min. • **MAKES:** 6 servings

- 2  lbs. sweet potato, peeled and cubed
- 2  cups fresh cauliflowerets
- 1  large onion, chopped
- 3  garlic cloves, minced
- 2  Tbsp. olive oil
- 2  tsp. curry powder, divided
- 1¼  tsp. salt, divided
- 1  tsp. lemon-pepper seasoning, divided
- 6  bone-in chicken thighs (about 2¼ lbs.), skin removed
- 1  tsp. smoked paprika
- ¼  cup chicken broth

**1.** Preheat oven to 425°. Line a 15x10x1-in. baking pan with heavy-duty foil. Place sweet potatoes, cauliflower, onion and garlic on prepared pan. Drizzle with oil; sprinkle with 1 tsp. curry powder, ¾ tsp. salt and ½ tsp. lemon pepper; toss to coat.
**2.** Arrange chicken over vegetables. In a small bowl, mix paprika and remaining 1 tsp. curry powder, ½ tsp. salt and ½ tsp. lemon pepper; sprinkle over chicken. Roast until the vegetables are almost tender, 30-35 minutes. Drizzle with broth; bake until thermometer inserted in chicken reads 170°-175° and the vegetables are tender, 7-10 minutes longer.
**1 SERVING:** 409 cal., 14g fat (3g sat. fat), 87mg chol., 686mg sod., 42g carb. (17g sugars, 6g fiber), 28g pro. **DIABETIC EXCHANGES:** 4 lean meat, 3 starch, 1 fat.

## ONE-DISH TURKEY DINNER

I'm still settling into married life and learning how to balance our busy schedules. This quick, one-dish dinner helps keep us on track throughout the week.
—*Shannon Barden, Alpharetta, GA*

-------------------------------------------------------------

**TAKES:** 30 min. • **MAKES:** 4 servings

- 1  lb. ground turkey
- 1  medium onion, chopped
- 1  shallot, finely chopped
- 3  garlic cloves, minced
- ¼  cup tomato paste
- 1  medium sweet potato, peeled and cubed
- 1  cup chicken broth
- 2  tsp. smoked paprika
- ½  tsp. salt
- ¼  tsp. pepper
- 3  cups chopped fresh kale
     Dash crushed red pepper flakes
- 1  medium ripe avocado, peeled and sliced
     Minced fresh mint, optional

**1.** In a large skillet, cook turkey, onion, shallot and garlic over medium heat until turkey is no longer pink and vegetables are tender, 8-10 minutes, breaking up turkey into crumbles; drain. Add tomato paste; cook and stir 1 minute longer.
**2.** Add sweet potato, broth, smoked paprika, salt and pepper. Bring to a boil; reduce heat. Simmer, covered, until sweet potato is tender, about 10 minutes, stirring occasionally. Add kale and red pepper flakes; cook and stir until kale is wilted, about 2 minutes. Serve with avocado and, if desired, mint.
**FREEZE OPTION:** Freeze cooled mixture in freezer containers. To use, partially thaw in refrigerator overnight. Heat through in a saucepan, stirring occasionally; add broth or water if necessary. Serve with avocado and, if desired, mint.
**1⅓ CUPS:** 318 cal., 14g fat (3g sat. fat), 76mg chol., 628mg sod., 24g carb. (8g sugars, 5g fiber), 26g pro. **DIABETIC EXCHANGES:** 3 lean meat, 2 fat, 1½ starch.

## HOT DOG CASSEROLE

When our children were small and I was busy trying to get all those extra things done that are part of a mom's normal schedule, I would make this quick hot dish. Kids love it!
—JoAnn Gunio, Franklin, NC

- - - - - - - - - - - - - - - - - - - - - - - - - - - - - - - - - - - - - - - - - - - - - - - - -

**PREP:** 10 min. • **BAKE:** 70 min. • **MAKES:** 8 servings

- 3   Tbsp. butter
- 2   Tbsp. all-purpose flour
- 1   to 1½ tsp. salt
- ¼   to ½ tsp. pepper
- 1½  cups 2% milk
- 5   medium red potatoes, thinly sliced
- 1   pkg. (1 lb.) hot dogs, halved lengthwise and cut into ½-in. slices
- 1   medium onion, chopped
- ⅓   cup shredded cheddar cheese
      Chopped green onions, optional

**1.** Preheat oven to 350°. In a small saucepan, melt butter. Stir in flour, salt and pepper until smooth. Gradually add milk. Bring to a boil; cook and stir until thickened and bubbly, 2 minutes.

**2.** In a greased 2½-qt. baking dish, layer a third of the potatoes, half the hot dogs and half the onion. Repeat layers. Top with remaining potatoes. Pour white sauce over all.

**3.** Bake, covered, for 1 hour. Uncover; sprinkle with cheese. Bake until potatoes are tender, 10-15 minutes longer. If desired, garnish with green onions.

**1 CUP:** 330 cal., 24g fat (11g sat. fat), 52mg chol., 967mg sod., 18g carb. (4g sugars, 2g fiber), 11g pro.

> **TIP**
> You can store this casserole in an airtight container in the fridge for up to three or four days. We don't recommend freezing this casserole recipe, so make sure you eat it up!

 **PM**

## ROTISSERIE-STYLE CHICKEN

My mother used to fix this when I lived at home, and we called it "church chicken" because Mom would put it in the oven Sunday morning before we left for church. When we got home, the aroma of roasted chicken would hit us as we opened the door.
—Brian Stevenson, Grand Rapids, MI

- - - - - - - - - - - - - - - - - - - - - - - - - - - - - - - - - - - - - - - - - - - - - - - - -

**PREP:** 15 min. + chilling • **BAKE:** 1¼ hours + standing
**MAKES:** 6 servings

- 2    tsp. salt
- 1¼   tsp. paprika
- 1    tsp. brown sugar
- ¾    tsp. dried thyme
- ¾    tsp. white pepper
- ¼    tsp. cayenne pepper
- ¼    tsp. pepper
- 1    broiler/fryer chicken (3 to 4 lbs.)
- 1    medium onion, quartered

**1.** Mix the first 7 ingredients. Rub over the outside and inside of chicken. Place in a large dish. Cover and refrigerate 8 hours or overnight.

**2.** Preheat oven to 350°. Place chicken on a rack in a shallow roasting pan, breast side up. Tuck wings under chicken; tie drumsticks together. Place onion around chicken in pan.

**3.** Roast until a thermometer inserted in thickest part of thigh reads 170°-175°, 1¼-1½ hours. Baste occasionally with pan drippings. (Cover loosely with foil if chicken browns too quickly.)

**4.** Remove chicken from oven; tent with foil. Let stand 15 minutes before slicing.

**5 OZ. COOKED CHICKEN:** 306 cal., 17g fat (5g sat. fat), 104mg chol., 878mg sod., 3g carb. (2g sugars, 1g fiber), 33g pro.

# MEDITERRANEAN ONE-DISH MEAL

I came up with this recipe one night while improvising with what I had on hand. I love to make simple, healthy one-dish dinners with lots of vegetables. Greek olives and feta give this meal a depth of flavor that people love.
—*Donna Jesser, Everett, WA*

- - - - - - - - - - - - - - - - - - - - - - - - - - - - - - - - - - - - - - - - - - - - - - - - - -

**PREP:** 15 min. • **COOK:** 25 min. • **MAKES:** 4 servings

- ¾ lb. Italian turkey sausage links, cut into 1-in. pieces
- 1 medium onion, chopped
- 2 garlic cloves, minced
- 1 can (14½ oz.) no-salt-added diced tomatoes, undrained
- ¼ cup Greek olives
- 1 tsp. dried oregano
- ½ cup quinoa, rinsed
- 3 cups fresh baby spinach
- ½ cup crumbled feta cheese

**1.** In a large saucepan coated with cooking spray, cook sausage and onion over medium heat until sausage is browned and onion is tender. Add garlic; cook 1 minute longer. Stir in the tomatoes, olives and oregano; bring to a boil.

**2.** Stir in quinoa. Top with spinach; do not stir. Reduce heat; cover and simmer for 12-15 minutes or until liquid is absorbed. Remove from the heat; fluff with a fork. Sprinkle with cheese.

**1 CUP:** 307 cal., 14g fat (3g sat. fat), 58mg chol., 845mg sod., 26g carb. (6g sugars, 5g fiber), 21g pro.

# EASY PEPPER STEAK

This popular beef dish is tasty as well as colorful.
—*Carolyn Butterfield, Atkinson, NE*

- - - - - - - - - - - - - - - - - - - - - - - - - - - - - - - - - - - - - - - - - - - - - - - - - -

**PREP:** 10 min. • **COOK:** 55 min. • **MAKES:** 4 servings

- 1 lb. beef top round steak, cut into ¼-in. x 2-in. strips
- 1 Tbsp. paprika
- 2 Tbsp. butter
- 1 can (10½ oz.) beef broth
- 2 garlic cloves, minced
- 2 medium green peppers, cut into strips
- 1 cup thinly sliced onion
- 2 Tbsp. cornstarch
- 2 Tbsp. reduced-sodium soy sauce
- ⅓ cup cold water
- 2 fresh tomatoes, peeled and cut into wedges
  Cooked rice

**1.** Sprinkle meat with paprika. In a large skillet, melt butter over medium-high heat. Brown beef. Add broth and garlic. Simmer, covered, for 30 minutes. Add green peppers and onion. Cover and continue to simmer for 5 minutes longer.

**2.** Combine cornstarch, soy sauce and water; stir into meat mixture. Cook and stir until thickened. Gently stir in tomatoes and heat through. Serve over rice.

**1 SERVING:** 365 cal., 4g fat (1g sat. fat), 65mg chol., 465mg sod., 48g carb. (5g sugars, 4g fiber), 32g pro.

**TIP**
Beef top round steak is a leaner, less tender cut of meat. One way to get a more tender result is to use a meat mallet prior to cooking. Starting at one end of the steak and gradually working toward the other end, use the spiked side of the mallet to hit and flatten the meat evenly without damaging it.

## FAVORITE COMPANY CASSEROLE

Even my friends who don't eat a lot of broccoli or mushrooms admit this casserole is a winner. It's so easy to throw together, and the leftovers are delicious.
—*Suzann Verdun, Lisle, IL*

PREP: 15 min. • BAKE: 45 min. • MAKES: 8 servings

- 1  pkg. (6 oz.) wild rice, cooked
- 3  cups frozen chopped broccoli, thawed
- 1½ cups cubed cooked chicken
- 1  cup cubed cooked ham
- 1  cup shredded cheddar cheese
- 1  jar (4½ oz.) sliced mushrooms, drained
- 1  cup mayonnaise
- 1  tsp. prepared mustard
- ½ to 1 tsp. curry powder
- 1  can (10¾ oz.) condensed cream of mushroom soup, undiluted
- ¼ cup grated Parmesan cheese

Preheat oven to 350°. In a greased 2-qt. baking dish, layer the first 6 ingredients in the order listed. Combine mayonnaise, mustard, curry and soup; spread over top. Sprinkle with Parmesan cheese. Bake, uncovered, until top is light golden brown, 45-60 minutes.
**1 CUP:** 405 cal., 32g fat (8g sat. fat), 61mg chol., 872mg sod., 11g carb. (1g sugars, 2g fiber), 18g pro.

## TACO SKILLET PIZZA WITH CORNBREAD CRUST

Our family loves taco pizza, and I have made so many versions of it. This recipe is like a deep-dish skillet pizza. It's a hearty meal and can be served straight out of the pan.
—*Pamela Shank, Parkersburg, WV*

PREP: 30 min. • BAKE: 15 min. • MAKES: 6 servings

- ½ lb. lean ground beef (90% lean)
- 1  cup refried beans
- ⅓ cup salsa
- 2  Tbsp. taco seasoning
- 1  pkg. (6 oz.) Mexican-style cornbread/muffin mix
- ⅓ cup tortilla chips, crushed
- 1  cup shredded cheddar cheese
  TOPPINGS: Torn romaine, chopped tomatoes, sour cream, chopped onion, chopped cilantro and fried tortilla strips

1. Preheat oven to 350°. In a 10-in. cast-iron or other ovenproof skillet, cook beef over medium heat until no longer pink, 6-8 minutes, breaking into crumbles; drain. Transfer to a small bowl. Stir in beans, salsa and taco seasoning; keep warm. Wipe skillet clean.
2. Prepare cornbread mix according to package directions; stir in crushed tortilla chips. Pour into skillet. Bake until set, 12-15 minutes. Spread ground beef mixture over cornbread to within 1 in. of edges; sprinkle with cheese. Bake until cheese is melted and crust is golden brown, 3-5 minutes. Serve with toppings.
**1 WEDGE:** 329 cal., 14g fat (6g sat. fat), 75mg chol., 1052mg sod., 31g carb. (3g sugars, 3g fiber), 19g pro.

TIP

If you can't find Mexican-style corn bread/muffin mix, make with a package of regular corn bread/muffin mix (8½ oz.). Mix according to the package directions and proceed with the recipe as directed.

## CHICKEN BULGUR SKILLET

This recipe was given to me by a friend, and I've altered it slightly to suit our tastes. We like it with a fresh green salad.
—Leann Hillmer, Sylvan Grove, KS

PREP: 15 min. • COOK: 30 min.
MAKES: 4 servings

- 1 lb. boneless skinless chicken breasts, cut into 1-in. cubes
- 2 tsp. olive oil
- 2 medium carrots, chopped
- ⅔ cup chopped onion
- 3 Tbsp. chopped walnuts
- ½ tsp. caraway seeds
- ¼ tsp. ground cumin
- 1½ cups bulgur
- 2 cups reduced-sodium chicken broth
- 2 Tbsp. raisins
- ¼ tsp. salt
- ⅛ tsp. ground cinnamon

1. In a large cast-iron or other heavy skillet, cook chicken in oil over medium-high heat until meat is no longer pink. Remove and keep warm. In the same skillet, cook and stir the carrots, onion, nuts, caraway seeds and cumin until the onion starts to brown, 3-4 minutes.
2. Stir in bulgur. Gradually add broth; bring to a boil over medium heat. Reduce heat; add the raisins, salt, cinnamon and chicken. Cover and simmer until bulgur is tender, 12-15 minutes.

1½ CUPS: 412 cal., 8g fat (1g sat. fat), 66mg chol., 561mg sod., 51g carb. (8g sugars, 12g fiber), 36g pro.

REVIEW

*"Very easy to make and yummy! Each bite had an amazing flavor. I served it in a bowl."*
—LORETTALIZZI, TASTEOFHOME.COM

## ROASTED CHICKEN THIGHS WITH PEPPERS & POTATOES

My family loves this easy-to-make dish! Peppers and herbs from the garden make the chicken and potatoes special.
—Pattie Prescott, Manchester, NH

PREP: 20 min. • BAKE: 35 min. • MAKES: 8 servings

- 2  lbs. red potatoes (about 6 medium)
- 2  large sweet red peppers
- 2  large green peppers
- 2  medium onions
- 2  Tbsp. olive oil, divided
- 4  tsp. minced fresh thyme or 1½ tsp. dried thyme, divided
- 3  tsp. minced fresh rosemary or 1 tsp. dried rosemary, crushed, divided
- 8  boneless skinless chicken thighs (about 2 lbs.)
- ½  tsp. salt
- ¼  tsp. pepper

1. Preheat oven to 450°. Cut potatoes, peppers and onions into 1-in. pieces. Place vegetables in a roasting pan. Drizzle with 1 Tbsp. oil; sprinkle with 2 tsp. each thyme and rosemary and toss to coat. Place chicken over vegetables. Brush chicken with remaining oil; sprinkle with remaining 2 tsp. thyme and 1 tsp. rosemary. Sprinkle vegetables and chicken with salt and pepper.
2. Roast until a thermometer inserted in chicken reads 170° and the vegetables are tender, 35-40 minutes.

**1 CHICKEN THIGH WITH 1 CUP VEGETABLES:** 308 cal., 12g fat (3g sat. fat), 76mg chol., 221mg sod., 25g carb. (5g sugars, 4g fiber), 24g pro.
**DIABETIC EXCHANGES:** 3 lean meat, 1 starch, 1 vegetable, ½ fat.

TIP · Common olive oil works better than virgin or extra-virgin olive oil for cooking at high heat. The higher grades have ideal flavor for cold foods, but they smoke at lower temperatures.

## HEARTY BEANS & RICE

Filling and fast, this dish has become a favorite in my family. It can be served as a side or main dish.
—Barbara Musgrove, Fort Atkinson, WI

PREP: 10 min. • COOK: 25 min. • MAKES: 5 servings

- 1  lb. lean ground beef (90% lean)
- 1  can (15 oz.) black beans, rinsed and drained
- 1  can (14½ oz.) diced tomatoes with mild green chiles, undrained
- 1⅓  cups frozen corn, thawed
- 1  cup water
- ¼  tsp. salt
- 1½  cups instant brown rice

In a large saucepan, cook beef over medium heat until no longer pink, breaking into crumbles, 6-8 minutes; drain. Stir in the beans, tomatoes, corn, water and salt. Bring to a boil. Stir in rice; return to a boil. Reduce heat; cover and simmer for 5 minutes. Remove from the heat; let stand, covered, for 5 minutes.
**1¼ CUPS:** 376 cal., 9g fat (3g sat. fat), 56mg chol., 647mg sod., 47g carb. (6g sugars, 7g fiber), 26g pro. **DIABETIC EXCHANGES:** 3 starch, 3 lean meat, 1 vegetable.

REVIEW · *"I added some kick with a few drops of hot sauce and tomato paste. My husband ate some right out of the pan!"*
—LIPPERTB5, TASTEOFHOME.COM

## SPANISH-STYLE PAELLA

If you enjoy cooking ethnic foods, this hearty rice dish is a great one. It's brimming with generous chunks of sausage, shrimp and veggies.

—Taste of Home *Test Kitchen*

- - - - - - - - - - - - - - - - - - - - - - - - - - - - - - - - - - - - - - -

**PREP:** 10 min. • **COOK:** 35 min. • **MAKES:** 8 servings

- ½ lb. Spanish chorizo links, sliced
- ½ lb. boneless skinless chicken breasts, cubed
- 1 Tbsp. olive oil
- 1 garlic clove, minced
- 1 cup uncooked short grain rice
- 1 cup chopped onion
- 1½ cups chicken broth
- 1 can (14½ oz.) stewed tomatoes, undrained
- ½ tsp. paprika
- ¼ tsp. ground cayenne pepper
- ¼ tsp. salt
- 10 strands saffron, crushed or ⅛ tsp. ground saffron
- ½ lb. uncooked medium shrimp, peeled and deveined
- ½ cup sweet red pepper strips
- ½ cup green pepper strips
- ½ cup frozen peas
  Optional: Minced fresh parsley and lemon wedges

**1.** In a large saucepan or skillet over medium-high heat, cook sausage and chicken in oil for 5 minutes or until sausage is lightly browned and chicken is no longer pink, stirring frequently. Add garlic; cook 1 minute longer. Drain if necessary.

**2.** Stir in rice and onion. Cook until onion is tender and rice is lightly browned, stirring frequently. Add the broth, tomatoes, paprika, cayenne, salt and saffron. Bring to a boil. Reduce heat to low; cover and cook for 10 minutes.

**3.** Stir in shrimp, peppers and peas. Cover and cook 10 minutes longer or until the rice is tender, shrimp are pink and liquid is absorbed. Top with fresh parsley and lemon wedges, if desired.

**1 CUP:** 237 cal., 7g fat (2g sat. fat), 62mg chol., 543mg sod., 27g carb. (5g sugars, 2g fiber), 16g pro.

## ONE-POT DUTCH OVEN PASTA BAKE

I was in a hurry one night, so I went on a pantry search to see what I had on hand. I found penne pasta and decided to go Italian! We all loved it; this is now one of my weeknight faves! This dish is so satisfying and easy, and it's a timesaver since the pasta cooks in the same pot.

—Tammy Reid, Oklahoma City, OK

- - - - - - - - - - - - - - - - - - - - - - - - - - - - - - - - - - - - - - -

**PREP:** 10 min. • **COOK:** 30 min. • **MAKES:** 4 servings

- 1 lb. ground beef
- ½ medium onion, chopped
- 2 garlic cloves, minced
- 1 can (8 oz.) tomato sauce
- 3 cups uncooked penne pasta
- 1 cup beef broth
- 3 cups water
- 1 can (14 oz.) diced tomatoes
- 1 tsp. onion powder
- 1 Tbsp. Italian seasoning
- 1 pkg. (5 oz.) fresh spinach
  Shredded Parmesan cheese, optional

Heat a Dutch oven over medium heat; add ground beef and onion. Cook and stir until beef is no longer pink, 5-7 minutes, crumbling meat; drain. Add garlic; cook 1 minute longer. Add tomato sauce, pasta, broth, water, diced tomatoes and seasonings. Stir; bring to a boil. Cover, reduce heat and simmer until pasta is tender, stirring occasionally. Top with spinach; cover just until wilted. Stir. If desired, sprinkle with Parmesan cheese.

**2 CUPS:** 452 cal., 15g fat (5g sat. fat), 70mg chol., 773mg sod., 50g carb. (7g sugars, 5g fiber), 30g pro.

# - 12 -

# DELECTABLE DESSERTS

Why not finish off your meal with a fabulous homemade dessert? If you're thinking that it takes too much time and effort to create a stupendous sweet, think again. Whether you're cooking for your family or making a treat for a party, these easy recipes are just what you need to satisfy everyone's craving for sweets.

**Lemon Chess Pie** (p. 255) **Sweetened Ricotta with Berries** (p. 268) **Air-Fryer Cookie Pie** (p. 259)
**Two-Minute Cookies** (p. 271) **Blue-Ribbon Apple Cake** (p. 270) **Classic Creme Brulee** (p. 262)
**Banana Fritters** (p. 263) **Caramel-Pecan Cookie Butter Bars** (p. 264) **Ice Cream Bowls** (p. 270)

## ANGEL BERRY TRIFLE

I usually serve this in summer when fresh berries are bountiful, but I recently prepared it using frozen cherries and some light cherry pie filling instead. It was delicious!
—*Brenda Paine, Clinton Township, MI*

**TAKES:** 25 min. • **MAKES:** 14 servings

- 1½ cups cold fat-free milk
- 1 pkg. (1 oz.) sugar-free instant vanilla pudding mix
- 1 cup fat-free vanilla yogurt
- 6 oz. reduced-fat cream cheese, cubed
- ½ cup reduced-fat sour cream
- 2 tsp. vanilla extract
- 1 carton (12 oz.) frozen reduced-fat whipped topping, thawed and divided
- 2 prepared angel food cakes (8 oz. each), cut into 1-in. cubes
- 1 pint fresh blackberries
- 1 pint fresh raspberries
- 1 pint fresh blueberries
  Fresh mint leaves, optional

**1.** Whisk the milk and pudding mix for 2 minutes. Let stand until soft-set, about 2 minutes more. Meanwhile, beat yogurt, cream cheese, sour cream and vanilla until smooth. Fold in the pudding mixture and 1 cup whipped topping.

**2.** Place a third of the cake cubes in a 4-qt. trifle bowl. Top with a third of pudding mixture, a third of berries and half the remaining whipped topping. Repeat layers once. Top with remaining cake, pudding and berries. If desired, garnish with additional whipped topping and fresh mint leaves. Serve immediately or refrigerate.

**¾ CUP:** 234 cal., 6g fat (5g sat. fat), 10mg chol., 342mg sod., 34g carb. (10g sugars, 3g fiber), 6g pro.

## PEACH POUND CAKE

Our state grows excellent peaches, and this is one recipe I'm quick to pull out when they are in season. It's a tender, moist cake that receives rave reviews wherever I take it.
—*Betty Jean Gosnell, Inman, SC*

**PREP:** 10 min. • **BAKE:** 1 hour + cooling • **MAKES:** 16 servings

- 1 cup butter, softened
- 2 cups sugar
- 6 large eggs, room temperature
- 1 tsp. almond extract
- 1 tsp. vanilla extract
- 3 cups all-purpose flour
- ¼ tsp. baking soda
- ¼ tsp. salt
- ½ cup sour cream
- 2 cups diced fresh or frozen peaches
  Whipped cream, optional

**1.** Preheat oven to 350°. Grease and flour a 10-in. fluted tube pan. In a large bowl, cream butter and sugar until light and fluffy, 5-7 minutes. Add the eggs, 1 at a time, beating well after each addition. Beat in extracts. Combine flour, baking soda and salt; add to batter alternately with sour cream, beating well after each addition. Fold in peaches.

**2.** Pour into prepared pan. Bake until a toothpick inserted in the center comes out clean, 60-70 minutes. Cool 10 minutes before removing from pan to a wire rack to cool completely. If desired, serve with whipped cream and additional peaches.

**1 PIECE:** 335 cal., 15g fat (9g sat. fat), 106mg chol., 178mg sod., 45g carb. (27g sugars, 1g fiber), 5g pro.

## CHERRY CREAM CHEESE PIE

My mom is known for her scrumptious desserts. This easy-to-make pie is one she has served often. It's one of my favorite desserts any time of year. I love the combination of cream cheese and cherry pie filling.
—Cindy Kufeldt, Orlando, FL

**PREP:** 10 min. + chilling
**BAKE:** 40 min. + cooling
**MAKES:** 8 servings

- ¾ cup all-purpose flour
- 3 Tbsp. plus ⅓ cup sugar
- ¼ tsp. salt
- ¼ cup butter, softened
- 1 can (21 oz.) cherry pie filling
- 1 pkg. (8 oz.) cream cheese, softened
- 1 large egg, room temperature
- 1 tsp. vanilla extract

**1.** Preheat oven to 350°. In a small bowl, combine flour, 3 Tbsp. sugar and salt. Add butter; stir until combined. Press onto the bottom and up the side of a 9-in. pie plate. Bake until lightly browned, 10-12 minutes. Pour pie filling into crust.

**2.** In a large bowl, beat the cream cheese, ⅓ cup sugar, egg and vanilla until smooth. Carefully spread around the outside edge of pie, leaving a 3-in. circle of cherries exposed in the center.

**3.** Bake until the edge begins to brown, 30-35 minutes. Cool pie on a wire rack. Refrigerate several hours before serving.

**1 PIECE:** 329 cal., 16g fat (10g sat. fat), 67mg chol., 232mg sod., 42g carb. (29g sugars, 1g fiber), 4g pro.

**TIPS**

- To ensure a lump-free pie, allow cream cheese to soften at room temperature before mixing so that it blends in smoothly with the rest of your batter.
- If you're short on time or want to experiment, try using crushed graham crackers or chocolate cookies to make a quick and easy crust. For a bright punch of color, consider switching the layers to put the cheesecake layer on the bottom and the cherries on top.

## LIMONCELLO TIRAMISU

We love everything about this wonderful dessert—from the light lemon flavor and creamy Mascarpone to the crunchy, crushed macaroon on top. We think you'll enjoy it too.
—Taste of Home Test Kitchen

**PREP:** 30 min. + chilling
**MAKES:** 16 servings

- ½ cup sugar
- ¼ cup water
- 2 Tbsp. limoncello

**LEMON CURD**
- 1½ cups sugar
- ⅓ cup plus 1 Tbsp. cornstarch
- 1½ cups cold water
- 3 large egg yolks, lightly beaten
- 3 Tbsp. butter, cubed
- ½ cup lemon juice
- 2 tsp. grated lemon zest

**CREAM FILLING**
- 1½ cups heavy whipping cream
- ¾ cup sugar
- 1 carton (8 oz.) Mascarpone cheese

**ASSEMBLY**
- 3 pkg. (3 oz. each) ladyfingers, split
- 4 macaroon cookies, crumbled
  Candied lemon peel, optional

**1.** In a small saucepan, bring sugar and water to a boil. Cook and stir until sugar is dissolved. Remove from the heat. Stir in limoncello; set aside.

**2.** For lemon curd, in another saucepan, combine sugar and cornstarch. Stir in water until smooth. Bring to a boil; cook and stir until thickened, about 1 minute. Remove from the heat.

**3.** Stir a small amount of hot mixture into egg yolks; return all to the pan, stirring constantly. Bring to a gentle boil; cook and stir 2 minutes longer. Remove from the heat. Stir in butter. Gently stir in lemon juice and zest. Cool to room temperature without stirring.

**4.** In a large bowl, beat cream until it begins to thicken. Add sugar; beat until stiff peaks form. Fold Mascarpone cheese and whipped cream into lemon curd.

**5.** Arrange a third of the ladyfingers on the bottom of a 9-in. springform pan. Drizzle with a third of the syrup; spread with a third of the filling. Repeat layers twice. Cover and refrigerate overnight. Carefully run a knife around edge of pan to loosen. Remove side of pan. Sprinkle with cookies and lemon peel.

**1 PIECE:** 396 cal., 20g fat (11g sat. fat), 128mg chol., 57mg sod., 51g carb. (37g sugars, 0 fiber), 4g pro.

# EASY APPLE CAKE

This old-fashioned cake is moist, dense and down-home delicious. Even better, it's quick to fix and, served warm with whipped cream or a dollop of frozen custard, one of my family's very favorite recipes for decades.
—Sherry Ashenfelter, Waterville, OH

PREP: 25 min. • BAKE: 35 min. + cooling
MAKES: 20 servings

1¾ cups sugar
1 cup vegetable oil
3 large eggs, room temperature
1 tsp. vanilla extract
2 cups all-purpose flour
1¼ tsp. baking powder
1 tsp. salt
1 tsp. ground cinnamon
¼ tsp. baking soda
2 cups finely chopped peeled tart apples
1 cup chopped walnuts
1¼ cups whipped topping

1. Preheat oven to 350°. In a large bowl, beat the sugar, oil, eggs and vanilla until well blended. Combine the flour, baking powder, salt, cinnamon and baking soda; gradually beat into sugar mixture until blended. Fold in apples and walnuts.
2. Transfer to a greased 13x9-in. baking dish. Bake until a toothpick inserted in the center comes out clean, 35-45 minutes. Cool on a wire rack. Serve the cake with whipped topping.

1 PIECE: 278 cal., 16g fat (3g sat. fat), 32mg chol., 169mg sod., 31g carb. (19g sugars, 1g fiber), 4g pro.

TIPS

• Granny Smith apples are the go-to apple for this cake, but other tart varieties, such as Braeburn and Jonathan, are great, too. Or, use a mix of tart and tart-sweet apples, such as Gala or Fuji.
• Grab the ice cream—especially vanilla, if you have it. Drizzle caramel syrup on top, or go with nuts and whipped cream. For a lighter take, dust a bit of confectioners' sugar over top.

## LEMON-LIME BARS

I baked these bars for a luncheon, and a gentleman made his way to the kitchen to compliment the cook who made them.
—*Holly Wilkins, Lake Elmore, VT*

**PREP:** 20 min. • **BAKE:** 20 min. + cooling • **MAKES:** 4 dozen

- 1 cup butter, softened
- ½ cup confectioners' sugar
- 2 tsp. grated lime zest
- 1¾ cups all-purpose flour
- ¼ tsp. salt

FILLING
- 4 large eggs, room temperature
- 1½ cups sugar
- ¼ cup all-purpose flour
- ½ tsp. baking powder
- ⅓ cup lemon juice
- 2 tsp. grated lemon zest
  Confectioners' sugar

**1.** Preheat oven to 350°. In a large bowl, cream butter and confectioners' sugar until light and fluffy. Beat in lime zest. Combine flour and salt; gradually add to the creamed mixture and mix well.

**2.** Press into a greased 13x9-in. baking dish. Bake just until the edges are lightly browned, 13-15 minutes.

**3.** Meanwhile, in another large bowl, beat the eggs and sugar. Combine flour and baking powder. Gradually add to egg mixture. Stir in lemon juice and zest; beat until frothy. Pour over hot crust.

**4.** Bake until light golden brown, 20-25 minutes. Cool on a wire rack. Dust with confectioners' sugar. Cut into squares. Store in the refrigerator.

**1 BAR:** 88 cal., 4g fat (2g sat. fat), 28mg chol., 60mg sod., 12g carb. (7g sugars, 0 fiber), 1g pro.

## TURTLE TART WITH CARAMEL SAUCE

Between the creamy chocolate filling, crunchy nut crust and gooey caramel sauce, this tart has a whole lot to love.
—*Leah Davis, Morrow, OH*

**PREP:** 15 min. + chilling • **BAKE:** 15 min. • **MAKES:** 12 servings

- 2 cups pecan halves, toasted
- ½ cup sugar
- 2 Tbsp. butter, melted

FILLING
- 2 cups semisweet chocolate chips
- 1½ cups heavy whipping cream
- ½ cup finely chopped pecans, toasted

CARAMEL SAUCE
- ½ cup butter, cubed
- 1 cup sugar
- 1 cup heavy whipping cream

**1.** Preheat oven to 350°. Place pecans and sugar in a food processor; pulse until pecans are finely ground. Add melted butter; pulse until combined. Press onto bottom and up side of a 9-in. fluted tart pan with removable bottom. Bake until golden brown, 12-15 minutes. Cool completely on a wire rack.

**2.** For filling, place chocolate chips in a small bowl. In a small saucepan, bring cream just to a boil. Pour over chocolate; stir with a whisk until smooth. Pour into cooled crust; cool slightly. Refrigerate until slightly set, about 30 minutes.

**3.** Sprinkle pecans over filling. Refrigerate, covered, until set, about 3 hours.

**4.** For sauce, in a large heavy saucepan, melt butter over medium heat; stir in sugar until dissolved. Bring to a boil; cook until deep golden brown, 10-12 minutes, stirring occasionally. Slowly whisk in cream until blended. Remove from heat; cool slightly. Serve with tart.

**1 PIECE WITH 2 TBSP. CARAMEL SAUCE:** 632 cal., 51g fat (24g sat. fat), 82mg chol., 93mg sod., 47g carb. (43g sugars, 4g fiber), 5g pro.

## HEAVENLY BLUEBERRY TART

Mmm—this tart is bursting with the fresh flavor of blueberries! Not only do I bake berries with the crust, but I also top the tart with more fresh fruit after I take it out of the oven.
—Lyin Schramm, Berwick, ME

- - - - - - - - - - - - - - - - - - - - - - - - - - - - - - - - - - - - - - - - - - - - - - - - -

**PREP:** 20 min. • **BAKE:** 40 min. + cooling • **MAKES:** 6 servings

- 1   cup all-purpose flour
- 2   Tbsp. sugar
- ⅛   tsp. salt
- ½   cup cold butter
- 1   Tbsp. vinegar

FILLING

- 4   cups fresh blueberries, divided
- ⅔   cup sugar
- 2   Tbsp. all-purpose flour
- ½   tsp. ground cinnamon
- ⅛   tsp. ground nutmeg

**1.** Preheat oven to 400°. In a small bowl, combine flour, sugar and salt; cut in butter until crumbly. Add vinegar, tossing with a fork to moisten. Press onto bottom and up the side of a lightly greased 9-in. tart pan with removable bottom.

**2.** For filling, lightly smash 2 cups blueberries in a bowl. Combine the sugar, flour, cinnamon and nutmeg; stir into the smashed blueberries. Spread mixture evenly into crust; sprinkle with 1 cup of the remaining whole blueberries. Place tart pan on a baking sheet.

**3.** Bake for 40-45 minutes or until crust is browned and filling is bubbly. Remove from the oven; arrange remaining berries over top. Cool on a wire rack. Store in the refrigerator.

**1 PIECE:** 380 cal., 16g fat (10g sat. fat), 41mg chol., 173mg sod., 59g carb. (36g sugars, 3g fiber), 3g pro.

## PEANUT BUTTER & JELLY ICE CREAM

What could be tastier than peanut butter and jelly ice cream? You'll love the sweet-salty combination. Use your favorite jelly, and switch to crunchy peanut butter if you like extra texture.
—Taste of Home *Test Kitchen*

- - - - - - - - - - - - - - - - - - - - - - - - - - - - - - - - - - - - - - - - - - - - - - - - -

**PREP:** 30 min. + freezing • **MAKES:** 10 servings (1¼ qt.)

- 1½   cups whole milk
- ⅔   cup packed brown sugar
- ½   tsp. salt
- 1   large egg, lightly beaten
- ⅔   cup creamy peanut butter
- 2   cups heavy whipping cream
- 2   tsp. vanilla extract
- ½   cup grape or strawberry jelly

**1.** In a large heavy saucepan, heat the milk, brown sugar and salt until bubbles form around side of pan. Whisk a small amount of the hot mixture into the egg. Return all to the pan, whisking constantly.

**2.** Cook and stir over low heat until mixture is thickened and coats the back of a spoon. Remove from the heat; whisk in the peanut butter. Quickly transfer to a bowl; place bowl in ice water and stir for 2 minutes. Stir in cream and vanilla. Press waxed paper onto surface of custard. Refrigerate for several hours or overnight.

**3.** Fill cylinder of ice cream freezer two-thirds full; freeze according to the manufacturer's directions.

**4.** When ice cream is frozen, spoon into a freezer container, layering with jelly; freeze for 2-4 hours before serving.

**½ CUP:** 393 cal., 28g fat (14g sat. fat), 77mg chol., 231mg sod., 32g carb. (29g sugars, 1g fiber), 7g pro.

VEGAN TROPICAL
MAGIC BARS

## RICOTTA CHEESECAKE

When I was a nurse, my co-workers and I regularly swapped recipes during lunch breaks. This creamy cheesecake was one of the best I ever received.
—*Georgiann Franklin, Canfield, OH*

- - - - - - - - - - - - - - - - - - - - - - - - - - - - -

**PREP:** 30 min. • **BAKE:** 50 min. + chilling
**MAKES:** 12 servings

- 1¼ cups graham cracker crumbs
- 3 Tbsp. sugar
- ⅓ cup butter, melted

FILLING
- 2 cartons (15 oz. each) ricotta cheese
- 1 cup sugar
- 3 large eggs, lightly beaten
- 2 Tbsp. all-purpose flour
- 1 tsp. vanilla extract
- Cherry pie filling, optional

**1.** Preheat oven to 400°. In a medium bowl, combine the graham cracker crumbs and sugar; stir in butter. Press onto the bottom and 1 in. up the side of a greased 9-in. springform pan.
**2.** Place on a baking sheet. Bake until crust is lightly browned around the edge, 6-8 minutes. Cool on a wire rack.
**3.** Beat ricotta cheese on medium speed for 1 minute. Add sugar; beat for 1 minute. Add eggs; beat just until combined. Beat in flour and vanilla. Pour into crust.
**4.** Place pan on a baking sheet. Bake at 350° for 50-60 minutes or until center is almost set. Cool on a wire rack for 10 minutes. Carefully run a knife around edge of pan to loosen; cool 1 hour longer. Refrigerate overnight.
**5.** Remove side of pan. If desired, serve with cherry pie filling. Refrigerate any leftover cheesecake.
**1 PIECE:** 234 cal., 11g fat (6g sat. fat), 81mg chol., 163mg sod., 29g carb. (23g sugars, 0 fiber), 6g pro.

> "Rich and creamy ... I added a bit of lemon juice and zest to give it a lemony taste. Excellent."
> —RIVERGULCH, TASTEOFHOME.COM

REVIEW

## VEGAN TROPICAL MAGIC BARS

Magic bars are one of the easiest treats you can make and I decided to give them a couple of twists. By using a plant-based butter and condensed coconut milk, I made them completely vegan. I also added some macadamia nuts and dried pineapple and mango to give them a tropical spin.
—*James Schend, Pleasant Prairie, WI*

- - - - - - - - - - - - - - - - - - - - - - - - - - - - -

**PREP:** 10 min. • **BAKE:** 30 min. + chilling
**MAKES:** 16 bars

- ½ cup vegan butter-style sticks
- 1 cup graham cracker crumbs
- 1 cup sweetened shredded coconut
- 1 cup dairy-free white baking chips
- 1 cup macadamia nuts, chopped
- ½ cup dried pineapple, chopped
- ½ cup dried mangoes, chopped
- 1 can (11.6 oz.) sweetened condensed coconut milk

**1.** Preheat oven to 350°. Melt butter in a 9-in. square baking pan. Over melted butter, sprinkle, in order: crumbs, coconut, baking chips, nuts, pineapple and mango. Pour well-stirred coconut milk over all. Do not stir.
**2.** Bake until a toothpick inserted in the center comes out clean, 30-35 minutes. Refrigerate at least 4 hours or overnight. Cut into bars and serve.
**1 BAR:** 323 cal., 20g fat (9g sat. fat), 2mg chol., 188mg sod., 34g carb. (27g sugars, 2g fiber), 2g pro.

## LEMON CHESS PIE

(SHOWN ON PAGE 249)
This luscious, lemony pie cuts beautifully and has a lovely, smooth texture. It's one of my favorites.
—*Hannah LaRue Rider, East Point, KY*

- - - - - - - - - - - - - - - - - - - - - - - - - - - - -

**PREP:** 15 min. • **BAKE:** 35 min. + chilling
**MAKES:** 8 servings

- 1 sheet refrigerated pie crust
- 4 large eggs, room temperature
- 1½ cups sugar
- ½ cup lemon juice
- ¼ cup butter, melted
- 1 Tbsp. cornmeal
- 2 tsp. all-purpose flour
- ⅛ tsp. salt
- Confectioners' sugar, optional

**1.** Preheat oven to 350°. Unroll crust into a 9-in. pie plate; flute edge. In a large bowl, beat eggs for 3 minutes. Gradually add sugar; beat until mixture becomes thick and lemon-colored, about 2 minutes. Beat in the lemon juice, butter, cornmeal, flour and salt.
**2.** Pour into crust. Bake until a knife inserted in the center comes out clean, 35-40 minutes. Cool on a wire rack for 1 hour. Refrigerate at least 3 hours before serving. If desired, garnish with confectioners' sugar.
**1 PIECE:** 363 cal., 15g fat (7g sat. fat), 113mg chol., 219mg sod., 54g carb. (39g sugars, 0 fiber), 4g pro.

## LEMON BREAD PUDDING

Sweet raisins and a smooth hot lemon sauce make this bread pudding extra special. Even today, I get requests for the recipe from people who tasted this traditional dessert years ago.
—*Mildred Sherrer, Fort Worth, TX*

- - - - - - - - - - - - - - - - - - - - - - - - - - -

**PREP:** 15 min. • **BAKE:** 50 min.
**MAKES:** 6 servings

- 3   slices day-old bread, cubed
- ¾   cup raisins
- 2   cups 2% milk
- ½   cup sugar
- 2   Tbsp. butter
- ¼   tsp. salt
- 2   large eggs
- 1   tsp. vanilla extract

LEMON SAUCE
- ¾   cup sugar
- 2   Tbsp. cornstarch
- 1   cup water
- 2   tsp. grated lemon zest
- 3   Tbsp. lemon juice
- 1   Tbsp. butter

**1.** Preheat oven to 350°. Toss bread and raisins in a greased 1½-qt. baking dish. In a small saucepan, combine milk, sugar, butter and salt; cook and stir until butter melts. Remove from the heat. Whisk eggs and vanilla in a small bowl. Stir a small amount of the hot milk mixture into the egg mixture; return all to pan, stirring constantly. Pour over bread and raisins.
**2.** Place baking dish in a larger baking pan. Fill larger pan with hot water to a depth of 1-in. Bake, uncovered, until a knife inserted in the center comes out clean, 50-60 minutes.
**3.** For sauce, in a small saucepan, combine sugar and cornstarch. Stir in water until smooth. Bring to a boil over medium heat; cook and stir until thickened, 1-2 minutes. Remove from heat. Stir in lemon zest, juice and butter until butter is melted. Serve over warm or cold pudding. Refrigerate leftovers.
**1 CUP:** 385 cal., 10g fat (5g sat. fat), 84mg chol., 280mg sod., 71g carb. (58g sugars, 1g fiber), 7g pro.

## GOLDEN M&M'S BARS

Our family loves to take drives, and I often bring these bars along for snacking in the car.
—*Martha Haseman, Hinckley, IL*

- - - - - - - - - - - - - - - - - - - - - - - - - - -

**PREP:** 15 min. • **BAKE:** 25 min. + cooling
**MAKES:** 2 dozen

- ½   cup butter, softened
- ¾   cup sugar
- ¾   cup packed brown sugar
- 2   tsp. vanilla extract
- 2   large eggs, room temperature
- 1½  cups all-purpose flour
- 1   tsp. baking powder
- ½   tsp. salt
- 1   cup white baking chips
- 1¾  cups plain M&M's, divided

**1.** Preheat oven to 350°. In a large bowl, cream butter, sugars and vanilla until light and fluffy, 5-7 minutes. Beat in the eggs, 1 at a time. Whisk together the flour, baking powder and salt; gradually add to the creamed mixture. Stir in chips and 1 cup of M&M's.
**2.** Spread evenly into a greased 13x9-in. baking pan. Sprinkle with the remaining ¾ cup M&M's. Bake until golden brown and a toothpick inserted in center comes out with moist crumbs, 25-30 minutes. Cool on a wire rack. Cut into bars.
**1 BAR:** 233 cal., 10g fat (6g sat. fat), 29mg chol., 123mg sod., 34g carb. (27g sugars, 1g fiber), 2g pro.

**TIPS**

- To keep these bars chewy, check them 5 minutes before the end of the recommended baking time to make sure they haven't dried out. Also, be sure to use the right size baking pan; using too large of pan can create a thin, dry bar.
- Try adding other mix-ins to recipe, such as caramel candies, Oreos, chocolate or toffee chips, or walnuts.
- You can store these bars for up to 5 days in an airtight container.

# - LEMON ICE -

Cool and refreshing, this recipe transforms the simplest ingredients into a light and elegant dessert—the perfect end to a summer meal.

In a saucepan over low heat, cook and stir **2 cups sugar** and **1 cup water** until sugar is dissolved. Remove from heat; stir in **2 cups lemon juice**. Pour into a freezer container. Freeze until slushy, 8 hours or overnight. If desired, garnish with **lemon slices** and **mint.**

# BEST ANGEL FOOD CAKE

For our daughter's wedding, a friend made this lovely, airy cake from a recipe she's used for decades. It really is one of the best angel food cake recipes I've found. Serve slices plain or dress them up with fresh fruit.
—*Marilyn Niemeyer, Doon, IA*

**PREP:** 15 min. + standing
**BAKE:** 35 min. + cooling
**MAKES:** 16 servings

1¼ cups egg whites (about 9 large)
1½ cups sugar, divided
1 cup cake flour
1¼ tsp. cream of tartar
1 tsp. vanilla extract
¼ tsp. almond extract
¼ tsp. salt

**1.** Place egg whites in a large bowl; let stand at room temperature 30 minutes. Sift ½ cup sugar and flour together twice; set aside.

**2.** Place oven rack in the lowest position. Preheat oven to 350°. Add cream of tartar, extracts and salt to egg whites; beat on medium speed until soft peaks form. Gradually add remaining 1 cup sugar, about 2 Tbsp. at a time, beating on high until stiff peaks form. Gradually fold in flour mixture, about ½ cup at a time.

**3.** Gently spoon batter into an ungreased 10-in. tube pan. Cut through batter with a knife to remove air pockets. Bake until lightly browned and the entire top appears dry, 35-40 minutes. Immediately invert pan; cool completely, about 1 hour.

**4.** Run a knife around side and center tube of pan. Remove cake to a serving plate.
**1 PIECE:** 115 cal., 0 fat (0 sat. fat), 0 chol., 68mg sod., 26g carb. (19g sugars, 0 fiber), 3g pro. **DIABETIC EXCHANGES:** 1½ starch.

**TIPS**

- Be sure to use an ungreased (but not a nonstick) tube pan for angel food cakes. The batter needs to climb the side of the pan for the cake to reach its light-as-air texture.
- Inverting the pan while cooling helps prevent the cake from compressing and losing volume. If your pan doesn't have feet to keep it suspended, suspend it on the neck of a wine bottle.

# AIR-FRYER COOKIE PIE

My mom used to make cookie bars for every school event when I was growing up. My updated version takes half the time and tastes just like Mom used to make.
—*Ashley Long, Mission, KS*

**PREP:** 15 min. + cooling • **COOK:** 10 min.
**MAKES:** 12 servings

½ cup unsalted butter, cubed
½ cup sugar
½ cup packed brown sugar
1 large egg, room temperature
1 Tbsp. vanilla extract
1½ cups all-purpose flour
½ tsp. sea salt
½ tsp. baking soda
1 cup brickle toffee bits
½ cup Nutella
Confectioners' sugar, optional

**1.** In a small heavy saucepan, melt butter over medium heat until golden brown, 5-7 minutes, stirring constantly. Remove from heat. Transfer to a large bowl. Cool completely until butter is solid.

**2.** Preheat air fryer to 350°. Grease an 8-in. round baking pan that will fit in air fryer; line it with parchment and grease the paper. Add sugars to melted butter; beat until crumbly, about 2 minutes. Beat in egg and vanilla. In another bowl, whisk flour, salt and baking soda; gradually beat into the butter mixture. Fold in toffee bits.

**3.** Press half the dough onto bottom and up side of prepared pan. Spread Nutella over dough to within ½ in. of edge. Press the remaining dough between sheets of parchment into an 8-in. circle. Remove paper and place dough over Nutella; pinch edge to seal. If desired, sprinkle with additional sea salt.

**4.** Cook until a toothpick inserted in center comes out clean, 10-12 minutes. Loosen side from pan with a knife. Cool in pan 10 minutes before removing to wire rack; remove paper. If desired, dust with confectioners' sugar before serving.
**1 PIECE:** 369 cal., 18g fat (8g sat. fat), 43mg chol., 261mg sod., 49g carb. (36g sugars, 1g fiber), 3g pro.

## CREAM CHEESE ICE CREAM

This is hands-down the best homemade ice cream I've ever eaten. It tastes like cheesecake with a refreshing hint of lemon.
—Johnnie McLeod, Bastrop, LA

- - - - - - - - - - - - - - - - - - - - - - - - - - - - - - - - - - - - - - - - - - - - -

**PREP:** 20 min. + chilling • **PROCESS:** 20 min./batch + freezing
**MAKES:** 1½ qt.

- 2½ cups half-and-half cream
- 1 cup whole milk
- 1¼ cups sugar
- 2 large eggs, lightly beaten
- 12 oz. cream cheese, cubed
- 1 Tbsp. lemon juice
- 1 tsp. vanilla extract

**1.** In a large saucepan, heat the cream and milk to 175°; stir in sugar until dissolved. Whisk a small amount of hot mixture into the eggs. Return all to the pan, whisking constantly. Cook and stir over low heat until mixture reaches at least 160° and coats the back of a metal spoon.
**2.** Remove from heat. Whisk in cream cheese until smooth. Cool quickly by placing pan in a bowl of ice water; stir for 2 minutes. Stir in lemon juice and vanilla. Press foil or waxed paper onto surface of custard. Refrigerate for several hours or overnight.
**3.** Fill the cylinder of ice cream freezer two-thirds full; freeze according to manufacturer's directions. Refrigerate remaining mixture until ready to freeze. Transfer to a freezer container; freeze for 2-4 hours before serving.
**½ CUP:** 273 cal., 16g fat (10g sat. fat), 87mg chol., 135mg sod., 25g carb. (25g sugars, 0 fiber), 5g pro.

## TURTLE ICE CREAM SAUCE

Making this rich caramel-fudge sauce is a family affair at our house—the kids love to unwrap the caramels! The sauce can be made ahead and frozen.
—Marci Cullen, Milton, WI

- - - - - - - - - - - - - - - - - - - - - - - - - - - - - - - - - - - - - - - - - - - - -

**PREP:** 10 min. • **COOK:** 15 min. + cooling • **MAKES:** 9 cups

- 2 cups butter, cubed
- 2 cans (12 oz. each) evaporated milk
- 2 cups sugar
- ⅓ cup dark corn syrup
- ⅛ tsp. salt
- 2 cups semisweet chocolate chips
- 1 pkg. (14 oz.) caramels
- 1 tsp. vanilla extract

**1.** In a Dutch oven, combine the first 7 ingredients. Cook, stirring constantly, over medium-low heat until the caramels are melted and mixture is smooth (do not boil). Reduce heat to low.
**2.** With an electric hand mixer on medium speed, beat in vanilla; continue beating for 5 minutes. Then beat on high for 2 minutes. Remove from the heat and cool for 30 minutes (sauce will thicken as it cools). Pour into food storage containers; refrigerate. Serve warm or cold.
**2 TBSP. SAUCE:** 83 cal., 3g fat (1g sat. fat), 4mg chol., 30mg sod., 15g carb. (14g sugars, 0 fiber), 1g pro.

**TIP**
When working with caramel, make sure you're using a heavy-bottomed pan to avoid uneven cooking. Caramel can burn when using a thin and shallow pot.

## DATE PUDDING COBBLER

There were eight children in my family when I was a girl, and all of us enjoyed this cobbler. I now serve it for everyday and special occasions alike.
—*Carolyn Miller, Guys Mills, PA*

**PREP:** 15 min. • **BAKE:** 25 min. • **MAKES:** 8 servings

1  cup all-purpose flour
1½  cups packed brown sugar, divided
2  tsp. baking powder
1  Tbsp. cold butter
½  cup 2% milk
¾  cup chopped dates
¾  cup chopped walnuts
1  cup water
    Optional: Whipped cream and
    ground cinnamon

**1.** Preheat oven to 350°. In a large bowl, combine the flour, ½ cup brown sugar and the baking powder. Cut in butter until crumbly. Gradually add milk, dates and walnuts.
**2.** In a large saucepan, combine water and the remaining 1 cup brown sugar; bring to a boil. Remove from the heat; add the date mixture and mix well.
**3.** Transfer to a greased 10-in. cast-iron skillet or 8-in. square baking pan. Bake for 25-30 minutes or until top is golden brown and fruit is tender. Serve warm, with whipped cream and cinnamon if desired.
**1 SERVING:** 347 cal., 9g fat (2g sat. fat), 5mg chol., 150mg sod., 65g carb. (50g sugars, 2g fiber), 4g pro.

## GLAZED LEMON CHIFFON CAKE

This fluffy cake is a real treat drizzled with the sweet-tart lemon glaze.
—*Rebecca Baird, Salt Lake City, UT*

**PREP:** 15 min. • **BAKE:** 45 min. + cooling • **MAKES:** 16 servings

½  cup fat-free evaporated milk
½  cup reduced-fat sour cream
¼  cup lemon juice
2  Tbsp. canola oil
2  tsp. vanilla extract
1  tsp. grated lemon zest
1  tsp. lemon extract
2  cups cake flour
1½  cups sugar
1  Tbsp. baking powder
½  tsp. salt
1  cup large egg whites (about 7), room temperature
½  tsp. cream of tartar
LEMON GLAZE
1¾  cups confectioners' sugar
3  Tbsp. lemon juice

**1.** Preheat oven to 325°. In a large bowl, combine the first 7 ingredients. Sift together the flour, sugar, baking powder and salt; gradually beat into the lemon mixture until smooth. In a small bowl, beat egg whites until foamy. Add cream of tartar; beat until stiff peaks form. Gently fold into the lemon mixture.
**2.** Pour batter into an ungreased 10-in. tube pan. Bake for 45-55 minutes or until cake springs back when lightly touched. Immediately invert pan; cool completely. Remove cake to a serving platter. Combine glaze ingredients; drizzle over cake.
**1 PIECE:** 230 cal., 3g fat (1g sat. fat), 3mg chol., 189mg sod., 47g carb. (33g sugars, 0 fiber), 4g pro.

## TRADITIONAL FUNNEL CAKES

When I was in high school, I made these funnel cakes every Sunday after church for my family. They are crisp and tender, just like the kind we always ate at the state fair.
—*Susan Tingley, Portland, OR*

**PREP:** 15 min. • **COOK:** 5 min./batch • **MAKES:** 8 servings

- 2 cups 2% milk
- 3 large eggs, room temperature
- ¼ cup sugar
- 2 cups all-purpose flour
- 2 tsp. baking powder
  - Oil for deep-fat frying
  - Confectioners' sugar
  - Lingonberry jam or red currant jelly

**1.** Combine milk, eggs and sugar. Combine flour and baking powder; beat into the egg mixture until smooth.
**2.** In a cast-iron or electric skillet, heat 2 in. oil to 375°. Cover the bottom of a funnel spout with your finger; ladle ½ cup batter into funnel. Holding the funnel several inches above the skillet, release your finger; move the funnel in a spiral motion until all the batter is released. Scrape funnel with a rubber spatula if needed.
**3.** Fry until golden brown, about 1 minute on each side. Drain on paper towels. Repeat with remaining batter. Dust with the confectioners' sugar. Serve warm with the jam.
**NOTE:** To pour batter easily into hot oil, you can also use a liquid measuring cup or a turkey baster.
**1 FUNNEL CAKE:** 300 cal., 15g fat (2g sat. fat), 84mg chol., 157mg sod., 33g carb. (10g sugars, 1g fiber), 8g pro.

## 5i
## CLASSIC CREME BRULEE

My favorite dessert is creme brulee, so I quickly learned how to successfully make this on my own. Recently I was at a party where the guests finished off their own desserts by broiling the sugar on their portions with a small torch. What a clever idea!
—*Joylyn Trickel, Helendale, CA*

**PREP:** 30 min. • **BAKE:** 25 min. + chilling • **MAKES:** 8 servings

- 4 cups heavy whipping cream
- 9 large egg yolks
- ¾ cup sugar
- 1 tsp. vanilla extract
  - Brown sugar

**1.** In a large saucepan, combine the cream, egg yolks and sugar. Cook and stir over medium heat until mixture reaches 160° or is thick enough to coat the back of a metal spoon. Stir in vanilla.
**2.** Transfer to eight 6-oz. ramekins or custard cups. Place cups in a baking pan; add 1 in. of boiling water to pan. Bake, uncovered, at 325° until centers are just set (mixture will jiggle), 25-30 minutes. Remove ramekins from water bath; cool for 10 minutes. Cover and refrigerate for at least 4 hours .
**3.** One hour before serving, place custards on a baking sheet. Sprinkle each with 1-2 tsp. brown sugar. Broil 8 in. from the heat until sugar is caramelized, 4-7 minutes. Refrigerate leftovers.
**1 SERVING:** 551 cal., 50g fat (29g sat. fat), 402mg chol., 53mg sod., 22g carb. (22g sugars, 0 fiber), 6g pro.

## POSSUM PIE

This recipe was found in a box of recipes in the cafe we own. The recipes were used in the early 1950s by a previous owner, and this pie has been on our menu since we discovered it.

—*David Heilemann, Eureka Springs, AR*

- - - - - - - - - - - - - - - - - - - - - - - - - - - -

**PREP:** 20 min. + chilling
**MAKES:** 8 servings

- 6 oz. cream cheese, softened
- ¾ cup confectioners' sugar
- 1 graham cracker crust (9 in.)
- ¼ cup chopped pecans
- 1¾ cups cold milk
- ¾ tsp. vanilla extract
- ¼ cup instant vanilla pudding mix
- ⅓ cup instant chocolate pudding mix
- ½ cup heavy whipping cream, whipped
- 12 to 16 pecan halves

**1.** In a small bowl, beat the cream cheese and sugar until smooth. Spoon into crust. Sprinkle with chopped pecans.
**2.** In a bowl, whisk the milk, vanilla and pudding mixes for 2 minutes. Let stand for 2 minutes or until soft-set. Spoon over the pecans. Refrigerate for at least 4 hours. Top with whipped cream and pecan halves.

**1 PIECE:** 388 cal., 24g fat (10g sat. fat), 44mg chol., 276mg sod., 40g carb. (32g sugars, 1g fiber), 5g pro.

## BANANA FRITTERS

(SHOWN ON PAGE 249)
Soon after I made these fritters for the first time, my husband began requesting them on a regular basis. I also like to serve them to overnight guests as a sweet breakfast treat.

—*Laurel Cosbie, Palm Desert, CA*

- - - - - - - - - - - - - - - - - - - - - - - - - - - -

**TAKES:** 30 min. • **MAKES:** 16 fritters

- 2 large eggs, room temperature
- ½ cup 2% milk
- 1 tsp. canola oil
- 1 cup all-purpose flour
- 1 tsp. baking powder
- 1 tsp. salt
- 4 large firm bananas
  Additional oil for deep-fat frying
  Confectioners' sugar, optional

**1.** In a bowl, beat eggs, milk and oil. Combine flour, baking powder and salt; stir into egg mixture until smooth. Cut bananas into quarters (about 2 in. long). Dip each banana piece into batter to coat.
**2.** In an electric skillet or deep-fat fryer, heat oil to 375°. Fry banana pieces, 2-3 at a time, until golden brown.
**3.** Drain on paper towels. If desired, dust with confectioners' sugar.

**1 FRITTER:** 124 cal., 7g fat (1g sat. fat), 24mg chol., 190mg sod., 14g carb. (5g sugars, 1g fiber), 2g pro.

## TART & TANGY LEMON TART

Our family adores lemon desserts. I like to make this lemony tart for brunch. For extra-special events, I bake it in my heart-shaped tart pan.

—*Joyce Moynihan, Lakeville, MN*

- - - - - - - - - - - - - - - - - - - - - - - - - - - -

**PREP:** 15 min. + chilling
**BAKE:** 45 min. + cooling
**MAKES:** 14 servings

- ¾ cup butter, softened
- ½ cup confectioners' sugar
- 1½ cups all-purpose flour
FILLING
- ¾ cup sugar
- 1 Tbsp. grated lemon zest
- ¾ cup lemon juice
- 3 large eggs, room temperature
- 3 large egg yolks, room temperature
- 4 oz. cream cheese, softened
- 1 Tbsp. cornstarch
  Sweetened whipped cream, optional

**1.** Preheat oven to 325°. In a large bowl, cream butter and confectioners' sugar until smooth. Gradually beat in flour. Press dough onto bottom and up side of an ungreased 11-in. fluted tart pan with removable bottom. Refrigerate for 15 minutes.
**2.** Line unpricked crust with a double thickness of foil. Fill with pie weights, dried beans or uncooked rice. Bake until edge is lightly browned, 18-22 minutes. Remove foil and weights; bake until bottom is golden brown, 5-7 minutes longer. Cool on a wire rack.
**3.** In a large bowl, beat sugar, lemon zest, lemon juice, eggs, egg yolks, cream cheese and cornstarch until blended; pour into crust. Bake until filling is set, 18-22 minutes. Cool on a wire rack. If desired, serve with whipped cream. Refrigerate leftovers.

**1 PIECE:** 254 cal., 15g fat (9g sat. fat), 114mg chol., 125mg sod., 27g carb. (16g sugars, 0 fiber), 4g pro.

REVIEW
*"This is an absolute winner! The filling is nice and tangy but not too tart and the crust melts in your mouth ... soooo tender!"*
—VICTORIAPAGE, TASTEOFHOME.COM

POSSUM PIE

## CARAMEL-PECAN COOKIE BUTTER BARS

I love cookie butter and used to spread it on toast, vanilla wafers or graham crackers. One day I was thinking about another way to use it. I came up with these bars, and they were an instant hit in my house. These cookies freeze well—they are so tempting to remove from the freezer one by one until there are no more left!
—Sheryl Little, Cabot, AR

--------------------------------------------

**PREP:** 15 min. • **BAKE:** 15 min. + cooling
**MAKES:** 2 dozen

- ½ cup butter, softened
- ½ cup sugar
- ½ cup packed brown sugar
- ½ cup Biscoff creamy cookie spread
- 1 large egg, room temperature
- 1¼ cups self-rising flour
- 2 cups pecan halves, coarsely chopped
- 1 pkg. (11 oz.) caramels
- 3 Tbsp. half-and-half cream
- 1 tsp. vanilla extract
- 1 cup (6 oz.) dark chocolate chips
- 1 Tbsp. shortening

**1.** Preheat oven to 375°. In a large bowl, cream butter, sugars and cookie butter until light and fluffy, 5-7 minutes. Beat in egg. Gradually beat in flour. Spread onto bottom of greased 13x9-in. baking pan. Sprinkle with pecans; press lightly into dough. Bake until edges are lightly browned, 15-20 minutes.
**2.** Meanwhile, in a large saucepan, combine caramels and cream. Cook and stir over medium-low heat until caramels are melted. Remove from the heat; stir in vanilla. Pour over crust. Cool completely in pan on a wire rack.
**3.** In a microwave, melt chocolate chips and shortening; stir until smooth. Drizzle over bars; let stand until set. Cut into bars.
**1 BAR:** 285 cal., 17g fat (6g sat. fat), 20mg chol., 149mg sod., 34g carb. (25g sugars, 2g fiber), 3g pro.

REVIEW

*"These ... are fabulous. There are several steps to this recipe but the bars are well worth it."*
—MARINEMOM_TEXAS, TASTEOFHOME.COM

## MACAROON CHERRY PIE

In summer, I use homegrown cherries in this amazing pie with a crunchy coconut topping. But canned tart cherries yield a dessert that's almost as delicious. I always bake this pie around Presidents Day or Valentine's Day, but it's popular with my family the whole year through.
—Lori Daniels, Beverly, WV

--------------------------------------------

**PREP:** 25 min. • **BAKE:** 35 min. + chilling
**MAKES:** 8 servings

  Dough for single-crust pie
- 3 cans (14½ oz. each) pitted tart cherries
- 1 cup sugar
- ⅓ cup cornstarch
- ½ tsp. ground cinnamon
- ¼ tsp. red food coloring, optional

TOPPING
- 1 large egg, room temperature, lightly beaten
- 2 Tbsp. 2% milk
- 1 Tbsp. butter, melted
- ¼ tsp. almond extract
- ¼ cup sugar
- ⅛ tsp. salt
- 1 cup sweetened shredded coconut
- ½ cup sliced almonds

**1.** Preheat oven to 400°. On a lightly floured surface, roll dough to a ⅛-in.-thick circle; transfer to a 9-in. cast-iron skillet or deep-dish pie plate. Trim to ½ in. beyond edge of plate; flute edge. Bake 6 minutes; set aside.
**2.** Drain cherries, reserving 1 cup juice. Set cherries aside. In a large saucepan, combine sugar and cornstarch; gradually stir in cherry juice until blended. Bring to a boil over medium heat; cook and stir until thickened, 2 minutes.
**3.** Remove from heat; stir in cinnamon and food coloring if desired. Gently fold in cherries. Pour into crust. Cover edge loosely with foil. Bake at 400° 20 minutes.
**4.** Meanwhile, in a large bowl, combine first 6 topping ingredients. Stir in coconut and almonds.
**5.** Remove foil from pie; spoon topping over pie. Reduce oven to 350°; bake until topping is lightly browned, 15-20 minutes. Cool on a wire rack 1 hour. Chill 4 hours or overnight before cutting.
**DOUGH FOR SINGLE-CRUST PIE (9 IN.):**
Combine 1¼ cups all-purpose flour and ¼ tsp. salt; cut in ½ cup cold butter until crumbly. Gradually add 3-5 Tbsp. ice water, tossing with a fork until dough holds together when pressed. Shape into a disk; wrap dough and refrigerate 1 hour.
**1 PIECE:** 434 cal., 16g fat (8g sat. fat), 36mg chol., 199mg sod., 70g carb. (48g sugars, 3g fiber), 5g pro.

## PUMPKIN CHEESECAKE BARS

This recipe caught my eye and was extremely popular at the annual Christmas party that's sponsored by our Extension Homemakers. It's also a great dessert for fall.
—Agnes Jasa, Malabar, FL

PREP: 15 min. • BAKE: 45 min. + cooling • MAKES: 16 bars

- 1   cup all-purpose flour
- ⅓   cup packed brown sugar
- 5   Tbsp. cold butter
- 1   cup finely chopped pecans
- 1   pkg. (8 oz.) cream cheese, softened
- ¾   cup sugar
- ½   cup canned pumpkin
- 2   large eggs, room temperature, lightly beaten
- 1   tsp. vanilla extract
- 1½  tsp. ground cinnamon
- 1   tsp. ground allspice

**1.** Preheat oven to 350°. Combine flour and brown sugar. Cut in butter until crumbly. Stir in pecans; set aside ¾ cup for topping.
**2.** Press remaining crumb mixture into a greased 8-in. square baking pan. Bake for 15 minutes or until edges are lightly browned. Cool on a wire rack.
**3.** In a large bowl, beat cream cheese and sugar until smooth. Beat in the pumpkin, eggs, vanilla, cinnamon and allspice. Pour over crust. Sprinkle with reserved crumb mixture.
**4.** Bake for 30-35 minutes or until golden brown. Cool on a wire rack. Cut into bars. Store in the refrigerator.
**1 BAR:** 228 cal., 15g fat (6g sat. fat), 52mg chol., 88mg sod., 22g carb. (15g sugars, 1g fiber), 4g pro.

## MADEIRA CAKE

This classic British cake is often served with Madeira wine, which is how it got its name. Similar to a pound cake, it is commonly flavored with lemon and can also be served with other sweet liqueurs or tea.
—Peggy Woodward, Shullsburg, WI

PREP: 15 min. • BAKE: 45 min. + cooling • MAKES: 12 servings

- 1    cup unsalted butter, softened
- 1    cup plus 2 Tbsp. sugar, divided
- 2    tsp. grated lemon zest
- 3    large eggs, room temperature
- 2¼  cups all-purpose flour
- 2    tsp. baking powder

**1.** Preheat oven to 325°. Line the bottom of a greased 8x4-in. loaf pan with parchment; grease the parchment.
**2.** In a large bowl, cream butter and 1 cup sugar until light and fluffy, 5-7 minutes. Beat in lemon zest. Add eggs, 1 at a time, beating well after each addition. In another bowl, whisk flour and baking powder; gradually add to the creamed mixture.
**3.** Transfer batter to prepared pan. Sprinkle with the remaining 2 Tbsp. sugar. Bake until a toothpick inserted in center comes out clean, 45-50 minutes. Cool in pan 10 minutes before removing to a wire rack to cool completely.
**1 PIECE:** 304 cal., 17g fat (10g sat. fat), 87mg chol., 100mg sod., 35g carb. (17g sugars, 1g fiber), 4g pro.

## SLOW-COOKER PINA COLADA BANANAS FOSTER

I took bananas Foster one step further and combined it with the flavors of my favorite tropical drink. Make sure your bananas are not super ripe—choose ones that are still nice and firm.
—*Trisha Kruse, Eagle, ID*

- - - - - - - - - - - - - - - - - - - - - - - - - - - - - - - - - - - - - - - - - - -

**PREP:** 10 min. • **COOK:** 2 hours • **MAKES:** 3 cups

- 4  medium firm bananas
- 1  can (8 oz.) pineapple tidbits, drained
- ¼  cup butter, melted
- 1  cup packed brown sugar
- ¼  cup rum
- ½  tsp. coconut extract
- ½  cup sweetened shredded coconut, toasted
   Optional: Coconut ice cream, vanilla wafers and cream-filled wafer cookies

Cut bananas in half lengthwise, then widthwise. Layer sliced bananas and pineapple in the bottom of a 1½-qt. slow cooker. Combine butter, brown sugar, rum and coconut extract in a small bowl; pour over fruit. Cover and cook on low until heated through, about 2 hours. Sprinkle with the toasted coconut. If desired, serve with coconut ice cream, vanilla wafers or cream-filled wafer cookies.

**NOTE:** If you want your bananas to stay somewhat firm, add them to the slow cooker during the last 20 minutes of cooking.

**½ CUP:** 358 cal., 11g fat (7g sat. fat), 20mg chol., 95mg sod., 63g carb. (53g sugars, 3g fiber), 1g pro.

## 🍓 🍎 PM
## FROSTY WATERMELON ICE

For a different way to serve watermelon, try this make-ahead frozen dessert. It's so refreshing on a summer day—and you don't have to worry about seeds while you're enjoying it.
—*Kaaren Jurack, Manassas, VA*

- - - - - - - - - - - - - - - - - - - - - - - - - - - - - - - - - - - - - - - - - - -

**PREP:** 20 min. + freezing • **MAKES:** 4 servings

- 1  tsp. unflavored gelatin
- 2  Tbsp. water
- 2  Tbsp. lime juice
- 2  Tbsp. honey
- 4  cups cubed seedless watermelon, divided

**1.** In a microwave-safe bowl, sprinkle gelatin over water; let stand 1 minute. Microwave on high for 40 seconds. Stir and let stand until gelatin is completely dissolved, 1-2 minutes.

**2.** Place lime juice, honey and gelatin mixture in a blender. Add 1 cup watermelon; cover and process until blended. Add the remaining watermelon, 1 cup at a time, processing until smooth after each addition.

**3.** Transfer to a shallow dish; freeze until almost firm. In a chilled bowl, beat with an electric mixer until mixture is bright pink. Divide among 4 serving dishes; freeze, covered, until firm. Remove from freezer 15-20 minutes before serving.

**¾ CUP:** 81 cal., 0 fat (0 sat. fat), 0 chol., 3mg sod., 21g carb. (18g sugars, 1g fiber), 1g pro. **DIABETIC EXCHANGES:** 1 fruit, ½ starch.

> **TIP**
> Working with gelatin requires a balance between temperatures. Before gelatin can be mixed with other ingredients, it first needs to absorb some cold water, a process called "blooming." Then it needs to be added to a warm mixture, or heated, so it doesn't set too fast.

# SWEETENED RICOTTA WITH BERRIES

Ricotta is a lovely fast cheese that can be made from whole milk, skim milk or whey. This creamy dessert is luscious topped with raspberries or strawberries.
—*Matthew Lawrence, Vashon, WA*

- - - - - - - - - - - - - - - - - - - - - - - - - - - - - - - - - - - - -

**PREP:** 40 min. + chilling
**MAKES:** 7 servings

**HOMEMADE RICOTTA**
- 8 cups whole milk
- 1 cup heavy whipping cream
- ½ cup lemon juice

**DESSERT**
- 1 cup fresh blackberries
- 1 cup fresh raspberries
- 1 tsp. sugar
- 3 Tbsp. honey
- ⅛ tsp. salt
- ¼ cup heavy whipping cream

**1.** In a Dutch oven, heat milk and cream to 180° over low heat, stirring constantly. Stir in lemon juice. Remove from the heat and let stand for 15 minutes (milk and whey will separate).

**2.** Line a large strainer with 4 layers of cheesecloth and place over a large bowl. Pour milk mixture into prepared strainer; strain for 1 hour or until most of the liquid is strained. Discard liquid. Wrap the ricotta in the cheesecloth. Refrigerate for at least 1 hour. Squeeze out any liquid; remove cheesecloth and discard liquid from bowl.

**3.** In a small bowl, combine berries and sugar; set aside. Place ricotta in a food processor. Add honey and salt; cover and process until blended. While processing, gradually add cream in a steady stream; process until creamy. Serve with berries.

**⅓ CUP RICOTTA WITH ¼ CUP BERRIES :** 366 cal., 25g fat (15g sat. fat), 86mg chol., 171mg sod., 27g carb. (23g sugars, 2g fiber), 10g pro.

**DID YOU KNOW?**
The name ricotta comes from the Italian word *recocta*, meaning "recooked." In Italy, most types of ricotta use reheated whey. It's thought that ricotta was first invented to find a use for the huge amount of whey produced by Italy's cheesemakers— which was actually causing environmental issues!

## CITRUS CORNMEAL CAKE

Cornmeal adds a rustic quality to this delicate dessert flavored with citrus and almond. It's sure to be a staple in your recipe collection and also makes a great holiday party hostess gift.
—*Roxanne Chan, Albany, CA*

**PREP:** 25 min. • **BAKE:** 25 min. + cooling • **MAKES:** 8 servings

- ½  cup lemon yogurt
- ⅓  cup honey
- ¼  cup olive oil
- 1  large egg, room temperature
- 2  large egg whites, room temperature
- ¼  tsp. almond extract
- ¾  cup all-purpose flour
- ½  cup cornmeal
- 1  tsp. baking powder
- ½  tsp. grated orange zest
- 1  can (15 oz.) mandarin oranges, drained
- 3  Tbsp. sliced almonds

**1.** Coat a 9-in. fluted tart pan with removable bottom with cooking spray. In a large bowl, beat the yogurt, honey, oil, egg, egg whites and extract until well blended. In a second bowl, combine flour, cornmeal and baking powder; gradually beat into the yogurt mixture until blended. Stir in orange zest.
**2.** Pour batter into prepared pan. Arrange oranges over batter; sprinkle with almonds. Bake at 350° until a toothpick inserted in the center comes out clean, 25-30 minutes. Cool on a wire rack for 10 minutes before cutting. Serve warm or room temperature.
**1 PIECE:** 240 cal., 9g fat (1g sat. fat), 27mg chol., 85mg sod., 36g carb. (20g sugars, 2g fiber), 5g pro.

## 🍎 BAKED PUMPKIN PUDDING

Even after you eat your favorite turkey dinner, you'll find room for this perfect pudding dessert—a treat served hot or cold. Mildly spiced, it will leave you sweetly satisfied, but not overly full.
—*Gerri Saylor, Graniteville, SC*

**PREP:** 10 min. • **BAKE:** 40 min. • **MAKES:** 5 servings

- ½  cup egg substitute
- 1  can (15 oz.) solid-pack pumpkin
- ¾  cup sugar
- 1  Tbsp. honey
- 1  tsp. ground cinnamon
- ½  tsp. ground ginger
- ¼  tsp. ground cloves
- 1½  cups fat-free evaporated milk
- 5  Tbsp. reduced-fat whipped topping

**1.** In a large bowl, beat the egg substitute, pumpkin, sugar, honey and spices until blended. Gradually beat in milk. Pour into five 8-oz. custard cups coated with cooking spray. Place in a 13x9-in. baking pan. Pour hot water into pan to act as a water bath.
**2.** Bake, uncovered, at 425° for 10 minutes. Reduce heat to 350°. Bake 30-35 minutes longer or until a knife inserted in the center comes out clean.
**3.** Serve warm or cold. Garnish with whipped topping. Store in the refrigerator.
**1 SERVING:** 244 cal., 1g fat (1g sat. fat), 3mg chol., 141mg sod., 52g carb. (46g sugars, 3g fiber), 9g pro.

## BLUE-RIBBON APPLE CAKE

A friend from New Hampshire gave me this recipe for her cake, which took a blue ribbon at the county fair.
—*Jennie Wilburn, Long Creek, OR*

- - - - - - - - - - - - - - - - - - - - - - - - - - - - - - - - - -

**PREP:** 15 min. • **BAKE:** 55 min. + cooling • **MAKES:** 16 servings

> 3 cups all-purpose flour
> 2¼ cups sugar, divided
> 1 Tbsp. baking powder
> ½ tsp. salt
> 4 large eggs, room temperature
> 1 cup canola oil
> ⅓ cup orange juice
> 2½ tsp. vanilla extract
> 4 medium tart apples, peeled and thinly sliced
> 2 tsp. ground cinnamon
> Confectioners' sugar

**1.** Preheat oven to 350°. Combine flour, 2 cups sugar, baking powder and salt. In a second bowl, combine the eggs, oil, orange juice and vanilla; add to the flour mixture and mix well. In a third bowl, toss apples with cinnamon and the remaining ¼ cup sugar.
**2.** Spread a third of the batter into a greased 10-in. tube pan. Top with half the apples. Repeat layers. Carefully spread the remaining batter over apples.
**3.** Bake until a toothpick inserted in the center comes out clean, 55-65 minutes. Cool 15 minutes before removing from pan to a wire rack; cool. Dust with confectioners' sugar.
**1 PIECE:** 353 cal., 15g fat (2g sat. fat), 53mg chol., 165mg sod., 51g carb. (32g sugars, 1g fiber), 4g pro.

## ICE CREAM BOWLS

Once you sample these homemade waffle ice cream bowls, you'll want to serve them time and again! You can either prepare them with pretty designs in a special pizzelle cookie maker or without designs in the oven.
—Taste of Home *Test Kitchen*

- - - - - - - - - - - - - - - - - - - - - - - - - - - - - - - - - -

**PREP:** 15 min. • **BAKE:** 35 min. • **MAKES:** 16 servings

> 3 large eggs, room temperature
> ¾ cup sugar
> ½ cup butter, melted
> 2 tsp. vanilla extract
> 1½ cups all-purpose flour
> 2 tsp. baking powder

**1.** In a small bowl, beat eggs on medium speed until blended. Gradually beat in sugar until thick and lemon colored. Add butter and vanilla. Combine flour and baking powder; gradually add to egg mixture. Invert two 6-oz. custard cups on paper towels; coat with cooking spray.
**2.** Prepare cookies in a preheated pizzelle maker according to manufacturer's directions, using 2 Tbsp. batter for each cookie. Immediately remove pizzelles and drape over inverted custard cups. To shape cookies into bowls, place another custard cup coated with cooking spray over each pizzelle. Let stand until set. Remove cookies from custard cups and set aside. Repeat with the remaining batter. Store in an airtight container.
**TO MAKE IN THE OVEN:** Line a baking sheet with parchment. Draw two 7-in. circles on the paper. Spread 2 Tbsp. batter over each circle. Bake at 400° for 4-5 minutes or until edges are golden brown. Immediately remove the cookies and drape over inverted custard cups. Shape into bowls as directed above.
**1 BOWL:** 145 cal., 7g fat (4g sat. fat), 50mg chol., 119mg sod., 19g carb. (10g sugars, 0 fiber), 2g pro.

MAGIC BARS

## MAGIC BARS

These rich bar cookies will melt in your mouth—like magic! They're ideal to have on hand for a snack.
—*Pauline Schrag, Theresa, NY*

------------------------------------------------

**PREP:** 15 min. • **BAKE:** 30 min. + cooling
**MAKES:** 16 bars

- ½ cup butter
- 1 cup graham cracker crumbs
- 1 cup sweetened shredded coconut
- 1 cup semisweet chocolate chips
- 1 cup chopped nuts
- 1 can (14 oz.) sweetened condensed milk

**1.** Preheat oven to 350°. Melt butter in a 9-in. square baking pan. On top of melted butter, sprinkle the crumbs, then coconut, then chocolate chips, then nuts. Pour milk over all. Do not stir.

**2.** Bake until a toothpick inserted in center comes out clean, about 30 minutes. Cool several hours before cutting.

**1 BAR:** 279 cal., 18g fat (9g sat. fat), 24mg chol., 138mg sod., 28g carb. (22g sugars, 1g fiber), 5g pro.

## 🕐 TWO-MINUTE COOKIES

(SHOWN ON PAGE 249)

My mom used to pack these cookies into our school lunches. They're inexpensive and easy to prepare, so all seven of us children learned to make them. Now they're also a favorite with my children.
—*Kerry Bouchard, Augusta, MT*

------------------------------------------------

**TAKES:** 15 min. • **MAKES:** about 3 dozen

- ½ cup butter, cubed
- ½ cups 2% milk
- 2 cups sugar
- 3 cups quick-cooking oats or old-fashioned oats
- 5 Tbsp. baking cocoa
- ½ cup raisins, chopped nuts or sweetened shredded coconut

**1.** In a large saucepan, heat butter, milk and sugar. Bring to a boil, stirring occasionally. Boil for 1 minute.

**2.** Remove from the heat. Stir in the oats, cocoa, and raisins, nuts or coconut. Drop by tablespoonfuls onto waxed paper. Cool.

**1 COOKIE:** 101 cal., 3g fat (2g sat. fat), 7mg chol., 22mg sod., 18g carb. (13g sugars, 1g fiber), 1g pro.

# - 13 -

# FEEDING
# A CROWD

When you need to bring a dish for a potluck, create a bevy of treats for
a bake sale, set a feast for extended family or lay out a party spread for
a house full of friends, these recipes are just the thing. From appetizers
to desserts, every recipe serves at least 12 people.

**Roasted Fall Vegetables** (p. 293) **Angel Strawberry Dessert** (p. 293) **Dijon-Rubbed Pork with Rhubarb Sauce** (p. 274)
**Savory Cucumber Sandwiches** (p. 284) **Herbed Rubbed Turkey** (p. 291) **Lemon Sheet Cake** (p. 289)
**Hot Chocolate Cookies** (p. 284) **Cashew Rice Pilaf** (p. 276) **Buffalo Wing Dip** (p. 288)

## OKLAHOMA COCONUT POKE CAKE

Coconut is the star of this cake. You get a double dose, first in the mixture that soaks into the cake and second with the coconut sprinkled on top. It's a lovely flavor treat with just enough coconut!
—Taste of Home *Test Kitchen*

PREP: 10 min. • BAKE: 25 min. + cooling
MAKES: 20 servings

- 1 pkg. white cake mix (regular size)
- 1 can (15 oz.) cream of coconut
- 1 can (14 oz.) sweetened condensed milk
- 1 carton (16 oz.) frozen whipped topping, thawed (6½ cups)
- 1 cup sweetened shredded coconut

**1.** Preheat oven to 350°. Prepare and bake cake mix according to package directions, using a 13x9-in. baking pan.
**2.** Meanwhile, in a small bowl, mix the cream of coconut and milk. Remove the cake from the oven; place on a wire rack. Using a wooden skewer, pierce top of cake to within 1 in. of edge; twist skewer gently to make slightly larger holes. Spoon milk mixture evenly over cake, being careful to fill each hole. Cool completely.
**3.** Spread the whipped topping over the cake; sprinkle with coconut. Refrigerate until serving.

**1 PIECE:** 320 cal., 12g fat (10g sat. fat), 7mg chol., 211mg sod., 50g carb. (40g sugars, 0 fiber), 3g pro.

**TIPS**

- You can substitute full-fat coconut milk for the cream of coconut in this recipe, but know that the texture and taste will be different because coconut milk has less fat than cream of coconut.
- Instead of a white cake mix, try chocolate, vanilla or strawberry.

## DIJON-RUBBED PORK WITH RHUBARB SAUCE

This moist and tender pork loin roast is served with a rhubarb sauce that's just delicious! It's great for company and makes a special weeknight meal.
—Marilyn Rodriguez, Sparks, NV

PREP: 15 min. • BAKE: 1 hour + standing
MAKES: 12 servings (1½ cups sauce)

- 1 boneless pork loin roast (3 lbs.)
- ¼ cup Dijon mustard
- 6 garlic cloves, minced
- 1 Tbsp. minced fresh rosemary or 1 tsp. dried rosemary, crushed
- ¾ tsp. salt
- ½ tsp. pepper

**SAUCE**
- 3 cups sliced fresh or frozen rhubarb
- ⅓ cup orange juice
- ⅓ cup sugar
- 1 Tbsp. cider vinegar

**1.** Score the surface of the pork, making diamond shapes ¼ in. deep. In a small bowl, combine mustard, garlic, rosemary, salt and pepper; rub over pork.
**2.** Coat roasting pan and rack with cooking spray; place the pork on rack in pan. Bake, uncovered, at 350° for 1 hour or until a thermometer reads 145°. Let stand for 10 minutes before slicing.
**3.** Meanwhile, in a small saucepan, bring the sauce ingredients to a boil. Reduce heat; cover and simmer for 8-12 minutes or until rhubarb is tender. Serve warm, with pork.

**NOTE:** To help give pork loin a uniform shape and ensure even cooking, tie with butcher's twine before roasting.

**3 OZ. COOKED PORK WITH 2 TBSP. SAUCE:** 181 cal., 6g fat (2g sat. fat), 56mg chol., 308mg sod., 9g carb. (7g sugars, 1g fiber), 23g pro.
**DIABETIC EXCHANGES:** 3 lean meat, ½ starch.

## FROSTED PEANUT COOKIES

Oats, chopped peanuts and peanut butter frosting make this a nice change of pace from a traditional peanut butter cookie. After folks sample these, compliments and recipe requests always follow.
—*Alicia Surma, Tacoma, WA*

**PREP:** 20 min. • **BAKE:** 10 min./batch + cooling • **MAKES:** 5 dozen

- 1   cup butter, softened
- 1½  cups packed brown sugar
- 2   large eggs, room temperature
- 1   tsp. vanilla extract
- 2   cups all-purpose flour
- 2   tsp. baking powder
- 1   cup quick-cooking oats
- 1   cup chopped salted peanuts

**FROSTING**

- ½   cup peanut butter
- 3   cups confectioners' sugar
- ⅓   to ½ cup 2% milk

**1.** In a large bowl, cream butter and brown sugar until light and fluffy, 5-7 minutes. Beat in eggs and vanilla. Combine flour and baking powder; gradually add to creamed mixture and mix well. Stir in oats and peanuts.

**2.** Drop by rounded teaspoonfuls 2 in. apart onto ungreased baking sheets. Bake at 350° for 10-12 minutes or until golden brown. Remove to wire racks to cool.

**3.** For frosting, in a bowl, beat peanut butter, confectioners' sugar and ⅓ cup milk; add additional milk if necessary. Frost cookies.

**1 COOKIE:** 122 cal., 6g fat (2g sat. fat), 14mg chol., 64mg sod., 17g carb. (12g sugars, 1g fiber), 2g pro.

## CHEESY CORN SPOON BREAD

Homey and comforting, this custard-like side dish is a much-requested recipe at potlucks and holiday dinners. The jalapeno pepper adds just the right bite. Second helpings of this tasty casserole are common—leftovers aren't.
—*Katherine Franklin, Carbondale, IL*

**PREP:** 15 min. • **BAKE:** 35 min. • **MAKES:** 15 servings

- ¼   cup butter, cubed
- 1   medium onion, chopped
- 2   large eggs
- 2   cups sour cream
- 1   can (15¼ oz.) whole kernel corn, drained
- 1   can (14¾ oz.) cream-style corn
- ¼   tsp. salt
- ¼   tsp. pepper
- 1   pkg. (8½ oz.) cornbread/muffin mix
- 2   medium jalapeno peppers, divided
- 2   cups shredded cheddar cheese, divided

**1.** Preheat oven to 375°. In a large skillet, heat the butter over medium-high heat. Add the onion; saute until tender. Set aside.

**2.** Beat eggs; add sour cream, both cans of corn, salt and pepper. Stir in cornbread mix just until blended. Mince 1 jalapeno pepper; fold into corn mixture with sauteed onion and 1½ cups cheese.

**3.** Transfer to a greased shallow 3-qt. baking dish. Sprinkle with remaining cheese. Bake, uncovered, until a toothpick inserted in center comes out clean, 35-40 minutes; cool slightly. Slice remaining jalapeno; sprinkle over dish.

**1 SERVING:** 266 cal., 17g fat (9g sat. fat), 56mg chol., 470mg sod., 21g carb. (7g sugars, 2g fiber), 8g pro.

## DAD'S CHOCOLATE CHIP COOKIES

When I was in college, I'd get care packages from home with cookies baked by my dad instead of my mom. These classics have long been a favorite in our family.
—*Art Winter, Trumbull, CT*

----

**PREP:** 15 min. • **BAKE:** 10 min./batch • **MAKES:** about 6 dozen

- ⅔ cup butter, softened
- ⅔ cup shortening
- 1 cup sugar
- 1 cup packed brown sugar
- 2 large eggs, room temperature
- 2 tsp. vanilla extract
- 3½ cups all-purpose flour
- 1 tsp. salt
- 1 tsp. baking soda
- 2 cups semisweet chocolate chips
- 1 cup chopped walnuts

**1.** Preheat oven to 350°. In a large bowl, cream butter, shortening and sugars until light and fluffy, 5-7 minutes. Beat in eggs and vanilla. Combine flour, salt and baking soda; gradually add to creamed mixture and mix well. Stir in chocolate chips and nuts.

**2.** Form dough into 1½-in. balls and place on ungreased baking sheets. Bake until golden brown, 10-13 minutes. Remove from pans to wire racks to cool.

**1 COOKIE:** 134 cal., 7g fat (3g sat. fat), 12mg chol., 81mg sod., 16g carb. (10g sugars, 1g fiber), 2g pro.

**CRANBERRY CHIP COOKIES:** Substitute 1 cup white baking chips for 1 cup of the semisweet chips. Stir in ½ cup dried cranberries.

**WHITE CHOCOLATE CHIP COOKIES:** Substitute white baking chips for the semisweet chips and toasted chopped hazelnuts for the walnuts.

**CHERRY CHIP COOKIES:** Stir in 1 cup chopped dried cherries.

## CASHEW RICE PILAF

This hearty dish will add pizazz to your plate, thanks to its beautiful blend of flavors and colors. I often serve it as a main course with salad and bread.
—*Tina Coburn, Tucson, AZ*

----

**PREP:** 5 min. • **COOK:** 35 min. • **MAKES:** 12 servings

- ¼ cup butter, cubed
- 1½ cups uncooked long grain rice
- 1 cup chopped onion
- 1 cup diced carrots
- 1 cup golden raisins
- 3 cups chicken broth
- 1 tsp. onion salt
- 2 cups frozen peas
- 1½ cups cooked wild rice
- 1 cup salted cashews
- ¼ cup thinly sliced green onions, optional

In a Dutch oven, melt butter over medium heat; add the rice, onion, carrots and raisins. Cook and stir until onion is tender, 5-7 minutes. Add broth and onion salt; bring to a boil. Reduce the heat; cover and simmer until liquid is absorbed and rice is tender, about 20 minutes. Stir in peas, wild rice and cashews; heat through. If desired, sprinkle with green onions.

**1 CUP:** 287 cal., 11g fat (4g sat. fat), 10mg chol., 541mg sod., 41g carb. (12g sugars, 3g fiber), 7g pro.

## RUSTIC SQUASH TARTS

These flaky, rustic-looking pastry shells hold a sweet and spicy pecan layer under the squash slices.

—Ann Marie Moch, Kintyre, ND

- - - - - - - - - - - - - - - - - - - - - - - - - - -

**PREP:** 30 min. • **BAKE:** 35 min.
**MAKES:** 2 tarts (8 servings each)

- 1  medium butternut squash, peeled, seeded and cut into ⅛-in. slices
- 1  medium acorn squash, peeled, seeded and cut into ⅛-in. slices
- 2  Tbsp. water
- ¼  cup olive oil
- 1  Tbsp. minced fresh thyme
- 1  Tbsp. minced fresh parsley
- ½  tsp. salt
- ¼  tsp. pepper
- ½  cup all-purpose flour
- ½  cup ground pecans
- 6  Tbsp. sugar
- ½  tsp. ground nutmeg
- ½  tsp. ground cinnamon
- 1  pkg. (17.3 oz.) frozen puff pastry, thawed
- 1  large egg, lightly beaten
- 2  Tbsp. butter

**1.** In a large microwave-safe bowl, combine squash and water. Cover and microwave on high for 5 minutes or until crisp-tender. Drain; return to bowl. In a small bowl, combine oil, thyme, parsley, salt and pepper; drizzle onto the squash and toss to coat. In another small bowl, combine flour, pecans, sugar, nutmeg and cinnamon; set aside.

**2.** Unfold puff pastry sheets on a lightly floured surface. Roll each sheet to ⅛-in. thickness; transfer each to an ungreased baking sheet. Sprinkle with the pecan mixture. Arrange squash slices to within 1½ in. of edges, alternating slices of the butternut and acorn squash.

**3.** Fold up the edges of the pastry over filling, leaving centers uncovered. Brush pastry with egg. Dot squash with butter. Bake at 375° for 35-40 minutes or until golden brown.

**1 PIECE:** 279 cal., 15g fat (4g sat. fat), 17mg chol., 196mg sod., 34g carb. (7g sugars, 5g fiber), 4g pro.

## NOODLE KUGEL

I make this traditional dish along with other Jewish specialties for an annual Hanukkah/Christmas party with our friends.

—Lauren Kargen, Buffalo, NY

- - - - - - - - - - - - - - - - - - - - - - - - - - -

**PREP:** 20 min.
**BAKE:** 50 min. + standing
**MAKES:** 15 servings

- 1  pkg. (1 lb.) egg noodles
- ½  cup butter, melted
- 8  large eggs
- 2  cups sugar
- 2  cups sour cream
- 2  cups 4% cottage cheese

**TOPPING**

- ¾  cup cinnamon graham cracker crumbs (about 4 whole crackers)
- 3  Tbsp. butter, melted

**1.** Cook noodles according to package directions; drain. Toss with butter; set aside. In a large bowl, beat the eggs, sugar, sour cream and cottage cheese until well blended. Stir in noodles.

**2.** Transfer to a greased 13x9-in. baking dish. Combine the cracker crumbs and butter; sprinkle over top.

**3.** Bake, uncovered, at 350° 50-55 minutes or until a thermometer reads 160°. Let the dish stand for 10 minutes before cutting. Serve warm or cold.

**1 CUP:** 432 cal., 19g fat (11g sat. fat), 191mg chol., 261mg sod., 54g carb. (30g sugars, 1g fiber), 12g pro.

**DID YOU KNOW?** Sweet noodle kugel is a traditional Jewish side dish casserole. It's commonly served with signature Jewish dishes, such as latkes, roast chicken or smoked brisket.

## GERMAN BRATWURST WITH SAUERKRAUT & APPLES

I created this old-world favorite based on a dish I had during my travels. The flavorful entree is perfect for weeknights or special occasions. I like to serve it with pasta.
—*Gerald Hetrick, Erie, PA*

**PREP:** 15 min. • **COOK:** 6 hours
**MAKES:** 15 servings

- 4 lbs. uncooked bratwurst links
- 3 bottles (12 oz. each) German-style beer or 4½ cups reduced-sodium chicken broth
- 1 jar (32 oz.) sauerkraut, rinsed and well drained
- 4 medium Granny Smith apples (about 1¼ lbs.), cut into wedges
- 1 medium onion, halved and thinly sliced
- 1½ tsp. caraway seeds
- ¼ tsp. pepper

**1.** In a large nonstick skillet, brown the bratwursts over medium-high heat in batches. Transfer to a 7-qt. slow cooker. Add remaining ingredients.
**2.** Cook, covered, on low 6-8 hours or until a thermometer inserted in sausage reads at least 160°.
**NOTE:** This recipe pairs well with spaetzle, or try serving the brats on pretzel buns.
**1 SERVING:** 445 cal., 35g fat (12g sat. fat), 90mg chol., 1424mg sod., 13g carb. (6g sugars, 3g fiber), 17g pro.

## SPICY CAJUN POTATO SALAD

Here in the South we have a lot of get-togethers, and if you want your dish to be chosen over all of the rest, it has to have a kick! This is a winner.
—*Amanda West, Shelbyville, TN*

-------------------------------------------------

**PREP:** 20 min. • **COOK:** 10 min. + chilling • **MAKES:** 20 servings

- 5 lbs. medium Yukon Gold potatoes, peeled and cut into ¾-in. cubes
- 1 large yellow onion
- ½ medium lemon
- ½ tsp. salt
- 8 hard-boiled large eggs, chopped
- 1½ cups mayonnaise with olive oil and coarsely ground pepper
- 1 cup dill pickle relish
- ¼ cup yellow mustard
- 1 to 2 Tbsp. Cajun seasoning
- ¼ cup minced fresh parsley
  Paprika

**1.** Place potatoes in a Dutch oven; add water to cover. Cut onion in half crosswise; add 1 half to saucepan. Bring to a boil. Add lemon and salt to cooking water. Reduce heat; cook, uncovered, until potatoes are tender, 5-6 minutes.
**2.** Meanwhile, chop the remaining onion half. Combine with eggs, mayonnaise, dill pickle relish, mustard and Cajun seasoning.
**3.** Drain potatoes; rinse under cold water. Discard onion and lemon. Add the potatoes to the egg mixture; gently toss until well mixed (do not overmix, or the potatoes will break down). Refrigerate, covered, 1-2 hours. Just before serving, sprinkle with parsley and paprika.

**¾ CUP:** 229 cal., 10g fat (2g sat. fat), 81mg chol., 400mg sod., 31g carb. (3g sugars, 2g fiber), 5g pro.

## MISSISSIPPI MUD CAKE

This cake starts with a fudgy brownie-like base topped with marshmallow creme and a nutty frosting. Serve up big slices with glasses of cold milk or steaming mugs of coffee.
—*Tammi Simpson, Greensburg, KY*

-------------------------------------------------

**PREP:** 20 min. • **BAKE:** 35 min. + cooling • **MAKES:** 20 servings

- 1 cup butter, softened
- 2 cups sugar
- 4 large eggs, room temperature
- 1½ cups self-rising flour
- ½ cup baking cocoa
- 1 cup chopped pecans
- 1 jar (7 oz.) marshmallow creme

**FROSTING**
- ½ cup butter, softened
- 3¾ cups confectioners' sugar
- 3 Tbsp. baking cocoa
- 1 Tbsp. vanilla extract
- 4 to 5 Tbsp. 2% milk
- 1 cup chopped pecans

**1.** In a large bowl, cream butter and sugar until light and fluffy, 5-7 minutes. Add eggs, 1 at a time, beating well after each addition. Combine flour and cocoa; gradually add to creamed mixture until blended. Fold in the pecans.
**2.** Transfer to a greased 13x9-in. baking pan. Bake at 350° until a toothpick inserted in center comes out clean, 35-40 minutes. Cool for 3 minutes (the cake will fall in the center). Spoon the marshmallow creme over cake; carefully spread to cover top. Cool completely.
**3.** For frosting, in a small bowl, cream butter and confectioners' sugar until light and fluffy. Beat in the cocoa, vanilla and enough milk to achieve frosting consistency. Fold in pecans. Spread over marshmallow creme layer. Store in the refrigerator.

**1 PIECE:** 457 cal., 24g fat (10g sat. fat), 80mg chol., 270mg sod., 61g carb. (48g sugars, 2g fiber), 4g pro.

## OLD-FASHIONED MACARONI & CHEESE

Bring back the taste of days gone by with this ooey-gooey mac-and-cheese classic. A little ground mustard and hot pepper sauce give this dish just the right spice.
—*James Backman, Centralia, WA*

**PREP:** 15 min. • **BAKE:** 45 min. • **MAKES:** 16 servings

3½ cups uncooked elbow macaroni (about 12 oz.)
¼ cup butter, cubed
¼ cup all-purpose flour
1 tsp. salt
¾ tsp. ground mustard
½ tsp. pepper
  Few dashes hot pepper sauce
3½ cups whole milk
5 cups shredded cheddar cheese, divided
  Optional: Crumbled cooked bacon and coarsely ground pepper

1. Preheat oven to 350°. Cook macaroni in boiling water until almost tender; drain. Meanwhile, in a Dutch oven, melt butter over medium heat. Stir in flour, salt, mustard, pepper and pepper sauce until smooth. Cook and stir until bubbly, about 1 minute. Stir in cooked macaroni, milk and 4 cups cheese.
2. Transfer to an ungreased 13x9-in. baking dish. Cover and bake until bubbly, 45-50 minutes. Uncover; sprinkle with the remaining 1 cup cheese. Let stand for 5 minutes before serving. If desired, top with bacon and pepper.
**1 CUP:** 267 cal., 17g fat (10g sat. fat), 48mg chol., 425mg sod., 17g carb. (3g sugars, 1g fiber), 12g pro.

## CHERRY ICEBOX COOKIES

Maraschino cherries add colorful flecks to these cookies. As a home economics teacher, I often supplied treats for school functions. These delectable cookies were always popular.
—*Patty Courtney, Jonesboro, TX*

**PREP:** 20 min. + chilling • **BAKE:** 10 min./batch • **MAKES:** 16 dozen

1 cup butter, softened
1 cup sugar
¼ cup packed brown sugar
1 large egg, room temperature
¼ cup maraschino cherry juice
4½ tsp. lemon juice
1 tsp. vanilla extract
3¼ cups all-purpose flour
½ tsp. baking soda
½ tsp. ground cinnamon
¼ tsp. cream of tartar
½ cup chopped walnuts
½ cup chopped maraschino cherries

1. In a large bowl, cream butter and sugars until light and fluffy, 5-7 minutes. Beat in the egg, cherry and lemon juices and vanilla. Combine dry ingredients; gradually add to creamed mixture and mix well. Stir in nuts and cherries.
2. Shape into four 12-in. rolls; securely wrap each in waxed paper. Refrigerate for 4 hours or until firm.
3. Unwrap the rolls and cut into ¼-in. slices. Place 2 in. apart on ungreased baking sheets. Bake at 375° until the edges begin to brown, 8-10 minutes. Remove to wire racks to cool.
**1 COOKIE:** 66 cal., 3g fat (2g sat. fat), 10mg chol., 37mg sod., 9g carb. (4g sugars, 0 fiber), 1g pro.

# - BAKED HAM WITH PINEAPPLE -

Widely known as a symbol of hospitality, pineapple
is the star ingredient on this lovely baked ham.

Place **1 fully cooked bone-in ham
(6-8 lbs.)** in a roasting pan. Score
surface with shallow diagonal cuts,
making diamond shapes; insert
**whole cloves** into diamonds. Cover
and bake at 325° for 1½ hours. Drain
**1 can (20 oz.) sliced pineapple**,
reserving ¼ cup juice. Combine
**½ brown sugar** and reserved
pineapple juice; pour over ham.
Arrange pineapple slices and
**12 maraschino cherries** on ham.
Bake, uncovered, until a
thermometer reads 140° and
the ham is heated through,
30-45 minutes longer.

## BUTTERSCOTCH PECAN DESSERT

Light and creamy, this terrific treat never lasts long when I serve it. The fluffy cream cheese layer topped with cool butterscotch pudding is a lip-smacking combination.
—*Becky Harrison, Albion, IL*

**PREP:** 15 min. + chilling • **BAKE:** 20 min. + cooling
**MAKES:** 20 servings

- ½ cup cold butter, cubed
- 1 cup all-purpose flour
- ¾ cup chopped pecans, divided
- 1 pkg. (8 oz.) cream cheese, softened
- 1 cup confectioners' sugar
- 1 carton (8 oz.) frozen whipped topping, thawed, divided
- 3½ cups cold 2% milk
- 2 pkg. (3.4 or 3.5 oz. each) instant butterscotch or vanilla pudding mix

**1.** Preheat oven to 350°. In a small bowl, cut butter into flour until crumbly; stir in ½ cup pecans. Press into an ungreased 13x9-in. baking dish. Bake until lightly browned, about 20 minutes. Cool.
**2.** In a small bowl, beat cream cheese and confectioners' sugar until fluffy. Fold in 1 cup whipped topping; spread over the crust.
**3.** In a large bowl, whisk milk and pudding mix for 2 minutes. Let stand for 2 minutes or until soft-set; pour over the cream cheese layer. Refrigerate until set, 15-20 minutes. Top with remaining whipped topping and pecans. Refrigerate for 1-2 hours.
**1 PIECE:** 242 cal., 14g fat (8g sat. fat), 27mg chol., 247mg sod., 23g carb. (18g sugars, 1g fiber), 3g pro.

## BRUSSELS SPROUTS & KALE SAUTE

This colorful side dish is filled with healthy greens. It pairs well with turkey, potatoes and other holiday staples. The crispy salami—my kid's favorite ingredient—makes it over-the-top delicious.
—*Jennifer McNabb, Brentwood, TN*

**TAKES:** 30 min. • **MAKES:** 12 servings

- ¼ lb. thinly sliced hard salami, cut into ¼-in. strips
- 1½ tsp. olive oil
- 2 Tbsp. butter
- 2 lbs. fresh Brussels sprouts, thinly sliced
- 2 cups shredded fresh kale
- 1 large onion, finely chopped
- ½ tsp. kosher salt
- ⅛ tsp. cayenne pepper
- ¼ tsp. coarsely ground pepper
- 1 garlic clove, minced
- ½ cup chicken broth
- ½ cup chopped walnuts
- 1 Tbsp. balsamic vinegar

**1.** In a Dutch oven, cook and stir salami in oil over medium-high heat until crisp, 3-5 minutes. Remove to paper towels with a slotted spoon; reserve drippings in pan.
**2.** Add butter to drippings; heat over medium-high heat. Add Brussels sprouts, kale, onion, salt, cayenne and black pepper; cook and stir until vegetables are crisp-tender. Add garlic; cook 1 minute longer.
**3.** Stir in the broth; bring to a boil. Reduce heat; cover and cook until Brussels sprouts are tender, 4-5 minutes. Stir in walnuts and vinegar. Serve with salami strips.
**½ CUP:** 126 cal., 9g fat (3g sat. fat), 14mg chol., 341mg sod., 9g carb. (3g sugars, 3g fiber), 6g pro. **DIABETIC EXCHANGES:** 2 fat, 1 vegetable.

## FIREFIGHTER'S CHICKEN SPAGHETTI

My husband is a firefighter in our town, and I'm often in the kitchen most of the day making something for the local fire department, neighbors or family to pass around. This spaghetti casserole is a firehouse favorite.
—*Krista Davis-Keith, New Castle, IN*

------------------------------------------------

**PREP:** 20 min. • **BAKE:** 45 min.
**MAKES:** 14 servings

- 12 oz. uncooked spaghetti, broken in half
- 1 can (10¾ oz.) condensed cream of chicken soup, undiluted
- 1 can (10¾ oz.) condensed cream of mushroom soup, undiluted
- 1 cup sour cream
- ½ cup whole milk
- ¼ cup butter, melted, divided
- 2 Tbsp. dried parsley flakes
- ½ tsp. garlic powder
- ½ tsp. salt
- ¼ tsp. pepper
- 2 cups shredded part-skim mozzarella cheese
- 1 cup grated Parmesan cheese
- 2 to 3 celery ribs, chopped
- 1 medium onion, chopped
- 1 can (4 oz.) mushroom stems and pieces, drained
- 5 cups cubed cooked chicken
- 1½ cups crushed cornflakes

**1.** Preheat oven to 350°. Cook spaghetti according to the package directions for al dente; drain.
**2.** In a large bowl, combine the soups, sour cream, milk, 2 Tbsp. butter and seasonings. Add the cheeses, celery, onion and mushrooms. Stir in chicken and spaghetti.
**3.** Transfer to a greased 3-qt. baking dish (dish will be full). Combine cornflakes and remaining butter; sprinkle over the top.
**4.** Bake, uncovered, for 45-50 minutes or until bubbly.
**1 CUP:** 407 cal., 18g fat (9g sat. fat), 76mg chol., 789mg sod., 34g carb. (4g sugars, 2g fiber), 25g pro.

## POTLUCK PAN ROLLS

The appealing homemade yeast-bread flavor of these golden rolls is unbeatable. Soft and light, they're great alongside any entree. Folks are disappointed if I don't bring them to potluck dinners.
—*Carol Mead, Los Alamos, NM*

------------------------------------------------

**PREP:** 20 min. + rising • **BAKE:** 20 min.
**MAKES:** 27 rolls

- 1 pkg. (¼ oz.) active dry yeast
- ⅓ cup plus 1 tsp. sugar, divided
- 1½ cups warm water (110° to 115°), divided
- ½ cup butter, melted
- 2 large eggs, room temperature
- ¼ cup instant nonfat dry milk powder
- 1¼ tsp. salt
- 5½ to 6 cups all-purpose flour

**1.** In a large bowl, dissolve yeast and 1 tsp. sugar in ½ cup water. Add the butter, eggs, milk powder, salt, 3 cups flour and the remaining sugar and water. Beat on medium speed 3 minutes. Stir in enough remaining flour to form a soft dough.
**2.** Turn onto a floured surface; knead until smooth and elastic, 6-8 minutes. Place in a greased bowl, turning once to grease top. Cover and let rise in a warm place until doubled, about 1½ hours.
**3.** Punch the dough down. Divide into 27 pieces; shape into balls. Place 18 of the balls in a greased 13x9-in. baking pan and remaining balls in a greased 9-in. square baking pan. Cover; let rise until doubled, about 45 minutes.
**4.** Preheat oven to 375°. Bake until golden brown, 17-20 minutes. Cool on wire racks.
**1 ROLL:** 141 cal., 4g fat (1g sat. fat), 14mg chol., 158mg sod., 23g carb. (3g sugars, 1g fiber), 3g pro.

**HOW-TO**

### PROOFING YEAST

In a large bowl, combine yeast, sugar and water. Let stand for 5-10 minutes. Once it's bubbly, it's ready to be incorporated with the other ingredients. If the yeast hasn't bubbled much after 10 minutes, the yeast might be old. You can still use it, but the rolls will take longer to rise.

## SAVORY CUCUMBER SANDWICHES

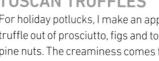

Italian salad dressing easily flavors this simple spread. Serve it as a dip with crackers and veggies, or use it as a sandwich filling.
—*Carol Henderson, Chagrin Falls, OH*

------------------------------------------

**PREP:** 15 min. + chilling • **MAKES:** 3 dozen

- 1 pkg. (8 oz.) cream cheese, softened
- ½ cup mayonnaise
- 1 envelope Italian salad dressing mix
- 36 slices snack rye bread
- 1 medium cucumber, sliced
  Snipped fresh dill, optional

**1.** In a small bowl, combine the cream cheese, mayonnaise and salad dressing mix. Refrigerate for 1 hour.
**2.** Just before serving, spread cream cheese mixture over each slice of rye bread; top each with a cucumber slice. If desired, sprinkle with dill.
**1 SANDWICH:** 62 cal., 5g fat (2g sat. fat), 7mg chol., 149mg sod., 4g carb. (1g sugars, 0 fiber), 1g pro.

## TUSCAN TRUFFLES

For holiday potlucks, I make an appetizer truffle out of prosciutto, figs and toasted pine nuts. The creaminess comes from mascarpone and goat cheese.
—*Roxanne Chan, Albany, CA*

------------------------------------------

**PREP:** 25 min. + chilling • **MAKES:** 3 dozen

- 2 logs (4 oz. each) fresh goat cheese
- 1 carton (8 oz.) mascarpone cheese
- 6 Tbsp. grated Parmesan cheese
- 3 garlic cloves, minced
- 1½ tsp. olive oil
- 1½ tsp. white balsamic vinegar
- ¾ tsp. grated lemon zest
- 3 oz. (6 Tbsp.) chopped prosciutto
- 3 oz. (6 Tbsp.) finely chopped dried figs
- 3 Tbsp. minced fresh parsley
- ¼ tsp. pepper
- 1 cup pine nuts, toasted and chopped

Combine the first 11 ingredients until well blended. Shape into 36 balls; roll in pine nuts. Refrigerate, covered, until serving.
**1 APPETIZER:** 80 cal., 7g fat (3g sat. fat), 15mg chol., 90mg sod., 3g carb. (1g sugars, 0 fiber), 3g pro.

## HOT CHOCOLATE COOKIES

Using hot chocolate mix and marshmallow bits in the cookie dough really makes these cookies taste just like hot cocoa.
—*Lisa Kaminski, Wauwatosa, WI*

------------------------------------------

**PREP:** 15 min.
**BAKE:** 10 min./batch + cooling
**MAKES:** 5 dozen

- ¾ cup butter, softened
- ¾ cup sugar
- ¾ cup packed brown sugar
- 2 large eggs, room temperature
- 1 tsp. vanilla extract
- 2¼ cups all-purpose flour
- ½ cup instant hot cocoa mix (about 3 packets)
- 3 Tbsp. baking cocoa
- 1 tsp. salt
- 1 tsp. baking soda
- ½ tsp. baking powder
- 1 cup vanilla marshmallow bits (not miniature marshmallows)
- 1 cup semisweet chocolate chips

**1.** Preheat oven to 375°. In a large bowl, cream butter and sugars until light and fluffy, 5-7 minutes. Beat in the eggs and vanilla. In another bowl, whisk the flour, cocoa mix, baking cocoa, salt, baking soda and baking powder; gradually beat into creamed mixture. Gently stir in marshmallow bits and chocolate chips.
**2.** Drop dough by tablespoonfuls 2 in. apart onto greased baking sheets. Bake until set, 10-12 minutes. Remove to wire racks to cool completely.
**1 COOKIE:** 81 cal., 4g fat (2g sat. fat), 12mg chol., 95mg sod., 12g carb. (8g sugars, 0 fiber), 1g pro.

**TIP**
Vanilla marshmallow bits are drier than mini marshmallows and will hold their shape better, making them easily identifiable in the finished cookies.

## ARROZ CON GANDULES (RICE WITH PIGEON PEAS)

Feed a crowd with this authentic Puerto Rican rice dish, which was handed down to me from my mom. It's a staple with the familia at all our gatherings.
—*Evelyn Robles, Oak Creek, WI*

**PREP:** 15 min. • **COOK:** 30 min.
**MAKES:** 18 servings

- ½ cup sofrito
- 2 Tbsp. canola oil
- 4 cups uncooked long grain rice
- 1 envelope Goya sazon with coriander and annatto
- 7 cups water
- 1 can (15 oz.) pigeon peas, drained
- 2 cans (5 oz. each) Vienna sausage, drained and chopped
- ½ cup tomato sauce
- 1¼ tsp. salt
- 1 envelope Goya ham-flavored concentrate
- ½ tsp. chicken bouillon granules
- ¼ tsp. pepper

In a Dutch oven, cook sofrito in oil over medium-low heat, stirring occasionally, 5 minutes. Add the rice and sazon; cook and stir until the rice is lightly toasted, 3-4 minutes. Add all the remaining ingredients. Bring to a boil. Reduce the heat; cover and simmer until the rice is tender, 15-20 minutes. Fluff with a fork.
**¾ CUP:** 220 cal., 5g fat (1g sat. fat), 14mg chol., 537mg sod., 38g carb. (1g sugars, 2g fiber), 6g pro.

> **HOW-TO**
>
> Sofrito is a base used in many Puerto Rican recipes. To make it: Separate and peel the cloves of **one head of garlic**. Quarter **1 medium green pepper**, **1 medium onion** and **1 plum tomato**. Place all in a food processor; add **½ cup fresh cilantro**. Cover and process until finely chopped. Use immediately, refrigerate up to 1 week or freeze for up to 1 month.

## GARDEN GREEN BEANS & POTATOES

Fresh green beans paired with red potatoes make for an easy and filling side dish. To make it even better, add crumbled bacon!
—*Kelly Zinn, Cicero, IN*

**PREP:** 10 min. • **COOK:** 6 hours
**MAKES:** 16 servings

- 2 lbs. fresh green beans, trimmed
- 1½ lbs. red potatoes, quartered
- 1 medium onion, chopped
- ½ cup beef broth
- 1½ tsp. salt
- 1 tsp. dried thyme
- ½ tsp. pepper
- ¼ cup butter, softened
- 1 Tbsp. lemon juice

In a 6-qt. slow cooker, combine the first 7 ingredients. Cook, covered, on low 6-8 hour or until beans are tender. Stir in butter and lemon juice. Remove with a slotted spoon.
**¾ CUP:** 77 cal., 3g fat (2g sat. fat), 8mg chol., 278mg sod., 12g carb. (2g sugars, 3g fiber), 2g pro. **DIABETIC EXCHANGES:** 1 vegetable, ½ starch, ½ fat.

## BUTTERSCOTCH TOFFEE COOKIES

With its big butterscotch and chocolate flavor, my cookie stands out. I like to enjoy it with a glass of milk or a cup of coffee. It's my fallback recipe when I'm short on time and need something delicious fast.
—*Allie Blinder, Norcross, GA*

**PREP:** 10 min. • **BAKE:** 10 min./batch
**MAKES:** 5 dozen

- 2 large eggs, room temperature
- ½ cup canola oil
- 1 pkg. butter pecan cake mix (regular size)
- 1 pkg. (10 to 11 oz.) butterscotch chips
- 1 pkg. (8 oz.) milk chocolate English toffee bits

**1.** Preheat oven to 350°. In a large bowl, beat eggs and oil until blended; gradually add cake mix and mix well. Fold in chips and toffee bits.
**2.** Drop by tablespoonfuls 2 in. apart onto greased baking sheets. Bake until golden brown, 10-12 minutes. Cool 1 minute before removing to wire racks.
**1 COOKIE:** 95 cal., 5g fat (3g sat. fat), 10mg chol., 70mg sod., 11g carb. (3g sugars, 0 fiber), 1g pro.

## BANANA CAKE WITH CREAM CHEESE FROSTING

As a mother of three sons, I always have sweets in my kitchen! I buy lots of ripe bananas on sale and freeze them with this cake in mind. I'm often asked to bring it to family picnics and dinners.
—Bonnie Krause, Irvona, PA

- - - - - - - - - - - - - - - - - - - - - - - - - - - -

**PREP:** 25 min. • **BAKE:** 30 min. + cooling
**MAKES:** 18 servings

- ⅔ cup shortening
- 1½ cups sugar
- 2 large eggs, separated, room temperature
- 2 cups mashed bananas (about 4 medium)
- 1 cup 2% milk
- 3 cups all-purpose flour
- 1¼ tsp. baking powder
- 1¼ tsp. baking soda
- ½ tsp. salt

### CREAM CHEESE FROSTING

- 1 pkg. (8 oz.) cream cheese, softened
- ¼ cup butter, softened
- 4 cups confectioners' sugar
- 1 tsp. vanilla extract
  Dash salt
  Sliced banana, optional

**1.** Preheat oven to 350°. In a large bowl, cream shortening and sugar until light and fluffy, 5-7 minutes. Add egg yolks, 1 at a time, beating well after each addition. Add bananas and milk; mix just until combined. Combine the flour, baking powder, baking soda and salt. Add to creamed mixture just until blended.

**2.** In another bowl, beat egg whites until soft peaks form. Fold into batter. Pour into a greased 13x9-in. baking pan. Bake until a toothpick inserted in the center comes out clean, 30-35 minutes. Cool completely on a wire rack.

**3.** In a large bowl, beat cream cheese and butter until fluffy. Add the confectioners' sugar, vanilla and salt; beat until smooth. Spread over cake. Store in the refrigerator. If desired, serve with sliced bananas.

**1 PIECE:** 416 cal., 15g fat (6g sat. fat), 42mg chol., 269mg sod., 66g carb. (47g sugars, 1g fiber), 4g pro.

## BUFFALO WING DIP

If you like spice, you'll love this dip. It's super cheesy, full of rich flavor and really has that Buffalo wing taste!
—Taste of Home *Test Kitchen*

- - - - - - - - - - - - - - - - - - - - - - - - - - - -

**PREP:** 20 min. • **COOK:** 2 hours
**MAKES:** 6 cups

- 2 pkg. (8 oz. each) cream cheese, softened
- ½ cup ranch salad dressing
- ½ cup sour cream
- 5 Tbsp. crumbled blue cheese
- 2 cups shredded cooked chicken
- ½ cup Buffalo wing sauce
- 2 cups shredded cheddar cheese, divided
- 1 green onion, sliced
  Tortilla chips and assorted fresh vegetables

**1.** In a small bowl, combine the cream cheese, dressing, sour cream and blue cheese. Transfer to a 3-qt. slow cooker. Layer with chicken, wing sauce and 1 cup cheese. Cover and cook on low 2-3 hours or until heated through.

**2.** Sprinkle with remaining 1 cup cheese and green onion. Serve with tortilla chips and vegetables.

**¼ CUP DIP:** 167 cal., 14g fat (8g sat. fat), 47mg chol., 348mg sod., 2g carb. (0 sugars, 0 fiber), 8g pro.

**BUFFALO BEAN VEGETARIAN DIP:** Instead of chicken, use 1 can of rinsed and drained black beans and ¾ cup chopped fresh mushrooms. Substitute Monterey Jack cheese for half or all of the cheddar.

## LEMON SHEET CAKE

Lemon pie filling lends a splash of citrus flavor to a convenient cake mix, and a rich cream cheese frosting gives it sweetness. My family likes this cake cold, so I cut it into squares and freeze it before serving.
—*Alyce Dubisar, North Bend, OR*

- - - - - - - - - - - - - - - - - - - - - - - - - - - - - - - - - - - - - - - - -

**PREP:** 10 min. • **BAKE:** 20 min. + cooling • **MAKES:** 35 servings

- 1   pkg. lemon cake mix (regular size)
- 4   large eggs, room temperature
- 1   can (15¾ oz.) lemon pie filling
- 3   oz. cream cheese, softened
- ½   cup butter, softened
- 2   cups confectioners' sugar
- 1½  tsp. vanilla extract
- 1   to 2 Tbsp. 2% milk
- Colored sugar, optional

**1.** In a large bowl, beat the cake mix and eggs until well blended. Fold in pie filling.

**2.** Spread batter into a greased 15x10x1-in. baking pan. Bake at 350° until a toothpick inserted in the center comes out clean, 18-20 minutes. Cool on a wire rack.

**3.** In a small bowl, beat cream cheese, butter and confectioners' sugar until smooth. Stir in the vanilla and enough milk to reach desired consistency. Spread over cake. If desired, sprinkle with colored sugar. Store cake in the refrigerator.

**1 PIECE:** 141 cal., 5g fat (3g sat. fat), 31mg chol., 166mg sod., 23g carb. (16g sugars, 0 fiber), 1g pro.

## SPICY GOULASH

Ground cumin, chili powder and a can of Mexican diced tomatoes jazz up my goulash recipe. Even the elbow macaroni is prepared in the slow cooker.
—*Melissa Polk, West Lafayette, IN*

- - - - - - - - - - - - - - - - - - - - - - - - - - - - - - - - - - - - - - - - -

**PREP:** 25 min. • **COOK:** 5½ hours • **MAKES:** 12 servings

- 1   lb. lean ground beef (90% lean)
- 4   cans (14½ oz. each) Mexican diced tomatoes, undrained
- 2   cans (16 oz. each) kidney beans, rinsed and drained
- 2   cups water
- 1   medium onion, chopped
- 1   medium green pepper, chopped
- ¼   cup red wine vinegar
- 2   Tbsp. chili powder
- 1   Tbsp. Worcestershire sauce
- 2   tsp. beef bouillon granules
- 1   tsp. dried basil
- 1   tsp. dried parsley flakes
- 1   tsp. ground cumin
- ¼   tsp. pepper
- 2   cups uncooked elbow macaroni

**1.** In a large skillet, cook beef over medium heat until no longer pink, crumbling meat; drain. Transfer to a 5-qt. slow cooker. Stir in tomatoes, beans, water, onion, green pepper, vinegar, chili powder, Worcestershire sauce, bouillon and seasonings.

**2.** Cover and cook on low for 5-6 hours or until heated through.

**3.** Stir in macaroni; cover and cook 30 minutes longer or until macaroni is tender.

**1 CUP:** 222 cal., 5g fat (2g sat. fat), 23mg chol., 585mg sod., 30g carb. (7g sugars, 6g fiber), 15g pro. **DIABETIC EXCHANGES:** 2 lean meat, 1½ starch, 1 vegetable.

# - PAN GRAVY -

This basic recipe is all you need to prepare a rich, tasty gravy from any meats and poultry that have been roasted in an uncovered pan.

Pour pan drippings from your roasting pan into a measuring cup. Loosen the browned bits from the pan and add to drippings. Skim fat. Reserve ¼ cup fat and transfer to a small saucepan; whisk in **¼ cup flour** until smooth. Add enough **chicken broth or water** to pan drippings to measure 2 cups. Gradually stir into flour mixture in saucepan. Bring to a boil; cook and stir for 2 minutes or until thickened. Season with **salt, pepper** and **browning sauce** if desired.

# HERBED RUBBED TURKEY

Rubs really have a way of locking in the flavor of meats. Here a wonderful blend of seasonings makes turkey extraordinary.
—*Twila Burkholder, Middleburg, PA*

------------------------------------------------

**PREP:** 10 min. • **BAKE:** 4 hours + standing
**MAKES:** 20 servings

- 2 **Tbsp. rubbed sage**
- 1 **Tbsp. salt**
- 2 **tsp. garlic powder**
- 2 **tsp. celery seed**
- 2 **tsp. dried parsley flakes**
- 2 **tsp. curry powder**
- 2 to 3 **tsp. pepper**
- 1 **tsp. paprika**
- ½ **tsp. ground mustard**
- ¼ **tsp. ground allspice**
- 3 **bay leaves**
- 1 **turkey (14 to 16 lbs.)**

**1.** Combine the first 10 ingredients. Rub half the seasoning mixture in the cavity of the turkey; add the bay leaves. Rub remaining mixture over the turkey skin.
**2.** Tie drumsticks together; place turkey in a roasting pan. Roast using your favorite cooking method until a thermometer inserted in thickest part of thigh reads 170°-175°. Cover turkey and let stand for 15 minutes before carving.

**6 OZ. COOKED TURKEY:** 376 cal., 17g fat (5g sat. fat), 172mg chol., 476mg sod., 1g carb. (0 sugars, 0 fiber), 51g pro.

**TIPS**

- To have this rub ready whenever it's time to roast your bird, freeze it in an airtight container for up to 6 months.
- For even more flavor, rub the seasoning mix on the turkey and refrigerate overnight to allow the flavors to permeate the meat.

## TEX-MEX CASSEROLE

Both family and friends enjoy this dish—even those who prefer a level of spiciness that's mild rather than wild, but still full of flavor!
—*Cheryl Ruesch, Waukegan, IL*

- - - - - - - - - - - - - - - - - - - - - - - - - - - - - - - - - - - - - - - - - -

**PREP:** 20 min. • **BAKE:** 40 min. • **MAKES:** 12 servings

   2   lbs. ground beef
   1   medium onion, chopped
   1   can (10½ oz.) condensed cream of mushroom soup, undiluted
   1   can (10½ oz.) condensed cream of chicken soup, undiluted
   2   cans (10 oz. each) green enchilada sauce
   ¾   cup 2% milk
   1   tsp. garlic powder
   30  taco shells, broken
   2   cups shredded cheddar cheese

**1.** Preheat oven to 350°. In a large skillet, cook ground beef and onion over medium heat until beef is no longer pink, 10-12 minutes, breaking beef into crumbles; drain. Stir in soups, enchilada sauce, milk and garlic powder.
**2.** Place half of the broken taco shells in a 13x9-in. baking dish. Layer with half of the meat mixture and half the cheese. Repeat layers using remaining taco shells, meat mixture and cheese. Bake until heated through, 40-45 minutes. Let stand 5 minutes before serving.
**1 SERVING:** 415 cal., 25g fat (10g sat. fat), 70mg chol., 861mg sod., 25g carb. (2g sugars, 2g fiber), 21g pro.

## OATMEAL S'MORE COOKIES

I can't count how many times I have made these cookies—they are our favorites. I love to bake all kinds of goodies with my two daughters, and my husband loves to sample the treats.
—*Carmen Rae, New Haven, IN*

- - - - - - - - - - - - - - - - - - - - - - - - - - - - - - - - - - - - - - - - - -

**PREP:** 20 min. + chilling • **BAKE:** 10 min./batch + cooling
**MAKES:** about 5½ dozen

   ½    cup butter, softened
   ½    cup shortening
   1    cup packed brown sugar
   ½    cup sugar
   2    large eggs, room temperature
   1½   tsp. vanilla extract
   3    cups all-purpose flour
   1    tsp. baking soda
   ¼    tsp. salt
   1½   cups old-fashioned oats
   1    cup semisweet chocolate chips
   1    cup miniature marshmallows

**1.** In a large bowl, cream the butter, shortening and sugars until light and fluffy, 5-7 minutes. Add eggs, 1 at a time, beating well after each addition. Beat in vanilla. Combine the flour, baking soda and salt; gradually add to creamed mixture and mix well. Stir in the oats, chocolate chips and marshmallows; refrigerate until dough is chilled, about 30 minutes.
**2.** Roll tablespoons of dough into balls; place 2 in. apart onto greased baking sheets. Bake at 350° for 8-10 minutes or until golden brown. Cool for 1-2 minutes before removing from pans to wire racks to cool completely.
**1 COOKIE:** 89 cal., 4g fat (2g sat. fat), 9mg chol., 43mg sod., 13g carb. (7g sugars, 0 fiber), 1g pro.

## ANGEL STRAWBERRY DESSERT

This is a wonderful treat when fresh strawberries are readily available. Every time I make this pretty dessert, someone asks for the recipe.
—*Theresa Mathis, Tucker, GA*

- - - - - - - - - - - - - - - - - - - - - - - - - - - - - - - - - - - - -

**PREP:** 30 min. + chilling • **MAKES:** 16 servings

    1½  cups sugar
    5   Tbsp. cornstarch
    1   pkg. (3 oz.) strawberry gelatin
    2   cups water
    2   lbs. fresh strawberries, divided
    1   pkg. (8 oz.) cream cheese, softened
    1   can (14 oz.) sweetened condensed milk
    1   carton (12 oz.) frozen whipped topping, thawed (4½ cups)
    1   prepared angel food cake (8 to 10 oz.), cut into 1-in. cubes

**1.** For glaze, in a large saucepan, combine sugar, cornstarch and gelatin; stir in water until smooth. Cook and stir over medium-high heat until mixture begins to boil. Cook and stir until thickened, 1-2 minutes longer. Remove from the heat; cool completely. Cut half the strawberries into quarters; fold into the glaze.

**2.** In a small bowl, beat the cream cheese until smooth. Beat in the condensed milk until blended. Fold in whipped topping.

**3.** In a 4-qt. clear glass bowl, layer half the cake cubes, glaze and cream mixture. Repeat layers. Cut remaining strawberries in half and arrange over the top. Cover and refrigerate for at least 2 hours or overnight.

**1 CUP:** 344 cal., 11g fat (8g sat. fat), 24mg chol., 202mg sod., 57g carb. (43g sugars, 1g fiber), 5g pro.

## ROASTED FALL VEGETABLES

I love serving these tender roasted veggies on a chilly fall night. The cayenne pepper lends a zippy flavor that's not overpowering.
—*Juli Meyers, Hinesville, GA*

- - - - - - - - - - - - - - - - - - - - - - - - - - - - - - - - - - - - -

**PREP:** 30 min. • **BAKE:** 40 min. • **MAKES:** 14 servings

    1   large acorn squash, peeled and cut into 1½-in. cubes
    1   large rutabaga, peeled and cut into 1-in. cubes
    1   medium pie pumpkin or butternut squash, peeled and cut into 1-in. cubes
    3   large carrots, peeled and cut into 1½-in. pieces
    1   medium parsnip, peeled and cut into 1-in. cubes
    ¼   cup grated Parmesan cheese
    ¼   cup canola oil
    3   Tbsp. minced fresh parsley
    2   Tbsp. paprika
    2   tsp. salt
    1   tsp. garlic powder
    ½   tsp. cayenne pepper

**1.** In a large bowl, combine first 5 ingredients. In a small bowl, combine the remaining ingredients. Pour over the vegetables; toss to coat.

**2.** Transfer vegetables to 2 greased 15x10x1-in. baking pans. Bake, uncovered, at 425° for 40-50 minutes or until tender, stirring occasionally.

**¾ CUP:** 110 cal., 5g fat (1g sat. fat), 1mg chol., 384mg sod., 17g carb. (6g sugars, 3g fiber), 3g pro. **DIABETIC EXCHANGES:** 1 vegetable, 1 fat, ½ starch.

# INDEX

## A

Air-Fryer Apple Danish........................ 167
Air-Fryer Bacon-Wrapped Scallops
    with Pineapple Quinoa.................... 144
Air-Fryer Beef Turnovers ................... 151
Air-Fryer Black Bean
    Chimichangas.............................. 175
Air-Fryer Boiled Eggs ........................174
Air-Fryer Buffalo Chicken Wings........176
Air-Fryer Calamari............................19
Air-Fryer Cookie Pie.......................... 259
Air-Fryer Fish & Chips .......................113
Air-Fryer Fish Tacos ......................... 168
Air-Fryer Garlic & Wine
    Lamb Chops ............................... 183
Air-Fryer Garlic-Butter Steak ............ 100
Air-Fryer Lime & Gin
    Coconut Macaroons......................... 181
Air-Fryer Nacho Dogs ....................... 179
Air-Fryer Okra with Smoked
    Paprika ...................................... 181
Air-Fryer Parmesan Breaded
    Squash....................................... 171
Air-Fryer Pretzel-Crusted Catfish ..... 177
Air-Fryer Rosemary-Lemon
    Chicken Thighs ........................... 177
Air-Fryer Southwestern
    Chicken Enchiladas........................ 164
Air-Fryer Spinach Feta Turnovers..... 170
Air-Fryer Steak Fajitas ...................... 178
Air-Fryer Thai Chicken Meatballs........ 21
Air-Fryer Turkey Club Roulades ......... 183
Almond Broccoli Salad ...................... 188
Angel Berry Trifle............................. 250
Angel Strawberry Dessert.................. 293
Apple Cider Pork Chops ..................... 133
Apple Martini ................................... 27
Apple-Cinnamon Baked
    French Toast ................................ 34
Arroz con Gandules
    (Rice with Pigeon Peas).................. 287
Asparagus & Shrimp with
    Angel Hair .................................. 134
At-Attention Grilled Chicken .............. 212
Aunt Edith's Baked Pancake ............... 43
Avocado Salsa................................. 202

## B

Baba Ganoush ...................................10
Bacon & Egg Gravy ............................ 34
Bacon & Asparagus Frittata ............... 232
Bacon Cheeseburger Balls...................16
Bacon-Cheese Puff Pie........................ 46
Baked Crab Cakes ............................ 109
Baked Ham with Pineapple ................ 281
Baked Lobster Tails ......................... 223
Baked Pumpkin Pudding..................... 269
Balsamic Brussels Sprouts with
    Pears ........................................ 78
Banana Cake with Cream Cheese
    Frosting...................................... 288
Banana Crumb Pudding ...................... 195
Banana Fritters................................ 263
Bang Bang Shrimp Cake Sliders........ 202
Barbecued Chicken Salad
    Sandwiches................................. 58
Barbecued Meatballs.......................... 189
Basil Shrimp ................................... 22
Basil Tomato Soup with Orzo ............. 75
BBQ Country-Style Ribs ...................... 146
BBQ Meat Loaf Minis ......................... 145
Bean & Burger Pockets ...................... 239
Beef Osso Bucco................................ 186
Best Angel Food Cake........................ 259
Best Ever Grilled Cheese
    Sandwiches................................. 75
Best Veal Scallopini........................... 100
Blue Cheese Garlic Bread................... 26
Blue Plate Beef Patties....................... 134
Blue-Ribbon Apple Cake ...................... 270
Blueberry Cantaloupe Salad ............... 36
Blueberry Cream Muffins....................47
Blueberry Iced Tea............................ 21
Blueberry Vinaigrette ....................... 91
Breakfast Enchiladas......................... 43
Brie with Almonds .............................19
Broccoli & Chicken Cheese
    Strata ....................................... 45
Broccoli Beef Braids.......................... 135
Broiled Lobster Tails ......................... 223
Broiled Parmesan Tilapia ................... 120
Brunch Egg Casserole ....................... 44
Brussels Sprouts & Kale Saute .......... 282
Buffalo Bean Vegetarian Dip.............. 288
Buffalo Bites with Blue Cheese
    Ranch Dip...................................17
Buffalo Chicken Chili ......................... 65
Buffalo Wing Dip............................... 288
Buffet Scrambled Eggs ....................... 36
Butterscotch Pecan Dessert .............. 282
Butterscotch Toffee Cookies.............. 287

## C

Caesar Salmon with Roasted
    Tomatoes & Artichokes ................... 151
Cajun Crab Poppers............................12
Canadian Cheese Soup........................ 63
Candied Bacon Palmiers..................... 186
Caramel Bubble Ring ............................ 45
Caramel-Pecan Cookie
    Butter Bars................................. 264
Caribbean Chicken Stir-Fry................ 145
Carolina Crab Boil ............................ 232
Cashew Rice Pilaf .............................. 276
Cheddar Twists .................................10
Cheesy Corn Spoon Bread .................. 275
Cherry Chip Cookies .......................... 276
Cherry Cream Cheese Pie ................... 251
Cherry Icebox Cookies ....................... 280
Chicken & Rice Casserole.................... 188
Chicken & Vegetable
    Curry Couscous .......................... 146
Chicken Bulgur Skillet........................ 245
Chicken Chiles Rellenos Alfredo......... 136
Chicken Chiles Rellenos Strata........... 195
Chicken Curry for Two ....................... 108
Chicken Florentine Panini................... 63
Chicken Mushroom Stew......................67
Chicken Paella ................................. 102
Chicken Parmesan Burgers................. 132

Chicken Provolone .................................. 153
Chicken Thai Pizza ................................. 137
Chicken with Peach-Avocado
    Salsa ................................................ 131
Chicken with Shallot Sauce ................. 149
Chicken Yakitori ..................................... 222
Chili-Lime Air-Fried Chickpeas ............. 22
Chocolate Chip Pancakes ........................ 49
Cilantro-Topped Salmon ....................... 140
Cinnamon Breakfast Bites ....................... 37
Cinnamon Swirl Quick Bread ................. 50
Citrus Cornmeal Cake ........................... 269
Classic Crab Cakes ................................ 127
Classic Creme Brulee ............................ 262
Classic Tartar Sauce ...............................112
Classic Wilted Lettuce Salad ................. 78
Cocoa-Crusted Beef Tenderloin ......... 143
Cod & Asparagus Bake ......................... 152
Colorful Brunch Frittata ......................... 53
Corn Pudding with Bacon &
    Cheddar ...........................................200
Corn Stuffing Balls ................................. 80
Corned Beef Hash & Eggs ..................... 46
Cowboy Casserole ..................................117
Crab & Shrimp Stuffed Sole .............. 213
Crab-Stuffed Manicotti ......................... 108
Cranberry Endive Appetizers ............... 29
Cranberry Chocolate Chip
    Cookies ........................................... 276
Cream Cheese Ice Cream ..................... 260
Creamed Peas ........................................... 97
Creamy Banana Crepes ........................... 53
Creamy Crab Wontons ............................ 29
Creamy Garlic & Mushroom
    Soup ...................................................67
Creamy Red Pepper Dip .......................... 29
Cuban Sandwich Burgers ..................... 219

**D**

Dad's Chocolate Chip Cookies ............. 276
Date Pudding Cobbler ............................ 261
Dijon-Rubbed Pork with
    Rhubarb Sauce ............................... 274
Dirty Rice ................................................. 97
Dreamy Polenta ........................................ 95
Dutch Oven Barbecued
    Pork Sandwiches .............................. 68

**E**

Early-Riser Oven Omelet ........................ 41
Easy Apple Cake ...................................... 252
Easy Egg Rolls ......................................... 199
Easy Mediterranean Chicken ............... 129
Easy Pepper Steak ................................. 243
Easy Pimiento Cheese .............................. 19
Easy Ropa Vieja Stew ............................ 199
Easy Shrimp Tacos ................................. 124
Eggplant Casserole ................................ 201

Eggs Benedict Baked Potatoes ........... 150
Elote (Mexican Street Corn) ................. 211
The Elvis Sandwich .................................. 66

**F**

Fajita-Style Shrimp & Grits ................. 129
Falafel ...................................................... 205
Favorite Company Casserole ............... 244
Favorite Marinated Mushrooms .......... 30
Festive French Pancakes ........................ 47
Feta Cheese & Pomegranate
    Guacamole ........................................ 13
Feta Chicken Burgers ........................... 189
Fettuccine with Sausage &
    Fresh Tomato Sauce ...................... 140
Fiesta Bean Casserole .......................... 102
Fiesta Turkey Tortilla Soup ................. 198
Firefighter's Chicken Spaghetti .........283
Flaky Chicken Wellington ..................... 190
Fluffy Pancakes ....................................... 49
Foil-Packet Potatoes &
    Sausage ........................................... 208
Freezer Mashed Potatoes .................... 198
French Potato Salad ................................ 81
Fried Chicken Strips ............................. 127

Frosted Peanut Cookies ....................... 275
Frosty Watermelon Ice ......................... 267
Frozen Margaritas ....................................17

**G**

Garden Green Beans & Potatoes ........ 287
Garlic & Artichoke Roasted
    Potatoes ............................................ 95
Garlic Lime Shrimp ............................... 132
German Brat Seafood Boil ................... 214
German Bratwurst with
    Sauerkraut & Apples ...................... 278
Gingerbread Coffee Cake ....................... 37
Glazed Cake Doughnuts ....................... 205
Glazed Cornish Hens ............................ 143
Glazed Lemon Chiffon Cake ................ 261
Golden M&M's Bars ...............................256
Grapefruit Gremolata Salmon ........... 133
Grapefruit Lettuce Salad ....................... 83
Green Bean, Corn &
    Buttermilk Salad .............................. 80
Green Chile Corn Fritters ...................... 83
Green Chile Prosciutto Rolls ................ 23
Grilled Broccoli ..................................... 213
Grilled Burgers ...................................... 225

Grilled Campfire Trout Dinner............220
Grilled Cheese &
    Pepperoni Sandwich.......................... 65
Grilled Flank Steak ................................220
Grilled Jerk Chicken .............................221
Grilled Lobster Tails .............................223
Grilled Mahi Mahi..................................219
Grilled Nectarine & Cheese
    Crostini .............................................. 214
Grilled Pistachio-Lemon
    Pesto Shrimp.................................... 215
Grilled Pork Tenderloin with
    Cherry Salsa Mole ........................... 215
Grilled Pork with Pear Salsa ..............222
Grilled Potatoes ....................................224
Grilled Pound Cake with Berries........221
Grilled Ribeye with Garlic
    Blue Cheese Mustard Sauce........... 147
Grilled Salmon Fillet ............................217

Grilling Marinades..................................218
    *Huli Huli; Northwoods; Honey-Garlic;*
    *Orange-Spice; Ranch; Heavenly Greek;*
    *Southwest Chili; Balsamic Mustard;*
    *Ginger-Peach; Tangy Barbecue*
Guacamole Chicken Salad
    Sandwiches...................................... 69
Guacamole Tossed Salad ..................... 94

**H**
Habanero Raspberry Ribs...................... 142
Haddock en Papillote ........................... 130
Ham & Egg Pockets ............................... 48
Ham & Swiss Bread Pudding................ 38
Harvard Beets ........................................ 84
Hearty Beans & Rice .............................246
Hearty Beef & Barley Soup .................. 68
Heavenly Blueberry Tart.......................254
Heirloom Tomato Salad.......................... 81

Heirloom Tomato Tart............................233
Herb-Stuffed Roasted
    Cornish Hens ....................................... 103
Herbed Rubbed Turkey..........................291
Honey-Mustard Glazed Salmon .........142
Hot Artichoke-Spinach Dip................... 25
Hot Chocolate Cookies...........................284
Hot Dog Casserole ................................. 242

**I**
Ice Cream Bowls.....................................270
Italian Sausage Bean Soup ................... 56
Italian Tomato Cucumber Salad ........... 94

**J**
Jackfruit Tacos with
    Green Apple Salsa ............................ 109
Jalapeno Popper Stuffed
    Chicken Breasts................................. 147

**K**
Key West Flank Steak ........................... 217

**L**
Lemon-Basil Grilled Shrimp
    & Couscous....................................... 225
Lemon Bread Pudding...........................256
Lemon Chess Pie...................................255
Lemon Chicken with Basil ................... 153
Lemon Ice ..............................................258
Lemon-Lime Bars..................................253
Lemon Olive Oil Cake ...........................200
Lemon Sheet Cake................................289
Lemony Chicken & Rice ........................ 197
Limoncello Tiramisu .............................251
Lisa's All-Day Sugar & Salt
    Pork Roast.......................................... 193
Lobster Tartlets .....................................16
Long Island Iced Tea............................. 23

**M**
Macaroon Cherry Pie ............................264
Madeira Cake .........................................266
Magic Bars.............................................271
Mango Lassi...........................................12
Maple Pancakes..................................... 49
Meatball Submarine Casserole ..........136
Mediterranean One-Dish Meal............243
Merlot Filet Mignon...............................103
Mexican-Inspired
    Chicken Soup......................................... 58
Mexican-Style
    Chicken Manicotti............................116
Mississippi Mud Cake...........................279
Mom's Roast Chicken ........................... 152
Mom's Sloppy Tacos.............................161
Mushroom & Olive Bruschetta...........197
Mushroom Asparagus Quiche.............. 50

## N

No-Fry Fried Ice Cream.........................196
Noodle Kugel.........................................277
North African Chicken & Rice..............234
Northwest Salmon Chowder.................69

## O

Oat Waffles.............................................41
Oatmeal S'more Cookies......................292
Oklahoma Coconut Poke Cake............274
Old-Fashioned Macaroni & Cheese....280
Old-Fashioned Poor Man's Steak.......149
Old-Time Cake Doughnuts...................205
One-Dish Turkey Dinner......................241
One-Pot Chili Mac................................233
One-Pot Dutch Oven Pasta Bake........247
One-Pot Spaghetti Dinner....................239
One-Skillet Pasta.................................230
Open-Faced Pizza Burgers...................203
Oven-Fried Ranch Steak.......................116
Overnight Yeast Waffles......................193

## P

Pan Gravy.............................................290
Pancetta & Mushroom-Stuffed
    Chicken Breast................................155
Peach Pound Cake................................250
Peanut Butter & Jelly Ice Cream.........254
Peanut Butter Banana Oatmeal............48
Pear & Fennel Pork..............................123
Pecan Pumpkin Biscuits........................39
Pepper Ricotta Primavera....................137
Pesto Twists...........................................10
Pico de Gallo..........................................20
Pineapple Smoothies.............................30
Pizza Monkey Bread...............................31
Pork Meatballs.....................................113
Pork Schnitzel with Sauce...................120
Portobello Mushroom &
    Cream Cheese Taquitos...................191
Possum Pie...........................................263
Potluck Pan Rolls.................................283
Pressure-Cooker Autumn
    Apple Chicken..................................169
Pressure-Cooker Balsamic
    Pork Tenderloin...............................166
Pressure-Cooker Boiled Eggs..............174
Pressure-Cooker Clam Sauce..............176
Pressure-Cooker Cranberry
    Stuffed Apples.................................170
Pressure-Cooker German
    Goulash...........................................175
Pressure-Cooker Herbed Chicken
    & Shrimp..........................................164
Pressure-Cooker Lava Cake.................169
Pressure-Cooker Meat Loaf.................173
Pressure-Cooker Mexican
    Stuffed Peppers...............................114

Pressure-Cooker
   Pineapple Chicken............................ 171
Pressure-Cooker Red Beans
   & Rice ............................................... 180
Pressure-Cooker Salsa
   London Broil ..................................... 178
Pressure-Cooker Smoked Sausage
   & White Beans .................................. 173
Pressure-Cooker Spicy Lime
   Chicken ............................................. 166
Pressure-Cooker Spicy Pork
   & Squash Ragu................................... 180
Pressure-Cooker Steamed Mussels
   with Peppers..................................... 167
Provolone-Stuffed Pork Chops
   with Tarragon Vinaigrette................ 224

Pumpkin Cheese Coffee Cake ............... 51
Pumpkin Cheesecake Bars ................. 266

## Q
Quick Fettuccine Alfredo...................... 125
Quick Stovetop Granola......................... 39
Quick Tangy Sloppy Joes ...................... 56

## R
Radish Cucumber Salad......................... 85
Ramen Corn Chowder.............................61
Ranch Pork Roast................................. 154
Red Pepper Cornmeal Souffle ............. 40
Reuben Sandwiches............................... 62
Ricotta Cheesecake ............................. 255
Roast Leg of Lamb with Rosemary ... 159

Roasted Chicken Thighs with
   Peppers & Potatoes........................... 246
Roasted Fall Vegetables......................293
Roasted Mushroom &
   Couscous Soup .................................. 70
Roasted Pear Salad................................ 84
Roasted Red Pepper Soup..................... 70
Roasted Sweet Potato
   & Chickpea Pitas............................... 72
Rosemary Sweet Potato Fries ............. 85
Rosemary Garlic Shrimp ..................... 131
Rosemary-Apricot Pork
   Tenderloin......................................... 157
Rotisserie-Style Chicken..................... 242
Russian Borscht ................................... 59
Rustic Squash Tarts ............................277

# S

Salmon Dip with Cream Cheese........... 26
Salmon with Horseradish
      Pistachio Crust.................... 122
Salmon with Spinach Sauce................114
Saucy Beef & Cabbage Dinner .........235
Sausage & Egg Grits.................... 40
Sausage Cheese Balls ........................... 24
Sausage, Pear & Sweet Potato
      Sheet-Pan Dinner....................237
Sausage-Stuffed Shells ......................115
Savory Cheese Ball.................... 31
Savory Cucumber Sandwiches..........284
Seafood Fettuccine Alfredo .................111
Sesame Almond Slaw ........................... 92
Sheepherder's Breakfast.......................51
Sheet-Pan Chicken Curry Dinner ....... 241
Sheet-Pan Tandoori Chicken ..............237
Shrimp Pad Thai.................... 122
Shrimp Patty Sandwiches.................... 71
Shrimp Quesadillas ......................... 104
Simple Shrimp Chowder.................... 73
Skillet Cabbage .................... 94
Slow-Cooked Beef & Veggies ............. 105
Slow-Cooked Beef Tips .................... 106
Slow-Cooked Cherry Pork Chops....... 160
Slow-Cooked Moroccan Chicken........230
Slow-Cooker Cassoulet
      with Crumb Topping ........................ 192
Slow-Cooker Pina Colada
      Bananas Foster.................... 267
Slow-Cooker Veggie Lasagna ............. 107
Smash Burgers.................... 73
Smoked Sausage Dinner .................... 107
Smoky Cauliflower Bites.................... 88
Smoky Grilled Shrimp Appetizers ..... 210
So-Tender Swiss Steak .................... 203
Sourdough Bread Bowl Sandwich.....227
Southwestern Rice .................... 235
Spaghetti with Eggs & Bacon ............. 156
Spanish-Style Paella.................... 247
Sparkling Ginger Lemonade.................. 27
Spiced Grilled Chicken with
      Cilantro Lime Butter.................... 227
Spicy Beef & Pepper Stir-Fry ............. 126
Spicy Cajun Potato Salad.................... 279
Spicy Chicken Nuggets .................... 154
Spicy Goulash.................... 289
Spicy Turkey Stir-Fry with
      Noodles.................... 105
Spicy Turkey Tenderloin.................... 106
Spinach Pizza Quesadillas .................... 59
Spinach Ravioli Bake..........................161
Spinach Salad with
      Hot Bacon Dressing.................... 92
Spinach Shrimp Fettuccine.................. 126
Spinach-Artichoke Rigatoni.................. 159
Spring Pea Soup.................... 62

Steak & Prosciutto Skewers with
      Creamy Basil-Tarragon Sauce........208
Strawberry Shakes .................... 24
Strawberry Shortcake Salad ............... 87
Strawberry Vinaigrette .................... 91
Strawberry Watermelon
      Lemonade..........................15
Stroganoff Soup.................... 72
Stuffed Grilled Zucchini.................... 211
Stuffed Pizza Rolls..........................15
Stuffed Pork Tenderloin..........................111
Sunday Supper Sandwiches....................61
Sunshine Chicken.................... 236
Super Quick Chicken Fried Rice ......... 157
Super Quick Shrimp &
      Green Chile Quesadillas .................... 125
Sweet Almond Twists ..........................10
Sweet & Spicy Chipotle Chicken ......... 156
Sweet Potato Pone.................... 82
Sweetened Ricotta with Berries........268
Swiss Potato Pancake .................... 87
Syrian Green Beans with
      Fresh Herbs .................... 91
Szechuan Sugar Snap Peas.................... 89

# T

Taco Skillet Pizza with
      Cornbread Crust....................244
Tapenade-Stuffed Chicken
      Breasts .................... 123
Tart & Tangy Lemon Tart .................... 263
Tasty Onion Chicken .................... 160

Tex-Mex Casserole.................... 292
Thai Chicken Thighs .................... 191
Thai Salad with Peanut
      Dressing.................... 90
Tostones..........................13
Traditional Funnel Cakes .................... 262
Turtle Ice Cream Sauce .................... 260
Turtle Tart with Caramel Sauce..........253
Tuscan Truffles.................... 284
Two-Minute Cookies .................... 271

# U

Ultimate Grilled Pork Chops ................ 210

# V

Veg Jambalaya..........................236
Vegan Tropical Magic Bars....................255
Vegetarian Stuffed Mushrooms ...........14
Veggie Brown Rice Wraps .................... 60
Veggie Dill Dip.................... 192

# W

Walnut Cranberry Orzo .................... 89
Weiner Schnitzel..........................100
White Bean, Sweet Potato
      & Pepper Ragout .................... 240
White Chocolate Chip Cookies............276
Wilted Spinach Salad .................... 78

# Z

Zucchini Fries.................... 93
Zucchini Patties .................... 90

# ICON INDEX

## ⏱ FAST FIX

Air-Fryer Bacon-Wrapped Scallops
with Pineapple Quinoa...................... 144
Air-Fryer Beef Turnovers ..................... 151
Air-Fryer Garlic-Butter Steak ............. 100
Air-Fryer Okra with Smoked
Paprika ..................................... 181
Air-Fryer Spinach Feta Turnovers..... 170
Air-Fryer Steak Fajitas ......................... 178
Almond Broccoli Salad......................... 188
Angel Berry Trifle.................................. 250
Apple Cider Pork Chops ....................... 133
Apple Martini ........................................ 27
Asparagus & Shrimp with
Angel Hair ................................... 134
Bacon & Egg Gravy ............................... 34
Banana Fritters..................................... 263
Basil Shrimp ........................................ 22
BBQ Meat Loaf Minis ............................ 145
Best Grilled Cheese Sandwiches ......... 75
Best Veal Scallopini ............................. 100
Blue Cheese Garlic Bread..................... 26

Blue Plate Beef Patties......................... 134
Blueberry Cantaloupe Salad ................ 36
Brie with Almonds ................................ 19
Broccoli Beef Braids............................. 135
Broiled Parmesan Tilapia..................... 120
Brussels Sprouts & Kale Saute .......... 282
Buffet Scrambled Eggs ......................... 36
Caesar Salmon with Roasted
Tomatoes & Artichokes .................... 151
Caribbean Chicken Stir-Fry................. 145
Chicken & Vegetable Curry
Couscous....................................... 146
Chicken Chiles Rellenos Alfredo......... 136
Chicken Florentine Panini..................... 63
Chicken Parmesan Burgers................. 132
Chicken Provolone ................................ 153
Chicken Thai Pizza ............................... 137
Chicken with Peach-Avocado Salsa.. 131
Chicken Yakitori ................................... 222
Cilantro-Topped Salmon ...................... 140
Cinnamon Breakfast Bites................... 37
Classic Crab Cakes .............................. 127

Classic Wilted Lettuce Salad ............... 78
Cocoa-Crusted Beef Tenderloin ......... 143
Cod & Asparagus Bake ......................... 152
Cranberry Endive Appetizers............... 29
Creamed Peas ...................................... 97
Creamy Crab Wontons ......................... 29
Creamy Red Pepper Dip ....................... 29
Dirty Rice .............................................. 97
Easy Mediterranean Chicken.............. 129
Easy Shrimp Tacos ............................... 124
Fajita-Style Shrimp & Grits................. 129
Festive French Pancakes ..................... 47
Feta Cheese & Pomegranate
Guacamole..................................... 13
Feta Chicken Burgers .......................... 189
Fiesta Turkey Tortilla Soup ................ 198
Fluffy Pancakes .................................... 49
French Potato Salad.............................. 81
Fried Chicken Strips ............................ 127
Frozen Margaritas................................ 17
Garlic Lime Shrimp ............................... 132
Grapefruit Gremolata Salmon ........... 133
Grapefruit Lettuce Salad ..................... 83
Green Chile Prosciutto Balls................ 23
Grilled Burgers..................................... 225
Grilled Cheese & Pepperoni
Sandwich ...................................... 65
Grilled Nectarine & Cheese Crostini.. 214
Grilled Pound Cake with Berries........ 221
Grilled Salmon Fillet ............................ 217
Guacamole Chicken Salad
Sandwiches.................................... 69
Guacamole Tossed Salad ..................... 94
Ham & Egg Pockets ............................... 48
Harvard Beets ...................................... 84
Honey-Mustard Glazed Salmon ......... 142
Hot Artichoke-Spinach Dip.................. 25
Italian Tomato Cucumber Salad .......... 94
Lemon-Basil Grilled Shrimp &
Couscous....................................... 225
Lobster Tartlets ................................... 16
Long Island Iced Tea ............................ 23
Mango Lassi .......................................... 12
Meatball Submarine Casserole .......... 136
Merlot Filet Mignon.............................. 103
Mom's Sloppy Tacos ............................. 161
Oat Waffles........................................... 41
One-Dish Turkey Dinner ...................... 241
Open-Faced Pizza Burgers ................. 203
Peanut Butter Banana Oatmeal.......... 48
Pear & Fennel Pork............................... 123

Pecan Pumpkin Biscuits ........................ 39
Pepper Ricotta Primavera.................... 137
Pesto Twists.........................................10
Pork Schnitzel with Sauce ................... 120
Pressure-Cooker Balsamic Pork
    Tenderloin..................................... 166
Pressure-Cooker Clam Sauce ...........176
Pressure-Cooker Cranberry Stuffed
    Apples ........................................... 170
Pressure-Cooker Salsa
    London Broil .................................. 178
Pressure-Cooker Spicy Lime
    Chicken ......................................... 166
Provolone-Stuffed Pork Chops with
    Tarragon Vinaigrette ..................... 224
Quick Fettucine Alfredo........................ 125
Quick Stovetop Granola........................ 39
Quick Tangy Sloppy Joes ...................... 56
Radish Cucumber Salad........................ 85
Ramen Corn Chowder............................61
Reuben Sandwiches.............................. 62
Roasted Sweet Potato & Chickpea
    Pitas............................................... 72
Rosemary Garlic Shrimp ..................... 131
Salmon with Horseradish
    Pistachio Crust.............................. 122
Salmon with Spinach Sauce.................114
Sausage Cheese Balls ......................... 24
Seafood Fettucine Alfredo ...................111
Sesame Almond Slaw ........................... 92
Sheepherder's Breakfast......................51
Shrimp Pad Thai.................................. 122
Shrimp Patty Sandwiches.................... 71
Shrimp Quesadillas ............................ 104
Simple Shrimp Chowder........................ 73
Skillet Cabbage ................................... 94
Smash Burgers.................................... 73
Smoked Sausage Dinner ..................... 107
Smoky Grilled Shrimp Appetizers ..... 210
Southwestern Rice ............................. 235
Spaghetti with Eggs & Bacon ............. 156
Spicy Beef & Pepper Stir-Fry ............. 126
Spicy Chicken Nuggets........................ 154
Spicy Turkey Stir-Fry with
    Vegetables.................................... 105
Spinach-Artichoke Rigatoni................ 159
Spinach Pizza Quesadillas .................. 59
Spinach Salad with Hot Bacon
    Dressing......................................... 92
Spinach Shrimp Fettucine................... 126
Strawberry Shakes .............................. 24
Strawberry Shortcake Salad ............... 87
Strawberry Watermelon Lemonade....15
Strawberry Vinaigrette ........................ 91
Stuffed Pizza Rolls...............................15
Super Quick Chicken Fried Rice ......... 157
Super Quick Shrimp & Green Chile
    Quesadillas................................... 125

Swiss Potato Pancake ........................... 87
Syrian Green Beans with Fresh
    Herbs............................................. 91
Szechuan Sugar Snap Peas.................. 89
Tapenade-Stuffed Chicken Breasts... 123
Tasty Onion Chicken ........................... 160
Thai Salad with Peanut Dressing........ 90
Two-Minute Cookies........................... 271
Veggie Brown Rice Wraps .................... 60
Walnut Cranberry Orzo ........................ 89

# 🍳 5 INGREDIENT

Air-Fryer Bacon-Wrapped Scallops
    with Pineapple Quinoa.................. 144
Air-Fryer Beef Turnovers ................... 151
Air-Fryer Garlic-Butter Steak ............ 100
Air-Fryer Okra with Smoked
    Paprika ......................................... 181
Air-Fryer Parmesan Breaded
    Squash .......................................... 171
Air-Fryer Spinach Feta Turnovers..... 170
Apple Martini ....................................... 27
Bacon & Egg Gravy............................... 34
Banana Fritters................................. 263
BBQ Country-Style Ribs ..................... 146
BBQ Meat Loaf Minis .......................... 145
Blueberry Iced Tea............................... 21
Brie with Almonds ...............................19
Buffet Scrambled Eggs ........................ 36
Butterscotch Toffee Cookies............... 287
Caesar Salmon with Roasted
    Tomatoes & Artichokes .................. 151
Candied Bacon Palmiers..................... 186
Caribbean Chicken Stir-Fry................ 145
Chicken & Vegetable Curry
    Couscous....................................... 146
Chicken Provolone .............................. 153
Chicken with Shallot Sauce................. 149
Cilantro-Topped Salmon .................... 140
Classic Creme Brulee ........................ 262
Cocoa-Crusted Beef Tenderloin ........ 143
Cod & Asparagus Bake........................ 152
Corned Beef Hash & Eggs.................... 46
Creamed Peas ..................................... 97
Creamy Crab Wontons ......................... 29
Feta Cheese & Pomegranate
    Guacamole......................................13
Fettucine with Sausage & Fresh
    Tomato Sauce................................ 140
Fiesta Turkey Tortilla Soup................ 198
Freezer Mashed Potatoes................... 198
Frosty Watermelon Ice ....................... 267
Glazed Cornish Hens .......................... 143
Grilled Broccoli .................................. 213
Grilled Burgers................................... 225
Grilled Lobster Tail.............................. 223
Grilled Nectarine & Cheese Crostini.. 214
Grilled Potatoes................................. 224

Grilled Ribeye with Garlic Blue Cheese
    Mustard Sauce............................... 147
Lemon Chicken with Basil .................. 153
Habanero Raspberry Ribs ................... 142
Hearty Beans & Rice........................... 246
Honey-Mustard Glazed Salmon ........ 142
Italian Tomato Cucumber Salad .......... 94
Jalapeno Popper Stuffed Chicken
    Breasts........................................... 147
Mango Lassi.........................................12
Merlot Filet Mignon............................. 103
Mom's Roast Chicken ......................... 152
Mom's Sloppy Tacos............................161
Oklahoma Coconut Poke Cake ........... 274
Old-Fashioned Poor Man's Steak ....... 149
Pancetta & Mushroom-Stuffed
    Chicken Breast .............................. 155
Peanut Butter Banana Oatmeal........... 48
Pesto Twists.........................................10
Pineapple Smoothies .......................... 30
Pressure-Cooker Cranberry
    Stuffed Apples ............................... 170
Pressure-Cooker Pineapple
    Chicken ......................................... 171
Pressure-Cooker Spicy Lime
    Chicken ......................................... 166
Ranch Pork Roast................................ 154
Roast Leg of Lamb with Rosemary ... 159
Rosemary-Apricot Pork Tenderloin .. 157
Rosemary Sweet Potato Fries ............. 85
Savory Cucumber Sandwiches...........284
Sheepherder's Breakfast......................51
Skillet Cabbage ................................... 94
Slow-Cooked Cherry Pork Chops....... 160
Smash Burgers.................................... 73
Smoky Grilled Shrimp Appetizers ..... 210
So-Tender Swiss Steak ...................... 203
Spaghetti with Eggs & Bacon ............. 156
Sparkling Ginger Lemonade................ 27
Spicy Chicken Nuggets........................ 154
Spinach-Artichoke Rigatoni................ 159
Spinach Pizza Quesadillas .................. 59
Spinach Ravioli Bake............................161
Spring Pea Soup................................... 62
Strawberry Shakes .............................. 24
Strawberry Watermelon Lemonade....15
Strawberry Vinaigrette ........................ 91
Super Quick Chicken Fried Rice ......... 157
Sweet & Spicy Chipotle Chicken ........ 156
Swiss Potato Pancake .......................... 87
Syrian Green Beans with Fresh
    Herbs............................................. 91
Tasty Onion Chicken ........................... 160

# 🍎 EAT SMART

Air-Fryer Black Bean
    Chimichangas................................ 175
Air-Fryer Fish Tacos........................... 168

**(EAT SMART CONTINUED)**

Air-Fryer Fish & Chips ...................113
Air-Fryer Okra with Smoked
    Paprika ................................... 181
Air-Fryer Parmesan Breaded
    Squash ................................... 171
Air-Fryer Steak Fajitas ................. 178
Angel Berry Trifle ......................... 250
Apple Cider Pork Chops ............... 133
Avocado Salsa .............................. 202
Baba Ganoush ................................10
Baked Crab Cakes ........................ 109
Baked Pumpkin Pudding ............... 269
Balsamic Brussels Sprouts with
    Pears ...................................... 78
Basil Shrimp ................................. 22
Best Angel Food Cake ................... 259
Blueberry Cantaloupe Salad ......... 36
Broiled Parmesan Tilapia ............. 120
Brussels Sprouts & Kale Saute ......... 282
Caesar Salmon with Roasted
    Tomatoes & Artichokes ............ 151
Canadian Cheese Soup .................. 63
Caribbean Chicken Stir-Fry ........... 145
Chicken & Vegetable Curry
    Couscous ................................ 146
Chicken Bulgur Skillet ................. 245

Chicken Mushroom Stew ......................67
Chicken with Peach-Avocado
    Salsa ...................................... 131
Chili-Lime Air-Fried Chickpeas........... 22
Cilantro-Topped Salmon ............... 140
Cocoa-Crusted Beef Tenderloin ......... 143
Cod & Asparagus Bake .................. 152
Crab-Stuffed Manicotti ................. 108
Dijon-Rubbed Pork with Rhubarb
    Sauce ..................................... 274
Early Riser Oven Omelet....................41
Easy Mediterranean Chicken.............. 129
Easy Pepper Steak......................... 243
Easy Shrimp Tacos ....................... 124
Favorite Marinated Mushrooms ......... 30
Feta Cheese & Pomegranate
    Guacamole...............................13
Feta Chicken Burgers ................... 189
French Potato Salad ....................... 81
Frosty Watermelon Ice .................. 267
Garden Green Beans & Potatoes....... 287
Glazed Lemon Chiffon Cake................ 261
Grapefruit Gremolata Salmon ........... 133
Grilled Broccoli ............................ 213
Grilled Mahi Mahi.......................... 219
Grilled Nectarine & Cheese Crostini.. 214
Grilled Pistachio-Lemon Pesto
    Shrimp .................................... 215

Grilled Pork Tenderloin with
    Cherry Salsa Mole ..................... 215
Grilled Pork with Pear Salsa ............222
Grilled Potatoes ........................... 224
Grilled Salmon Fillet ..................... 217
Guacamole Chicken Salad
    Sandwiches ............................. 69
Hearty Beans & Rice ..................... 246
Hearty Beef & Barley Soup ................. 68
Heirloom Tomato Salad................... 81
Italian Tomato Cucumber Salad ......... 94
Key West Flank Steak ................... 217
Lemon-Basil Grilled Shrimp &
    Couscous ................................. 225
Lemon Chicken with Basil ............. 153
Mediterranean One-Dish Meal........... 243
Mexican-Style Chicken Manicotti ......116
Mom's Sloppy Tacos .....................161
North African Chicken & Rice ............ 234
One-Dish Turkey Dinner................ 241
One-Pot Chili Mac......................... 233
Peanut Butter Banana Oatmeal............ 48
Pepper Ricotta Primavera................ 137
Pineapple Smoothies ...................... 30
Pressure-Cooker Autumn Apple
    Chicken ................................... 169
Pressure-Cooker Clam Sauce ............176
Pressure-Cooker Cranberry
    Stuffed Apples ......................... 170
Pressure-Cooker Lava Cake............. 169
Pressure-Cooker Mexican Stuffed
    Peppers ...................................114
Pressure-Cooker Pineapple
    Chicken ................................... 171
Pressure-Cooker Red Beans &
    Rice ........................................ 180
Pressure-Cooker Salsa
    London Broil ............................ 178
Pressure-Cooker Spicy Lime
    Chicken ................................... 166
Pressure-Cooker Spicy Pork &
    Squash Ragu............................. 180
Pressure-Cooker Steamed Mussels
    with Peppers ........................... 167
Radish Cucumber Salad.................. 85
Ranch Pork Roast ......................... 154
Roasted Chicken Thighs with
    Peppers & Potatoes................... 246
Roasted Fall Vegetables................. 293
Roasted Sweet Potato & Chickpea
    Pitas ...................................... 72
Rosemary-Apricot Pork Tenderloin .. 157
Rosemary Garlic Shrimp ................ 131
Rosemary Sweet Potato Fries ............. 85
Salmon with Horseradish Pistachio
    Crust....................................... 122
Saucy Beef & Cabbage Dinner ........... 235
Sausage & Egg Grits...................... 40

Sheet-Pan Chicken Curry Dinner ....... 241
Slow-Cooked Beef Tips ......................... 106
Slow-Cooked Moroccan Chicken ........ 230
Slow-Cooker Veggie Lasagna ............. 107
Spicy Beef & Pepper Stir-Fry .............. 126
Spicy Goulash ...................................... 289
Spicy Turkey Stir-Fry with
    Vegetables ...................................... 105
Spicy Turkey Tenderloin ...................... 106
Spinach Pizza Quesadillas .................... 59
Spinach Shrimp Fettucine ................... 126
Strawberry Vinaigrette ......................... 91
Stuffed Grilled Zucchini ...................... 211
Sunshine Chicken ................................ 236
Syrian Green Beans with Fresh
    Herbs ................................................ 91
Tapenade-Stuffed Chicken Breasts ... 123
Thai Chicken Thighs ............................ 191
Thai Salad with Peanut Dressing ......... 90
Veg Jambalaya ..................................... 236
Veggie Brown Rice Wraps ..................... 60
Veggie Dill Dip ..................................... 192
Zucchini Fries ........................................ 93

## ❄ FREEZER FRIENDLY

BBQ Meat Loaf Minis ........................... 145
Candied Bacon Palmiers ...................... 186
Classic Crab Cakes .............................. 127
Easy Ropa Vieja Stew .......................... 199
Feta Chicken Burgers .......................... 189
Fettucine with Sausage & Fresh
    Tomato Sauce .................................. 140
Flaky Chicken Wellington ..................... 190
Freezer Mashed Potatoes .................... 198
Lemon Chicken with Basil ................... 153
Lisa's All-Day Sugar & Salt
    Pork Roast ....................................... 193
Mushroom & Olive Bruschetta ............ 197
Mushroom Asparagus Quiche ............... 50
Old-Time Cake Doughnuts ................... 205
One-Dish Turkey Dinner ...................... 241
Open-Faced Pizza Burgers .................. 203
Pork Meatballs .................................... 113
Pressure-Cooker German Goulash ... 175
Pressure-Cooker Red Beans & Rice . 180
Pressure-Cooker Spicy Lime
    Chicken ........................................... 166
Pressure-Cooker Spicy Pork &
    Squash Ragu .................................... 180
Ranch Pork Roast ................................ 154
Sausage Cheese Balls ........................... 24
So-Tender Swiss Steak ........................ 203

## 🍲 SLOW COOKER

BBQ Country-Style Ribs ...................... 146
Beef Osso Bucco .................................. 186
Blueberry Iced Tea ................................ 21
Buffalo Chicken Chili ............................ 65

Buffalo Wing Dip .................................. 288
Chicken Curry for Two ......................... 108
Chicken Mushroom Stew ....................... 67
Dreamy Polenta ..................................... 95
Easy Ropa Vieja Stew .......................... 199
Garden Green Beans & Potatoes ........ 287
German Bratwurst with
    Sauerkraut & Apples ....................... 278
Lemon Chicken with Basil ................... 153
Mexican-Inspired Chicken Soup ........... 58
North African Chicken & Rice ............. 234
Old-Fashioned Poor Man's Steak ....... 149
Slow-Cooked Beef & Veggies ............. 105
Slow-Cooked Beef Tips ....................... 106
Slow-Cooked Cherry Pork Chops ....... 160
Slow-Cooked Moroccan Chicken ........ 230
Slow-Cooker Cassoulet with
    Crumb Topping ................................ 192
Slow-Cooker Pina Colada
    Bananas Foster ............................... 267
Slow-Cooker Veggie Lasagna ............. 107
Spicy Goulash ...................................... 289
Thai Chicken Thighs ............................ 191

## 🍲 INSTANT POT

Pressure-Cooker Autumn Apple
    Chicken ........................................... 169
Pressure-Cooker Balsamic Pork
    Tenderloin ....................................... 166
Pressure-Cooker Clam Sauce ............ 176
Pressure-Cooker Cranberry Stuffed
    Apples ............................................. 170

Pressure-Cooker German Goulash ... 175
Pressure-Cooker Herbed Chicken &
    Shrimp ............................................ 164
Pressure-Cooker Lava Cake ............... 169
Pressure-Cooker Meat Loaf ............... 173
Pressure-Cooker Mexican Stuffed
    Peppers ........................................... 114
Pressure-Cooker Pineapple
    Chicken ........................................... 171
Pressure-Cooker Red Beans & Rice . 180
Pressure-Cooker Salsa
    London Broil .................................... 178
Pressure-Cooker Smoked Sausage &
    White Beans .................................... 173
Pressure-Cooker Spicy Lime
    Chicken ........................................... 166
Pressure-Cooker Spicy Pork &
    Squash Ragu .................................... 180
Pressure-Cooker Steamed Mussels
    with Peppers ................................... 167
Salmon with Spinach Sauce ............... 114

## 🍳 AIR FRYER

Air-Fryer Apple Danish ........................ 167
Air-Fryer Bacon-Wrapped Scallops
    with Pineapple Quinoa .................... 144
Air-Fryer Beef Turnovers .................... 151
Air-Fryer Black Bean Chimichangas . 175
Air-Fryer Buffalo Chicken Wings ........ 176
Air-Fryer Calamari ................................ 19
Air-Fryer Cookie Pie ........................... 259
Air-Fryer Fish & Chips ........................ 113

*(AIR FRYER CONTINUED)*

Air-Fryer Fish Tacos.............................. 168
Air-Fryer Garlic & Wine Lamb
    Chops ............................................. 183
Air-Fryer Garlic-Butter Steak ............. 100
Air-Fryer Lime & Gin Coconut
    Macaroons...................................... 181
Air-Fryer Nacho Dogs ......................... 179
Air-Fryer Okra with Smoked
    Paprika ........................................... 181
Air-Fryer Parmesan Breaded
    Squash ........................................... 171
Air-Fryer Pretzel-Crusted Catfish ..... 177
Air-Fryer Rosemary-Lemon
    Chicken Thighs............................... 177
Air-Fryer Southwestern Chicken
    Enchiladas...................................... 164
Air-Fryer Spinach Feta Turnovers..... 170
Air-Fryer Steak Fajitas ....................... 178
Air-Fryer Thai Chicken Meatballs ........ 21
Air-Fryer Turkey Club Roulades ......... 183
Buffalo Bites with Blue Cheese Dip ...... 17

Chili-Lime Air-Fried Chickpeas............. 22
Fried Chicken Strips ............................ 127
Jalapeno Popper Stuffed Chicken
    Breasts ........................................... 147
Zucchini Fries ....................................... 93

### 🅟🅜 OVERNIGHT

Air-Fryer Garlic & Wine Lamb
    Chops ............................................. 183
Angel Strawberry Dessert................... 293
Apple-Cinnamon Baked
    French Toast ..................................... 34
Arroz con Gandules
    (Rice with Pigeon Peas).................... 287
At-Attention Grilled Chicken ............... 212
Avocado Salsa...................................... 202
Banana Crumb Pudding ....................... 195
Barbecued Chicken Salad
    Sandwiches....................................... 58
Broccoli & Chicken Cheese Strata ....... 45
Caramel-Pecan Cookie Butter Bars .. 264
Cherry Cream Cheese Pie ................... 251
Chicken Chiles Rellenos Strata........... 195

Cream Cheese Ice Cream ..................... 260
Falafel .................................................. 205
Favorite Marinated Mushrooms ........... 30
Frosty Watermelon Ice ........................ 267
Grilled Flank Steak .............................. 220
Grilled Pork with Pear Salsa ............... 222
Herbed Rubbed Turkey......................... 291
Key West Flank Steak .......................... 217
Lemon Sheet Cake................................ 289
Lemony Chicken & Rice ........................ 197
Limoncello Tiramisu ............................ 251
Lisa's All-Day Sugar & Salt
    Pork Roast ...................................... 193
Macaroon Cherry Pie ........................... 264
Mom's Roast Chicken .......................... 152
Oven-Fried Ranch Steak.......................116
Overnight Yeast Waffles....................... 193
Peanut Butter & Jelly Ice Cream ........254
Ricotta Cheesecake ............................. 255
Rotisserie-Style Chicken...................... 242
Ultimate Grilled Pork Chops ............... 210
Vegan Tropical Magic Bars.................. 255
Veggie Dill Dip...................................... 192